5th Workshop on Insights from Negative Results in NLP (Insights 2025)

Albuquerque, New Mexico, USA
4 May 2025

ISBN: 979-8-3313-1919-9

Printed from e-media with permission by:

Curran Associates, Inc.
57 Morehouse Lane
Red Hook, NY 12571

Some format issues inherent in the e-media version may also appear in this print version.

Printed with permission by Curran Associates, Inc. (2026)

For permission requests, please contact the Association for Computational Linguistics at the address below.

Association for Computational Linguistics
209 N. Eighth Street
Stroudsburg, Pennsylvania 18360

Phone: 1-570-476-8006
Fax: 1-570-476-0860

acl@aclweb.org

Additional copies of this publication are available from:

Curran Associates, Inc.
57 Morehouse Lane
Red Hook, NY 12571 USA
Phone: 845-758-0400
Fax: 845-758-2633
Email: curran@proceedings.com
Web: www.proceedings.com

NAACL 2025

The 5th Workshop on Insights from Negative Results in NLP

Proceedings of the Workshop

May 4, 2025

Order copies of this and other ACL proceedings from:

Association for Computational Linguistics (ACL)
317 Sidney Baker St. S
Suite 400 - 134
Kerrville, TX 78028
USA
Tel: +1-855-225-1962
acl@aclweb.org

Introduction

Publication of negative results is difficult in most fields, and the current focus on benchmark-driven performance improvement exacerbates this situation and implicitly discourages hypothesis-driven research. As a result, the development of NLP models often devolves into a product of tinkering and tweaking, rather than science. Furthermore, it increases the time, effort, and carbon emissions spent on developing and tuning models, as the researchers have little opportunity to learn from what has already been tried and failed.
The mission of the workshop on Insights from Negative Results in NLP is to provide a venue for many kinds of negative results, with the hope that they could yield useful insights and provide a much-needed reality check on the successes of deep learning models in NLP. In particular, we solicit the following types of contributions:

- broadly applicable recommendations for training/fine-tuning, especially if X that didn't work is something that many practitioners would think reasonable to try, and if the demonstration of X's failure is accompanied by some explanation/hypothesis;
- ablation studies of components in previously proposed models, showing that their contributions are different from what was initially reported;
- datasets or probing tasks showing that previous approaches do not generalize to other domains or language phenomena;
- trivial baselines that work suspiciously well for a given task/dataset;
- cross-lingual studies showing that a technique X is only successful for a certain language or language family;
- experiments on (in)stability of the previously published results due to hardware, random initializations, preprocessing pipeline components, etc;
- theoretical arguments and/or proofs for why X should not be expected to work;
- demonstration of issues with under-reporting of training details of pre-trained models, including test data contamination and invalid comparisons.

The fifth iteration of the Workshop on Insights from Negative Results attracted 23 submissions and 2 from ACL Rolling Reviews. We accepted 16 papers, resulting in 64% acceptance rate. We hope the workshop will continue to contribute to the many reality-check discussions on progress in NLP. If we do not talk about things that do not work, it is harder to see what the biggest problems are and where the community effort is the most needed

Table of Contents

Program

Sunday, May 4, 2025

09:00 - 09:10	*Opening Remarks*
09:10 - 09:50	*Technical session 1*
09:50 - 10:30	*Technical session 2*
10:30 - 11:30	*Coffee Break*
11:30 - 12:00	*Invited Talk 1*
12:30 - 14:00	*Lunch*
14:10 - 14:50	*Technical session 3*
14:50 - 15:30	*Technical session 4*
15:30 - 16:00	*Coffee Break*
16:00 - 16:30	*Invited Talk 2*
16:30 - 17:30	*Poster Session*

Challenging Assumptions in Learning Generic Text Style Embeddings

Phil Ostheimer, Marius Kloft, Sophie Fellenz
RPTU Kaiserslautern-Landau
surname@cs.uni-kl.de

Abstract

Recent advancements in language representation learning primarily emphasize language modeling for deriving meaningful representations, often neglecting style-specific considerations. This study addresses this gap by creating generic, sentence-level style embeddings crucial for style-centric tasks. Our approach is grounded on the premise that low-level text style changes can compose any high-level style. We hypothesize that applying this concept to representation learning enables the development of versatile text style embeddings. By fine-tuning a general-purpose text encoder using contrastive learning and standard cross-entropy loss, we aim to capture these low-level style shifts, anticipating that they offer insights applicable to high-level text styles. The outcomes prompt us to reconsider the underlying assumptions as the results do not always show that the learned style representations capture high-level text styles.

1 Introduction

Learning meaningful representations of text has received much attention recently as models pre-trained on large corpora have become the standard for extracting representations that capture prior knowledge (i.a. Devlin et al., 2019; Radford and Narasimhan, 2018). However, most pre-trained models focus on general aspects, as they are trained with causal or masked language modeling objectives. Therefore, they are suboptimal for NLP tasks focusing on a specific aspect, such as style. There are many notable NLP tasks, such as identifying chatbot-written text based on its style (e.g., Soto et al. (2024)) or style transfer where models rely on dedicated style representations (e.g., John et al. (2019)).

Existing work on style transfer focuses on high-level stylistic aspects such as sentiment (Shen et al., 2017) or formality (Rao and Tetreault, 2018), taking style definitions based on the dataset's structure. Lyu et al. (2021) view those high-level text style changes as compositions of more fine-grained, low-level style changes. Generic style representations incorporating low-level aspects such as lexical, syntactic, semantic, and thematic stylistic traits (McDonald and Pustejovsky, 1985; DiMarco and Hirstt, 1993) but also high-level, composed stylistic traits might significantly improve style-focused tasks.

Based on the hypothesis that low-level style changes compose high-level style changes, this work explores learning generic, sentence-level style representations. We take a pre-trained encoder model producing general-purpose representations and fine-tune it to distinguish between low-level stylistic changes using contrastive learning and cross-entropy loss. We hypothesize that the resulting text encoder generalizes to high-level styles, applying the view by Lyu et al. (2021) on how low-level stylistic changes compose high-level changes to representation learning for styles.

We train our method using contrastive learning and cross-entropy loss on the StylePTB dataset (Lyu et al., 2021) comprising low-level, fine-grained style changes to obtain high-level, generic style embeddings. We evaluate our method by training a simple classifier on the representations of the learned style. The results show an ambiguous picture of the resulting style embeddings, challenging the underlying assumptions.

2 Related Work

Explicitly Learning Style Representations Only a few works learn style representations explicitly. StyleDistance (Patel et al., 2024) uses a contrastive triplet loss and synthetic parallel data created by Large Language Models to learn generic style representations, showing strong performance in multiple benchmarks.

Style Representations as a Byproduct Text style transfer is conducted by prominent models by

The Sixth Workshop on Insights from Negative Results in NLP, pages 1–6
May 4, 2025 ©2025 Association for Computational Linguistics

disentangling content and style to learn separate task-specific representations to control them independently (Fu et al., 2018; Hu et al., 2017; Kim and Sohn, 2020; John et al., 2019; Cheng et al., 2020). Other text style transfer models learn content representations and multiple decoders (one for each style) (Shen et al., 2017; Fu et al., 2018). Another group of models uses a structured style code to enforce a particular style in the decoder, either given as a structured code (Hu et al., 2017; Lample et al., 2019) or learned (Fu et al., 2018; Kim and Sohn, 2020).

For text style classification, TextCNN (Kim, 2014) is the most widely used method (Ostheimer et al., 2023). BERT (Devlin et al., 2019) and RoBERTa (Liu et al., 2019), fine-tuned for style classification, are strong baselines.

In contrast, our proposed method learns style representations at the sentence level from low-level, linguistically motivated style changes. This is much more fine-grained and allows applications to unseen styles.

Contrastive Learning for Text Representations To learn meaningful content representations on the sentence level from unlabeled text corpora, the QT model (Logeswaran and Lee, 2018) was introduced. The QT model relies on the distributional hypothesis to get meaningful content representations. It uses a contrastive objective to map nearby (context) sentences to similar and distant (non-context) sentences to far-apart representations.

For fine-tuning sentence representations, notable approaches are SimCSE (Gao et al., 2021) and Mirror-BERT (Liu et al., 2021), incorporating minimal data augmentation with dropout. In contrast, SBERT (Reimers and Gurevych, 2019) uses siamese and triplet network structures to generate meaningful sentence representations for calculating semantic sentence similarities using standard measures like cosine distance. Kim et al. (2021) improve the quality of the sentence representations by contrasting the representations of different layers of BERT (Devlin et al., 2019).

However, these approaches focus on improving the sentence-level representations for general language understanding or semantics. We, in contrast, focus on the style of the sentences.

3 Method

This section describes the underlying assumptions of the proposed method to compute (sentence-level) style representations of texts and the method itself.

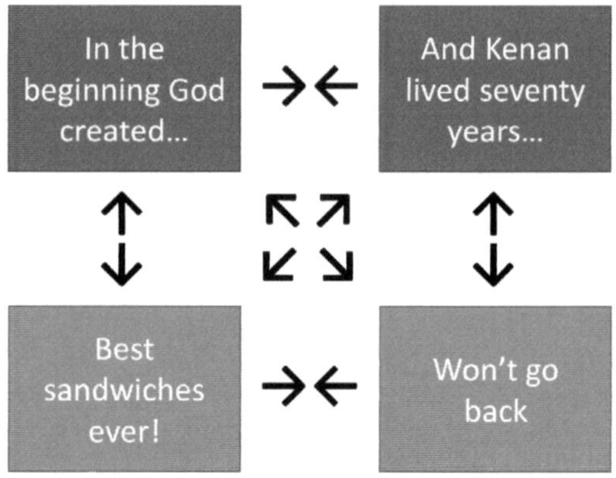

Figure 1: Our training objective pushes sentence representations of the same style close together. In this example, reviews (in orange) are pushed close together, and sentences of one Bible version (in blue) are pushed close together, while the representations of different styles (Bible vs reviews) are pushed to be far apart.

Assumption 1 *Low-level stylistic changes can be composed to form high-level styles in line with previous work (Lyu et al., 2021).*

Assumption 2 *Learning style embeddings can be achieved by contrasting different styles (Patel et al., 2024).*

We combine the aforementioned assumptions to come up with the following method.

Method The core idea—illustrated in Figure 1—is to embed the data into a space where texts of the same style resemble each other, while texts of different styles are easily distinguishable. Formally, we want to learn a neural encoder f mapping any two input sentences x and $\tilde{x}$ onto vector representations $f(x)$ and $f(\tilde{x})$ such that $f(x) \approx f(\tilde{x})$ if and only if x and $\tilde{x}$ are of the same style: $\text{style}(x) = \text{style}(\tilde{x}) = s$. To achieve this, we first form pairs of sentences, some equal and others of a different style. Then, we use a contrastive objective to push the vector representations of sentences of the same style closer together and ones of different styles far apart.

For a given sentence x with $\text{style}(x) = s$, our set of candidate sentences X_{cand} contains sentences of the same style and different style(s): $X_{\text{cand}} = X_s \cup \overline{X_s}$. We employ a simple architecture to compute the similarity between the outputs $f(x)$ and $f(\tilde{x})$, namely the inner product $f(x)^\top f(\tilde{x})$. Other functions to consider are, e.g., the cosine similarity or kernel functions. We compute the similarity using a simple architecture to avoid learning a rich similarity measure compensating for the encoder producing poor style representations.

Therefore, we have the following formulation for the probability of each candidate sentence $\tilde{x} \in X_{\text{cand}}$ to have the same style as x:

$$p(\tilde{x}|x, X_{\text{cand}}) = \frac{\exp[f(x)^\top f(\tilde{x})]}{\sum_{\tilde{x}' \in X_{\text{cand}}} \exp[f(x)^\top f(\tilde{x}')]} \quad (1)$$

Our training objective is to maximize the probability of identifying all sentences $\tilde{x} \in X_{\text{cand}}$ where $\text{style}(x) = \text{style}(\tilde{x}) = s$ for each sentence x in the training data D:

$$\sum_{x \in D} \sum_{\tilde{x} \in X_s} \log p(\tilde{x}|x, X_{\text{cand}}) \quad (2)$$

We also experiment with a cross-entropy loss and its combination with a contrastive loss.

4 Experiments

In this section, we describe how we evaluated the effectiveness in learning style representations for multiple styles.

4.1 Experimental Setup

Fine-Tuning Data We use the StylePTB (Lyu et al., 2021) dataset containing 21 individual and 32 compositional fine-grained style changes to train our generic text style embeddings.

Evaluation Data We evaluate the learned style embeddings on datasets that take a data-driven approach, containing high-level stylistic changes, to define a text style. These are used in many recent works on text style transfer. We experiment with the Bible corpus (Carlson et al., 2018) with eight different styles of the Bible (249K sentences), Grammarly's Yahoo Answers Formality Corpus (GYAFC) (Rao and Tetreault, 2018) (113K sentences) in two styles, a collection of Shakespeare plays in Shakespearean and modern English (Xu et al., 2012) (42K sentences), Amazon (558K) and Yelp (448K) sentiment datasets[1] (two styles each). We follow prior work by using the existing train-dev-test splits.

Training We experiment with both $\text{RoBERTa}_{\text{Large}}$ (Liu et al., 2019) and $\text{BERT}_{\text{Large}}$ (Devlin et al., 2019) as pre-trained encoders for f. The sentence representation is the activation from the last hidden layer for the "CLS" token. We add a linear transformation and a l_2 normalization before applying the objective function. Training stops after a maximum of 10 epochs, and the best model is used based on the loss on the validation dataset. Hyperparameters were chosen using the loss on the validation dataset. We used a batch size of 16, a learning rate of 1e-5 with a linear warmup for the first 10% steps, followed by a linear cooldown for the remaining steps. We used an Adam optimizer and a dropout rate of 0.1. A logistic classifier is trained on the training data and evaluated on the test data using the representations obtained by the encoder f.

Batch Construction We initially experimented with contrasting more than two styles per batch. However, this resulted in no meaningful representations. Therefore, we resorted to two styles per batch. We use a random sampler with replacements to randomly select sentences of each style. We also use two random samplers without replacement: one where we assure for each style pair that only unseen sentence pairs are contrasted and one where we only assure on the corpus level that per epoch, the sentences are only contrasted once. Half of the batch consists of style s while the other half contains style $\overline{s}$.

Obtaining Generic Style Embeddings To get generic style embeddings, we fine-tune pre-trained encoders f on StylePTB (Lyu et al., 2021) and apply the resulting encoders to the previously mentioned high-level style datasets. The hypothesis is the following: Since StylePTB contains fine-grained (and compositional) style changes, it should also generalize to high-level and unseen styles.

4.2 Results

In Table 1, we summarize our style classification results. Using pre-trained BERT and RoBERTa encoders as f, we apply a logistic regression for classification without fine-tuning, serving as our baseline. Baseline accuracies for datasets like Yelp, Amazon, GYAFC, and Shakespeare (two styles each) are already nearly 80% or higher. The Bible dataset, with eight styles, exhibits lower accuracy, as expected. Generally, BERT outperforms RoBERTa in style classification. Our approach considers three sampling strategies (Section 4.1), crucial for contrastive loss performance.

[1]https://github.com/lijuncen/Sentiment-and-Style-Transfer

	Dataset	PT	CEL	Random Sampler CEL+CL	Random Sampler CL	Pairwise Sampler CEL+CL	Pairwise Sampler CL	Corpus Sampler CEL+CL	Corpus Sampler CL
BERT	Yelp	**94.3**	92.9	90.5	90.1	72.9	87.0	71.4	88.1
	Amazon	**77.4**	74.9	72.1	74.5	59.6	68.3	58.1	69.3
	GYAFC	**88.4**	88.0	82.1	82.1	71.5	86.2	74.3	78.3
	Shakespeare	85.7	**86.4**	83.4	83.5	75.1	83.7	73.7	81.7
	Bible	50.9	**52.8**	42.9	46.7	31.1	52.4	33.9	41.2
RoBERTa	Yelp	86.2	**87.5**	85.3	74.2	55.1	50.8	56.0	71.9
	Amazon	**75.2**	67.1	64.4	60.3	54.1	65.4	55.9	58.1
	GYAFC	79.4	**85.5**	80.2	76.3	55.5	59.0	60.4	66.9
	Shakespeare	80.1	**85.1**	81.7	76.1	64.8	74.0	67.4	77.6
	Bible	55.9	**60.8**	53.8	44.4	18.9	24.2	19.1	38.5

Table 1: Shown is the style classification accuracy of a logistic regression fitted to the two text encoders f BERT and RoBERTa as a pre-trained (PT) encoder, fine-tuned on StylePTB and applied to the mentioned datasets using a Cross-Entropy Loss (CEL), Contrastive Loss (CL), or both (CEL+CL) with the three mentioned sampling strategies.

Fine-tuning BERT and RoBERTa with the cross-entropy loss yields slight accuracy improvements for the Shakespeare and Bible corpora. Moreover, fine-tuning RoBERTa further enhances accuracies on Yelp and GYAFC. However, incorporating the contrastive loss reduces accuracy compared to cross-entropy fine-tuning. Solely fine-tuning with a contrastive loss also leads to less accuracy.

4.3 Discussion

While fine-tuning an encoder f on the StylePTB dataset using cross-entropy loss slightly improves some settings' accuracy, contrastive learning does not. These findings of our study question the representational capacity of the learned style embeddings, especially for contrastive learning.

Contrastive Objective Is Too Aggressive Contrary to our expectations, applying the contrastive loss does not improve the accuracy compared to the cross-entropy loss across various settings we explored. One possible reason is that the contrastive loss might push dissimilar styles too far apart. Contrary to previous work (Patel et al., 2024), we do not use synthetic parallel data but contrast non-parallel data. This might hamper the model's ability to learn the relationship between different styles and style levels.

RoBERTa's "CLS" Tokens Need Fine-Tuning The improvements with the cross-entropy loss can be attributed to the fact that the "CLS" token is not pre-trained using the next sentence prediction task and, therefore, any fine-tuning might improve the "CLS" token representations.

Differentiated Picture for Cross-Entropy Loss One possible reason for the differentiated results can be seen in the examples from StylePTB in Table 2. While some low-level changes, like info addition, relate directly to a formality change, others, such as tense changes, do not align with the investigated styles. Mixing low-level styles may confuse the encoding mechanisms that distinguish higher-level styles.

Aspect	Original	Transferred
Info addition	Morgan Freeman did the new one	Morgan Freeman did *perform* the new one.
To future tense	It is also planning another night of original series.	It will be also planning another night of original series.

Table 2: Examples from the StylePTB dataset

5 Conclusion

Learning generic, high-level text style representations from low-level, linguistically motivated changes and generalizing to high-level styles according to Assumption 1 by Lyu et al. (2021) using contrastive learning according to Assumption 2 by Patel et al. (2024) presents challenges. Although the approach does not yield the expected results using contrastive learning, cross-entropy loss shows improvements for some settings. However, our approach does not yield the expected results compared to previous work (Patel et al., 2024) using contrastive learning to learn generic style representations.

Limitations

One limitation of this study is the reliance on the StylePTB dataset, which, to our knowledge, is the only available dataset containing low-level and composed stylistic changes. The dataset is restricted to English, limiting the generalizability of our findings to other languages. As style may manifest differently across languages, a more diverse, multilingual dataset would allow for broader application and a more comprehensive evaluation of the proposed method.

Additionally, our study focuses on contrastive learning to capture text style representations. This choice was made because it intuitively aligns with the underlying assumptions of the task, but it may not be the optimal approach for all settings.

Acknowledgements

Part of this work was conducted within the DFG Research Unit FOR 5359 on Deep Learning on Sparse Chemical Process Data (BU 4042/2-1, KL 2698/6-1, and KL 2698/7-1) and the DFG TRR 375 (no. 511263698). SF and MK acknowledge support by the Carl-Zeiss Foundation (AI-Care, Process Engineering 4.0), the BMBF award 01|S2407A, and the DFG awards FE 2282/6-1, FE 2282/1-2, KL 2698/5-2, and KL 2698/11-1.

References

Keith Carlson, Allen Riddell, and Daniel Rockmore. 2018. Evaluating prose style transfer with the Bible. *Royal Society Open Science*, 5(10):171920.

Pengyu Cheng, Martin Renqiang Min, Dinghan Shen, Christopher Malon, Yizhe Zhang, Yitong Li, and Lawrence Carin. 2020. Improving disentangled text representation learning with information-theoretic guidance. In *Proceedings of the 58th Annual Meeting of the Association for Computational Linguistics, ACL 2020, Online, July 5-10, 2020*, pages 7530–7541. Association for Computational Linguistics.

Jacob Devlin, Ming-Wei Chang, Kenton Lee, and Kristina Toutanova. 2019. BERT: pre-training of deep bidirectional transformers for language understanding. In *Proceedings of the 2019 Conference of the North American Chapter of the Association for Computational Linguistics: Human Language Technologies, NAACL-HLT 2019, Minneapolis, MN, USA, June 2-7, 2019, Volume 1 (Long and Short Papers)*, pages 4171–4186. Association for Computational Linguistics.

Chrysanne DiMarco and Graeme Hirstt. 1993. A Computational Theory of Goal-Directed Style in Syntax. *Computational Linguistics*, 19(3):50.

Zhenxin Fu, Xiaoye Tan, Nanyun Peng, Dongyan Zhao, and Rui Yan. 2018. Style transfer in text: Exploration and evaluation. In *Proceedings of the Thirty-Second AAAI Conference on Artificial Intelligence, (AAAI-18), the 30th innovative Applications of Artificial Intelligence (IAAI-18), and the 8th AAAI Symposium on Educational Advances in Artificial Intelligence (EAAI-18), New Orleans, Louisiana, USA, February 2-7, 2018*, pages 663–670. AAAI Press.

Tianyu Gao, Xingcheng Yao, and Danqi Chen. 2021. SimCSE: Simple Contrastive Learning of Sentence Embeddings. In *Proceedings of the 2021 Conference on Empirical Methods in Natural Language Processing, EMNLP 2021, Virtual Event / Punta Cana, Dominican Republic, 7-11 November, 2021*. Association for Computational Linguistics.

Zhiting Hu, Zichao Yang, Xiaodan Liang, Ruslan Salakhutdinov, and Eric P. Xing. 2017. Toward controlled generation of text. In *Proceedings of the 34th International Conference on Machine Learning, ICML 2017, Sydney, NSW, Australia, 6-11 August 2017*, volume 70 of *Proceedings of Machine Learning Research*, pages 1587–1596. PMLR.

Vineet John, Lili Mou, Hareesh Bahuleyan, and Olga Vechtomova. 2019. Disentangled representation learning for non-parallel text style transfer. In *Proceedings of the 57th Conference of the Association for Computational Linguistics, ACL 2019, Florence, Italy, July 28- August 2, 2019, Volume 1: Long Papers*, pages 424–434. Association for Computational Linguistics.

Heejin Kim and Kyung-Ah Sohn. 2020. How positive are you: Text style transfer using adaptive style embedding. In *Proceedings of the 28th International Conference on Computational Linguistics, COLING 2020, Barcelona, Spain (Online), December 8-13, 2020*, pages 2115–2125. International Committee on Computational Linguistics.

Taeuk Kim, Kang Min Yoo, and Sang-goo Lee. 2021. Self-guided contrastive learning for BERT sentence representations. In *Proceedings of the 59th Annual Meeting of the Association for Computational Linguistics and the 11th International Joint Conference on Natural Language Processing, ACL/IJCNLP 2021, (Volume 1: Long Papers), Virtual Event, August 1-6, 2021*, pages 2528–2540. Association for Computational Linguistics.

Yoon Kim. 2014. Convolutional Neural Networks for Sentence Classification. In *Proceedings of the 2014 Conference on Empirical Methods in Natural Language Processing (EMNLP)*, pages 1746–1751, Doha, Qatar. Association for Computational Linguistics.

Guillaume Lample, Sandeep Subramanian, Eric Michael Smith, Ludovic Denoyer, Marc'Aurelio

Ranzato, and Y-Lan Boureau. 2019. Multiple-attribute text rewriting. In *7th International Conference on Learning Representations, ICLR 2019, New Orleans, LA, USA, May 6-9, 2019*. OpenReview.net.

Fangyu Liu, Ivan Vulić, Anna Korhonen, and Nigel Collier. 2021. Fast, Effective, and Self-Supervised: Transforming Masked Language Models into Universal Lexical and Sentence Encoders. In *Proceedings of the 2021 Conference on Empirical Methods in Natural Language Processing*, pages 1442–1459, Online and Punta Cana, Dominican Republic. Association for Computational Linguistics.

Yinhan Liu, Myle Ott, Naman Goyal, Jingfei Du, Mandar Joshi, Danqi Chen, Omer Levy, Mike Lewis, Luke Zettlemoyer, and Veselin Stoyanov. 2019. Roberta: A robustly optimized BERT pretraining approach. *CoRR*, abs/1907.11692.

Lajanugen Logeswaran and Honglak Lee. 2018. An efficient framework for learning sentence representations. In *6th International Conference on Learning Representations, ICLR 2018, Vancouver, BC, Canada, April 30 - May 3, 2018, Conference Track Proceedings*. OpenReview.net.

Yiwei Lyu, Paul Pu Liang, Hai Pham, Eduard H. Hovy, Barnabás Póczos, Ruslan Salakhutdinov, and Louis-Philippe Morency. 2021. Styleptb: A compositional benchmark for fine-grained controllable text style transfer. In *Proceedings of the 2021 Conference of the North American Chapter of the Association for Computational Linguistics: Human Language Technologies, NAACL-HLT 2021, Online, June 6-11, 2021*, pages 2116–2138. Association for Computational Linguistics.

David D McDonald and James Pustejovsky. 1985. A computational theory of prose style for natural language generation. In *Second Conference of the European Chapter of the Association for Computational Linguistics*.

Phil Ostheimer, Mayank Kumar Nagda, Marius Kloft, and Sophie Fellenz. 2023. A call for standardization and validation of text style transfer evaluation. In *Findings of the Association for Computational Linguistics: ACL 2023, Toronto, Canada, July 9-14, 2023*, pages 10791–10815. Association for Computational Linguistics.

Ajay Patel, Jiacheng Zhu, Justin Qiu, Zachary Horvitz, Marianna Apidianaki, Kathleen McKeown, and Chris Callison-Burch. 2024. Styledistance: Stronger content-independent style embeddings with synthetic parallel examples. *arXiv preprint arXiv:2410.12757*.

Alec Radford and Karthik Narasimhan. 2018. Improving language understanding by generative pre-training.

Sudha Rao and Joel R. Tetreault. 2018. Dear sir or madam, may I introduce the GYAFC dataset: Corpus, benchmarks and metrics for formality style transfer. In *Proceedings of the 2018 Conference of the North American Chapter of the Association for Computational Linguistics: Human Language Technologies, NAACL-HLT 2018, New Orleans, Louisiana, USA, June 1-6, 2018, Volume 1 (Long Papers)*, pages 129–140. Association for Computational Linguistics.

Nils Reimers and Iryna Gurevych. 2019. Sentence-BERT: Sentence Embeddings using Siamese BERT-Networks. In *Proceedings of the 2019 Conference on Empirical Methods in Natural Language Processing and the 9th International Joint Conference on Natural Language Processing, EMNLP-IJCNLP 2019, Hong Kong, China, November 3-7, 2019*, pages 3980–3990. Association for Computational Linguistics.

Tianxiao Shen, Tao Lei, Regina Barzilay, and Tommi S. Jaakkola. 2017. Style transfer from non-parallel text by cross-alignment. In *Advances in Neural Information Processing Systems 30: Annual Conference on Neural Information Processing Systems 2017, December 4-9, 2017, Long Beach, CA, USA*, pages 6830–6841.

Rafael Alberto Rivera Soto, Kailin Koch, Aleem Khan, Barry Y. Chen, Marcus Bishop, and Nicholas Andrews. 2024. Few-shot detection of machine-generated text using style representations. In *The Twelfth International Conference on Learning Representations*.

Wei Xu, Alan Ritter, Bill Dolan, Ralph Grishman, and Colin Cherry. 2012. Paraphrasing for style. In *COLING 2012, 24th International Conference on Computational Linguistics, Proceedings of the Conference: Technical Papers, 8-15 December 2012, Mumbai, India*, pages 2899–2914. Indian Institute of Technology Bombay.

In-Context Learning on a Budget: A Case Study in Token Classification

Uri Berger[1,2], **Tal Baumel**[3], **Gabriel Stanovsky**[1]
[1]School of Computer Science and Engineering, The Hebrew University of Jerusalem
[2]School of Computing and Information Systems, University of Melbourne
[3]Microsoft Corporation
{uri.berger2, gabriel.stanovsky}@mail.huji.ac.il
tal.baumel@microsoft.com

Abstract

Few shot in-context learning (ICL) typically assumes access to large annotated training sets. However, in many real world scenarios, such as domain adaptation, there is only a limited budget to annotate a small number of samples, with the goal of maximizing downstream performance. We study various methods for selecting samples to annotate within a predefined budget, focusing on token classification tasks, which are expensive to annotate and are relatively less studied in ICL setups. Across various tasks, models, and datasets, we observe that no method significantly outperforms the others, with most yielding similar results, including random sample selection for annotation. Moreover, we demonstrate that a relatively small annotated sample pool can achieve performance comparable to using the entire training set. We hope that future work adopts our realistic paradigm which takes annotation budget into account.

1 Introduction

In-context learning (ICL) has emerged as a highly efficient and robust method for various textual tasks. In this paradigm, a large language model (LLM) is exposed to a small number of annotated samples, termed *demonstration examples*, which are provided as part of the prompt, before the sample which the model is required to annotate, which we will refer to as *inference sample* henceforth. While the reasons for ICL's success are still contested (Min et al., 2022; Liu et al., 2022), it has been observed that ICL prompts commonly outperform zero-shot prompts, where no demonstration examples are provided (Brown et al., 2020).

Furthermore, a recent line of work has found that the choice of demonstration examples can lead to improved results over random demonstration selection. For example, Liu et al. (2022) found that choosing the nearest neighbors of the inference sample in the training set leads to improvements over random demonstration selection on 6 tasks, such as sentiment analysis or question answering. In all of these, the demonstration examples are chosen from large annotated training sets, ranging from 3.5K samples up to 78K samples.

In this work, we address the following research question: *How can we maximize ICL performance on a given annotation budget?* This question is particularly relevant for real-world domain adaptation settings, where a large pool of annotated samples is unavailable for selecting demonstration examples. Instead, there are large sets of unannotated samples (e.g., raw text in the target domain), and a fixed budget to annotate only a small portion of them. As depicted in Figure 1, we define the task as *pool selection*, i.e., selecting a small pool of k examples out of a large corpus of raw texts. These samples are annotated and serve as the available pool for demonstration examples.

We implement several methods for pool selection, e.g., clustering the train set and selecting a representative example from each cluster, and test them on three token classification tasks: named entity recognition, dependency parsing, and part-of-speech tagging. We select these tasks as they are relatively understudied in the context of ICL and are expensive to annotate due to the need for linguistic expertise and domain-specific knowledge (Chen et al., 2015; Zhang et al., 2017).

We evaluate several state-of-the-art LLMs on token classification benchmarks. We observe that none of the methods consistently outperforms the others, and, surprisingly, *randomly selecting* samples for the annotation pool performs comparably to more carefully designed approaches in certain scenarios. Furthermore, we find that a relatively small pool ($\sim$200 samples) allows LLMs to perform over 88% as when demonstrations are selected from the full training set.

We hope that our paradigm is adopted in future

The Sixth Workshop on Insights from Negative Results in NLP, pages 7–14
May 4, 2025 ©2025 Association for Computational Linguistics

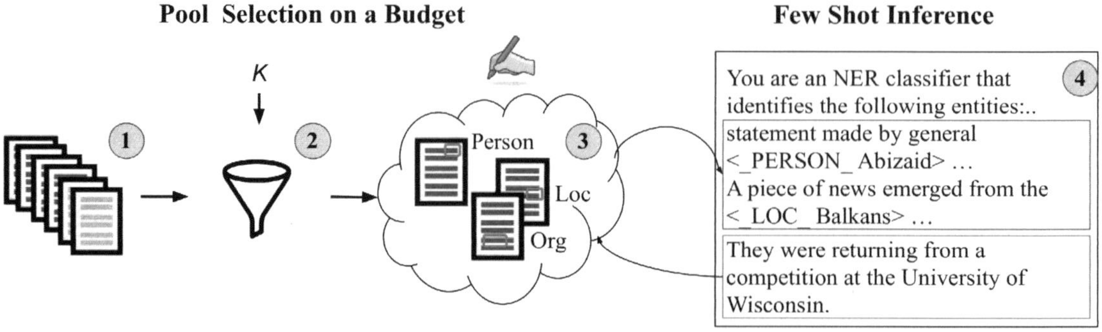

Figure 1: Our proposed approach for ICL on a budget, illustrated in four steps: (1) we assume a large pool of *raw* train and potentially test texts in the target domain; (2) a *pool selection strategy* chooses a subset of k train texts to maximize downstream ICL performance; (3) annotations are collected for the selected pool; (4) an inference prompt is instantiated by choosing the nearest examples in the pool to the inference sample. We focus on step (2), experimenting with various pool selection strategies.

work in order to report more realistic ICL performance, and explore new methods for sample selection for other tasks and domains.

2 ICL on a Budget

Here we propose a conceptual framework for ICL in a realistic domain adaptation setting (depicted in Figure 1), where there are no apriori annotated datasets for the target task. Instead, we assume that there is a large corpus of raw texts in the target domain, and a fixed budget for annotating a small portion of them, such that they can serve as potential demonstration examples during inference. Intuitively, the goal of the annotation process is to maximize downstream ICL performance.

Below we formalize the task of pool selection, and describe 4 selection strategies, which aim to maximize different aspects, e.g., coverage of the training set versus coverage of the test set. In the following section we evaluate these approaches for token classification tasks.

2.1 Pool Selection: Task Definition

Formally, a *pool selection strategy* is a function:

$$S_k : \mathcal{P}(\mathcal{D}) \mapsto \mathcal{D}^k \quad (1)$$

Where $\mathcal{D}$ represents an unannotated distribution (e.g., all texts in a certain domain), $\mathcal{P}(\mathcal{D})$ is the power set of $\mathcal{D}$, and $k \in \mathbb{N}_+$ is the annotation budget, i.e., the number of samples to annotate. Intuitively, S maps raw sample sets to k train samples (the pool), which are then annotated. In all that follows we denote the input samples set by $D \in \mathcal{P}(\mathcal{D})$. Typically, $k << |D|$, indicating that the annotation budget for a new domain can only annotate a small portion of its available texts.

Furthermore, we assume a similarity function ϕ:

$$\phi : \big(\mathcal{D} \times \mathcal{D}\big) \mapsto \mathbb{R} \quad (2)$$

In the scope of this work (similar to previous work (Liu et al., 2022)) samples are embedded into $\mathbb{R}^m$, where m is the text embedding dimension, and ϕ is the cosine similarity of these vectors. In particular, we use a sentence transformer (Reimers and Gurevych, 2019) trained over MPNet (Song et al., 2020).

2.2 Pool Selection Strategies

Below we describe 4 pool selection strategies which follow the definition in Equation 1.

Central. Select the k samples from D that are closest to the Euclidean center of D.

Cluster. Cluster D into k clusters and for each cluster center choose the most similar sample from D. This method aims to maximize the coverage of the expected training distribution. This strategy was proposed in Chang et al. (2021) for selecting examples for fine-tuning.

Vote-k (Su et al., 2022). Selects a k-sized subset of D such that the samples are diverse and dissimilar from one another, through a two-step process which uses the LLM's confidence to bucket the different samples. See Su et al. (2022) for more details.

Random. Randomly select k samples from D.

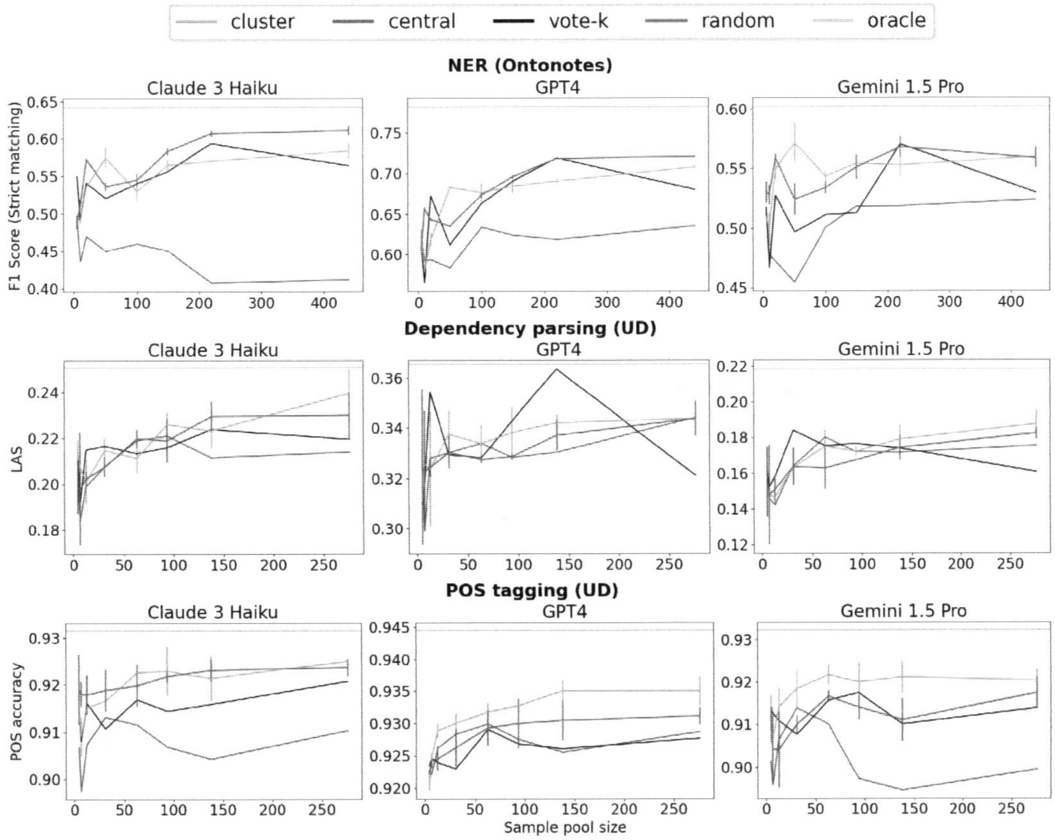

Figure 2: Results for NER (top), dependency parsing (center), and POS tagging (bottom) using Claude 3 Haiku (left), GPT4 (middle) and Gemini 1.5 Pro (right), as a function of the size of sample pool. In methods with a random component we run 3 trials and plot error bars showing the standard deviation. Oracle: using the full training set as the pool.

3 Evaluation

We focus on token classification tasks, as they are both understudied in the context of ICL, while traditionally expensive to annotate at scale. Importantly, as is commonly done in active learning scenarios (e.g., Shen et al., 2018; Liu et al., 2020), we use existing datasets to *simulate* the process shown in Figure 1, where instead of collecting manual annotations, we sample from the existing annotations.

3.1 Experimental Setup

Tasks, datasets, and models. We test three tasks using two English datasets: Ontonotes 5.0 for NER (Hovy et al., 2006), and the Universal Dependencies corpus for dependency parsing and POS tagging (UD; Nivre et al., 2016).[1] Both datasets contain texts from various domains, including news, conversational, weblogs, web forums, and more. Due to budget constrains we limit the size of each test set by randomly sampling 1000 samples. We experiment with a diverse set of 9 different LLMs, ranging from open to closed models in various parameter sizes: Llama-2 (Touvron et al., 2023), Mistral (Jiang et al., 2023), Starling (Zhu et al., 2023), Vicuna (Chiang et al., 2023), Mixtral (Jiang et al., 2024), phi-2 (Javaheripi et al., 2023), GPT-4 (Achiam et al., 2023), Claude 3 Haiku,[2] and Gemini 1.5 Pro (Reid et al., 2024).

Prompt and evaluation metric. For each task, we prompt the models by describing the task and the expected output format, followed by 5 demonstration examples and the current inference sample. Since POS tagging serves as a precursor to dependency parsing, both tasks are handled using

[1]We use the HuggingFace versions for both datasets with the *english_v12* configuration for Ontonotes and the *en_ewt* configuration for UD.

[2]www.anthropic.com/news/claude-3-family

a shared prompt. Following Zhao et al. (2021), we sort the examples such that the most similar example is the last one, based on the similarity function ϕ described in Equation 2. See Appendix A for the full prompt templates.

For NER evaulation we use *strict* matching (Segura-Bedmar et al., 2013), where a predicted entity is considered correct if it matches both exact span boundaries and entity type. For dependency parsing we use *labeled attachment score (LAS)*, which measures the accuracy of both the correct head and dependency label for each token. For POS tagging, we use the *POS accuracy*.

Pool sizes. We experiment with sample pools of size 0.1% - 10% of the maximum pool size, defined as the number of unique samples used when considering the full training set as the sample pool.

Oracle. As a reference, we report the performance of using the full training set for each dataset and model, compared to our budget-constrained approach.

3.2 Results

Results for the three best-performing models (Claude 3 Haiku, GPT-4, and Gemini 1.5 Pro) on all tasks are presented in Figure 2. The other smaller models we test are not able to produce outputs of the requested format in more than 50% of the cases, and hence cannot be meaningfully compared against these models, which adhere to the correct format in roughly 97% of the cases. We now discuss findings reflected in these results and conduct further analysis.

The choice of few-shot examples matter in token classification tasks. We observe a large variation in performance when selecting different demonstration examples in all configurations. While this was observed in other tasks (Zhang et al., 2022), to the best of our knowledge, this is the first time this was shown for token classification tasks.

Most pool selection methods perform similarly, random is surprisingly good. None of the four methods consistently outperform the others. Surprisingly, we note that random performs similarly to other methods.

Very small pool sizes can approximate the full training corpus. All sampling methods require a pool of only 220 samples for Ontonotes, and 138 samples for UD, to achieve over 88% of the oracle performance across all configurations.

	NER	DP	POS
Central	67	40	96
Cluster	75	41	96
Vote-k	78	44	96
Random	78	41	96

Table 1: GPT-4 percentage in performance out of the state-of-the-art, when using 5% of the samples used in the fully labeled train set method.

ICL on a budget lags behind state-of-the-art. We compare the ICL results to state-of-the-art results in Table 1. In NER and dependency parsing, fine-tuned methods vastly outperforms using a limited annotation budget. In POS tagging which is considered an easier task, using 138 samples achieves 96% of the state-of-the-art.

4 Related Work

Similar to pool selection, active learning (Shen et al., 2017) also aims to select samples for annotation rather than assuming all samples are annotated. However, active learning operates during training and relies on access to an oracle or intermediate model results (e.g., confidence scores), whereas pool selection assumes no access to the model during training and only relies on observing the outputs of the model.

Recently, Su et al. (2022) introduced a pool selection method as a method for improving downstream performance, which we evaluate as one of our approaches for annotation pool selection (*cluster*). Our work is conceptually different in that it proposes a realistic paradigm under which to examine ICL performance where there are no annotated samples. Subsequently, we differ from them in that we study three different token level tasks, different pool selection methods, and particularly focus on the effect of the pool size on downstream performance.

5 Conclusion

We proposed the framework of ICL on a budget and studied different methods for pool selection, focusing on token classification tasks. We hope this work will inspire more realistic assumptions on the amount of labeled data used in different ICL settings.

6 Limitations

We tested our ICL on a budget approach on a single class of tasks (token classification), because it has high annotation cost and it was relatively less studied in the context of ICL. It is possible that other tasks will show different trends, hence we stress that the contribution here is the methodological approach, rather than advocating for one particular sampling strategy.

References

Josh Achiam, Steven Adler, Sandhini Agarwal, Lama Ahmad, Ilge Akkaya, Florencia Leoni Aleman, Diogo Almeida, Janko Altenschmidt, Sam Altman, Shyamal Anadkat, et al. 2023. Gpt-4 technical report. *ArXiv preprint*, abs/2303.08774.

Tom B. Brown, Benjamin Mann, Nick Ryder, Melanie Subbiah, Jared Kaplan, Prafulla Dhariwal, Arvind Neelakantan, Pranav Shyam, Girish Sastry, Amanda Askell, Sandhini Agarwal, Ariel Herbert-Voss, Gretchen Krueger, Tom Henighan, Rewon Child, Aditya Ramesh, Daniel M. Ziegler, Jeffrey Wu, Clemens Winter, Christopher Hesse, Mark Chen, Eric Sigler, Mateusz Litwin, Scott Gray, Benjamin Chess, Jack Clark, Christopher Berner, Sam McCandlish, Alec Radford, Ilya Sutskever, and Dario Amodei. 2020. Language models are few-shot learners. In *Advances in Neural Information Processing Systems 33: Annual Conference on Neural Information Processing Systems 2020, NeurIPS 2020, December 6-12, 2020, virtual.*

Ernie Chang, Xiaoyu Shen, Hui-Syuan Yeh, and Vera Demberg. 2021. On training instance selection for few-shot neural text generation. In *Proceedings of the 59th Annual Meeting of the Association for Computational Linguistics and the 11th International Joint Conference on Natural Language Processing (Volume 2: Short Papers)*, pages 8–13, Online. Association for Computational Linguistics.

Yukun Chen, Thomas A Lasko, Qiaozhu Mei, Joshua C Denny, and Hua Xu. 2015. A study of active learning methods for named entity recognition in clinical text. *Journal of biomedical informatics*, 58:11–18.

Wei-Lin Chiang, Zhuohan Li, Zi Lin, Ying Sheng, Zhanghao Wu, Hao Zhang, Lianmin Zheng, Siyuan Zhuang, Yonghao Zhuang, Joseph E. Gonzalez, Ion Stoica, and Eric P. Xing. 2023. Vicuna: An open-source chatbot impressing gpt-4 with 90%* chatgpt quality.

Eduard Hovy, Mitchell Marcus, Martha Palmer, Lance Ramshaw, and Ralph Weischedel. 2006. OntoNotes: The 90% solution. In *Proceedings of the Human Language Technology Conference of the NAACL, Companion Volume: Short Papers*, pages 57–60, New York City, USA. Association for Computational Linguistics.

Mojan Javaheripi, Sébastien Bubeck, Marah Abdin, Jyoti Aneja, Sebastien Bubeck, Caio César Teodoro Mendes, Weizhu Chen, Allie Del Giorno, Ronen Eldan, Sivakanth Gopi, et al. 2023. Phi-2: The surprising power of small language models. *Microsoft Research Blog*.

Albert Q Jiang, Alexandre Sablayrolles, Arthur Mensch, Chris Bamford, Devendra Singh Chaplot, Diego de las Casas, Florian Bressand, Gianna Lengyel, Guillaume Lample, Lucile Saulnier, et al. 2023. Mistral 7b. *ArXiv preprint*, abs/2310.06825.

Albert Q Jiang, Alexandre Sablayrolles, Antoine Roux, Arthur Mensch, Blanche Savary, Chris Bamford, Devendra Singh Chaplot, Diego de las Casas, Emma Bou Hanna, Florian Bressand, et al. 2024. Mixtral of experts. *ArXiv preprint*, abs/2401.04088.

Jiachang Liu, Dinghan Shen, Yizhe Zhang, Bill Dolan, Lawrence Carin, and Weizhu Chen. 2022. What makes good in-context examples for GPT-3? In *Proceedings of Deep Learning Inside Out (DeeLIO 2022): The 3rd Workshop on Knowledge Extraction and Integration for Deep Learning Architectures*, pages 100–114, Dublin, Ireland and Online. Association for Computational Linguistics.

Mingyi Liu, Zhiying Tu, Zhongjie Wang, and Xiaofei Xu. 2020. Ltp: a new active learning strategy for bert-crf based named entity recognition. *ArXiv preprint*, abs/2001.02524.

Sewon Min, Xinxi Lyu, Ari Holtzman, Mikel Artetxe, Mike Lewis, Hannaneh Hajishirzi, and Luke Zettlemoyer. 2022. Rethinking the role of demonstrations: What makes in-context learning work? In *Proceedings of the 2022 Conference on Empirical Methods in Natural Language Processing*, pages 11048–11064, Abu Dhabi, United Arab Emirates. Association for Computational Linguistics.

Joakim Nivre, Marie-Catherine de Marneffe, Filip Ginter, Yoav Goldberg, Jan Hajič, Christopher D. Manning, Ryan McDonald, Slav Petrov, Sampo Pyysalo, Natalia Silveira, Reut Tsarfaty, and Daniel Zeman. 2016. Universal Dependencies v1: A multilingual treebank collection. In *Proceedings of the Tenth International Conference on Language Resources and Evaluation (LREC'16)*, pages 1659–1666, Portorož, Slovenia. European Language Resources Association (ELRA).

Machel Reid, Nikolay Savinov, Denis Teplyashin, Dmitry Lepikhin, Timothy Lillicrap, Jean-baptiste Alayrac, Radu Soricut, Angeliki Lazaridou, Orhan Firat, Julian Schrittwieser, et al. 2024. Gemini 1.5: Unlocking multimodal understanding across millions of tokens of context. *ArXiv preprint*, abs/2403.05530.

Nils Reimers and Iryna Gurevych. 2019. Sentence-BERT: Sentence embeddings using Siamese BERT-networks. In *Proceedings of the 2019 Conference on Empirical Methods in Natural Language Processing and the 9th International Joint Conference on Natural Language Processing (EMNLP-IJCNLP)*, pages

3982–3992, Hong Kong, China. Association for Computational Linguistics.

Isabel Segura-Bedmar, Paloma Martínez, and María Herrero-Zazo. 2013. SemEval-2013 task 9 : Extraction of drug-drug interactions from biomedical texts (DDIExtraction 2013). In *Second Joint Conference on Lexical and Computational Semantics (*SEM), Volume 2: Proceedings of the Seventh International Workshop on Semantic Evaluation (SemEval 2013)*, pages 341–350, Atlanta, Georgia, USA. Association for Computational Linguistics.

Yanyao Shen, Hyokun Yun, Zachary Lipton, Yakov Kronrod, and Animashree Anandkumar. 2017. Deep active learning for named entity recognition. In *Proceedings of the 2nd Workshop on Representation Learning for NLP*, pages 252–256, Vancouver, Canada. Association for Computational Linguistics.

Yanyao Shen, Hyokun Yun, Zachary C. Lipton, Yakov Kronrod, and Animashree Anandkumar. 2018. Deep active learning for named entity recognition. In *6th International Conference on Learning Representations, ICLR 2018, Vancouver, BC, Canada, April 30 - May 3, 2018, Conference Track Proceedings*. OpenReview.net.

Kaitao Song, Xu Tan, Tao Qin, Jianfeng Lu, and Tie-Yan Liu. 2020. Mpnet: Masked and permuted pre-training for language understanding. In *Advances in Neural Information Processing Systems 33: Annual Conference on Neural Information Processing Systems 2020, NeurIPS 2020, December 6-12, 2020, virtual*.

Hongjin Su, Jungo Kasai, Chen Henry Wu, Weijia Shi, Tianlu Wang, Jiayi Xin, Rui Zhang, Mari Ostendorf, Luke Zettlemoyer, Noah A Smith, et al. 2022. Selective annotation makes language models better few-shot learners. *ArXiv preprint*, abs/2209.01975.

Hugo Touvron, Louis Martin, Kevin Stone, Peter Albert, Amjad Almahairi, Yasmine Babaei, Nikolay Bashlykov, Soumya Batra, Prajjwal Bhargava, Shruti Bhosale, et al. 2023. Llama 2: Open foundation and fine-tuned chat models. *ArXiv preprint*, abs/2307.09288.

Yiming Zhang, Shi Feng, and Chenhao Tan. 2022. Active example selection for in-context learning. In *Proceedings of the 2022 Conference on Empirical Methods in Natural Language Processing*, pages 9134–9148, Abu Dhabi, United Arab Emirates. Association for Computational Linguistics.

Yue Zhang, Zhenghua Li, Jun Lang, Qingrong Xia, and Min Zhang. 2017. Dependency parsing with partial annotations: An empirical comparison. In *Proceedings of the Eighth International Joint Conference on Natural Language Processing (Volume 1: Long Papers)*, pages 49–58, Taipei, Taiwan. Asian Federation of Natural Language Processing.

Zihao Zhao, Eric Wallace, Shi Feng, Dan Klein, and Sameer Singh. 2021. Calibrate before use: Improving few-shot performance of language models. In *Proceedings of the 38th International Conference on Machine Learning, ICML 2021, 18-24 July 2021, Virtual Event*, volume 139 of *Proceedings of Machine Learning Research*, pages 12697–12706. PMLR.

Banghua Zhu, Evan Frick, Tianhao Wu, Hanlin Zhu, and Jiantao Jiao. 2023. Starling-7b: Improving llm helpfulness & harmlessness with rlaif.

A Prompt Template

In this section we describe the prompt templates we use in our experiments.

A.1 NER task description

You are an NER classifier that identifies the following entities: Person __PER__, Organization __ORG__, Geo-Political __GPE__, Location __LOC__, Facility __FAC__, Work-of-Art __WOA__, Event __EVE__, Product __DUC__, Language __ANG__ use angle brackets to tag in-line, please don't include any additional information other than the annotated sentence and keep original spacing.

A.2 Dependency parsing and POS tagging task description

Your task is to parse the input sentence into a dependency tree by providing a (token, part-of-speech tag, head, deprel) for each token. In the input sentence, tokens are separated by spaces. Possible part-of-speech tags are:

VBN, WDT, GW, NN, TO, IN, JJR, WP, EX, VB, HYPH, JJ, SYM, :, RBR, MD, VBP, JJS, LS, WP$, $, VBD, VBZ, NFP, PRP, NNPS, CC, XX, „ “, NNP, -RRB-, CD, VBG, -LRB-, RP, NNS, PDT, AFX, RB, PRP$, UH, ., WRB, DT, FW, RBS, ADD, POS, ”

Output the parse and nothing else. Here are some examples:

A.3 Prompt design

We first describe the task in question, as outlined above. Next, we add the demonstration examples. For GPT and Claude we add the demonstration examples as follows. For each demonstration example, we use LangChain's[3] HumanMessage class for the original sentence, followed by an AIMessage for the annotated sentence. Finally, we add the inference sample as a HumanMessage.

[3]langchain.com

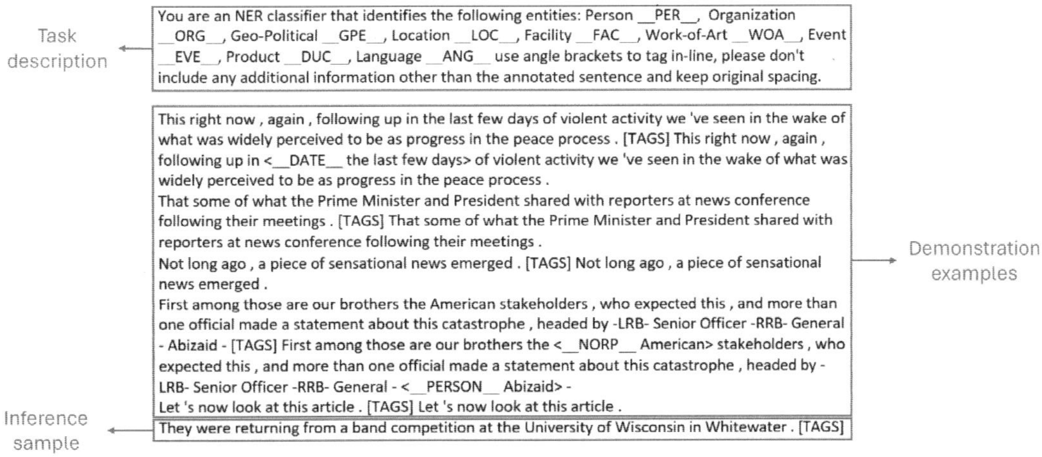

Figure 3: An example NER prompt used in our study.

In Gemini, for which these classes are not implemented, we choose a different strategy: for each demonstration example, we add the original sentence followed by the separator token ([TAGS] for NER, [PARSE] for dependency parsing and POS tagging), and then the annotated sentence. Finally, we add the inference sample, followed by the separator token. Figures 3 and 4 demonstrates an NER and dependency parsing prompts for Gemini, respectively.

B Performance-Diversity Correlation

Min et al. (2022) study the factors that impact performance in ICL and find that the coverage of the label space by the demonstration examples has a strong effect on performance. Drawing inspiration from their findings, we examine whether the diversity in the labels of demonstration examples is correlated with performance. To this end, for each dataset, pool selection method and pool size, we count how many instances of each label (entity for NER, dependency label for dependency parsing, POS tag for POS tagging) were presented in the demonstration examples in the sample pool, and compute the entropy of these counts as a proxy for diversity. For each model, we then compute the Pearson correlation between these entropy values and the model's scores. Table 2 presents the correlations. Correlation is high (> 0.5) for all models in the dependency parsing and POS tagging tasks.

	GPT	Claude	Gemini
NER	0.54	0.36	0.46
DP	0.64	0.62	0.64
POS	0.53	0.63	0.80

Table 2: Pearson correlation of performance with label diversity in the sample pool, as measured by the entropy of entities. All results are significant.

Task description

Your task is to parse the input sentence into a dependency tree by providing a (token, part-of-speech tag, head, deprel) for each token. In the input sentence, tokens are separated by spaces. Possible part-of-speech tags are: VBN, WDT, GW, NN, TO, IN, JJR, WP, EX, VB, HYPH, JJ, SYM, :, RBR, MD, VBP, JJS, LS, WP$, $, VBD, VBZ, NFP, PRP, NNPS, CC, XX, ,, ``, NNP, -RRB-, CD, VBG, -LRB-, RP, NNS, PDT, AFX, RB, PRP$, UH, ., WRB, DT, FW, RBS, ADD, POS.
Output the parse and nothing else. Here are some examples:

Demonstration examples

[input] (An outside water park !)
[parse] ((, -LRB-, 5, punct), (An, DT, 5, det), (outside, JJ, 5, amod), (water, NN, 5, compound), (park, NN, 0, root), (!, ., 5, punct), (), -RRB-, 5, punct)

[input] Besides the obvious tourist spots which I already have planned for .
[parse] (Besides, IN, 5, case), (the, DT, 5, det), (obvious, JJ, 5, amod), (tourist, NN, 5, compound), (spots, NNS, 0, root), (which, WDT, 10, obl), (I, PRP, 10, nsubj), (already, RB, 10, advmod), (have, VBP, 10, aux), (planned, VBN, 5, acl:relcl), (for, IN, 6, case), (., ., 5, punct)

[input] Maybe we can go drinking too .
[parse] (Maybe, RB, 4, advmod), (we, PRP, 4, nsubj), (can, MD, 4, aux), (go, VB, 0, root), (drinking, VBG, 4, xcomp), (too, RB, 4, advmod), (., ., 4, punct)

[input] To relax and to rejuvenate Disney cruise are the best option .
[parse] (To, TO, 2, mark), (relax, VB, 11, advcl), (and, CC, 5, cc), (to, TO, 5, mark), (rejuvenate, VB, 2, conj), (Disney, NNP, 7, compound), (cruise, NN, 11, nsubj), (are, VBP, 11, cop), (the, DT, 11, det), (best, JJS, 11, amod), (option, NN, 0, root), (., ., 11, punct)

[input] Explore which cruise may fit your needs the best .
[parse] (Explore, VB, 0, root), (which, WDT, 3, det), (cruise, NN, 5, nsubj), (may, MD, 5, aux), (fit, VB, 1, ccomp), (your, PRP$, 7, nmod:poss), (needs, NNS, 5, obj), (the, DT, 9, det), (best, RBS, 5, obl:npmod), (., ., 1, punct)

Inference sample

Parse the following sentence:
[input] Why not put together a bottle of champagne , a picnic and have a date on Treasure Island .
[parse]

Figure 4: An example dependency parsing prompt used in our study.

Reassessing Graph Linearization for Sequence-to-sequence AMR Parsing: On the Advantages and Limitations of Triple-Based Encoding

Jeongwoo Kang[1] **Maximin Coavoux**[1] **Cédric Lopez**[2] **Didier Schwab**[1]
[1]Univ. Grenoble Alpes, CNRS, Grenoble INP, LIG, 38000 Grenoble, France
[2]Emvista, Immeuble Le 610, 10 Rue Louis Breguet Bâtiment D, 34830 Jacou, France
[1]{firstname}.{lastname}@univ-grenoble-alpes.fr
[2]{firstname}.{lastname}@emvista.com

Abstract

Sequence-to-sequence models are widely used to train Abstract Meaning Representation (Banarescu et al., 2013, AMR) parsers. To train such models, AMR graphs have to be linearized into a one-line text format. While Penman encoding is typically used for this purpose, we argue that it has limitations: (1) for deep graphs, some closely related nodes are located far apart in the linearized text (2) Penman's tree-based encoding necessitates inverse roles to handle node re-entrancy, doubling the number of relation types to predict. To address these issues, we propose a triple-based linearization method and compare its efficiency with Penman linearization. Although triples are well suited to represent a graph, our results suggest room for improvement in triple encoding to better compete with Penman's concise and explicit representation of a nested graph structure.

1 Introduction

Abstract Meaning Representation (AMR) captures text meaning, such as "who does what to whom," and represents it in graphs (see Figure 1). Structured information is easier for computers to process and therefore, AMR is widely used in NLP applications, e.g., machine translation (Wein and Schneider, 2024), text generation (Huang et al., 2023), or human-robot interaction systems (Bonial et al., 2019, 2023).

Sequence-to-sequence (seq2seq) approaches have recently gained popularity for AMR parsing due to strong performance and easy implementation. For prediction, the model receives an input sentence and outputs an AMR graph in text format. To train seq2seq models for AMR parsing, graph linearization to represent an AMR graph in a one-line text format is a prerequisite. Penman encoding is the most common method for AMR graph linearization, representing graphs as *tree*-like structures. It uses variables (e.g. s, s2 in Figure 2)

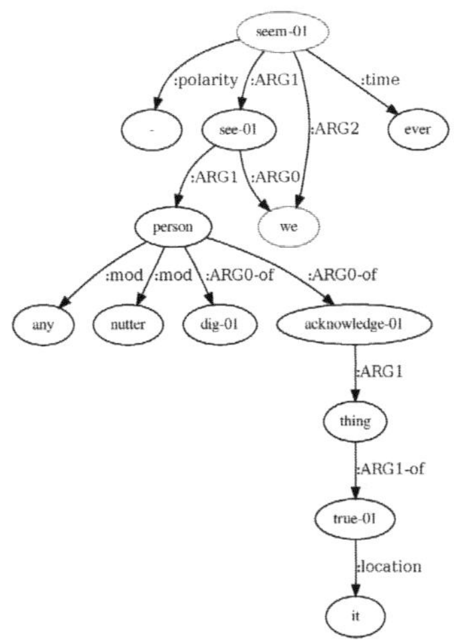

Figure 1: AMR graph for "We never seem to see any of the dug-in nutters acknowledge the truth in it." Example from the AMR 3.0 dataset (Knight et al., 2020).

```
(s / seem-01 :polarity -
      :ARG1 (s2 / see-01
           :ARG0 w
           :ARG1 (p / person
                   :mod (a / any)
                   :mod (n / nutter)
                   :ARG0-of (d / dig-01)
                   :ARG0-of (a2 / acknowledge-01
                       :ARG1 (t / thing
                               :ARG1-of (t2 / true-01
                                   :location (i / it))))))
      :ARG2 (w / we)
      :time (e / ever))
```

Figure 2: AMR in Penman encoding for Figure 2.

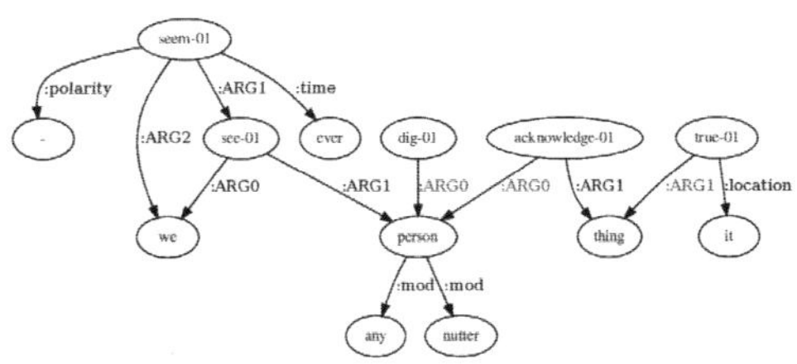

Figure 3: AMR graph without inverse roles.

The Sixth Workshop on Insights from Negative Results in NLP, pages 15–23
May 4, 2025 ©2025 Association for Computational Linguistics

as node IDs to manage co-references. In addition, parentheses represent nested structures of AMR graphs. However, Penman has key limitations to training a seq2seq model:

1) **Parent-Child Distance**: Parent and child nodes may appear far apart in the linearized text, despite being closely connected in the graph. For example, in Figure 2, `seem-01` and `we` are encoded distant in Penman format (highlighted in red) despite their proximity in the graph of Figure 2. This is observed when a preceding sibling node has a deep sub-graph. We hypothesize that this long distance increases the difficulty of learning strong parent-child connections, especially in deeper graphs. 2) **Inverse Roles**: Penman represents a graph in a tree-based format. To be specific, when a node has multiple parent nodes (node re-entrancy), the child node is duplicated to maintain a single-rooted tree structure. To fit an AMR graph into a tree structure, Penman introduces inverse roles by rewriting `:relation` as `:relation-of` (see Figure 2 where inverse roles are highlighted in blue). This increases the number of relations the model must learn, potentially complicating training and reducing model performance. Figure 3 shows how inverse roles are unnecessary in a graph-based representation.

To address these issues, we propose an alternative triple-based format for AMR graph linearization. A triple consists of a parent node, a child node, and a relation type between them, ensuring that parent and child nodes remain adjacent in the linearized text. This format also eliminates inverse roles by replacing `(node A, relation-of, node B)` with `(node B, relation, node A)`. In the rest of the paper, we compare Penman and triple-based formats with examples, highlighting their strengths and limitations in training a seq2seq AMR parser. Our contributions to seq2seq AMR parsing are:

- A triple-based linearization method for training seq2seq AMR parsers.
- A detailed comparison with Penman linearization, focusing on performance across varying graph depths and lengths, and identifying areas for improvement.

2 Related Work

Triple encoding has been used in relation extraction (Huguet Cabot and Navigli, 2021; Ye et al., 2021; Saxena et al., 2022) and discourse representation structure (DRS) parsing (van Noord et al., 2018a,b). The closest to our approach is van Noord et al. (2018a), who convert AMR graphs into DRS triples. However, their representation differs from ours by mapping AMR relations to DRS roles and adding extra information that does not exist in AMR. In addition, they did not include training an AMR parser in their work. While triple encoding is widely used in relation extraction and DRS parsing, it has not been used for seq2seq AMR parsers. In our work, we propose using it to linearize AMR graphs, analyzing its strengths and weaknesses as an encoding method.

```
s instance seem-01             s2 instance see-01   p instance person
a instance any                 n instance nutter    d instance dig-01
a2 instance acknowledge-01     t instance thing     t2 instance true-01
i instance it                  w instance we        e instance ever
s polarity -                   s ARG1 s2            s2 ARG0 w
s2 ARG1 p                      p mod a              p mod n
d ARG0 p                       a2 ARG0 p            a2 ARG1 t
t2 ARG1 t                      t2 location i        s ARG2 w
s time e
```

Figure 4: Triple linearization of the graph in Figure 2.

3 Methodology: Triple Linearization

Triple representation mitigates the challenges of Penman linearization (described in Section 1) by encoding a graph as a set of triples. Figure 4 illustrates that the parent-child nodes, which were distantly located in Figure 2, are now adjacent in the triple representation (highlighted in red). We hypothesize this helps the model learn direct parent-child relationships, especially in deeper graphs. Triples also eliminate inverse roles by reversing the order of two nodes, as shown in Figure 4 (highlighted in blue).

The triple format, widely used for graph representation (e.g., RDF), aligns better with AMR's graph structure than Penman's tree-based encoding. Its flexibility supports graphs with multiple roots or re-entrancies, making it potentially suitable for broader semantic frameworks. To assess its utility, we trained seq2seq AMR parsers using triple and Penman formats.

Despite its advantages, triple linearization can result in verbose linearization, slowing down the learning process, and may be less effective at capturing nested structures of graphs compared to Penman. This study evaluates both linearization methods to train seq2seq AMR parsers, exploring: **(1)** whether triple representation improves AMR parsing; **(2)** which graphs benefit most from triple representation, such as those with deep structures or large size, and **(3)** if combining triple and Penman representations enhances parsing performance.

Experiments involve training models respectively with triple, Penman, and both formats (multi-task learning). Using both formats may serve as a form of data augmentation, as it effectively doubles the training data by representing one example in two linearized formats. We train and evaluate our model with English AMR 3.0 (Knight et al., 2020) data. We evaluate our model using SMATCH (Cai and Knight, 2013) score by counting the matching triples between two graphs. We analyze results by graph depth and size to determine which types of graphs benefit from different encoding methods.

Triple linearization strategies To linearize AMR graphs in triples, we extract all triples and unfold them in depth-first search order using the PENMAN library.[1] Four linearization strategies are applied, varying in whether variables[2] or inverse roles are retained. We provide an example for each linearization type in Table 3 and Figure 7 of Appendix A. Each model is named based on linearization type as follows:

- **Triple_X_var_X_invrole**: Variables and inverse roles are removed. Variables are replaced by node names, and inverse roles are converted by reversing node order.[3] Reversing inverse roles reduces the number of relation types from 155 to 115 in our training data. Triples are separated by a pipe symbol (|).
- **Triple_X_var_O_invrole**: Variables are removed, but inverse roles are retained.
- **Triple_O_var_O_invrole**: Both variables and inverse roles are retained. Variables and their instances are represented as triples with the `instance` relation (e.g., `f instance fruit`). This approach is the most comprehensive, as no information is lost from the original graph during linearization.
- **Triple_O_var_X_invrole**: Variables are retained, but inverse roles are removed.

[1]`https://penman.readthedocs.io/en/`, version 1.3.0

[2]Removing variables is a common pre-processing strategy for seq2seq AMR parsing (Konstas et al., 2017; van Noord and Bos, 2017). This leads to information loss but effectively reduces data sparsity for training.

[3]For the models discussed in this article, variables and inverse roles are removed in this manner.

4 Experimental Setup

Models are trained using the large mBART model (Tang et al., 2021) on each linearization type.[4]

4.1 Baseline

To compare our method with existing approaches using Penman encoding, we trained a model on AMR graphs linearized using Penman encoding, which serves as our baseline. Note that maintaining inverse roles is a necessary aspect of Penman encoding and **X_invrole** types are not available for Penman encoding. For training, we employed the same mBART model and trained two models as follows (see Table 3 for examples):

- **Penman_X_var_O_invrole**: Variables are removed, but inverse roles are retained.[5]
- **Penman_O_var_O_invrole**: Both variables and inverse roles are retained.

4.2 Multi-task Learning

As mentioned in Section 1, combining triple and Penman encodings may offer complementary benefits. To test this, we trained models in a multi-task learning framework by merging two differently encoded datasets. During training, the model learns from shuffled examples with a token indicating the encoding type. For predictions, the model is instructed to use either triple or Penman encoding to use the corresponding decoding strategy to reconstruct graphs. We trained four models:

- **Multi_tri_O_var_O_invrole**: Both variables and inverse roles are retained. The main task is triple encoding, with Penman encoding as an auxiliary task. This means that the best model is selected based on the performance on the validation set using triple encoding, while Penman encoding is treated as an auxiliary task to help the triple learning.
- **Multi_penman_O_var_O_invrole**: Both variables and inverse roles are retained. The main task is Penman encoding, with triple encoding as an auxiliary.
- **Multi_tri_X_var_O_invrole**: Variables are removed but inverse roles are retained. The best model is chosen based on the model's performance in triple prediction.

[4]The model was chosen based on our goal of developing a multilingual system, which was not covered in this article.

[5]We used the script from van Noord and Bos (2017).

Model	*The Little Prince*	AMR 3.0
Triple_O_var_O_invrole	76.2 ± 0.3	80.0 ± 0.2
Triple_O_var_X_invrole	76.1 ± 0.5	80.3 ± 0.1
Triple_X_var_O_invrole	76.5 ± 0.2	78.7 ± 0.1
Triple_X_var_X_invrole	76.2 ± 0.2	78.9 ± 0.8
Penman_O_var_O_invrole	**77.0** ± 0.4	**80.9** ± 0.2
Penman_X_var_O_invrole	76.7 ± 0.1	80.2 ± 0.1
Multi_tri_O_var_O_invrole	<u>76.9</u> ± 0.2	80.3 ± 0.1
Multi_tri_X_var_O_invrole	76.3 ± 0.2	78.9 ± 0.1
Multi_penman_O_O_invrole	76.7 ± 0.2	<u>80.6</u> ± 0.3
Multi_penman_X_var_O_invrole	76.1 ± 0.1	79.8 ± 0.1

Table 1: SMATCH scores for evaluation (with the highest scores in **bold** and the second-highest scores <u>underlined</u>).

- **Multi_penman_X_var_O_invrole**: Variables are removed but inverse roles are retained. The best model is selected based on performance in Penman prediction.

5 Results and Insights

Global results. Table 1 presents results on two test sets: *The Little Prince*[6] and AMR 3.0. The Penman single-task model with variables (**Penman_O_var_O_invrole**) performs best on both test sets (77.0 and 80.9, respectively). Among single-task triple models, **Tri_O_var_O_invrole** achieves the best results, with a marginal gap from the best model ($\leq$1 SMATCH).

Preserving variables consistently improves performance, contradicting the assumption that removing them aids learning by reducing data sparsity. This suggests variable removal leads to critical information loss. In addition, learning from Penman encoding while performing an auxiliary triple task reduces performance, whereas the reverse improves it. This indicates Penman encoding provides structural information beneficial to triple encoding but not vice versa.

Within triple linearization, removing inverse roles improves performance on AMR 3.0 but not *The Little Prince*. Given that AMR 3.0 includes longer sentences, removing inverse roles may benefit longer sentences while harming shorter ones. However, the inconsistency across test sets could also suggest inverse roles have only a marginal effect.

Triple linearization does not improve learning for deeper graphs. We hypothesized that triple linearization could enhance training by positioning child and parent nodes closer, especially when a preceding sibling has a deep subgraph. In Penman encoding, such cases place these nodes farther apart. Assuming this issue is more common in deeper graphs, we analyzed results by reference graph depth (distance from the root to the furthest node), focusing on AMR 3.0, which has greater depth variety than *The Little Prince*.

Our results (Figure 5, Appendix) show SMATCH scores by depth align with overall scores, indicating no learning benefit for deeper graphs with triple encoding. The best model, **Penman_O_var_O_inverserole**, consistently performed best across depths. This contradicts our hypothesis that triple encoding benefits seq2seq AMR learning by bringing parent-child nodes closer together. Instead, the results emphasize the benefit of Penman's concise graph representation and its ability to explicitly encode nested structures, which play a more critical role in model performance.

Triple linearization does not improve learning for longer graphs. We also analyzed performance by graph length (i.e., token count in the linearized reference graph), assuming verbose triple encoding would degrade performance on longer graphs. Since graph depth and length are not always correlated, results may differ from the depth analysis. Figure 6 in the Appendix shows the results per graph length with token counts of reference graphs grouped into buckets of 50 for clarity. For shorter graphs, the gap between models is smaller, but as the graphs become longer, the performance of triple models decreases more noticeably, resulting in a wider gap. This supports our earlier hypothesis regarding the limitations of triple encoding: its verbose representation likely contributes to the observed performance degradation on lengthy graphs.

6 Conclusion

We introduced triple linearization as an alternative to Penman linearization, hypothesizing that it could improve training for several reasons: (1) parent and child nodes are always located together in a triple, (2) the elimination of inverse roles may simplify training by reducing the number of relations, (3) and triples more closely resemble the underlying graph structure, while Penman encoding represents a graph in a more tree-like format. Contrary to our hypothesis, Penman has proven to be a more effective linearization method to train a seq2seq parsing.

[6]https://github.com/flipz357/AMR-World

However, the gap between the best Penman model and certain triple-based models is marginal. Our results show a potential to train a seq2seq AMR parser that predicts a graph directly (not a tree-based representation) while maintaining equivalent performance. Notably, the model's output in triples more naturally aligns with AMR's graph structure than Penman. Our code to train and evaluate the model is available on `https://github.com/Emvista/Triple_AMR_Parser.git`.

Acknowledgments

We thank reviewers for their helpful comments and Cécile Macaire for proof-reading this article. Jeongwoo Kang and Maximin Coavoux gratefully acknowledge the support of the French National Research Agency (grant ANR-23-CE23-0017-01). This work was granted access to the HPC resources of IDRIS under the allocation 2024-AD011012853R2 made by GENCI.

References

Laura Banarescu, Claire Bonial, Shu Cai, Madalina Georgescu, Kira Griffitt, Ulf Hermjakob, Kevin Knight, Philipp Koehn, Martha Palmer, and Nathan Schneider. 2013. Abstract Meaning Representation for sembanking. In *Proceedings of the 7th Linguistic Annotation Workshop and Interoperability with Discourse*, pages 178–186, Sofia, Bulgaria. Association for Computational Linguistics.

Claire Bonial, Julie Foresta, Nicholas C. Fung, Cory J. Hayes, Philip Osteen, Jacob Arkin, Benned Hedegaard, and Thomas Howard. 2023. Abstract Meaning Representation for grounded human-robot communication. In *Proceedings of the Fourth International Workshop on Designing Meaning Representations*, pages 34–44, Nancy, France. Association for Computational Linguistics.

Claire N. Bonial, Lucia Donatelli, Jessica Ervin, and Clare R. Voss. 2019. Abstract Meaning Representation for human-robot dialogue. In *Proceedings of the Society for Computation in Linguistics (SCiL) 2019*, pages 236–246.

Shu Cai and Kevin Knight. 2013. Smatch: an evaluation metric for semantic feature structures. In *Proceedings of the 51st Annual Meeting of the Association for Computational Linguistics (Volume 2: Short Papers)*, pages 748–752, Sofia, Bulgaria. Association for Computational Linguistics.

Kuan-Hao Huang, Varun Iyer, I-Hung Hsu, Anoop Kumar, Kai-Wei Chang, and Aram Galstyan. 2023. ParaAMR: A large-scale syntactically diverse paraphrase dataset by AMR back-translation. In *Proceedings of the 61st Annual Meeting of the Association for Computational Linguistics (Volume 1: Long Papers)*, pages 8047–8061, Toronto, Canada. Association for Computational Linguistics.

Pere-Lluís Huguet Cabot and Roberto Navigli. 2021. REBEL: Relation extraction by end-to-end language generation. In *Findings of the Association for Computational Linguistics: EMNLP 2021*, pages 2370–2381, Punta Cana, Dominican Republic. Association for Computational Linguistics.

Kevin Knight, Bianca Badarau, Laura Baranescu, Claire Bonial, Madalina Bardocz, Kira Griffitt, Ulf Hermjakob, Daniel Marcu, Martha Palmer, Tim O'Gorman, and Nathan Schneider. 2020. Abstract meaning representation (amr) annotation release 3.0 ldc2020t02. Philadelphia: Linguistic Data Consortium.

Ioannis Konstas, Srinivasan Iyer, Mark Yatskar, Yejin Choi, and Luke Zettlemoyer. 2017. Neural AMR: Sequence-to-sequence models for parsing and generation. In *Proceedings of the 55th Annual Meeting of the Association for Computational Linguistics (Volume 1: Long Papers)*, pages 146–157, Vancouver, Canada. Association for Computational Linguistics.

Apoorv Saxena, Adrian Kochsiek, and Rainer Gemulla. 2022. Sequence-to-sequence knowledge graph completion and question answering. In *Proceedings of the 60th Annual Meeting of the Association for Computational Linguistics (Volume 1: Long Papers)*, pages 2814–2828, Dublin, Ireland. Association for Computational Linguistics.

Yuqing Tang, Chau Tran, Xian Li, Peng-Jen Chen, Naman Goyal, Vishrav Chaudhary, Jiatao Gu, and Angela Fan. 2021. Multilingual translation from denoising pre-training. In *Findings of the Association for Computational Linguistics: ACL-IJCNLP 2021*, pages 3450–3466, Online. Association for Computational Linguistics.

Rik van Noord, Lasha Abzianidze, Hessel Haagsma, and Johan Bos. 2018a. Evaluating scoped meaning representations. In *Proceedings of the Eleventh International Conference on Language Resources and Evaluation (LREC 2018)*, Miyazaki, Japan. European Language Resources Association (ELRA).

Rik van Noord, Lasha Abzianidze, Antonio Toral, and Johan Bos. 2018b. Exploring neural methods for parsing discourse representation structures. *Transactions of the Association for Computational Linguistics*, 6:619–633.

Rik van Noord and Johan Bos. 2017. Neural semantic parsing by character-based translation: Experiments with abstract meaning representations. *Computational Linguistics in the Netherlands Journal*, 7:93–108.

Shira Wein and Nathan Schneider. 2024. Lost in translationese? reducing translation effect using Abstract Meaning Representation. In *Proceedings of the 18th Conference of the European Chapter of the Association for Computational Linguistics (Volume 1: Long*

Papers), pages 753–765, St. Julian's, Malta. Association for Computational Linguistics.

Hongbin Ye, Ningyu Zhang, Shumin Deng, Mosha Chen, Chuanqi Tan, Fei Huang, and Huajun Chen. 2021. Contrastive triple extraction with generative transformer. In *Proceedings of the AAAI conference on artificial intelligence*, volume 35, pages 14257–14265.

A Appendix

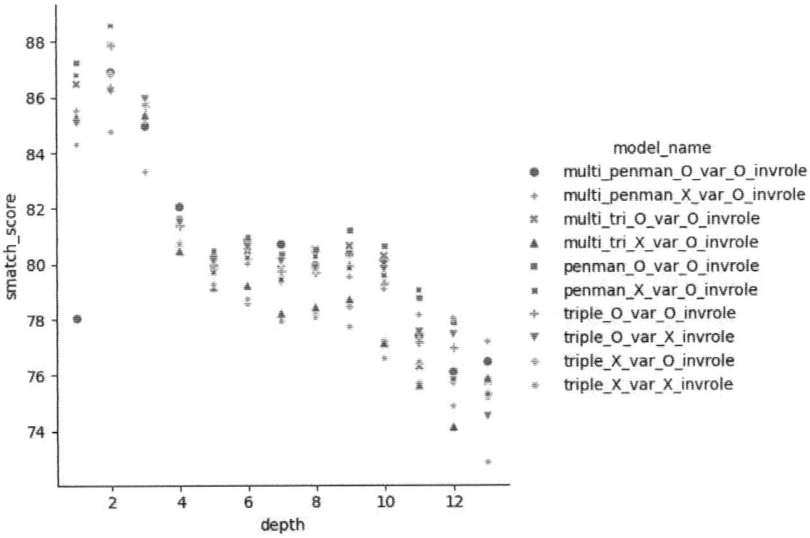

Figure 5: SMATCH score per graph depth.

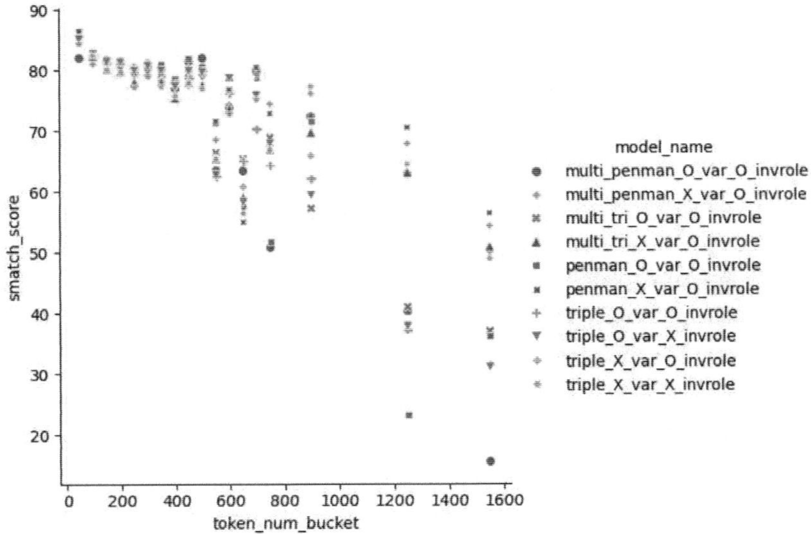

Figure 6: SMATCH score per graph length. The length is measured by the number of tokens in a linearized graph and token counts are grouped into buckets of 50 for clarity.

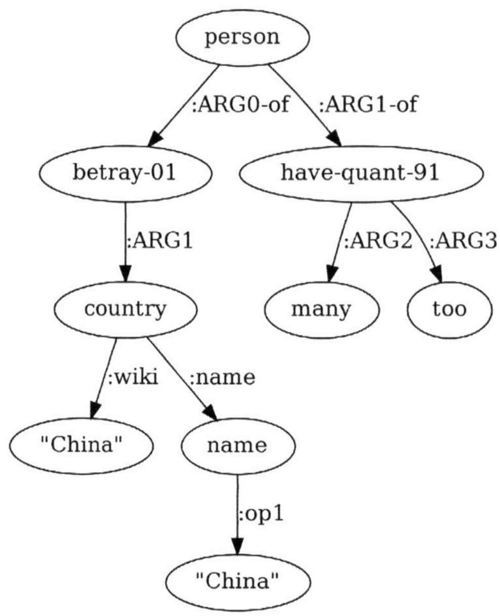

Figure 7: AMR graph for “There are too many traitors of China!”. This example is drawn from AMR 3.0 dataset (Knight et al., 2020).

Triple_X_var_X_invrole	Triple_X_var_O_invrole	Triple_O_var_O_invrole	Triple_O_var_X_invrole
person ARG0-of betray-01 | betray-01 ARG1 country | country name " China " | person ARG1-of have-quant-91 | have-quant-91 ARG2 many | have-quant-91 ARG3 too	betray-01 ARG0 person | betray-01 ARG1 country | country name " China " | have-quant-91 ARG1 person | have-quant-91 ARG2 many | have-quant-91 ARG3 too	p instance person | b instance betray-01 | c instance country | h instance have-quant-91 | m instance many | t instance too | p ARG0-of b | b ARG1 c | c name " China " | p ARG1-of h | h ARG2 m | h ARG3 t	p instance person | b instance betray-01 | c instance country | h instance have-quant-91 | m instance many | t instance too | b ARG0 p | b ARG1 c | c name " China " | h ARG1 p | h ARG2 m | h ARG3 t

Table 2: Triple encoding examples of Figure 7.

Penman_X_var_O_invrole	Penman_O_var_O_invrole
(person :ARG0-of (betray-01 :ARG1 (country :name " China ")) :ARG1-of (have-quant-91 :ARG2 (many) :ARG3 (too)))	(p / person :ARG0-of (b / betray-01 :ARG1 (c / country :name " China " Salut Maximin, j'ai soumis la version actuelle (changement du titre, ajouter des commentaires de Cédroc dans la conclusion) au workshop)) :ARG1-of (h / have-quant-91 :ARG2 (m / many) :ARG3 (t / too)))

Table 3: Penman encoding examples of Figure 7.

Corrective In-Context Learning: Evaluating Self-Correction in Large Language Models

Mario Sanz-Guerrero[1] and **Katharina von der Wense**[1,2]
[1]Johannes Gutenberg University Mainz, Germany
[2]University of Colorado Boulder, USA
{msanzgue, k.vonderwense}@uni-mainz.de

Abstract

In-context learning (ICL) has transformed the use of large language models (LLMs) for NLP tasks, enabling few-shot learning by conditioning on labeled examples without finetuning. Despite its effectiveness, ICL is prone to errors, especially for challenging examples. With the goal of improving the performance of ICL, we propose *corrective in-context learning* (CICL), an approach that incorporates a model's incorrect predictions alongside ground truth corrections into the prompt, aiming to enhance classification accuracy through self-correction. However, contrary to our hypothesis, extensive experiments on text classification tasks demonstrate that CICL consistently underperforms standard ICL, with performance degrading as the proportion of corrections in the prompt increases. Our findings indicate that CICL introduces confusion by disrupting the model's task understanding, rather than refining its predictions. Additionally, we observe that presenting harder examples in standard ICL does not improve performance, suggesting that example difficulty alone may not be a reliable criterion for effective selection. By presenting these negative results, we provide important insights into the limitations of self-corrective mechanisms in LLMs and offer directions for future research.[1]

1 Introduction

In-context learning (ICL; Brown et al., 2020) has emerged as a powerful paradigm for leveraging large language models (LLMs) for various NLP tasks, including text classification. Unlike traditional approaches that require finetuning on task-specific data, ICL allows models to make predictions based on a small number of examples presented in the prompt, effectively transforming LLMs into flexible tools for few-shot learning. This paradigm has demonstrated remarkable performance in numerous scenarios, often approaching or surpassing finetuned models on specific tasks (Brown et al., 2020).

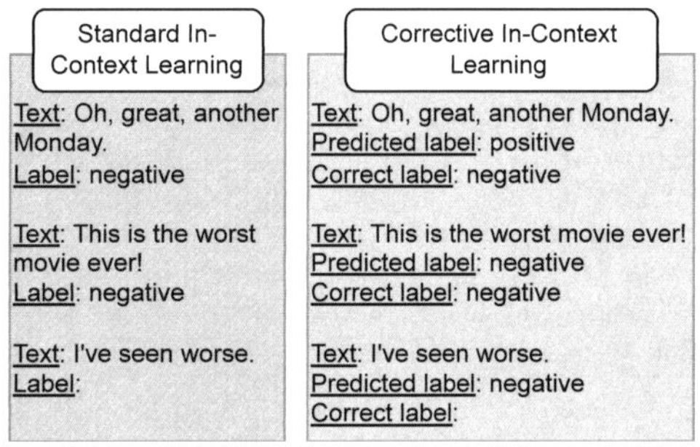

Figure 1: CICL prompt example. The model is tasked with predicting the correct label based on its own prediction, using examples that include both the prediction and its correction.

Although effective, ICL is susceptible to errors, particularly with difficult examples. We set out to further improve ICL by introducing a novel extension of it, which we term *corrective in-context learning* (CICL). Our approach is based on the idea that providing the model with its initial predictions alongside the correct ground truth labels can serve as a feedback mechanism, enabling the model to refine its understanding and improve subsequent predictions.

CICL builds on the intuition that LLMs, when exposed to their own errors in conjunction with the correct answers, might learn from these mistakes within the confines of a single interaction. For instance, if a model predicts "positive" for a sentence that is actually "negative," presenting this prediction–error pair could prompt the model to recalibrate its internal representations and make better-informed predictions for similar inputs.

However, our empirical evaluation reveals a different story. While the approach is theoretically promising, our experiments show that CICL fails to deliver the anticipated improvements. In some cases, performance even deteriorates compared to

[1]Code and data are available at https://github.com/mario-sanz/CICL.

The Sixth Workshop on Insights from Negative Results in NLP, pages 24–33
May 4, 2025

standard ICL. This underscores the complexity of self-correction in LLMs and the importance of rigorously evaluating intuitive extensions to ICL.

In this paper, we present a detailed investigation of CICL for text classification tasks. We outline our methodology, describe the experimental setup, and analyze the results, focusing on understanding why this approach falls short of expectations. By sharing these negative results, we aim to contribute to the growing discourse on the limitations of LLMs and to inspire future research to develop more effective self-correction mechanisms.

2 Related Work

In-Context Learning Introduced by Brown et al. (2020), ICL enables LLMs to perform tasks via few-shot prompting without parameter updates. Subsequent work has explored factors influencing ICL performance, including example selection (Liu et al., 2022) and ordering (Lu et al., 2022), raising questions about its robustness to errors or ambiguous examples. To enhance ICL, prompt tuning methods (Lester et al., 2021; Li and Liang, 2021) optimize soft prompts, improving adaptation while maintaining frozen model parameters, bridging the gap between ICL and finetuning.

Self-Correction in LLMs Prior work explores self-correction through iterative refinement (Madaan et al., 2023), finetuning on self-generated data (Huang et al., 2023), or reinforcement learning (Kumar et al., 2024). These approaches, however, require multi-step processes, parameter updates, or external rewards. In contrast, we investigate whether LLMs can self-correct *in-context* by directly incorporating corrections into the prompt. Closest to our setting, Monea et al. (2024) show that LLMs struggle to improve from binary reward signals (correct/incorrect) in ICL scenarios. While their feedback is implicit, we extend this observation to *explicit ground truth corrections* and similarly find degraded performance.

3 Methodology

3.1 Standard In-Context Learning

ICL leverages the few-shot capabilities of LLMs by conditioning predictions on a prompt constructed from a small set of labeled examples. Formally, given a dataset of examples $\{x_i, y_i\}$, where x_i represents a text input and y_i is a class label verbalized as one of the possible labels in the set $\mathcal{L}$, the model M predicts the label for a query x using a context prompt C_k of k examples:

$$\hat{y} = \arg\max_{y \in \mathcal{L}} P_M(y \mid C_k, x) \qquad (1)$$

ICL operates under the assumption that the few-shot examples encapsulate task-relevant patterns, allowing the model to generalize to unseen queries. This paradigm has demonstrated remarkable versatility and competitive performance across numerous tasks and datasets (Brown et al., 2020). However, its effectiveness is heavily dependent on the quality and representativeness of the examples in the prompt (Liu et al., 2022). Furthermore, biases in the selection or ordering of examples, as well as the inherent biases of the model, can significantly influence predictions, posing challenges for consistent and reliable performance (Zhao et al., 2021).

In this study, standard ICL is the baseline against which we compare the proposed CICL approach, providing insights into whether iterative feedback mechanisms can address some of these challenges. The structure of the ICL prompt, along with an example, is provided in Appendix B.1.

3.2 Corrective In-Context Learning

CICL extends the standard ICL paradigm by introducing a second round of predictions informed by feedback from the first round. The algorithm is as follows:

1. *Initial prediction*: A prompt is constructed from k randomly selected examples from the training data, each consisting of an input–output pair (x_i, y_i), for $i \in 1, ..., k$. This prompt is used to generate prediction $\hat{y}$ for the test input x via standard ICL.

2. *Feedback incorporation*: We perform ICL for the k examples selected in Step 1, getting the model's predictions $\hat{y}_i$ for each example (x_i, y_i), with the remaining $k-1$ examples acting as few-shot examples. Using these predictions, a feedback-augmented prompt (CICL) is constructed from triplets of the form $(x_i, \hat{y}_i, y_i)$, where x_i is the input text, $\hat{y}_i$ is the predicted label, and y_i is the true label. These triplets explicitly highlight the model's errors (when $\hat{y}_i \neq y_i$) and correct predictions (when $\hat{y}_i = y_i$), providing the model with a context to learn from its earlier outputs.

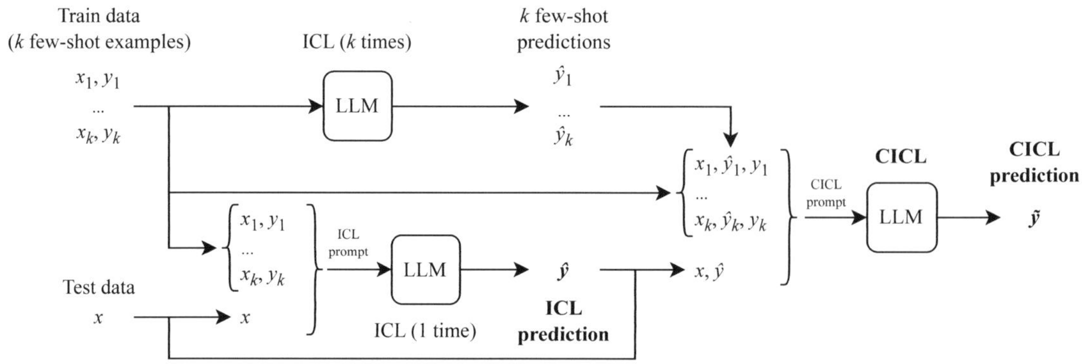

Figure 2: Diagram of the CICL methodology. For each test instance x, k few-shot examples $(x_1, y_1), \ldots, (x_k, y_k)$ are selected. Standard ICL generates predictions $\hat{y}_1, \ldots, \hat{y}_k$ for these examples, which are used to build the CICL prompt. This, combined with the initial ICL prediction $\hat{y}$ for x, allows the model to predict the corrected label $\tilde{y}$.

3. *Corrective prediction*: To perform the CICL prediction for the input x, the feedback prompt built in Step 2 is expanded to include x along with its initial prediction $\hat{y}$ (obtained in Step 1). The task for the model is then to predict a corrected label $\tilde{y}$ for x, leveraging the feedback triplets to generalize how errors were corrected in the few-shot examples.

This iterative setup allows the model to "see" its own mistakes and explicitly incorporate the correct answers during the second round, hypothesizing that this feedback mechanism can improve its performance. Figure 2 shows a diagram of the proposed methodology for CICL, and the structure of the CICL prompt, along with an example, is provided in Appendix B.2.

4 Experiments

4.1 Experimental Setup

Datasets We evaluate CICL using 17 text classification datasets widely adopted in previous work. These datasets span a variety of tasks, including sentiment analysis, topic classification, and more. Further details are provided in Appendix A.

Models To explore the effectiveness of CICL across different models and ensure findings are not model-specific, we use four recent LLMs: Llama-3.1 (8B; Dubey et al., 2024), GPT-J (6B; Wang and Komatsuzaki, 2021), Mistral 7B v0.3 (Jiang et al., 2023) and Qwen2.5 (7B; Qwen et al., 2024). The choice of these relatively small-sized models allows for extensive experimentation while maintaining computational feasibility. However, preliminary experiments with the larger 70B version of Llama-3.1 yielded similar results to the smaller versions.

Implementation Details Following prior work on ICL for text classification, we use simple and unified templates for all datasets and do not include task instructions, keeping human engineering to a minimal level (Min et al., 2022; Fei et al., 2023). Also following prior work, we set $k = 8$ few-shot examples, which enables incorporating a fair number of corrections in the prompt while keeping computational costs manageable. Preliminary experiments with larger k values showed similar results, so we stick with $k = 8$ for simplicity.

To assess how CICL performs with different levels of corrected examples, we introduce varying proportions of corrected examples in the CICL prompt, ranging from 0% (no corrected examples) to 100% (all examples corrected) in increments of 25%. Each proportion determines how many of the k examples in the CICL prompt are corrected (i.e., their initial ICL prediction was incorrect). This approach allows us to evaluate how the ratio of corrected feedback influences the model's ability to refine its predictions. To minimize the impact of randomness in the results, every experimental configuration is run using 5 different random seeds.

Metric We compare standard ICL and CICL performance using macro-F1 score, which accounts for class imbalance.

4.2 Results

Figure 3 compares the performance of standard ICL and CICL across different models. The results present the mean and standard deviation of

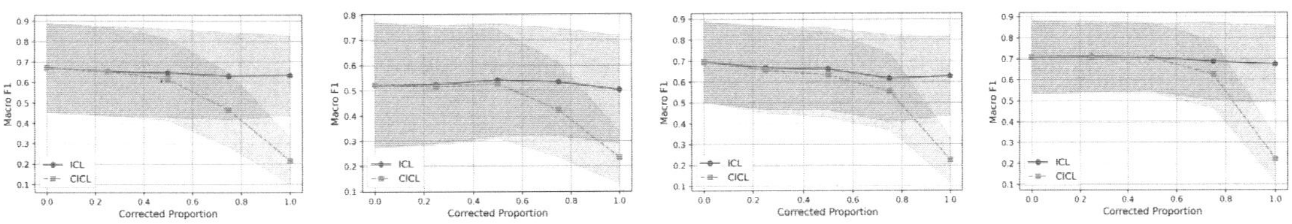

(a) Llama-3.1 (8B). (b) GPT-J (6B). (c) Mistral 7B v0.3. (d) Qwen2.5 (7B).

Figure 3: Mean Macro-F1 ($\pm$ Std Dev) across all datasets for each model, comparing standard ICL (blue) and CICL (orange). As the proportion of corrected examples increases (x-axis), the performance of CICL decreases (y-axis).

Macro-F1 scores across all datasets, evaluated for varying proportions of corrected examples in CICL. Detailed results are available in Appendix C.

Contrary to our hypothesis, CICL consistently underperforms standard ICL. When the proportion of corrected examples is 0%—or even 25% for some models—both methods yield equivalent performance, as the "corrective" task essentially reduces to replicating the previously predicted label. However, as the proportion of corrected examples increases, CICL's performance deteriorates further, highlighting the model's struggle to integrate feedback from corrected examples effectively.

Our findings suggest that the corrective nature of CICL introduces confusion rather than guiding the model towards improved predictions. Swapping (correcting) labels in the few-shot examples appears to disrupt the model's internal representations, making it harder to generalize and refine predictions, especially when encountering harder examples.

4.3 Statistical Analyses

To assess the significance of these performance differences, we conduct statistical tests. A Shapiro-Wilk test for normality reveals no statistical evidence supporting normality in the distributions of ICL and CICL results. Therefore, we employ non-parametric tests to evaluate the impact of correction proportions on performance.

A Wilcoxon signed-rank test is used to determine the threshold at which ICL becomes statistically superior to CICL. As shown in Table 1, from a correction proportion of 25% onward, ICL demonstrates statistically significant superiority over CICL, reinforcing our conclusion that CICL's self-corrective mechanism is ineffective.

Additionally, a Kruskal-Wallis test is conducted to examine variation in performance across correction proportions (for CICL) and example conditions (for ICL). Table 2 highlights significant

Corrected Proportion	Statistic	P-value
0%	178.00	0.7916
25%	9453.00	4e-03*
50%	20439.00	7e-04*
75%	13553.00	1e-16*
100%	984.00	9e-54*

Table 1: Wilcoxon signed-rank test results for different correction proportions. * indicates significant differences at the 0.01 level.

Method	Statistic	P-value
ICL	12.18	0.02
CICL	677.54	3e-145*

Table 2: Kruskal-Wallis test results for ICL and CICL. * indicates significant differences at the 0.01 level.

variation in CICL performance as the proportion of corrected examples increases, whereas ICL shows minimal variation across differing example conditions. These results underscore the robustness of ICL across diverse contexts, contrasting with CICL's instability under varying correction levels.

5 Impact of Harder Examples on ICL

Although not the primary objective of this study, an intriguing finding emerges from our results. As shown in Figure 3, increasing the proportion of incorrectly classified examples (i.e., higher "corrected proportions") in the few-shot context does not improve the performance of standard ICL. In fact, for some models, performance slightly declines as the corrected proportion increases.

Intuitively, one might expect that presenting the model with harder examples—those it initially misclassified—would enhance performance. The rationale is that such examples could help refine the model's decision boundaries and establish clearer classification thresholds, improving overall accuracy. However, our results do not support this.

When examining the performance trends of standard ICL (blue lines in Figure 3), we observe that including harder examples in the few-shot context fails to yield any consistent improvement. In some cases, performance remains unchanged or even decreases slightly. Furthermore, statistical analysis using the Kruskal-Wallis test reveals no significant variation in standard ICL performance across different corrected proportions (Table 2, first line). These findings suggest that simply exposing the model to harder examples does not provide the anticipated benefits for few-shot classification tasks.

This observation warrants further investigation into how example difficulty interacts with ICL, particularly in understanding why harder examples fail to contribute to improved model calibration or decision-making in this context.

6 Conclusion

In this paper, we introduced CICL, a novel approach aimed at leveraging incorrect model predictions to improve performance through self-correction. By including misclassified examples along with their correct labels in the prompt, CICL sought to refine the model's predictions in text classification tasks. However, contrary to our initial hypothesis, CICL consistently underperformed ICL across all models and datasets. Our findings revealed that the corrective nature of CICL often led to confusion rather than improvement. The swapping of labels in the few-shot examples disrupted the model's understanding of the task, resulting in degraded performance as the proportion of corrected examples increased.

Additionally, we explored an auxiliary finding regarding the impact of harder few-shot examples on standard ICL performance. Despite the expectation that presenting harder, misclassified examples could enhance the model's decision-making, our results showed no significant improvement across varying proportions of examples that required correction. This challenges the assumption that harder examples inherently contribute to better generalization in few-shot learning.

Overall, our study highlights the challenges of incorporating self-corrective mechanisms into LLMs through ICL and demonstrates that harder examples are not necessarily more useful than easier ones in standard ICL. These findings provide valuable insights for the development of more robust and effective few-shot learning methods with LLMs.

Limitations

Despite the intuitive appeal of CICL, our findings indicate that it performs worse than standard ICL for text classification tasks. Several factors may contribute to this result. First, our experiments are restricted to small-scale open-source LLMs due to computational constraints. Larger models may exhibit stronger reasoning and adaptation capabilities, potentially improving CICL performance. While preliminary experiments with the 70B version of Llama-3.1 yielded similar results to the smaller models, the impact of even larger models remains an open question. Second, CICL may be more effective for tasks requiring multi-step reasoning, e.g., via chain-of-thought prompting, where the model can benefit from explicit corrective feedback to refine intermediate steps. Third, LLMs are highly sensitive to prompt design. It is possible that alternative prompt formats or different ways of structuring corrective feedback could lead to better results.

Acknowledgments

The research in this paper was funded by the Carl Zeiss Foundation, grant number P2022-08-009 (MAINCE project).

References

Francesco Barbieri, Jose Camacho-Collados, Luis Espinosa Anke, and Leonardo Neves. 2020. TweetEval: Unified benchmark and comparative evaluation for tweet classification. In *Findings of the Association for Computational Linguistics: EMNLP 2020*, pages 1644–1650, Online. Association for Computational Linguistics.

Tom Brown, Benjamin Mann, Nick Ryder, Melanie Subbiah, Jared D Kaplan, Prafulla Dhariwal, Arvind Neelakantan, Pranav Shyam, Girish Sastry, Amanda Askell, et al. 2020. Language models are few-shot learners. In *Advances in Neural Information Processing Systems*, volume 33, pages 1877–1901. Curran Associates, Inc.

Abhimanyu Dubey, Abhinav Jauhri, Abhinav Pandey, Abhishek Kadian, Ahmad Al-Dahle, Aiesha Letman, Akhil Mathur, Alan Schelten, Amy Yang, Angela Fan, et al. 2024. The Llama 3 Herd of Models. *Preprint*, arXiv:2407.21783.

Yu Fei, Yifan Hou, Zeming Chen, and Antoine Bosselut. 2023. Mitigating label biases for in-context learning. In *Proceedings of the 61st Annual Meeting of the Association for Computational Linguistics (Volume 1: Long Papers)*, pages 14014–14031, Toronto, Canada. Association for Computational Linguistics.

Minqing Hu and Bing Liu. 2004. Mining and summarizing customer reviews. In *Proceedings of the Tenth ACM SIGKDD International Conference on Knowledge Discovery and Data Mining*, KDD '04, page 168–177, New York, NY, USA. Association for Computing Machinery.

Jiaxin Huang, Shixiang Gu, Le Hou, Yuexin Wu, Xuezhi Wang, Hongkun Yu, and Jiawei Han. 2023. Large language models can self-improve. In *Proceedings of the 2023 Conference on Empirical Methods in Natural Language Processing*, pages 1051–1068, Singapore. Association for Computational Linguistics.

Albert Q. Jiang, Alexandre Sablayrolles, Arthur Mensch, Chris Bamford, Devendra Singh Chaplot, Diego de las Casas, Florian Bressand, Gianna Lengyel, Guillaume Lample, Lucile Saulnier, et al. 2023. Mistral 7b. *Preprint*, arXiv:2310.06825.

Aviral Kumar, Vincent Zhuang, Rishabh Agarwal, Yi Su, John D Co-Reyes, Avi Singh, Kate Baumli, Shariq Iqbal, Colton Bishop, Rebecca Roelofs, Lei M Zhang, Kay McKinney, Disha Shrivastava, Cosmin Paduraru, George Tucker, Doina Precup, Feryal Behbahani, and Aleksandra Faust. 2024. Training language models to self-correct via reinforcement learning. *Preprint*, arXiv:2409.12917.

Brian Lester, Rami Al-Rfou, and Noah Constant. 2021. The power of scale for parameter-efficient prompt tuning. In *Proceedings of the 2021 Conference on Empirical Methods in Natural Language Processing*, pages 3045–3059, Online and Punta Cana, Dominican Republic. Association for Computational Linguistics.

Quentin Lhoest, Albert Villanova del Moral, Yacine Jernite, Abhishek Thakur, Patrick von Platen, Suraj Patil, Julien Chaumond, Mariama Drame, Julien Plu, Lewis Tunstall, et al. 2021. Datasets: A community library for natural language processing. In *Proceedings of the 2021 Conference on Empirical Methods in Natural Language Processing: System Demonstrations*, pages 175–184, Online and Punta Cana, Dominican Republic. Association for Computational Linguistics.

Xiang Lisa Li and Percy Liang. 2021. Prefix-tuning: Optimizing continuous prompts for generation. In *Proceedings of the 59th Annual Meeting of the Association for Computational Linguistics and the 11th International Joint Conference on Natural Language Processing (Volume 1: Long Papers)*, pages 4582–4597, Online. Association for Computational Linguistics.

Jiachang Liu, Dinghan Shen, Yizhe Zhang, Bill Dolan, Lawrence Carin, and Weizhu Chen. 2022. What makes good in-context examples for GPT-3? In *Proceedings of Deep Learning Inside Out (DeeLIO 2022): The 3rd Workshop on Knowledge Extraction and Integration for Deep Learning Architectures*, pages 100–114, Dublin, Ireland and Online. Association for Computational Linguistics.

Yao Lu, Max Bartolo, Alastair Moore, Sebastian Riedel, and Pontus Stenetorp. 2022. Fantastically ordered prompts and where to find them: Overcoming few-shot prompt order sensitivity. In *Proceedings of the 60th Annual Meeting of the Association for Computational Linguistics (Volume 1: Long Papers)*, pages 8086–8098, Dublin, Ireland. Association for Computational Linguistics.

Aman Madaan, Niket Tandon, Prakhar Gupta, Skyler Hallinan, Luyu Gao, Sarah Wiegreffe, Uri Alon, Nouha Dziri, Shrimai Prabhumoye, Yiming Yang, Shashank Gupta, Bodhisattwa Prasad Majumder, Katherine Hermann, Sean Welleck, Amir Yazdanbakhsh, and Peter Clark. 2023. Self-refine: Iterative refinement with self-feedback. In *Thirty-seventh Conference on Neural Information Processing Systems*.

Pekka Malo, Ankur Sinha, Pekka Korhonen, Jyrki Wallenius, and Pyry Takala. 2014. Good debt or bad debt: Detecting semantic orientations in economic texts. *Journal of the Association for Information Science and Technology*, 65(4):782–796.

Sewon Min, Xinxi Lyu, Ari Holtzman, Mikel Artetxe, Mike Lewis, Hannaneh Hajishirzi, and Luke Zettlemoyer. 2022. Rethinking the role of demonstrations: What makes in-context learning work? In *Proceedings of the 2022 Conference on Empirical Methods in Natural Language Processing*, pages 11048–11064, Abu Dhabi, United Arab Emirates. Association for Computational Linguistics.

Giovanni Monea, Antoine Bosselut, Kianté Brantley, and Yoav Artzi. 2024. Llms are in-context reinforcement learners. *Preprint*, arXiv:2410.05362v1.

Bo Pang and Lillian Lee. 2004. A sentimental education: Sentiment analysis using subjectivity summarization based on minimum cuts. In *Proceedings of the 42nd Annual Meeting of the Association for Computational Linguistics (ACL-04)*, pages 271–278, Barcelona, Spain.

Bo Pang and Lillian Lee. 2005. Seeing stars: Exploiting class relationships for sentiment categorization with respect to rating scales. In *Proceedings of the 43rd Annual Meeting of the Association for Computational Linguistics (ACL'05)*, pages 115–124, Ann Arbor, Michigan. Association for Computational Linguistics.

Qwen, An Yang, Baosong Yang, Beichen Zhang, Binyuan Hui, Bo Zheng, Bowen Yu, Chengyuan Li, Dayiheng Liu, Fei Huang, et al. 2024. Qwen2.5 technical report. *Preprint*, arXiv:2412.15115.

Emily Sheng and David Uthus. 2020. Investigating societal biases in a poetry composition system. In *Proceedings of the Second Workshop on Gender Bias in Natural Language Processing*, pages 93–106, Barcelona, Spain (Online). Association for Computational Linguistics.

Richard Socher, Alex Perelygin, Jean Wu, Jason Chuang, Christopher D. Manning, Andrew Ng, and Christopher Potts. 2013. Recursive deep models for semantic compositionality over a sentiment treebank. In *Proceedings of the 2013 Conference on Empirical Methods in Natural Language Processing*, pages 1631–1642, Seattle, Washington, USA. Association for Computational Linguistics.

Ellen M. Voorhees and Dawn M. Tice. 2000. Building a question answering test collection. In *Proceedings of the 23rd Annual International ACM SIGIR Conference on Research and Development in Information Retrieval*, SIGIR '00, page 200–207, New York, NY, USA. Association for Computing Machinery.

Ben Wang and Aran Komatsuzaki. 2021. GPT-J-6B: A 6 Billion Parameter Autoregressive Language Model. https://github.com/kingoflolz/mesh-transformer-jax.

Xiang Zhang, Junbo Zhao, and Yann LeCun. 2015. Character-level convolutional networks for text classification. In *Advances in Neural Information Processing Systems*, volume 28. Curran Associates, Inc.

Zihao Zhao, Eric Wallace, Shi Feng, Dan Klein, and Sameer Singh. 2021. Calibrate before use: Improving few-shot performance of language models. In *Proceedings of the 38th International Conference on Machine Learning*, volume 139 of *Proceedings of Machine Learning Research*, pages 12697–12706. PMLR.

A Datasets Details

Our experiments utilize 17 datasets spanning various text classification tasks, all of which are commonly used in prior research (Min et al., 2022; Lu et al., 2022; Zhao et al., 2021; Fei et al., 2023). All datasets are accessed through the HuggingFace Datasets library (Lhoest et al., 2021). For evaluation, we use the provided test sets when available. If no test set is provided, we create a stratified development set by sampling from the training data, ensuring the class distribution is preserved. Detailed dataset information, including task type, class counts, and data distribution, is summarized in Table 3.

As shown in Table 3, most datasets are imbalanced. To account for this, we use macro F1 as the evaluation metric, as it equally weighs all classes and ensures a fair assessment of the model's performance across both frequent and rare classes.

B Prompt Formats

B.1 In-Context Learning Prompt

```
Text: {example_1}
Label: {ground_truth_1}

Text: {example_2}
Label: {ground_truth_2}
...
Text: {example_k}
Label: {ground_truth_k}

Text: {input_text}
Label:
```

Figure 4: Prompt format for standard ICL, showing ground truth labels for k examples.

Example

Below is an example of a standard ICL prompt for the TREC dataset with $k = 8$ few-shot examples.

```
Text: What is the name of the tallest mountain in the world?
Label: location

Text: How many eyes does a bat have?
Label: numeric

Text: What does Ms., Miss, and Mrs. stand for?
Label: abbreviation

Text: What does IQ stand for?
Label: abbreviation

Text: What were the achievements of Richard Nixon?
Label: entity

Text: What is the C programming language?
Label: description

Text: Who was considered to be the father of psychology?
Label: human

Text: What are the top five oil-producing countries in the world?
Label: location

Text: What are the stars made of?
Label:
```

Dataset	# Classes	Balanced
Sentiment and topic classification		
SST-2 (Socher et al., 2013)	2	✓
SST-5 (Socher et al., 2013)	5	✗
MR (Pang and Lee, 2005)	2	✓
CR (Hu and Liu, 2004)	2	✓
financial_phrasebank (Malo et al., 2014)	3	✗
poem_sentiment (Sheng and Uthus, 2020)	4	✗
Subj (Pang and Lee, 2004)	2	✗
AG News (Zhang et al., 2015)	4	✓
DBpedia (Zhang et al., 2015)	14	✓
TREC (Voorhees and Tice, 2000)	6	✗
Detection		
tweet_eval-hate (Barbieri et al., 2020)	2	✗
tweet_eval-irony (Barbieri et al., 2020)	2	✗
tweet_eval-offensive (Barbieri et al., 2020)	2	✗
tweet_eval-stance_atheism (Barbieri et al., 2020)	3	✗
tweet_eval-stance_feminist (Barbieri et al., 2020)	3	✗
hate_speech18 (Barbieri et al., 2020)	2	✗
ethos-binary (Barbieri et al., 2020)	2	✗

Table 3: Full dataset information.

B.2 Corrective In-Context Learning Prompt

```
Text: {example_1}
Predicted label: {predicted_label_1}
Correct label: {ground_truth_1}

Text: {example_2}
Predicted label: {predicted_label_2}
Correct label: {ground_truth_2}
...
Text: {example_k}
Predicted label: {predicted_label_k}
Correct label: {ground_truth_k}

Text: {input_text}
Predicted label: {predicted_label}
Correct label:
```

Figure 5: Prompt format for CICL, showing predicted and ground truth ("correct") labels for k examples.

Example

Below is an example of a CICL prompt for the TREC dataset. There are $k = 8$ few-shot examples, with 50% being corrected examples. This means 4 examples are correctly predicted by ICL (in positions 2, 4, 6, and 7), and 4 are corrected examples (in positions 1, 3, 5, and 8). The final instance represents the current input, where ICL predicted the label "description." The task of the LLM is to predict the correct label based on the input text, the predicted label, and the corrections made in previous examples. The true label for this instance is "entity," and the goal of CICL is to make this correction.

```
Text: What is the name of the tallest mountain in the world?
Predicted label: entity
Correct label: location

Text: How many eyes does a bat have?
Predicted label: numeric
Correct label: numeric

Text: What does Ms., Miss, and Mrs. stand for?
Predicted label: description
Correct label: abbreviation

Text: What does IQ stand for?
Predicted label: abbreviation
Correct label: abbreviation

Text: What were the achievements of Richard Nixon?
Predicted label: human
Correct label: entity
```

```
Text: What is the C programming language?
Predicted label: description
Correct label: description

Text: Who was considered to be the father
of psychology?
Predicted label: human
Correct label: human

Text: What are the top five oil-producing
countries in the world?
Predicted label: numeric
Correct label: location

Text: What are the stars made of?
Predicted label: description
Correct label:
```

C Detailed Results

Table 4 presents the detailed results for all combinations of models, datasets, corrected example proportions, and approaches (ICL and CICL). Each configuration is evaluated five times using different random seeds to ensure diverse selections of examples, minimizing the impact of randomness on the results. The table reports the mean and standard deviation for each configuration, providing a comprehensive view of the performance across variations.

Dataset	Corrected Proportion	Llama-3.1		Mistral 7B		Qwen2.5		GPT-J	
		ICL	CICL	ICL	CICL	ICL	CICL	ICL	CICL
AG News	0%	$87.3_{1.6}$	$87.3_{1.6}$	$85.5_{1.0}$	$85.5_{1.0}$	$83.4_{1.7}$	$83.6_{1.6}$	$73.9_{4.4}$	$73.9_{4.4}$
	25%	$83.7_{4.0}$	$84.0_{3.6}$	$86.6_{1.0}$	$86.5_{0.7}$	$85.3_{1.1}$	$85.7_{1.2}$	$74.2_{0.8}$	$74.2_{0.8}$
	50%	$84.1_{3.4}$	$83.0_{4.4}$	$85.0_{2.3}$	$76.4_{13.0}$	$83.2_{2.4}$	$82.0_{2.4}$	$73.9_{7.3}$	$70.5_{7.8}$
	75%	$68.7_{20.2}$	$56.0_{24.0}$	$80.9_{3.9}$	$47.6_{22.8}$	$80.0_{6.1}$	$70.4_{8.7}$	$75.9_{2.4}$	$47.6_{7.3}$
	100%	$83.6_{2.8}$	$13.5_{2.1}$	$85.0_{3.2}$	$12.2_{2.2}$	$85.1_{1.9}$	$15.3_{5.1}$	$77.1_{3.8}$	$14.6_{2.0}$
CR	0%	$93.2_{0.5}$	$93.2_{0.5}$	$93.2_{0.4}$	$93.2_{0.4}$	$93.2_{0.5}$	$93.1_{0.5}$	$87.6_{2.0}$	$87.6_{2.0}$
	25%	$92.0_{1.3}$	$91.8_{1.5}$	$92.0_{0.7}$	$91.5_{0.7}$	$91.8_{1.8}$	$92.0_{0.8}$	$87.8_{2.7}$	$84.8_{7.9}$
	50%	$93.5_{0.7}$	$83.6_{7.3}$	$91.7_{1.9}$	$89.5_{1.0}$	$91.4_{1.4}$	$91.5_{0.9}$	$87.1_{2.3}$	$84.5_{5.4}$
	75%	$91.1_{1.9}$	$55.7_{18.9}$	$87.2_{6.7}$	$71.8_{14.1}$	$89.2_{5.7}$	$75.3_{18.2}$	$84.3_{5.6}$	$58.2_{20.3}$
	100%	$91.1_{1.0}$	$8.0_{0.8}$	$91.4_{1.0}$	$7.8_{0.6}$	$84.3_{7.5}$	$14.9_{5.3}$	$86.2_{5.8}$	$11.9_{4.4}$
DBpedia	0%	$85.6_{1.4}$	$85.6_{1.4}$	$82.6_{2.4}$	$82.6_{2.4}$	$75.7_{2.2}$	$75.8_{2.1}$	$77.4_{1.0}$	$77.4_{1.0}$
	25%	$84.0_{3.0}$	$84.2_{2.9}$	$80.7_{0.9}$	$81.0_{1.3}$	$75.5_{1.4}$	$76.9_{1.3}$	$75.1_{1.6}$	$74.7_{2.2}$
	50%	$80.5_{1.1}$	$84.6_{1.8}$	$76.2_{7.1}$	$79.1_{5.3}$	$74.1_{1.4}$	$81.4_{6.0}$	$75.1_{2.4}$	$73.3_{4.7}$
	75%	$81.6_{1.1}$	$86.6_{3.2}$	$78.0_{1.0}$	$79.3_{4.6}$	$71.2_{1.9}$	$74.7_{6.3}$	$73.8_{1.7}$	$59.0_{11.2}$
	100%	$78.8_{2.1}$	$12.8_{3.4}$	$66.1_{11.8}$	$9.6_{4.4}$	$68.8_{3.4}$	$13.6_{4.8}$	$72.8_{2.6}$	$12.3_{3.8}$
ethos-binary	0%	$72.8_{3.3}$	$72.8_{3.3}$	$79.6_{3.6}$	$79.6_{3.6}$	$80.6_{2.2}$	$80.6_{2.2}$	$56.9_{9.5}$	$56.6_{9.3}$
	25%	$63.2_{10.8}$	$62.7_{10.7}$	$76.1_{5.7}$	$73.1_{4.6}$	$77.7_{4.1}$	$77.9_{3.9}$	$44.6_{15.0}$	$45.3_{14.6}$
	50%	$67.6_{4.6}$	$62.6_{7.8}$	$69.2_{7.0}$	$60.8_{17.6}$	$77.5_{3.0}$	$77.8_{1.8}$	$58.7_{8.4}$	$57.4_{10.9}$
	75%	$55.6_{16.2}$	$46.7_{15.7}$	$70.6_{12.9}$	$55.0_{14.8}$	$78.9_{3.7}$	$71.8_{9.8}$	$55.8_{14.4}$	$53.1_{18.8}$
	100%	$51.4_{7.3}$	$30.8_{2.8}$	$64.3_{13.8}$	$26.7_{4.5}$	$77.9_{2.3}$	$23.8_{3.4}$	$36.3_{0.0}$	$30.1_{0.0}$
financial_phrasebank	0%	$77.9_{8.3}$	$77.9_{8.3}$	$84.1_{0.9}$	$84.1_{0.9}$	$85.4_{3.1}$	$85.2_{3.0}$	$59.5_{12.0}$	$59.5_{12.0}$
	25%	$78.6_{4.8}$	$78.7_{4.8}$	$82.5_{1.2}$	$82.4_{1.3}$	$82.4_{4.3}$	$82.4_{2.9}$	$58.0_{12.0}$	$57.6_{12.3}$
	50%	$74.9_{9.3}$	$68.8_{8.5}$	$83.5_{1.3}$	$83.3_{1.7}$	$84.2_{1.2}$	$83.6_{1.8}$	$61.9_{11.1}$	$61.8_{9.7}$
	75%	$79.4_{8.8}$	$43.4_{10.4}$	$82.2_{3.0}$	$70.3_{11.9}$	$84.7_{1.5}$	$82.3_{2.5}$	$50.2_{8.3}$	$17.3_{6.0}$
	100%	$81.1_{5.5}$	$10.5_{4.3}$	$78.5_{5.3}$	$25.9_{7.8}$	$84.1_{4.0}$	$23.2_{14.9}$	$49.6_{13.8}$	$13.8_{7.9}$
hate_speech18	0%	$53.5_{4.1}$	$53.5_{4.1}$	$67.5_{1.8}$	$67.5_{1.8}$	$68.4_{2.1}$	$68.3_{2.1}$	$38.9_{13.1}$	$38.7_{12.9}$
	25%	$47.9_{8.8}$	$47.4_{8.6}$	$57.2_{6.2}$	$51.3_{13.0}$	$66.0_{2.5}$	$65.7_{2.6}$	$37.2_{10.0}$	$34.4_{10.8}$
	50%	$46.4_{11.1}$	$46.1_{10.7}$	$62.2_{5.0}$	$60.9_{5.7}$	$63.4_{3.3}$	$64.9_{2.1}$	$38.1_{4.6}$	$37.5_{4.6}$
	75%	$36.9_{5.5}$	$39.8_{12.5}$	$52.8_{14.0}$	$49.2_{18.1}$	$64.2_{3.5}$	$58.3_{7.3}$	$37.5_{11.7}$	$42.9_{17.2}$
	100%	$42.8_{13.9}$	$34.3_{6.8}$	$57.8_{4.7}$	$24.2_{4.9}$	$63.6_{2.1}$	$21.4_{4.6}$	$45.5_{3.0}$	$15.8_{11.4}$
MR	0%	$93.6_{0.5}$	$93.6_{0.5}$	$93.8_{0.4}$	$93.8_{0.4}$	$92.6_{0.7}$	$92.6_{0.7}$	$90.7_{1.0}$	$90.7_{1.0}$
	25%	$93.1_{1.3}$	$93.0_{1.0}$	$94.1_{0.3}$	$94.0_{0.4}$	$93.0_{0.6}$	$92.7_{0.6}$	$88.6_{2.8}$	$88.3_{2.6}$
	50%	$93.1_{0.9}$	$89.8_{3.7}$	$93.9_{0.6}$	$92.7_{1.4}$	$92.4_{0.5}$	$91.0_{0.8}$	$81.6_{8.4}$	$81.8_{8.1}$
	75%	$91.7_{4.1}$	$44.5_{8.3}$	$91.6_{2.9}$	$79.4_{10.4}$	$92.6_{0.5}$	$69.0_{14.0}$	$76.0_{21.6}$	$62.7_{15.7}$
	100%	$81.8_{11.3}$	$14.8_{6.9}$	$80.7_{21.7}$	$13.3_{9.7}$	$90.2_{4.2}$	$9.8_{3.0}$	$75.1_{19.1}$	$17.7_{7.9}$
poem_sentiment	0%	$39.4_{3.6}$	$39.4_{3.6}$	$54.0_{5.6}$	$54.0_{5.6}$	$54.0_{3.5}$	$54.0_{3.5}$	$13.0_{4.2}$	$13.0_{4.2}$
	25%	$42.2_{7.1}$	$42.2_{7.1}$	$53.4_{11.3}$	$53.9_{10.3}$	$50.9_{6.6}$	$51.4_{6.3}$	$20.7_{11.0}$	$22.1_{11.1}$
	50%	$41.7_{12.8}$	$40.6_{12.6}$	$57.8_{6.1}$	$57.2_{4.9}$	$53.6_{5.9}$	$54.5_{5.6}$	$22.5_{8.0}$	$28.0_{2.2}$
	75%	$47.2_{12.0}$	$25.1_{9.0}$	$49.5_{11.1}$	$50.3_{9.7}$	$51.5_{7.9}$	$47.0_{6.1}$	$40.4_{4.9}$	$27.7_{12.5}$
	100%	$54.7_{8.6}$	$9.8_{3.6}$	$57.7_{11.6}$	$17.8_{7.8}$	$52.0_{7.0}$	$21.6_{4.2}$	$25.4_{11.7}$	$28.5_{5.0}$
SST-2	0%	$91.6_{1.3}$	$91.6_{1.3}$	$92.4_{1.5}$	$92.4_{1.5}$	$93.8_{1.0}$	$93.8_{1.0}$	$83.0_{9.0}$	$83.0_{9.0}$
	25%	$91.2_{1.1}$	$90.7_{1.8}$	$91.1_{0.9}$	$91.1_{0.8}$	$91.9_{2.8}$	$92.7_{2.6}$	$72.5_{17.6}$	$73.9_{18.0}$
	50%	$90.2_{1.5}$	$86.3_{4.0}$	$89.8_{2.1}$	$89.0_{2.6}$	$92.4_{1.1}$	$94.5_{0.5}$	$80.8_{8.4}$	$80.7_{5.4}$
	75%	$85.2_{9.3}$	$40.5_{8.6}$	$86.1_{7.1}$	$68.8_{21.6}$	$92.0_{3.0}$	$86.0_{5.6}$	$68.9_{20.1}$	$41.2_{23.6}$
	100%	$86.0_{5.0}$	$12.9_{3.8}$	$87.9_{4.5}$	$11.4_{3.3}$	$90.6_{1.1}$	$9.9_{0.4}$	$71.7_{7.8}$	$21.0_{4.2}$
SST-5	0%	$45.4_{2.4}$	$45.4_{2.4}$	$42.6_{4.3}$	$42.6_{4.3}$	$42.0_{2.1}$	$42.0_{2.1}$	$31.5_{9.8}$	$31.5_{9.8}$
	25%	$43.7_{2.1}$	$43.6_{1.5}$	$39.0_{4.6}$	$38.9_{4.7}$	$41.5_{2.2}$	$41.6_{2.2}$	$27.4_{3.4}$	$23.6_{7.2}$
	50%	$39.0_{4.4}$	$40.0_{4.7}$	$40.5_{4.3}$	$39.8_{3.9}$	$42.3_{4.2}$	$38.1_{3.4}$	$34.5_{6.3}$	$31.9_{8.6}$
	75%	$43.3_{2.4}$	$39.4_{3.9}$	$38.8_{4.6}$	$37.3_{2.7}$	$39.1_{6.0}$	$42.0_{3.5}$	$33.2_{3.1}$	$28.3_{7.2}$
	100%	$41.4_{2.2}$	$26.3_{1.2}$	$44.3_{4.1}$	$31.9_{4.2}$	$41.1_{6.6}$	$29.6_{1.9}$	$28.2_{4.5}$	$20.9_{5.2}$
Subj	0%	$87.1_{7.9}$	$87.1_{7.9}$	$75.3_{19.5}$	$75.3_{19.5}$	$79.7_{6.3}$	$79.4_{6.3}$	$43.0_{12.0}$	$43.0_{12.0}$
	25%	$86.9_{3.3}$	$86.0_{3.2}$	$68.3_{13.3}$	$62.4_{14.2}$	$80.8_{3.7}$	$70.6_{3.9}$	$55.7_{18.3}$	$42.9_{14.1}$
	50%	$83.6_{4.5}$	$57.2_{13.2}$	$59.0_{19.0}$	$51.5_{21.2}$	$82.1_{2.4}$	$68.4_{3.6}$	$57.2_{15.4}$	$49.8_{11.4}$
	75%	$82.0_{6.8}$	$25.0_{7.2}$	$37.4_{4.9}$	$54.8_{18.1}$	$78.4_{6.8}$	$47.8_{12.7}$	$70.4_{3.6}$	$44.3_{14.7}$
	100%	$82.4_{9.3}$	$15.2_{5.9}$	$47.9_{20.3}$	$28.2_{8.1}$	$84.4_{2.6}$	$14.6_{1.9}$	$39.9_{9.7}$	$32.8_{1.2}$
TREC-6	0%	$75.0_{7.3}$	$75.0_{7.3}$	$56.6_{7.6}$	$56.6_{7.6}$	$74.7_{3.6}$	$74.7_{3.6}$	$51.2_{7.7}$	$51.2_{7.7}$
	25%	$74.6_{7.4}$	$74.5_{7.7}$	$56.9_{12.2}$	$57.2_{12.2}$	$81.6_{3.9}$	$81.1_{3.6}$	$46.8_{3.6}$	$47.0_{3.3}$
	50%	$75.8_{3.5}$	$75.6_{2.9}$	$60.1_{4.9}$	$59.4_{3.0}$	$74.8_{5.0}$	$77.1_{3.3}$	$49.9_{7.1}$	$49.4_{2.2}$
	75%	$77.7_{3.0}$	$69.6_{8.4}$	$49.9_{16.4}$	$52.2_{6.7}$	$81.7_{1.9}$	$63.9_{10.3}$	$48.7_{7.7}$	$44.7_{9.9}$
	100%	$66.8_{9.0}$	$13.4_{6.0}$	$50.6_{13.6}$	$22.6_{7.2}$	$77.0_{2.6}$	$9.1_{4.3}$	$42.9_{6.4}$	$20.9_{1.5}$
tweet_eval_atheism	0%	$21.2_{10.1}$	$21.2_{10.1}$	$27.6_{10.3}$	$27.6_{10.3}$	$34.0_{4.3}$	$34.0_{4.3}$	$12.1_{1.3}$	$12.1_{1.3}$
	25%	$26.6_{4.8}$	$28.3_{3.1}$	$33.2_{11.5}$	$33.2_{11.5}$	$37.1_{5.9}$	$37.7_{5.6}$	$20.1_{10.6}$	$21.5_{7.7}$
	50%	$31.5_{9.0}$	$34.4_{8.1}$	$33.7_{6.5}$	$35.8_{8.0}$	$40.9_{7.9}$	$37.9_{6.0}$	$16.6_{5.6}$	$23.1_{10.7}$
	75%	$42.5_{7.0}$	$38.4_{10.8}$	$37.4_{7.3}$	$30.0_{7.1}$	$36.6_{11.7}$	$36.6_{11.1}$	$18.4_{6.1}$	$23.0_{4.3}$
	100%	$41.0_{8.1}$	$22.5_{4.9}$	$39.0_{10.9}$	$16.8_{3.6}$	$35.2_{8.1}$	$23.5_{3.2}$	$17.5_{7.1}$	$29.1_{4.4}$
tweet_eval_feminist	0%	$48.7_{10.1}$	$48.7_{10.1}$	$56.3_{6.0}$	$56.3_{6.0}$	$55.6_{4.2}$	$55.6_{4.2}$	$25.6_{8.5}$	$28.7_{7.2}$
	25%	$39.6_{10.8}$	$39.6_{10.8}$	$41.8_{7.0}$	$42.7_{7.8}$	$62.1_{3.7}$	$61.6_{3.1}$	$25.5_{7.7}$	$26.1_{7.0}$
	50%	$37.7_{6.5}$	$41.2_{5.2}$	$41.1_{16.4}$	$43.9_{13.9}$	$56.8_{3.7}$	$57.7_{3.3}$	$28.4_{7.7}$	$23.8_{10.0}$
	75%	$43.5_{8.5}$	$47.3_{6.0}$	$43.4_{12.2}$	$51.6_{8.9}$	$56.7_{4.1}$	$56.9_{2.9}$	$27.7_{8.8}$	$21.0_{6.8}$
	100%	$44.4_{5.6}$	$33.8_{12.0}$	$49.7_{9.5}$	$29.1_{11.7}$	$47.3_{6.1}$	$33.9_{6.8}$	$37.7_{7.5}$	$16.9_{2.1}$
tweet_eval_hate	0%	$52.3_{5.3}$	$52.3_{5.3}$	$67.5_{3.6}$	$67.5_{3.6}$	$61.3_{1.8}$	$61.3_{1.8}$	$40.4_{5.1}$	$40.3_{5.2}$
	25%	$51.0_{4.5}$	$50.9_{4.5}$	$66.5_{4.5}$	$60.7_{12.4}$	$61.1_{4.0}$	$61.5_{3.9}$	$46.2_{6.5}$	$43.8_{6.5}$
	50%	$51.8_{8.5}$	$49.9_{7.5}$	$66.7_{4.2}$	$52.0_{8.5}$	$62.4_{2.3}$	$64.8_{1.6}$	$46.6_{6.7}$	$34.2_{4.5}$
	75%	$44.7_{5.2}$	$53.5_{7.7}$	$54.2_{7.5}$	$51.6_{5.2}$	$55.7_{10.1}$	$62.4_{1.6}$	$42.6_{11.5}$	$47.0_{10.5}$
	100%	$51.0_{11.6}$	$37.1_{6.6}$	$52.7_{7.9}$	$35.9_{2.8}$	$51.1_{4.8}$	$40.0_{4.5}$	$43.3_{9.7}$	$36.1_{5.5}$
tweet_eval_irony	0%	$57.0_{1.9}$	$57.0_{1.9}$	$58.9_{3.2}$	$58.9_{3.2}$	$63.6_{2.6}$	$63.6_{2.6}$	$49.6_{2.6}$	$49.6_{2.6}$
	25%	$51.0_{7.3}$	$50.9_{7.2}$	$56.4_{8.6}$	$55.5_{10.2}$	$63.0_{3.8}$	$63.2_{3.4}$	$51.1_{3.1}$	$52.2_{2.9}$
	50%	$48.6_{6.8}$	$43.5_{8.1}$	$51.2_{12.4}$	$43.0_{10.7}$	$62.6_{3.6}$	$65.3_{2.4}$	$47.9_{8.2}$	$46.4_{7.8}$
	75%	$46.7_{7.2}$	$40.3_{5.5}$	$53.8_{9.8}$	$43.9_{8.3}$	$59.3_{6.3}$	$55.3_{8.4}$	$47.2_{5.1}$	$43.6_{4.7}$
	100%	$43.7_{8.1}$	$32.3_{1.3}$	$51.6_{8.0}$	$35.3_{2.4}$	$52.1_{9.3}$	$34.7_{0.7}$	$44.5_{6.4}$	$43.0_{6.4}$
tweet_eval_offensive	0%	$59.4_{4.8}$	$59.4_{4.8}$	$64.5_{1.4}$	$64.5_{1.4}$	$65.0_{1.8}$	$65.1_{1.8}$	$53.2_{5.3}$	$53.2_{5.4}$
	25%	$62.7_{2.0}$	$62.7_{2.0}$	$60.0_{4.5}$	$59.9_{4.5}$	$66.2_{0.9}$	$66.4_{1.1}$	$60.3_{5.9}$	$62.7_{3.0}$
	50%	$60.2_{4.9}$	$58.0_{4.8}$	$62.8_{2.2}$	$61.5_{3.2}$	$65.7_{1.9}$	$67.0_{1.7}$	$60.4_{6.8}$	$61.6_{4.3}$
	75%	$55.0_{13.8}$	$39.4_{5.7}$	$53.5_{12.0}$	$48.7_{5.8}$	$56.5_{13.9}$	$63.2_{3.7}$	$56.6_{14.4}$	$56.9_{7.7}$
	100%	$54.4_{9.1}$	$35.9_{2.6}$	$61.1_{2.9}$	$32.9_{2.7}$	$60.5_{3.7}$	$36.4_{4.3}$	$60.9_{6.6}$	$31.5_{3.4}$

Table 4: Results (Macro-F1) across datasets, models, and corrected proportions for ICL and CICL.

Do Prevalent Bias Metrics Capture Allocational Harms from LLMs?

Hannah Cyberey, Yangfeng Ji, David Evans
Department of Computer Science
University of Virginia
Charlottesville, VA 22904
{yc4dx,yangfeng,evans}@virginia.edu

Abstract

Allocational harms occur when resources or opportunities are unfairly withheld from specific groups. Many proposed bias measures ignore the discrepancy between *predictions*, which are what the proposed methods consider, and *decisions* that are made as a result of those predictions. Our work examines the reliability of current bias metrics in assessing allocational harms arising from predictions of large language models (LLMs). We evaluate their predictive validity and utility for model selection across ten LLMs and two allocation tasks. Our results reveal that commonly-used bias metrics based on average performance gap and distribution distance fail to reliably capture group disparities in allocation outcomes. Our work highlights the need to account for how model predictions are used in decisions, in particular in contexts where they are influenced by how limited resources are allocated.

1 Introduction

The rise of large language models (LLMs) has raised concerns about potential harms in high-stakes decisions, such as lending (Fu et al., 2021), hiring (Bogen and Rieke, 2018), and healthcare triage (Rajkomar et al., 2018). Recent orders in Europe (European Parliament, 2024) and the U.S. (Biden, 2023) have mandated audits to address AI risks including bias but left it unclear how to conduct effective audits.

Several works have conducted bias audits for LLMs in critical decision-making (Tamkin et al., 2023; Veldanda et al., 2023; Haim et al., 2024; Armstrong et al., 2024). Yet, they focus on the *predictions* models make, without considering how those predictions would be used to make decisions. Even when predictions appear to be unbiased, actual harms can arise from how they are used to make decisions (Corbett-Davies et al., 2017; Mitchell et al., 2018; Kleinberg et al., 2018). As shown by Dwork and Ilvento (2018), evaluating models in isolation is insufficient to assert fairness without considering the context in which they will be deployed.

Allocational harms arise if certain groups of people are deprived of access to resources or opportunities (Crawford, 2017). In settings where resources are limited and a model is used to prioritize options, there is a gap between *predictions* and *decisions*. It is unclear whether prevailing metrics, which measure bias in prediction outcomes, are sufficient to measure bias risks in applications where predictions are used for resource allocation.

Contributions. To assess the potential harms of using LLMs for decision-making, we evaluate how well commmon bias metrics predict actual disparities in allocation outcomes. These metrics typically rely on average performance and distribution differences. We conduct this evaluation across ten LLMs on two allocation tasks (Section 3). Our findings demonstrate that bias metrics based on predictions may not reliably reflect true disparities in outcomes (Section 4.1). In addition, these metrics may sometimes identify models with greater disparities as less biased and exhibit inconsistent predictive abilities across different groups (Section 4.2). As a more reliable alternative, we propose the rank-biserial correlation, which demonstrates a strong correlation with actual allocation disparities.

2 Background

Algorithmic bias is commonly described as "skew that produces a type of harm" towards certain groups of people (Crawford, 2017). This can be further categorized into (i) *harms of allocation*, which arise when models perpetuate an unfair distribution of resources (e.g., healthcare) or opportunities (e.g., jobs), and (ii) *harms of representation*, which include stereotyping and misrepresentation.

The Sixth Workshop on Insights from Negative Results in NLP, pages 34–45

2.1 Measuring Bias

Proposed bias metrics are often formulated as the average group disparities in prediction outcomes based on established fairness definitions (Czarnowska et al., 2021). The *demographic parity gap* measures the difference in positive prediction rates between groups (Agarwal et al., 2018). *Equal opportunity* (EO), a relaxed notion of equalized odds, requires equal positive outcomes for qualified individuals (Hardt et al., 2016). The EO gap is thus the true positive rate differences between groups. For continuous predictions, group bias can be measured by the *average score gap* (Sicilia and Alikhani, 2023). Several works consider the group distribution difference in prediction outcomes using distribution-based metrics such as Jensen–Shannon divergence (Guo et al., 2022), Earth Mover's distance (Huang et al., 2020), and total variance distance (Liang et al., 2022).

2.2 Allocational Harms

Blodgett et al. (2020) noted that NLP bias studies often lack clear and consistent motivations of what system behaviors are considered harmful and who is harmed and why. Out of thirty papers referencing allocational harms as motivation, they found only four actually propose measures or mitigations to address the harms (De-Arteaga et al., 2019; Zhao et al., 2020; Romanov et al., 2019; Prost et al., 2019). Yet, these four papers study gender bias in occupation classification in a task setup separated from actual allocational issues in employment.

We find similar cases in subsequent works where the evaluation setups differ from allocation decision tasks in practice (Kirk et al., 2021; Lalor et al., 2022; Shen et al., 2022; Borchers et al., 2022; Van Aken et al., 2022). Recent work has studied bias in LLMs used for hiring (Veldanda et al., 2023; Armstrong et al., 2024; Gaebler et al., 2024) and other high-stakes decision scenarios (Tamkin et al., 2023; Haim et al., 2024). The evaluation methods adopted in these works only consider the average performance gap, measured from binary outputs or graded ratings. However, we show that this type of approach does not reliably reflect disparities in decision outcomes. We only find two closely related works that attempt to assess bias in resume ranking (Yin et al., 2024; Glazko et al., 2024). Glazko et al. (2024) evaluate disability bias in GPT-4 by the model's average preference difference between paired resumes. Yin et al. (2024) inquires GPT-3.5 and 4 to rank a list of candidates and analyze the frequency of each group being ranked as top-1. We extend their work with more variations in resumes and conduct experiments on a wide range of open-weight LLMs.

3 Method

We consider the allocation task as a top-k ranking problem (Cossock and Zhang, 2006; Clémençon and Vayatis, 2007), where a fixed quota of $k \in \mathbb{N}$ candidates are selected among a pool of $n \gg k$ candidates. The goal is to determine a set of "best" candidates, with no particular emphasis on the relative order. We follow the LLM ranking method of Zhuang et al. (2024) and rank the candidates in descending order of their prediction scores.

3.1 Measuring Allocation Gaps

Bias scores can be viewed as predictions of the allocation gaps in the following decision outcomes made with a model. An effective bias metric should yield a higher score for a group or a model when the outcome shows greater disparities. Given the decision outcomes of model $\mathcal{M}$ and allocation quota k, we measure allocation gaps using two common fairness criteria: demographic parity (DP) (Agarwal et al., 2018) and equal opportunity (EO) (Hardt et al., 2016).

The *demographic parity gap* between group $\mathcal{A}$ and $\mathcal{B}$ is defined as:

$$\Delta\text{DP}_{\mathcal{M}}(\mathcal{A}, \mathcal{B}) = \phi_{\mathcal{M}}(\mathcal{A}, k) - \phi_{\mathcal{M}}(\mathcal{B}, k)$$

where $\phi_{\mathcal{M}}(\mathcal{X}, k)$ is the proportion of group $\mathcal{X}$'s candidates selected.

We compute the *equal opportunity gap* between group $\mathcal{A}$ and $\mathcal{B}$ as follows:

$$\Delta\text{EO}_{\mathcal{M}}(\mathcal{A}, \mathcal{B}) = \psi_{\mathcal{M}}(\mathcal{A}, k) - \psi_{\mathcal{M}}(\mathcal{B}, k)$$

where $\psi_{\mathcal{M}}(\mathcal{X}, k)$ is the rate of qualified candidates in group $\mathcal{X}$ being selected.

3.2 Bias Metrics

Proposed bias metrics are often formulated as the average score or distribution difference between groups in prediction outcomes (Czarnowska et al., 2021; Gallegos et al., 2024).

Average Performance Gap computes the average score difference between group $\mathcal{A}$ and $\mathcal{B}$ as follows (Sicilia and Alikhani, 2023):

$$\delta_{\mathcal{M}}(\mathcal{A}, \mathcal{B}) = \frac{1}{|\mathcal{A}|} \sum_{a \in \mathcal{A}} s_a - \frac{1}{|\mathcal{B}|} \sum_{b \in \mathcal{B}} s_b$$

where s_a is the prediction of candidate $a \in \mathcal{A}$.

Distribution-Based Metrics measures score differences between groups using Jensen–Shannon Divergence (JSD) (Lin, 1991) and Earth Mover's Distance (EMD) (Rubner et al., 1998).

Rank-Biserial Correlation. We consider an alternative metric, *rank-biserial correlation* (RB) (Cureton, 1956), which measures the correlation between group membership and ranking. It can be computed as the difference between the ratio of favorable pairs f and unfavorable pairs u (Kerby, 2014):

$$RB_{\mathcal{M}}(\mathcal{A}, \mathcal{B}) = f - u \quad (1)$$

where f is the proportion of candidate pairs that model $\mathcal{M}$ prefers candidates from $\mathcal{A}$ over $\mathcal{B}$.

3.3 Tasks

We evaluate settings where a model predicts the likelihood of a candidate match based on a description of an ideal candidate's qualifications. Appendix A provide further task details.

Resume Screening. Given a resume, the model evaluates a candidate's fit for a job position and outputs $\{\text{No}, \text{Yes}\}$. We use four job positions from real job listings (Yin et al., 2024). We use GPT-3.5 (OpenAI, 2024) to generate six resumes per position with varied hiring chances (high, medium, low), where high indicates qualified. Each candidate is represented by a first and last name on the resume. Each candidate pool includes one candidate sampled from each of the eight groups: $\{\text{Female}, \text{Male}\} \times \{\text{White}, \text{Black}, \text{Asian}, \text{Hispanic}\}$.

Essay Grading. The model is asked to rate each essay on a scale of $[1, 5]$. We use the International Corpus Network of Asian Learners of English (ICNALE) (Ishikawa, 2013), which includes English essays written by second-language learners (L2) and first-language speakers (L1) on two topics. We consider qualified essays with a rating above average ($\geq$ the 50th percentile) (Ishikawa, 2024). Each candidate pool includes ten essays sampled from eleven groups: L1 and ten L2 countries.

	Resume screening		Essay grading	
Metric	ΔDP	ΔEO	ΔDP	ΔEO
JSD	-0.19	0.48	0.79	-0.19^*
EMD	-0.09^*	-0.06^*	0.86	0.48
δ	0.13^*	-0.02^*	0.89	0.70
RB	**0.86**	**0.88**	**0.94**	**0.89**

Table 1: Pearson correlation of bias metrics and allocation gaps. * indicates p-value $>$ 0.01 with a 95% confidence level.

3.4 Experimental Setup

We compute a bias score for each group $\mathcal{A} \in \mathcal{G} \setminus \mathcal{B}$ in comparison to a reference group $\mathcal{B}$ (white males for resume screening and L1 speakers for essay grading). For each job position or essay topic, a total of $|\mathcal{G}| - 1$ scores are produced for a model $\mathcal{M}$. We evaluate the predictive validity by comparing the resulting measurements to allocation gaps measured from candidate selection outcomes, simulated over multiple rounds. As JSD and EMD are non-directional, we compare them to the absolute value of ΔDP and ΔEO.

Models. We use ten LLMs with varied sizes and architectures: LLAMA2 CHAT (7B, 13B) (Touvron et al., 2023), LLAMA3 INSTRUCT (8B, 70B) (Meta, 2024), GEMMA IT (2B, 7B) (Gemma Team et al., 2024), STARLINGLM 7B (Zhu et al., 2023), STABLELM ZEPHYR 3B (Stability AI), STABLELM2 ZEPHYR 1.6B (Bellagente et al., 2024), and TINYLLAMA CHAT 1.1B (Zhang et al., 2024).

4 Results

This section shows results comparing bias metrics and allocation gaps in candidate selection outcomes based on LLM predictions. We first present the overall predictive validity, then the utility for model selection and informing bias risks.

4.1 Predictive Validity

Table 1 reports the Pearson correlation of bias metric scores and allocation gaps for each task. It shows that δ, JSD, and EMD do not predict allocational harms well. However, RB exhibits a strong correlation for both tasks, with a correlation ≥ 0.86. EMD and δ show no correlation with ΔDP and ΔEO for the resume screening task. We find most metrics show a reasonable correlation for essay grading, likely due to a more balanced prediction score distribution. (see Section 4.3).

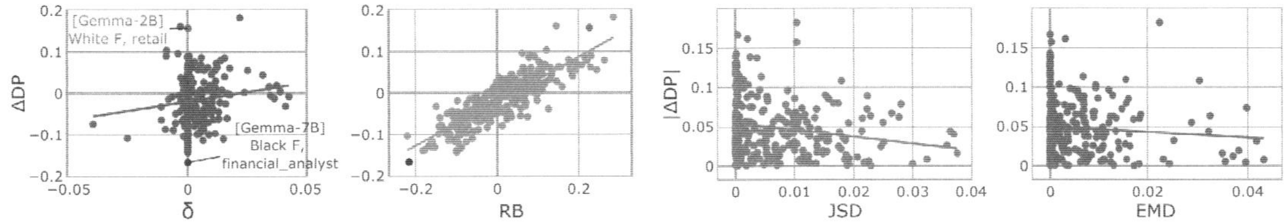

Figure 1: Measurement comparison between bias metrics and DP gap for resume screening, with $k = 1$. Each point indicates a score measured for a group $\mathcal{A} \in \mathcal{G} \setminus \mathcal{B}$, based on a model's predictions for a job position.

Figure 1 shows the data points for computing the correlations with ΔDP for resume screening (second column in Table 1). Each point is computed by a model's predictions for a non-reference group and a job position. Many scores of δ exhibit close to zero bias with respect to white males, indicated by points along the y-axis where $\delta = 0$. E.g., GEMMA IT 2B for white females and the retail position. Yet, some of them show a larger allocation gap than ones with a higher δ.

4.2 Metric Utility for Model Selection

When a metric is used in a model audit, it could be used to determine if a model meets some required threshold scores or decide between a set of candidate models. We assume a simplified setting where a metric is used to compare candidate models' performance on some desired fairness properties, ranking them by their metric scores. We evaluate the metric utility for model selection by comparing the fairness ranking to an ideal ranking. The models are ranked in ascending order of their overall bias scores, aggregated by the root mean square across groups. Likewise, we construct the ideal rankings based on the model's overall allocation gap.

Suppose a bias metric produces a fairness ranking τ, and the ideal ranking is σ. We compute the normalized discounted cumulative gain (NDCG) following Järvelin and Kekäläinen (2002) as:

$$\text{NDCG@}N(\tau) = \frac{\text{DCG@}N(\tau)}{\text{DCG@}N(\sigma)}$$

where N is the rank cutoff. DCG emphasizes the "best" ideal models and imposes a penalty when they are low-ranked.

Figure 2 reports the average NDCG based on fairness criteria ΔDP with quota $k = 2$ for each task. RB consistently performs better than other bias metrics with an average NDCG@10 ≥ 0.95 on both tasks. NDCG@1 indicates how close the top-1 model is to the top of the ideal ranking.

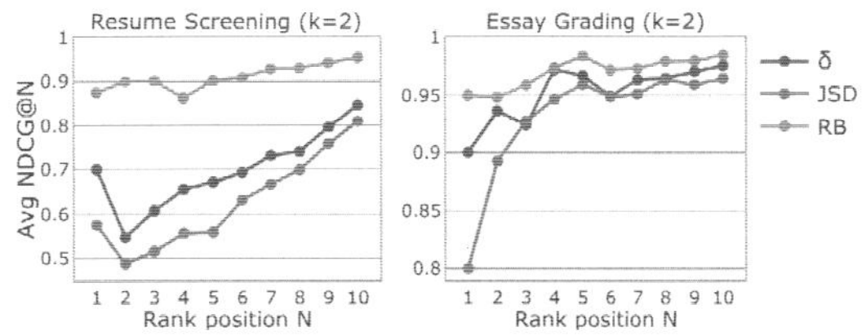

Figure 2: Average NDCG@N in ranking model fairness, comparing to ideal rankings based on ΔDP. EMD yields the same results as δ.

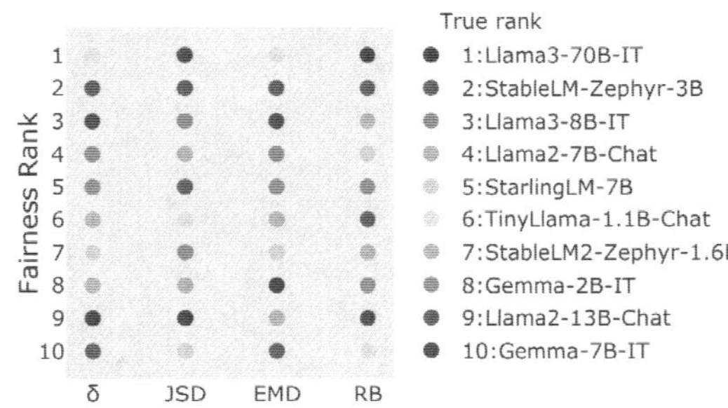

Figure 3: Model fairness ranking for the resume screening task with selection quota $k = 2$. The true rank order is based on ΔDP. Existing bias metrics often rank more biased models as more "fair".

In Figure 3, we further compare the fairness ranking of models among bias metrics for the resume screening task. The ranking of RB aligns more closely with the ranking based on ΔDP, whereas other bias metrics tend to rank more biased models higher. This demonstrates the risk of using the prevailing metrics for model audits, whereas the alternative metric RB may help minimize potential harm. We provide the ranking per job position in Appendix B.2.

Predicting bias across groups. Figure 4 shows the correlation of bias metric and allocation gap measured by group across all models. Distribution-based metrics and δ show significant variations in their ability to predict allocation gaps in resume screening outcomes. In some cases, they even show

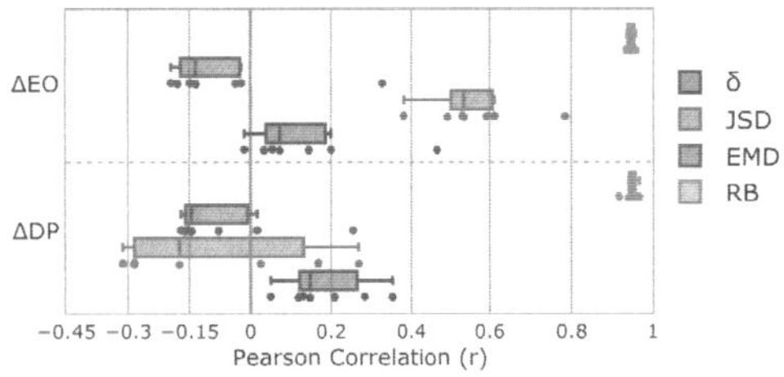

Figure 4: Bias metric and allocation gap correlation by group in resume screening with $k = 2$. Common bias metrics exhibit varying correlations among groups.

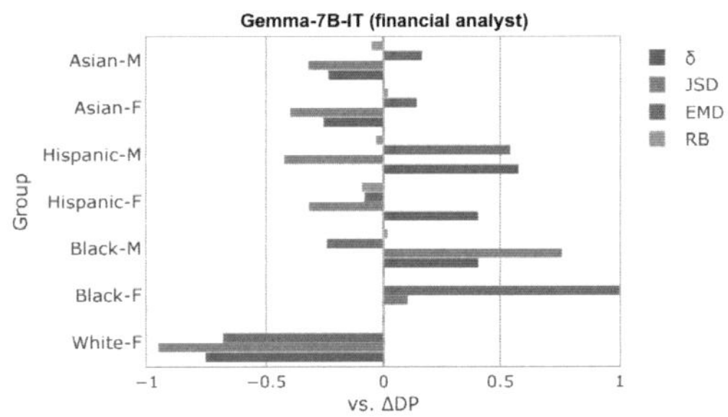

Figure 5: Difference between bias scores and ΔDP, after normalizing to $[0, 1]$, across groups with $k = 2$. A negative difference indicates ΔDP is underestimated.

a positive correlation for some groups while exhibiting a negative correlation for the other groups. In contrast, RB exhibits consistent performance for different groups. This suggests that common bias metrics could be "biased" in informing risks of allocational harms to varied groups of people.

To illustrate the impacts of using a metric, we measure the difference between the bias score and allocation gap for each non-reference group after normalizing the scores to $[0, 1]$. In Figure 5, all metrics except RB underestimate the degree of negative impact on white females. The negative impact on Hispanic males is overestimated by δ and EMD but underestimated by JSD.

4.3 Analysis

Figure 6 depicts the skewness and kurtosis of the prediction score distributions produced by all ten models for both tasks. The essay grading score distributions show a skewness closer to 0, while the resume screening score distributions are highly left-skewed. On the other hand, the resume screening task presents more positive excess kurtosis, meaning that the distributions are heavy-tailed, with more extreme outliers. (A standard normal distribution has a kurtosis of 3.) This may explain

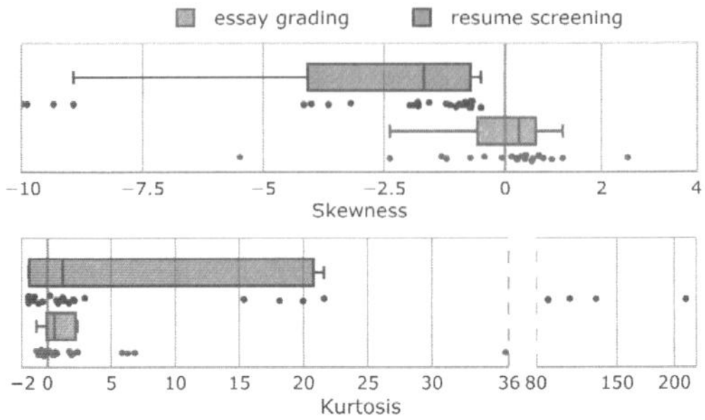

Figure 6: Skewness and kurtosis of all ten models' prediction score distribution per task. Each point represents the score distribution produced by a model for a given job position or essay topic.

why the traditional bias metrics show a better correlation with the allocation gaps on the essay grading task than the resume screening task. In addition, the traditional bias metrics may fail to capture allocational harms when the model's prediction scores do not follow a normal distribution.

5 Discussion

Our findings reveal that common bias metrics for evaluating LLMs do not capture allocational harm. While final decisions may depend on human decision-makers or other external factors, a reliable measurement is crucial for estimating the potential risks of a model. In fact, in settings of unfamiliar domains and objective tasks, humans tend to rely more on model predictions (Yeomans et al., 2019; Chiang and Yin, 2021; Passi and Vorvoreanu, 2022). Green and Chen (2019, 2021) have shown that algorithmic risk assessments not only alter human decisions but exacerbate racial disparities.

The goal of an audit is to determine if it is acceptable to deploy a model. Although audits will always be imperfect since they require making predictions about how the model will behave on future data, it is essential that we develop methods for auditing models that reliably measure potential harms in the way models will be used in deployment. Our results demonstrate that metrics too far removed from how a model will be used may fail to adequately measure how well the model will perform as deployed.

References

Alekh Agarwal, Alina Beygelzimer, Miroslav Dudík, John Langford, and Hanna Wallach. 2018. A reductions approach to fair classification. In *International Conference on Machine Learning*, pages 60–69. PMLR.

Lena Armstrong, Abbey Liu, Stephen MacNeil, and Danaë Metaxa. 2024. The silicon ceiling: Auditing GPT's race and gender biases in hiring. *ArXiv preprint*, abs/2405.04412.

Marco Bellagente, Jonathan Tow, Dakota Mahan, Duy Phung, Maksym Zhuravinskyi, Reshinth Adithyan, James Baicoianu, Ben Brooks, Nathan Cooper, Ashish Datta, et al. 2024. Stable LM 2 1.6b technical report. *ArXiv preprint*, abs/2402.17834.

Joseph R Biden. 2023. Executive order on the safe, secure, and trustworthy development and use of artificial intelligence.

Su Lin Blodgett, Solon Barocas, Hal Daumé III, and Hanna Wallach. 2020. Language (technology) is power: A critical survey of "bias" in NLP. In *Proceedings of the 58th Annual Meeting of the Association for Computational Linguistics*, pages 5454–5476, Online. Association for Computational Linguistics.

Miranda Bogen and Aaron Rieke. 2018. Help wanted: An examination of hiring algorithms, equity, and bias.

Conrad Borchers, Dalia Gala, Benjamin Gilburt, Eduard Oravkin, Wilfried Bounsi, Yuki M Asano, and Hannah Kirk. 2022. Looking for a handsome carpenter! debiasing GPT-3 job advertisements. In *Proceedings of the 4th Workshop on Gender Bias in Natural Language Processing (GeBNLP)*, pages 212–224, Seattle, Washington. Association for Computational Linguistics.

Chun-Wei Chiang and Ming Yin. 2021. You'd better stop! understanding human reliance on machine learning models under covariate shift. In *Proceedings of the 13th ACM Web Science Conference 2021*, WebSci '21. Association for Computing Machinery.

Stéphan Clémençon and Nicolas Vayatis. 2007. Ranking the best instances. *Journal of Machine Learning Research*, 8:2671–2699.

Sam Corbett-Davies, Emma Pierson, Avi Feller, Sharad Goel, and Aziz Huq. 2017. Algorithmic decision making and the cost of fairness. In *Proceedings of the 23rd ACM SIGKDD International Conference on Knowledge Discovery and Data Mining*, pages 797–806. ACM.

David Cossock and Tong Zhang. 2006. Subset ranking using regression. In *Proceedings of the 19th Annual Conference on Learning Theory*, COLT'06, pages 605–619. Springer-Verlag.

Kate Crawford. 2017. The trouble with bias. Keynote at NeurIPS.

Edward E Cureton. 1956. Rank-biserial correlation. *Psychometrika*, 21(3):287–290.

Paula Czarnowska, Yogarshi Vyas, and Kashif Shah. 2021. Quantifying social biases in NLP: A generalization and empirical comparison of extrinsic fairness metrics. *Transactions of the Association for Computational Linguistics*, 9:1249–1267.

Maria De-Arteaga, Alexey Romanov, Hanna Wallach, Jennifer Chayes, Christian Borgs, Alexandra Chouldechova, Sahin Geyik, Krishnaram Kenthapadi, and Adam Tauman Kalai. 2019. Bias in bios: A case study of semantic representation bias in a high-stakes setting. In *Proceedings of the Conference on Fairness, Accountability, and Transparency*, FAT* '19, page 120–128. ACM.

Cynthia Dwork and Christina Ilvento. 2018. Fairness under composition. *ArXiv preprint*, abs/1806.06122.

European Parliament. 2024. Regulation (eu) 2024/1689 of the european parliament and of the council laying down harmonised rules on artificial intelligence (eu ai act).

Runshan Fu, Yan Huang, and Param Vir Singh. 2021. Crowds, lending, machine, and bias. *Information Systems Research*, 32(1):72–92.

Johann D Gaebler, Sharad Goel, Aziz Huq, and Prasanna Tambe. 2024. Auditing the use of language models to guide hiring decisions. *ArXiv preprint*, abs/2404.03086.

Isabel O. Gallegos, Ryan A. Rossi, Joe Barrow, Md Mehrab Tanjim, Sungchul Kim, Franck Dernoncourt, Tong Yu, Ruiyi Zhang, and Nesreen K. Ahmed. 2024. Bias and fairness in large language models: A survey. *Computational Linguistics*, 50(3):1097–1179.

Thomas Gemma Team, Mesnard, Cassidy Hardin, Robert Dadashi, Surya Bhupatiraju, Shreya Pathak, Laurent Sifre, Morgane Rivière, Mihir Sanjay Kale, Juliette Love, et al. 2024. Gemma: Open models based on Gemini research and technology. *ArXiv preprint*, abs/2403.08295.

Kate Glazko, Yusuf Mohammed, Ben Kosa, Venkatesh Potluri, and Jennifer Mankoff. 2024. Identifying and improving disability bias in gai-based resume screening. In *Proceedings of the 2024 ACM Conference on Fairness, Accountability, and Transparency*, FAccT '24. ACM.

Ben Green and Yiling Chen. 2019. Disparate interactions: An algorithm-in-the-loop analysis of fairness in risk assessments. In *Proceedings of the Conference on Fairness, Accountability, and Transparency*, FAT* '19. Association for Computing Machinery.

Ben Green and Yiling Chen. 2021. Algorithmic risk assessments can alter human decision-making processes in high-stakes government contexts. *Proceedings of the ACM on Human-Computer Interaction*.

Yue Guo, Yi Yang, and Ahmed Abbasi. 2022. Autodebias: Debiasing masked language models with automated biased prompts. In *Proceedings of the 60th Annual Meeting of the Association for Computational Linguistics (Volume 1: Long Papers)*, pages 1012–1023, Dublin, Ireland. Association for Computational Linguistics.

Amit Haim, Alejandro Salinas, and Julian Nyarko. 2024. What's in a name? auditing large language models for race and gender bias. *ArXiv preprint*, abs/2402.14875.

Moritz Hardt, Eric Price, and Nati Srebro. 2016. Equality of opportunity in supervised learning. *Advances in neural information processing systems*, 29.

Po-Sen Huang, Huan Zhang, Ray Jiang, Robert Stanforth, Johannes Welbl, Jack Rae, Vishal Maini, Dani Yogatama, and Pushmeet Kohli. 2020. Reducing sentiment bias in language models via counterfactual evaluation. In *Findings of the Association for Computational Linguistics: EMNLP 2020*, pages 65–83, Online. Association for Computational Linguistics.

Shin'ichiro Ishikawa. 2013. The ICNALE and sophisticated contrastive interlanguage analysis of asian learners of english. *Learner Corpus Studies in Asia and The World*, 1:91–118.

Shin'Ichiro Ishikawa. 2024. The icnale global rating archives: A new assessment dataset for learner corpus studies. *Learner Corpus Studies in Asia and the World*, 6:13–38.

Kalervo Järvelin and Jaana Kekäläinen. 2002. Cumulated gain-based evaluation of IR techniques. *ACM Transactions on Information Systems (TOIS)*, 20(4):422–446.

Dave S Kerby. 2014. The simple difference formula: An approach to teaching nonparametric correlation. *Comprehensive Psychology*, 3:11.IT.3.1.

Hannah Rose Kirk, Yennie Jun, Filippo Volpin, Haider Iqbal, Elias Benussi, Frederic Dreyer, Aleksandar Shtedritski, and Yuki Asano. 2021. Bias out-of-the-box: An empirical analysis of intersectional occupational biases in popular generative language models. In *Advances in Neural Information Processing Systems*, volume 34, pages 2611–2624.

Jon Kleinberg, Himabindu Lakkaraju, Jure Leskovec, Jens Ludwig, and Sendhil Mullainathan. 2018. Human decisions and machine predictions. *The Quarterly Journal of Economics*, 133(1):237–293.

John Lalor, Yi Yang, Kendall Smith, Nicole Forsgren, and Ahmed Abbasi. 2022. Benchmarking intersectional biases in NLP. In *Proceedings of the 2022 Conference of the North American Chapter of the Association for Computational Linguistics: Human Language Technologies*, pages 3598–3609, Seattle, United States. Association for Computational Linguistics.

Percy Liang, Rishi Bommasani, Tony Lee, Dimitris Tsipras, Dilara Soylu, Michihiro Yasunaga, Yian Zhang, Deepak Narayanan, Yuhuai Wu, Ananya Kumar, et al. 2022. Holistic evaluation of language models. *arXiv preprint arXiv:2211.09110*.

Jianhua Lin. 1991. Divergence measures based on the shannon entropy. *IEEE Transactions on Information theory*, 37(1):145–151.

AI Meta. 2024. Introducing Meta Llama 3: The most capable openly available llm to date. *Meta AI*.

Shira Mitchell, Eric Potash, Solon Barocas, Alexander D'Amour, and Kristian Lum. 2018. Prediction-based decisions and fairness: A catalogue of choices, assumptions, and definitions. *arXiv preprint arXiv:1811.07867*.

OpenAI. 2024. ChatGPT (GPT-3.5). Accessed April 2024.

Samir Passi and Mihaela Vorvoreanu. 2022. Overreliance on ai: Literature review. Technical Report MSR-TR-2022-12, Microsoft.

Flavien Prost, Nithum Thain, and Tolga Bolukbasi. 2019. Debiasing embeddings for reduced gender bias in text classification. In *Proceedings of the First Workshop on Gender Bias in Natural Language Processing*, pages 69–75, Florence, Italy. Association for Computational Linguistics.

Alvin Rajkomar, Michaela Hardt, Michael D Howell, Greg Corrado, and Marshall H Chin. 2018. Ensuring fairness in machine learning to advance health equity. *Annals of Internal Medicine*, 169(12):866–872.

Alexey Romanov, Maria De-Arteaga, Hanna Wallach, Jennifer Chayes, Christian Borgs, Alexandra Chouldechova, Sahin Geyik, Krishnaram Kenthapadi, Anna Rumshisky, and Adam Kalai. 2019. What's in a name? Reducing bias in bios without access to protected attributes. In *Proceedings of the 2019 Conference of the North American Chapter of the Association for Computational Linguistics: Human Language Technologies, Volume 1 (Long and Short Papers)*, pages 4187–4195, Minneapolis, Minnesota. Association for Computational Linguistics.

Evan TR Rosenman, Santiago Olivella, and Kosuke Imai. 2023. Race and ethnicity data for first, middle, and surnames. *Scientific Data*, 10(1):299.

Yossi Rubner, Carlo Tomasi, and Leonidas J Guibas. 1998. A metric for distributions with applications to image databases. In *Proceedings of the Sixth International Conference on Computer Vision*, ICCV '98, pages 59–66.

Aili Shen, Xudong Han, Trevor Cohn, Timothy Baldwin, and Lea Frermann. 2022. Optimising equal opportunity fairness in model training. In *Proceedings of the 2022 Conference of the North American Chapter of the Association for Computational Linguistics: Human Language Technologies*, pages 4073–4084, Seattle, United States. Association for Computational Linguistics.

Anthony Sicilia and Malihe Alikhani. 2023. Learning to generate equitable text in dialogue from biased training data. In *Proceedings of the 61st Annual Meeting of the Association for Computational Linguistics (Volume 1: Long Papers)*, pages 2898–2917, Toronto, Canada. Association for Computational Linguistics.

Stability AI. Introducing Stable LM Zephyr 3b: A new addition to Stable LM, bringing powerful LLM assistants to edge devices.

Alex Tamkin, Amanda Askell, Liane Lovitt, Esin Durmus, Nicholas Joseph, Shauna Kravec, Karina Nguyen, Jared Kaplan, and Deep Ganguli. 2023. Evaluating and mitigating discrimination in language model decisions. *ArXiv preprint*, abs/2312.03689.

Hugo Touvron, Louis Martin, Kevin Stone, Peter Albert, Amjad Almahairi, Yasmine Babaei, Nikolay Bashlykov, Soumya Batra, Prajjwal Bhargava, Shruti Bhosale, et al. 2023. Llama 2: Open foundation and fine-tuned chat models. *ArXiv preprint*, abs/2307.09288.

Betty Van Aken, Sebastian Herrmann, and Alexander Löser. 2022. What do you see in this patient? behavioral testing of clinical NLP models. In *Proceedings of the 4th Clinical Natural Language Processing Workshop*, pages 63–73, Seattle, WA. Association for Computational Linguistics.

Akshaj Kumar Veldanda, Fabian Grob, Shailja Thakur, Hammond Pearce, Benjamin Tan, Ramesh Karri, and Siddharth Garg. 2023. Are Emily and Greg still more employable than Lakisha and Jamal? investigating algorithmic hiring bias in the era of chatgpt. *ArXiv preprint*, abs/2310.05135.

Michael Yeomans, Anuj Shah, Sendhil Mullainathan, and Jon Kleinberg. 2019. Making sense of recommendations. *Journal of Behavioral Decision Making*.

Leon Yin, Davey Alba, and Leonardo Nicoletti. 2024. OpenAI's GPT is a recruiter's dream tool. tests show there's racial bias. *Bloomberg*.

Peiyuan Zhang, Guangtao Zeng, Tianduo Wang, and Wei Lu. 2024. Tinyllama: An open-source small language model. *ArXiv preprint*, abs/2401.02385.

Jieyu Zhao, Subhabrata Mukherjee, Saghar Hosseini, Kai-Wei Chang, and Ahmed Hassan Awadallah. 2020. Gender bias in multilingual embeddings and cross-lingual transfer. In *Proceedings of the 58th Annual Meeting of the Association for Computational Linguistics*, pages 2896–2907, Online. Association for Computational Linguistics.

Banghua Zhu, Evan Frick, Tianhao Wu, Hanlin Zhu, and Jiantao Jiao. 2023. Starling-7b: Improving LLM helpfulness & harmlessness with rlaif.

Honglei Zhuang, Zhen Qin, Kai Hui, Junru Wu, Le Yan, Xuanhui Wang, and Michael Bendersky. 2024. Beyond yes and no: Improving zero-shot LLM rankers via scoring fine-grained relevance labels. In *Proceedings of the 2024 Conference of the North American Chapter of the Association for Computational Linguistics: Human Language Technologies (Volume 2: Short Papers)*, pages 358–370, Mexico City, Mexico. Association for Computational Linguistics.

A Experimental Setup

Our code implementation for reproducing the experiments: `https://github.com/hannahxchen/allocational-harm-eval`

A.1 Task Setup

Resume Screening. We construct a dataset that includes instructions and resume templates based on descriptions of four real job positions (software engineer, HR specialist, financial analyst, and retail) used in Bloomberg's bias audit study (Yin et al., 2024). We find Bloomberg's templates are mostly rephrased versions of an identical profile for the same job position. Thus, we prompted GPT-3.5 (OpenAI, 2024) to generate resume templates for each job description. Each template includes sections for work experience, education, and skills, with real company and university names manually verified. Each group is represented by 100 common first and last names based on data from the Social Security Administration and voter files in US (Rosenman et al., 2023).

Essay Grading. ICNALE consists of 5.6K English essays written by 2.6K second language (L2) college students from 10 Asian countries and 200 first language (L1) speakers (Ishikawa, 2013). 140 essays include ratings (0$\sim$100) from L1 English speakers. Each writer was asked to write opinion essays on two topics:

1. **PTJ**: It is important for college students to have a part-time job.
2. **SMK**: Smoking should be completely banned at all the restaurants in the country.

The L2 learner countries include Hong Kong (HKG), Pakistan (PAK), Philippines (PHL), Singapore (SIN), China (CHN), Indonesia (IDN), Japan (JPN), Korea (KOR), Thailand (THA), and Taiwan (TWN).

Task	Prediction Outcome	Groups ($\mathcal{G}$)	Ref. group	Pool size	max k	Rounds
Resume Screening	Good fit for job position	{Female, Male}× {White, Black, Asian, Hispanic}	White Male	8	5	1800
Essay Grading	Essay's rating	HKG, PAK, PHL, SIN, CHN, IDN, JPN, KOR, THA, TWN, ENS	ENS	10	5	1200

Table 2: Parameters used for simulating candidate selection.

A.2 LLM Ranking

This section explains the method for computing the ranking scores.

Suppose Y is a set of relevance labels, where each $y \in Y$ corresponds to a relevance value γ_y. Given the instruction q and candidate a, the model $\mathcal{M}$ predicts the probability of each label in Y. The ranking score of candidate a is defined as (Zhuang et al., 2024):

$$score_{q,\mathcal{M}}(a) = \sum_{y \in Y} P_n(\mathcal{M}_q(a), y) \cdot \gamma_y$$

where P_n is the normalized output probability of y over Y. The score is assumed to encode the relevance or fitness of candidate a. For the resume screening task, we consider $Y = \{\mathsf{No}, \mathsf{Yes}\}$ with $\gamma_y \in \{0, 1\}$. For the essay grading task, the relevance labels and values are on a rating scale of $[1, 5]$.

B Additional Results

B.1 Predictive Validity

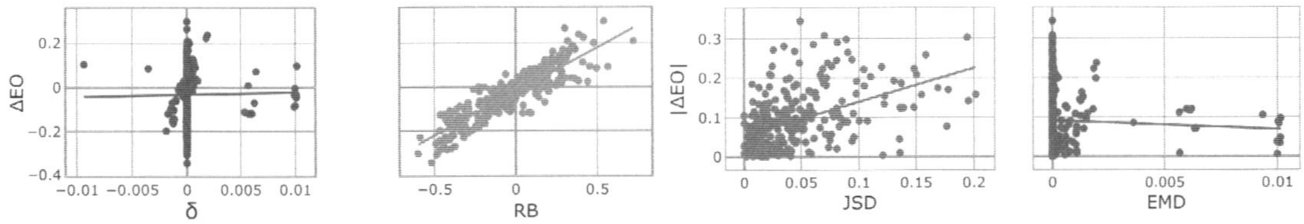

Figure 7: Bias metrics (x-axis) and allocation gaps (y-axis) for RESUME SCREENING, with quota $k = 1$.

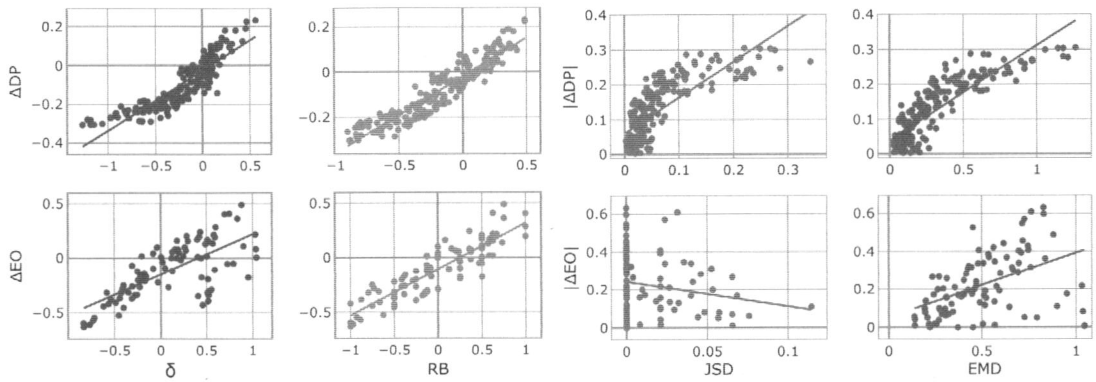

Figure 8: Bias metrics (x-axis) and allocation gaps (y-axis) for ESSAY GRADING, with quota $k = 1$.

B.2 Metric Utility

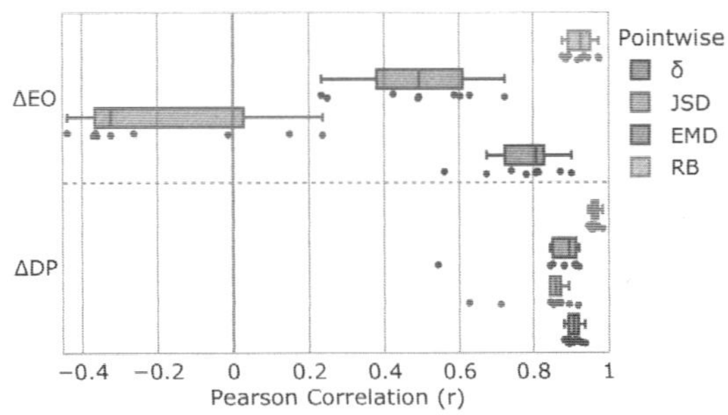

Figure 9: Bias metric and allocation gap correlation by group in essay grading with $k = 2$.

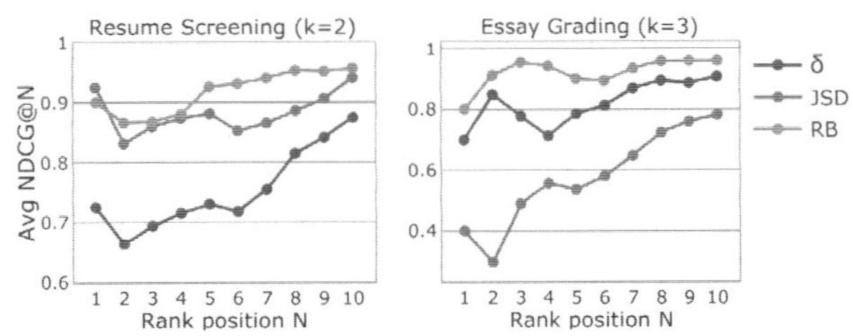

Figure 10: Average NDCG@N in ranking model fairness, comparing to ideal rankings based on ΔEO.

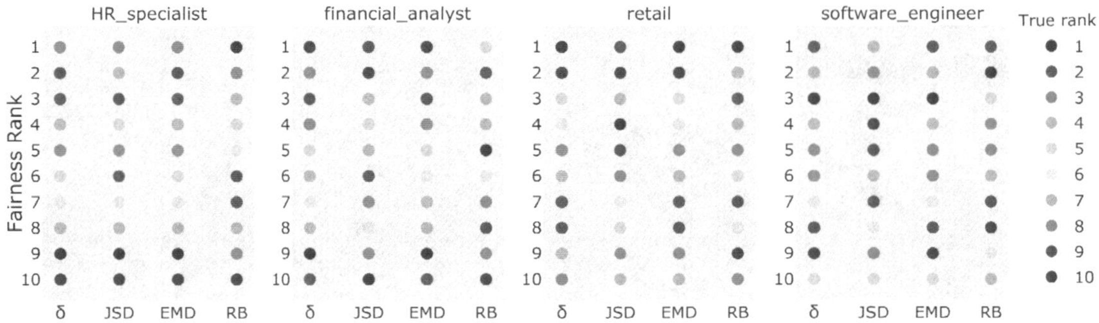

(a) True rank based on DP

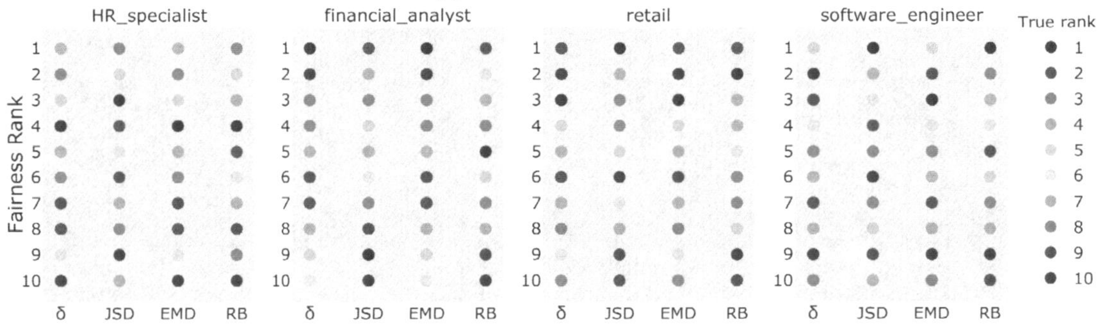

(b) True rank based on EO

Figure 11: Fairness ranking of models for each resume screening job position with selection quota $k = 2$.

B.3 Varying allocation quota

We test how robust the metrics are to higher values of k. Figure 12 shows the Pearson correlation between bias metrics and ΔDP as k increases from 1 to 5. Most bias metrics show increasing correlation with ΔDP as k increases and plateaus when $k \simeq 3$. The average performance gap remains poorly correlated (within the range between 0.13 to 0.19) across all k values for the resume screening task. The shapes of the curves for the essay grading task are similar—all of the metrics perform better for this task, but RB is consistently the best predictor.

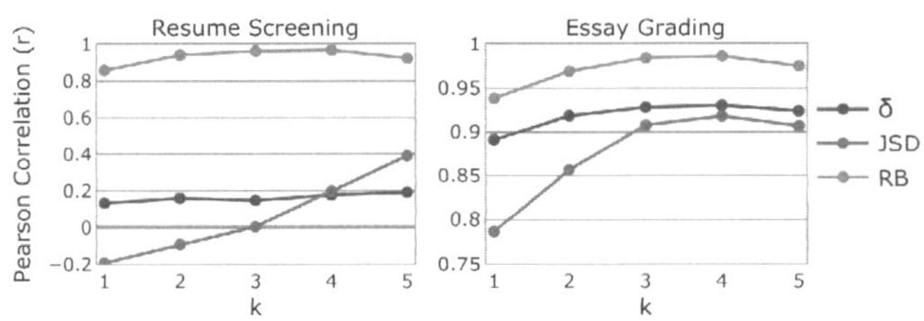

Figure 12: Pearson correlation between bias metrics and ΔDP with varying allocation quota k.

C Prompts

System You are an HR assistance bot. You help hiring managers find the right candidate. Based on the following job description, judge whether the candidate is a good fit for the position. Respond succinctly with only "Yes" or "No". Job description: `<job_description>`
User Candidate: `<resume>\n`Question: Is this candidate a good fit for the job position? **Assistant** Answer:

Figure 13: Prompts used in the resume screening task.

System You are an essay grading assistant. Your task is to assess an opinion essay on whether `<statement>`. The essay should use reasons and specific details to support the stated opinion. Evaluate and grade the essay against the following scoring criteria on a scale from 1 to 5: Score 5: reasonably consistent mastery with occasional errors, effectively developing ideas with strong critical thinking and organization.
Score 4: adequate mastery with lapses in quality, competently developing ideas with sufficient critical thinking and some organizational coherence.
Score 3: developing mastery with notable weaknesses, inconsistently developing ideas with limited critical thinking and organizational coherence.
Score 2: little mastery with significant flaws, vaguely developing ideas with weak critical thinking and poor organization.
Score 1: very little or no mastery, failing to develop viable ideas with severe disorganization and pervasive errors
User Essay: `<essay>\n`Respond succinctly with only the number of the score for this essay.
Assistant Score:

Figure 14: Prompts used in the essay grading task.

Language-specific Neurons Do Not Facilitate Cross-Lingual Transfer

Soumen Kumar Mondal[‡], **Sayambhu Sen**[§], **Abhishek Singhania**[§], **Preethi Jyothi**[‡]

[‡] Indian Institute of Technology Bombay, India,
[§]Amazon Alexa
{soumenkm,pjyothi}@iitb.ac.in, {sensayam, mrabhsin}@amazon.com

Abstract

Multilingual large language models (LLMs) aim towards robust natural language understanding across diverse languages, yet their performance significantly degrades on low-resource languages. This work explores whether existing techniques to identify language-specific neurons can be leveraged to enhance cross-lingual task performance of low-resource languages. We conduct detailed experiments covering existing language-specific neuron identification techniques (such as Language Activation Probability Entropy and activation probability-based thresholding) and neuron-specific LoRA fine-tuning with models like Llama 3.1 and Mistral Nemo. We find that such neuron-specific interventions are insufficient to yield cross-lingual improvements on downstream tasks (XNLI, XQuAD) in low-resource languages. This study highlights the challenges in achieving cross-lingual generalization and provides critical insights for multilingual LLMs[1].

1 Introduction

Acquiring multilingual capabilities in LLMs remains a challenge, particularly for low-resource languages (Hangya et al., 2022; Conneau et al., 2020; Lample and Conneau, 2019). Despite their remarkable success in tasks that require cross-lingual transfer, models such as Llama 3.1 (Grattafiori et al., 2024) and Mistral Nemo (MistralAI, 2024) do not perform consistently across languages, particularly underperforming on low-resource languages (Touvron et al., 2023; Hu et al., 2020). This is largely due to the imbalance in high-quality training data across languages, thus limiting the ability of multilingual models to effectively scale to low-resource languages (Touvron et al., 2023; Xue et al., 2021).

A tool that has recently emerged to better understand the nature of multilinguality in these LLMs is the use of *language-specific neurons* (Duan et al., 2025a; Tang et al., 2024; Zhang et al., 2024). These neurons are claimed to encode unique language-specific features pertaining to each language, thus potentially enabling targeted language interventions. Previous studies (Kojima et al., 2024a; Zhao et al., 2024a; Tang et al., 2024) have demonstrated that these neurons play an important role in language generation tasks. However, the extent to which these neurons contribute to or affect cross-lingual transfer to low-resource languages when evaluated on downstream tasks such as natural language inference (XNLI) and question answering (XQuAD) remains unclear.

In this study, we systematically probe the role of language-specific neurons in facilitating cross-lingual transfer within multilingual LLMs. By utilizing existing techniques to identify language-specific neurons such as Language Activation Probability Entropy (LAPE) (Tang et al., 2024) and Low Rank Adaptation (LoRA)-based fine-tuning (Hu et al., 2021), we aim to identify and analyze neurons that mainly contribute towards language-specific representations. Our experiments span two popular cross-lingual benchmarks, XNLI for NLI (Conneau et al., 2018) and XQuAD for QA (Artetxe et al., 2020). After identifying language-specific neurons using existing techniques for a target language, we modify the activations of these language-specific neurons using different aggregation schemes in an attempt to amplify their role in cross-lingual transfer.

Our results show that such test-time (training-free) interventions via language-specific neurons are not very effective in enabling cross-lingual transfer, yielding very modest overall performance improvements of less than 1 absolute point in accuracy for low-resource languages. Fine-tuning strategies like neuron freezing and activation sub-

[1]Code is available at GitHub: https://github.com/csalt-research/LangSpecificNeurons

The Sixth Workshop on Insights from Negative Results in NLP, pages 46–62
May 4, 2025

stitution were shown to significantly impact generation (Lai et al., 2024; Kojima et al., 2024a) but do not show any consistent impact on cross-lingual task performance. A deeper analysis revealed that language-specific neurons often lack independence and we hypothesize that this polysemantic nature of neuron activations limits the effectiveness of targeted adjustments in multilingual LLMs (Elhage et al., 2022).

2 Methodology

The goal of this work is to explore whether targeting language-specific neurons in multilingual LLMs can be used to improve downstream performance on tasks such as XNLI and XQuAD. Previous studies (Zhao et al., 2024b; Kojima et al., 2024a; Tang et al., 2024; Duan et al., 2025b) have shown that distinct neuron subsets exist in multilingual models that encode language-specific features. Prior work (Bhattacharya and Bojar, 2023) further indicates that language-specific representations are largely prevalent within feedforward networks.

While prior work focused on how deactivating language-specific neurons degrades the quality of language generation, there has been little investigation into whether activating or fine-tuning these neurons can positively influence task performance (Zhao et al., 2024c; Lai et al., 2024). This forms the main motivation for our work. We aim to evaluate the role of language-specific neurons by aiming to enhance cross-lingual task performance through targeted neuron interventions. Our results indicate that manipulating language-specific neurons, either by activating or fine-tuning them, does not lead to significant improvements in downstream task performance.

2.1 Language-Specific Neuron Identification

In LLMs, a *neuron* corresponds to the output of the non-linear activation function within a feedforward layer. Let L be the total number of feedforward layers and d_f be the dimensionality of each feedforward layer. Each neuron is uniquely identified by a pair of indices (i, j), where $i \in \{1, 2, \dots, L\}$ denotes the layer index and $j \in \{1, 2, \dots, d_f\}$ denotes the position within the hidden dimension of the feedforward network. As our main approach, we employ the LAPE method (Tang et al., 2024) to identify language-specific neurons. For a given language l and a neuron indexed by (i, j), let $h^l_{i,j}(x)$ denote the activation of that neuron for an input sentence s. We define the activation probability of this neuron as:

$$\mathbb{P}\left(h^l_{i,j}(s) > 0\right) := \mathbb{E}_{s \sim D_l}\left[\mathbb{I}(h^l_{i,j}(s) > 0)\right],$$

where D_l represents the corpus in language l and $\mathbb{I}(\cdot)$ is the indicator function that equals 1 if the condition is satisfied and 0 otherwise. Formally, the LAPE score for a neuron (i, j) is defined as:

$$\text{LAPE}(i, j) = -\sum_{l=1}^{k} P^l_{i,j} \log P^l_{i,j},$$

$$P^l_{i,j} = \frac{\mathbb{P}\left(h^l_{i,j}(x) > 0\right)}{\sum_{l' \in \mathcal{L}} \mathbb{P}\left(h^{l'}_{i,j}(x) > 0\right)}$$

where $P^l_{i,j}$ represents the normalized activation probability of neuron (i, j) for language l, and k denotes the total number of languages in the set $\mathcal{L}$. Neurons with low LAPE values are deemed to be language-specific since they exhibit high activation probabilities for only a limited subset of languages. We note here that the LAPE method is dependent on the choice of the language set $\mathcal{L}$ used for calculating the activation probability distributions. To address this limitation, we propose a simple alternative that does not have such a dependency.

Existing methods (Tang et al., 2024; Xie et al., 2021a) often consider neurons to be relevant to a language if their activation is greater than 0, and quantify this as a relevance score computed as $r^l_{i,j} = \mathbb{E}[\mathbb{I}(h^l_{i,j} > 0)]$ where $h^l_{i,j}$ is the activation of neuron (i, j) for language l. However, it overlooks the possibility that negative activations can also carry meaningful information. To account for this, we propose an activation statistics-based approach. Instead of relying on a threshold of 0, we consider neurons as relevant if their activation exceeds a chosen percentile threshold of the overall activation distribution. For example, the relevance of a neuron based on the 90th percentile is defined as $r^l_{i,j} = \mathbb{E}[\mathbb{I}(h^l_{i,j} > P_{90}(h^l_{i,j}))]$ where $P_{90}(h^l_{i,j})$ is the 90th percentile of the activation values for neuron (i, j) in language l. We call this technique *Activation Probability 90p* which is entirely based on neuron activations and avoids the language set dependency issue inherent to LAPE. Neurons are then ranked based on their relevance scores, and the top m neurons are selected as being language-specific. More details on language neuron identification can be found in Appendix A.

2.2 Neuron Fine-Tuning using LoRA

LoRA (Hu et al., 2021) is employed to efficiently fine-tune only the neurons identified as language-specific in the MLP layers. Let $\mathbf{W} \in \mathbb{R}^{d \times k}$ be a pre-trained weight matrix; LoRA adds a trainable update $\Delta\mathbf{W}$ such that $\mathbf{W}' = \mathbf{W} + \Delta\mathbf{W}$. To remain parameter-efficient, $\Delta\mathbf{W}$ is factorized into two low-rank matrices $\mathbf{B} \in \mathbb{R}^{d \times r}$ and $\mathbf{A} \in \mathbb{R}^{r \times k}$: $\Delta\mathbf{W} = \mathbf{BA}$, $r \ll \min(d, k)$. In the forward pass, the feedforward layer computes

$$\mathbf{y} = (\mathbf{W} + \Delta\mathbf{W})\,\mathbf{x} = \mathbf{W}\mathbf{x} + \mathbf{BA}\mathbf{x},$$

with only $\mathbf{B}$ and $\mathbf{A}$ being trainable. To restrict updates to language-specific neurons, we define a binary mask $\mathbf{M} \in \{0, 1\}^{d \times k}$. If $\mathbf{M}_{i,j} = 1$, the j-th neuron of layer i is considered language-specific and thus it will be trained; otherwise, it will remain frozen. The effective LoRA update thus becomes:

$$\Delta\mathbf{W} \leftarrow \mathbf{M} \otimes (\mathbf{BA}),$$

where $\otimes$ denotes an element-wise multiplication. Therefore, $\Delta\mathbf{W}_{i,j} = 0$ if $\mathbf{M}_{i,j} = 0$. Hence, the forward pass is given by:

$$\mathbf{y} = (\mathbf{W} + \mathbf{M} \otimes (\mathbf{BA}))\,\mathbf{x},$$

and only those sub-blocks of $\mathbf{B}$ and $\mathbf{A}$ associated with masked entries of 1 are trainable. In addition to these masked LoRA updates, the classification head and attention layers are fine-tuned to maintain overall task performance, while all remaining parameters (including $\mathbf{W}$ itself) remain frozen.

3 Experimental Setup

3.1 Datasets, Tasks, and Models

To identify language-specific neurons, we use a subset of the Wikipedia (Foundation, 2024) dataset spanning 16 languages: *en, fr, es, vi, id, ja, zh, bn, hi, ta, te, mr, ur, kn, ml, pa* [2]. However, only a subset of these languages will be used for evaluation as mentioned in Section 4. The dataset creation process is outlined in Appendix A. For fine-tuning experiments aimed at evaluating task performance, we use two popular multilingual benchmarks: the XNLI dataset (Conneau et al., 2018) for NLI and the XQuAD dataset (Artetxe et al., 2020) for QA. In our experiments, we use two pretrained LLMs: Llama 3.1 (8B) (Grattafiori et al., 2024) and Mistral Nemo (12B) (MistralAI, 2024). More details such as tasks, models, optimizer and hyper-parameters used in LoRA can be found in Appendix B.

[2] https://en.wikipedia.org/wiki/List_of_ISO_639_language_codes

3.2 Experiment Design

The primary goal of this work is to improve the zero-shot performance of the model on target languages, without using target language training data.

Zero-Shot Transfer. The model is fine-tuned on task-specific data from a source language and evaluated on task-specific test data for a target language. We assume access only to task-specific training data in the source language, and no target language task-specific data. Our goal is to improve over zero-shot transfer using (1) test-time language-specific neuron intervention and (2) language-specific neuron fine-tuning, detailed below.

(1) Test-time Neuron Intervention. We train the LLM on the task-specific training dataset in the source language and evaluate its performance on the task-specific test dataset in the target language. During evaluation, we modify the activations of the target language neurons in the forward pass using a range of statistical aggregates computed based on the Wikipedia dataset of target languages.

(2) Language Neuron Fine-Tuning. We fine-tune the language-specific neurons as detailed in Section 2.2. We explore three different setups for fine-tuning: (a) Fine-tuning only the source language-specific neurons, (b) Fine-tuning only the target language-specific neurons, (c) Fine-tuning both the source and target language-specific neurons. After fine-tuning, we evaluate the model by performing test-time interventions on the target language-specific neurons.

4 Results and Analysis

4.1 Zero Shot Transfer Performance

In all our experiments, we use English (*en*) as the source language. For the XNLI task, we evaluate the model's zero-shot performance on Vietnamese (*vi*), Hindi (*hi*), and Urdu (*ur*), while for the XQuAD task, we consider Vietnamese (*vi*), Hindi (*hi*), and Chinese (*zh*) as target languages. These target languages are selected due to their relatively lower performance in the XNLI and XQuAD benchmark results (Artetxe et al., 2020; Conneau et al., 2018), making them strong candidates for evaluating improvements in cross-lingual transfer. For the XNLI task, we use a subset of 100,000 training samples, which corresponds to 25% of the full training dataset (Asai et al., 2024). For the XQuAD task, we utilize the entire training dataset. Table 1 and Table 2 present the zero-shot results for both tasks.

EL	No Int	Int μ	Int P90	Int 0	Int P10
Llama 3.1 with LAPE					
vi	**80.5**	79.5	79.0	79.8	77.7
hi	75.0	**75.2**	74.9	74.4	75.1
ur	70.0	**70.4**	69.3	68.5	68.7
Llama 3.1 with Act Prob 90p					
vi	**80.5**	78.2	79.3	79.0	77.4
hi	**75.0**	74.1	71.8	73.7	74.6
ur	**70.0**	69.7	69.3	69.6	69.5
Mistral Nemo with LAPE					
vi	80.5	80.4	**80.6**	79.2	80.5
hi	**76.1**	69.8	66.9	74.9	72.4
ur	66.8	66.5	67.0	**66.9**	65.4
Mistral Nemo with Act Prob 90p					
vi	80.5	67.4	**81.1**	79.8	40.7
hi	**76.1**	72.2	74.5	74.5	66.3
ur	**66.8**	65.9	61.3	66.4	61.6

Table 1: XNLI performance across different models and intervention methods. "No Int" represents zero-shot performance without intervention, while "Int μ", "Int P90", "Int 0", and "Int P10" denote test-time interventions using mean, 90th percentile, zero, and 10th percentile activations, respectively. The best performance for each evaluation language (EL) is highlighted in bold.

EL	No Int	Int μ	Int P90	Int 0	Int P10
Llama 3.1 with LAPE					
vi	**41 (73.5)**	40 (72.9)	31 (69.5)	32 (69.2)	10 (43.2)
hi	38 (64.1)	**40 (65.5)**	36 (65.4)	23 (49.9)	37 (62.8)
zh	**56 (77.5)**	10 (62.8)	3 (56.1)	33 (63.2)	33 (63.2)
Llama 3.1 with Act Prob 90p					
vi	41 (73.6)	39 (73.0)	23 (64.9)	**42 (73.8)**	36 (70.3)
hi	**38 (64.1)**	34 (60.7)	36 (62.8)	38 (62.9)	31 (58.6)
zh	56 (77.5)	**61 (80.7)**	56 (78.8)	55 (78.5)	50 (73.6)
Mistral Nemo with LAPE					
vi	39 (74.6)	**42 (76.8)**	40 (75.0)	13 (45.0)	11 (41.2)
hi	**38 (66.9)**	35 (65.9)	37 (66.6)	22 (51.7)	36 (66.1)
zh	**47 (74.9)**	24 (74.0)	0 (61.6)	14 (53.3)	24 (68.9)
Mistral Nemo with Act Prob 90p					
vi	**39 (74.6)**	11 (43.3)	29 (63.9)	39 (74.5)	0 (6.5)
hi	**38 (66.9)**	26 (54.4)	37 (68.9)	33 (63.8)	0 (11.9)
zh	47 (74.9)	46 (77.4)	20 (59.8)	**48 (76.2)**	0 (17.0)

Table 2: XQuAD performance across different models and intervention methods. The intervention strategies are the same as described in Table 1. The values indicate Exact Match (EM) scores, with F1 scores in parentheses.

4.2 Impact of Test-Time Intervention

Test-Time Interventions Do Not Improve Performance. Tables 1 and 2 show that test-time interventions fail to consistently improve zero-shot transfer performance. Instead, they often disrupt the task-specific information encoded in the activations. This suggests that language-specific neurons in LLMs are not purely language-dependent but also contribute to task-relevant computations. Overwriting their activations with statistical values removes essential information required for solving the task due to the polysemantic nature of neuron activations (Elhage et al., 2022). We also experiment with different approaches for identifying language neurons, including LAPE and activation probability-based methods (e.g., 90th percentile); no significant improvements are observed. From the results for Chinese (*zh*) in XQuAD shown in Table 2, we observe that the *Act Prob 90p* method outperforms LAPE. This difference in performance can be attributed to the fact that the neurons identified by LAPE and *Act Prob 90p* are largely disjoint, as shown in Figures 18 and 19.

Deactivation of Zero Does not Degrade Performance Significantly: Prior studies (Kojima et al., 2024a; Tang et al., 2024) commonly deactivate neurons by setting their activations to zero. However, we argue that zero is not necessarily a true indicator of deactivation. While replacing activations with far lower percentiles (such as the 10th percentile) leads to a clear drop in performance (Table 2), setting activations to zero does not show a similar degradation. Figure 1 illustrates the perplexity change (PPXC(i, j)), defined as the difference in perplexity for language j when language neurons for language i are deactivated versus when they remain active, thereby quantifying the impact of targeted neuron deactivation on language understanding and their role in cross-lingual performance. As illustrated in Figure 1, deactivation at zero significantly increases perplexity (thus degrading generation quality); however, this degradation in perplexity does not directly translate to a decline in task performance. This suggests that setting activations to zero may not be an effective choice for deactivation. Detailed experimentation results can be found in Appendix C.

4.3 Impact of Neuron Fine-Tuning

We fine-tuned the identified language-specific neurons using LoRA but observed no improvement in performance (Table 3). When applying test-time interventions to the fine-tuned models, the results remained consistent with the zero-shot transfer (Table 1), reinforcing that fine-tuning language neurons does not enhance task performance. We also fine-tuned randomly selected neurons in the MLP layers. The results were similar to both language neuron fine-tuning and the original model (Table 8), indicating that LoRA applied to attention layers is already effective for task-specific tuning.

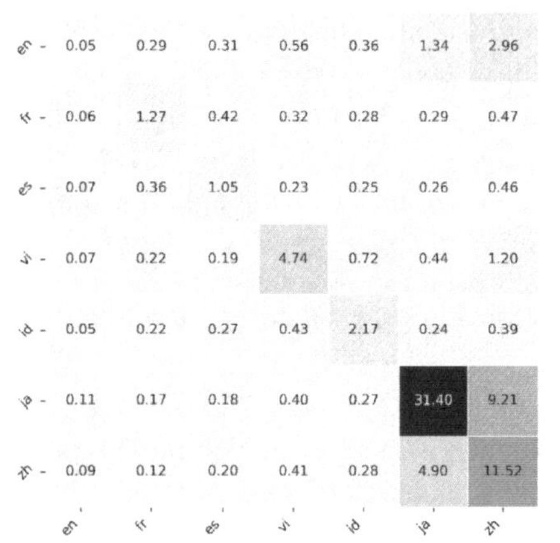

Figure 1: Perplexity Change (PPXC): Measures the effect of interventions on target language perplexity, defined as $\text{PPXC}(i,j) = \text{PPX}(j \mid \text{Intervention by 0 at } i) - \text{PPX}(j)$. Lower $\text{PPXC}(i,j)$ values indicate minimal interference, while higher values signify a significant impact on the model's understanding of language j (on 1 Million tokens).

FTL	EL	No Int	Int μ	Int P90	Int 0	Int P10
Llama 3.1 with LAPE						
en	vi	**80.2**	79.6	78.5	79.2	78.0
vi	vi	**80.1**	79.5	78.6	79.2	78.0
en+vi	vi	**80.1**	79.4	78.5	79.1	78.0
en	hi	**74.9**	74.6	74.6	74.1	74.6
hi	hi	**74.9**	74.6	74.5	74.3	74.6
en+hi	hi	**74.9**	74.5	74.5	74.3	74.7
en	ur	69.8	**70.4**	69.6	70.2	69.0
ur	ur	**69.8**	70.5	69.5	70.4	69.1
en+ur	ur	70.0	**70.6**	69.5	70.3	68.9

Table 3: Fine-tuning results for language-specific neurons on XNLI. The results follow the same format as Table 1, comparing zero-shot performance with test-time interventions across different fine-tuning language neuron (FTL) as per Section 2.2. A complete version is provided in Table 7.

5 Related Works

Other from Tang et al. (2024), Zhu et al. (2024) also introduce LANDeRMT that routes language-aware neurons to mitigate catastrophic forgetting, improving translation quality. Similarly, Xie et al. (2021b) propose a neuron allocation strategy to balance general and language-specific knowledge, thereby enhancing translation without increasing complexity. Lai et al. (2024) present Neuron-TST, which enhances text style transfer by identifying and deactivating source-style neurons to guide target-style generation. Kojima et al. (2024b) analyze language-specific neurons in decoder PLMs, showing that manipulating a small subset can control output language. Huo et al. (2024) study domain-specific neurons in Multimodal LLMs, showing a 10% accuracy gain in domain-specific tasks through neuron manipulation, akin to language-specific neuron use. Durrani et al. (2020) analyze encoder models, and find small neuron subsets capture linguistic tasks, with lower-level tasks requiring fewer neurons. No prior work has examined the effect of language-specific neurons on cross-lingual downstream tasks, which we attempt in this work.

6 Conclusion

In this work, we investigate if language-specific neurons in multilingual LLMs could be manipulated to improve cross-lingual task performance. Our results show that test-time interventions and fine-tuning of language-specific neurons do not yield meaningful improvements. Altering these activations often disrupt task-relevant information likely due to the polysemantic nature of LLM neurons. We found the same behaviour across different methods for identifying language neurons, such as LAPE and activation probability. Additionally, setting activations to zero did not significantly degrade performance, suggesting that zero is not a true indicator of deactivation. These findings indicate that language-specific neurons do not function independently but interact with broader model components, and need further investigation as tools of cross-lingual transfer.

Limitations

This work focuses on language-specific neurons in the MLP layers of multilingual LLMs, excluding attention mechanisms, which may also play a significant role. The experiments use a limited number of languages and datasets, limiting the generalizability of the findings. The interventions rely on statistical activations computed from Wikipedia text, which might not fully capture task-specific behavior. Additionally, the study does not explore alternate methods of fine-tuning techniques that might yield better results. Factors beyond language-specificity in neurons such as training data quality and architectural details of models should also be closely examined for effective cross-lingual transfer.

Acknowledgments

We are grateful to the anonymous reviewers for their insightful feedback. The last author gratefully acknowledges the generous support provided by the joint AI/ML initiative of Amazon and the Indian Institute of Technology Bombay.

References

Mikel Artetxe, Sebastian Ruder, and Dani Yogatama. 2020. On the cross-lingual transferability of monolingual representations. In *Proceedings of the 58th Annual Meeting of the Association for Computational Linguistics*. Association for Computational Linguistics.

Akari Asai, Sneha Kudugunta, Xinyan Yu, Terra Blevins, Hila Gonen, Machel Reid, Yulia Tsvetkov, Sebastian Ruder, and Hannaneh Hajishirzi. 2024. BUFFET: Benchmarking large language models for few-shot cross-lingual transfer. In *Proceedings of the 2024 Conference of the North American Chapter of the Association for Computational Linguistics: Human Language Technologies (Volume 1: Long Papers)*, pages 1771–1800, Mexico City, Mexico. Association for Computational Linguistics.

Sunit Bhattacharya and Ondrej Bojar. 2023. Unveiling multilinguality in transformer models: Exploring language specificity in feed-forward networks. *Preprint*, arXiv:2310.15552.

Alexis Conneau, Kartikay Khandelwal, Naman Goyal, Vishrav Chaudhary, Guillaume Wenzek, Francisco Guzmán, Edouard Grave, Myle Ott, Luke Zettlemoyer, and Veselin Stoyanov. 2020. Unsupervised cross-lingual representation learning at scale. In *Proceedings of the 58th Annual Meeting of the Association for Computational Linguistics*, pages 8440–8451, Online. Association for Computational Linguistics.

Alexis Conneau, Guillaume Lample, Ruty Rinott, Adina Williams, Samuel R. Bowman, Holger Schwenk, and Veselin Stoyanov. 2018. Xnli: Evaluating cross-lingual sentence representations. *Preprint*, arXiv:1809.05053.

Xufeng Duan, Xinyu Zhou, Bei Xiao, and Zhenguang Cai. 2025a. Unveiling language competence neurons: A psycholinguistic approach to model interpretability. In *Proceedings of the 31st International Conference on Computational Linguistics*, pages 10148–10157, Abu Dhabi, UAE. Association for Computational Linguistics.

Xufeng Duan, Xinyu Zhou, Bei Xiao, and Zhenguang Cai. 2025b. Unveiling language competence neurons: A psycholinguistic approach to model interpretability. In *Proceedings of the 31st International Conference on Computational Linguistics*, pages 10148–10157, Abu Dhabi, UAE. Association for Computational Linguistics.

Nadir Durrani, Hassan Sajjad, Fahim Dalvi, and Yonatan Belinkov. 2020. Analyzing individual neurons in pre-trained language models. In *Proceedings of the 2020 Conference on Empirical Methods in Natural Language Processing (EMNLP)*, pages 4865–4880, Online. Association for Computational Linguistics.

Nelson Elhage, Tristan Hume, Catherine Olsson, Nicholas Schiefer, Tom Henighan, Shauna Kravec, Zac Hatfield-Dodds, Robert Lasenby, Dawn Drain, Carol Chen, Roger Grosse, Sam McCandlish, Jared Kaplan, Dario Amodei, Martin Wattenberg, and Christopher Olah. 2022. Toy models of superposition. *Transformer Circuits Thread*.

Wikimedia Foundation. 2024. Wikimedia downloads.

Aaron Grattafiori, Abhimanyu Dubey, and Abhinav Jauhri. 2024. The llama 3 herd of models. *Preprint*, arXiv:2407.21783.

Viktor Hangya, Hossain Shaikh Saadi, and Alexander Fraser. 2022. Improving low-resource languages in pre-trained multilingual language models. In *Proceedings of the 2022 Conference on Empirical Methods in Natural Language Processing*, pages 11993–12006, Abu Dhabi, United Arab Emirates. Association for Computational Linguistics.

Edward J. Hu, Yelong Shen, Phillip Wallis, Zeyuan Allen-Zhu, Yuanzhi Li, Shean Wang, Lu Wang, and Weizhu Chen. 2021. Lora: Low-rank adaptation of large language models. *Preprint*, arXiv:2106.09685.

Junjie Hu, Sebastian Ruder, Aditya Siddhant, Graham Neubig, Orhan Firat, and Melvin Johnson. 2020. Xtreme: A massively multilingual multi-task benchmark for evaluating cross-lingual generalization. *Preprint*, arXiv:2003.11080.

Jiahao Huo, Yibo Yan, Boren Hu, Yutao Yue, and Xuming Hu. 2024. MMNeuron: Discovering neuron-level domain-specific interpretation in multimodal large language model. In *Proceedings of the 2024 Conference on Empirical Methods in Natural Language Processing*, pages 6801–6816, Miami, Florida, USA. Association for Computational Linguistics.

Takeshi Kojima, Itsuki Okimura, Yusuke Iwasawa, Hitomi Yanaka, and Yutaka Matsuo. 2024a. On the multilingual ability of decoder-based pre-trained language models: Finding and controlling language-specific neurons. In *Proceedings of the 2024 Conference of the North American Chapter of the Association for Computational Linguistics: Human Language Technologies (Volume 1: Long Papers)*, pages 6919–6971, Mexico City, Mexico. Association for Computational Linguistics.

Takeshi Kojima, Itsuki Okimura, Yusuke Iwasawa, Hitomi Yanaka, and Yutaka Matsuo. 2024b. On the multilingual ability of decoder-based pre-trained language models: Finding and controlling language-specific neurons. In *Proceedings of the 2024 Conference of the North American Chapter of the Association for Computational Linguistics: Human Language Technologies (Volume 1: Long Papers)*, pages 6919–6971, Mexico City, Mexico. Association for Computational Linguistics.

Wen Lai, Viktor Hangya, and Alexander Fraser. 2024. Style-specific neurons for steering LLMs in text style transfer. In *Proceedings of the 2024 Conference on*

Empirical Methods in Natural Language Processing, pages 13427–13443, Miami, Florida, USA. Association for Computational Linguistics.

Guillaume Lample and Alexis Conneau. 2019. Cross-lingual language model pretraining. *Preprint*, arXiv:1901.07291.

MistralAI. 2024. Mistral nemo.

Tianyi Tang, Wenyang Luo, Haoyang Huang, Dongdong Zhang, Xiaolei Wang, Xin Zhao, Furu Wei, and Ji-Rong Wen. 2024. Language-specific neurons: The key to multilingual capabilities in large language models. In *Proceedings of the 62nd Annual Meeting of the Association for Computational Linguistics (Volume 1: Long Papers)*, pages 5701–5715, Bangkok, Thailand. Association for Computational Linguistics.

Hugo Touvron, Thibaut Lavril, Gautier Izacard, Xavier Martinet, Marie-Anne Lachaux, Timothée Lacroix, Baptiste Rozière, Naman Goyal, Eric Hambro, Faisal Azhar, Aurelien Rodriguez, Armand Joulin, Edouard Grave, and Guillaume Lample. 2023. Llama: Open and efficient foundation language models. *Preprint*, arXiv:2302.13971.

Wanying Xie, Yang Feng, Shuhao Gu, and Dong Yu. 2021a. Importance-based neuron allocation for multilingual neural machine translation. *Preprint*, arXiv:2107.06569.

Wanying Xie, Yang Feng, Shuhao Gu, and Dong Yu. 2021b. Importance-based neuron allocation for multilingual neural machine translation. In *Proceedings of the 59th Annual Meeting of the Association for Computational Linguistics and the 11th International Joint Conference on Natural Language Processing (Volume 1: Long Papers)*, pages 5725–5737, Online. Association for Computational Linguistics.

Linting Xue, Noah Constant, Adam Roberts, Mihir Kale, Rami Al-Rfou, Aditya Siddhant, Aditya Barua, and Colin Raffel. 2021. mT5: A massively multilingual pre-trained text-to-text transformer. In *Proceedings of the 2021 Conference of the North American Chapter of the Association for Computational Linguistics: Human Language Technologies*, pages 483–498, Online. Association for Computational Linguistics.

Xue Zhang, Yunlong Liang, Fandong Meng, Songming Zhang, Yufeng Chen, Jinan Xu, and Jie Zhou. 2024. Multilingual knowledge editing with language-agnostic factual neurons. *Preprint*, arXiv:2406.16416.

Xin Zhao, Naoki Yoshinaga, and Daisuke Oba. 2024a. Tracing the roots of facts in multilingual language models: Independent, shared, and transferred knowledge. *Preprint*, arXiv:2403.05189.

Yiran Zhao, Wenxuan Zhang, Guizhen Chen, Kenji Kawaguchi, and Lidong Bing. 2024b. How do large language models handle multilingualism? *Preprint*, arXiv:2402.18815.

Yiran Zhao, Wenxuan Zhang, Guizhen Chen, Kenji Kawaguchi, and Lidong Bing. 2024c. How do large language models handle multilingualism? *Preprint*, arXiv:2402.18815.

Shaolin Zhu, Leiyu Pan, Bo Li, and Deyi Xiong. 2024. LANDeRMT: Dectecting and routing language-aware neurons for selectively finetuning LLMs to machine translation. In *Proceedings of the 62nd Annual Meeting of the Association for Computational Linguistics (Volume 1: Long Papers)*, pages 12135–12148, Bangkok, Thailand. Association for Computational Linguistics.

A Language Neuron Identification

A.1 Dataset Collection and Preprocessing

The dataset is constructed from publicly available Wikipedia dumps, specifically from the Foundation (2024) dataset. For each language, the following preprocessing steps are applied:

- The dataset is randomly shuffled to ensure diverse text coverage.
- Only the first 100 million tokens per language are retained for computational efficiency.
- Each sequence is truncated to a maximum context length of $T_{\max} = 512$ tokens.

A.2 Activation Computation

To identify language-specific neurons, we compute activation statistics from the Wikipedia dataset for each language. This involves calculating both the mean activation and the 90th percentile activation (*P90*) for every neuron in the model. These statistics provide insights into how neurons behave across different languages and form the basis for selecting language-specific neurons.

A.2.1 Mean Activation Computation

For a given language l, let the activation of neuron (i, j) at token position t in sequence s be denoted as $h_{i,j}^{(s,t)} \in \mathbb{R}$. The mean activation of a neuron across all token positions for a single sequence is computed as:

$$\bar{h}_{i,j}^{(s)} = \frac{1}{T} \sum_{t=1}^{T} h_{i,j}^{(s,t)},$$

where T represents the sequence length (maximum of 512 tokens). To obtain the overall mean activation for a language l, we aggregate across all sequences S_l in the Wikipedia dataset:

$$\mu_{i,j}^l = \frac{1}{|S_l|} \sum_{s \in S_l} \bar{h}_{i,j}^{(s)}.$$

This provides a language-specific average activation for each neuron, which helps in identifying neurons that consistently activate for a particular language.

A.2.2 90th Percentile Activation Computation

In addition to mean activation, we compute the 90th percentile activation (*P90*) to capture the upper range of neuron activity. The 90th percentile is useful in determining neurons that are highly responsive in a given language. The *P90* activation for neuron (i, j) in language l is computed as:

$$P_{90}(h_{i,j}^l) = \inf \left\{ x \mid F_{h_{i,j}^{(s)}}(x) \geq 0.90, s \in S_l \right\},$$

where $F_{h_{i,j}^{(s)}}(x)$ is the cumulative distribution function (CDF) of the activations of neuron (i, j) for all sequences in language l. In practice, this is computed by sorting activation values for all sequences and selecting the value at the 90th percentile position.

A.3 LAPE and Act Prob 90p Details

In our experiments, we focus on two specific language sets: *Set1* and *Set6*. Although we have explored different combinations of language sets during our analysis, for clarity and brevity we present results corresponding only to *Set1* and *Set6*.

Set1: Core Languages. This set consists of languages that were part of the original LAPE analysis (Tang et al., 2024). It includes: {en, fr, es, vi, id, ja, zh}. This selection covers a broad range of linguistic families, including *Indo-European (en, fr, es), Austroasiatic (vi), Austronesian (id), Japonic (ja), and Sino-Tibetan (zh)*. These languages are well-represented in large-scale multilingual corpora and serve as strong candidates for evaluating multilingual neuron activations.

Set6: Indian Language-Dominant Set. While *Set1* includes a mix of global languages, *Set6* is specifically designed to focus on *Indian languages*: {en, bn, hi, ta, te, mr, ur, kn, ml, pa}. The motivation behind selecting *Set6* is to investigate how LLMs encode representations for typologically and script-wise diverse Indian languages. The inclusion of *Bengali (bn), Hindi (hi), Tamil (ta), Telugu (te), Marathi (mr), Urdu (ur), Kannada (kn), Malayalam (ml), and Punjabi (pa)* ensures a wide coverage of Indo-Aryan and Dravidian language families.

The LAPE method is evaluated on both *Set1* and *Set6* to determine how neuron activations vary across these two distinct sets. Since *Set1* was originally introduced in prior work, our experiments on *Set6* extend the understanding of LAPE to Indian languages, which are underrepresented in pre-trained LLMs.

For the *Activation Probability 90p* (Act Prob 90p) method, we select {en, vi, hi, ur, zh}. This selection was based on language diversity, cross-lingual representation, and performance disparities in downstream tasks. Since Act Prob 90p is a set-independent method, we focus on selecting languages that exhibit poor performance in task-specific evaluations. Specifically, for the XNLI task, the lowest-performing languages were *Hindi (hi), Urdu (ur), and Vietnamese (vi)*, leading to their inclusion. Similarly, for the XQuAD task, the weakest-performing languages were *Vietnamese (vi), Hindi (hi), and Chinese (zh)*, which motivated their selection.

B Task, Models and Experiment Details

In this section, we provide detailed descriptions of the two evaluation tasks used in our experiments, namely XNLI and XQuAD, as well as the two large language models (LLMs) used for our study: Llama 3.1 and Mistral Nemo. We also formalize the task setup using mathematical notations.

B.1 Tasks

B.1.1 XNLI

The XNLI dataset (Conneau et al., 2018) is a cross-lingual extension of the MultiNLI dataset, designed for evaluating natural language inference (NLI) across multiple languages. Given a premise p and a hypothesis h, the task is to determine whether the hypothesis is *entailment*, *contradiction*, or *neutral* with respect to the premise. Formally, given a dataset $\mathcal{D} = \{(p_i, h_i, y_i)\}_{i=1}^N$, where: $p_i \in \mathcal{X}$ is the premise, $h_i \in \mathcal{X}$ is the hypothesis, $y_i \in \{0, 1, 2\}$ represents the label: entailment (0), contradiction (1), or neutral (2). We conduct zero-shot evaluation on target languages (*vi, hi, ur*), using English (*en*) as the source language. We limit the training dataset to 100,000 samples (25% of the full dataset) for efficiency.

B.1.2 XQuAD: Cross-lingual Question Answering

XQuAD (Artetxe et al., 2020) is a multilingual question-answering dataset based on the Stanford Question Answering Dataset (SQuAD). The task requires extracting an answer span a from a given context c for a question q. Given a dataset $\mathcal{D} = \{(c_i, q_i, a_i)\}_{i=1}^{M}$, where: $c_i \in \mathcal{X}$ is the passage (context), $q_i \in \mathcal{X}$ is the question, $a_i \in \mathcal{X}$ is the ground-truth answer. We evaluate on target languages (*vi*, *hi*, *zh*) and use the full training dataset for fine-tuning.

B.2 Models

B.2.1 Llama 3.1

Llama 3.1[3] is an 8 billion parameter multilingual model from Meta, trained on diverse text corpora across multiple languages (Grattafiori et al., 2024). The model consists of stacked transformer layers, each comprising self-attention and feedforward MLP components. Llama 3.1 is optimized for computational efficiency and supports a wide range of languages, making it a strong candidate for evaluating multilingual transfer performance.

B.2.2 Mistral Nemo

Mistral Nemo[4] is a 12 billion parameter transformer based model designed for multilingual tasks, with a particular emphasis on high-performance fine-tuning capabilities (MistralAI, 2024). Similar to Llama 3.1, it consists of transformer layers with self-attention and MLP modules.

B.3 Implementation Details for LoRA Fine-Tuning

In this section, we provide an overview of the implementation details for our fine-tuning experiments on the XNLI and XQuAD tasks using LoRA.

For model configuration, our experiments were conducted using the Meta-Llama-3.1-8B and Mistral-Nemo-Base-2407 models. Both models were loaded in 4-bit precision to optimize efficiency. Specifically, we employed the `nf4` quantization type, used `bfloat16` as the compute data type, and enabled double quantization.

Regarding task-specific dataset preparation, for the XNLI dataset—which involves natural language inference by predicting entailment, contradiction, or neutral relationships—we used 25% of the training data and 100% of the evaluation data. The maximum context length was set to 256 tokens. For the XQuAD dataset, which focuses on question answering by extracting answer spans from a given context, we utilized the full training data (100%) along with 100% of the evaluation data, with a maximum context length of 512 tokens.

LoRA was applied to fine-tune specific layers in the attention module of the models for both tasks. The fine-tuning was performed with a LoRA rank $r = 64$ and a LoRA scaling factor $\alpha = 128$. The learning rate was set to 1×10^{-6} for XNLI and 5×10^{-5} for XQuAD, with a weight decay of 0.1 and gradient clipping at a threshold of 10.0. The AdamW optimizer was used with parameters $\beta_1 = 0.95$ and $\beta_2 = 0.999$.

For the training configuration, we trained the model for 2 epochs on XNLI using a batch size of 8, and for 10 epochs on XQuAD using a batch size of 4. A linear warm-up was employed for 1% of the total steps, followed by a linear decay of the learning rate. Mixed precision training was enabled with `bfloat16` to improve memory efficiency.

C Results of Language Neuron Analysis

Figure 2 to 7 presents the number of neurons assigned per language, comparing the LAPE and Activation Probability 90p methods. The overlap of language-specific neurons across different languages is illustrated in Figure 8 to 13, highlighting the extent of shared neurons between languages. The layer-wise distribution of these neurons is shown in Figure 14 to 19, providing insights into where language-specific representations are most prominent in the model. Finally, the impact of neuron interventions on perplexity is analyzed in Figure 20 to 24, which displays the perplexity change across different languages when language neurons are manipulated. These figures collectively summarize the key findings from our language neuron analysis.

Table 4 presents the full XNLI results, extending the analysis from Table 1, incorporating additional statistical interventions, including percentiles at P75, P90, P95, P5, P10, and P25. Similarly, Table 5 provides the full XQuAD results, expanding upon Table 2, detailing both exact match (EM) and F1 scores across various intervention methods. The complete activation statistics for both Llama 3.1 and Mistral Nemo are listed in Table 6, offering a

[3] `https://huggingface.co/meta-llama/Llama-3.1-8B`

[4] `https://huggingface.co/mistralai/Mistral-Nemo-Base-2407`

breakdown of mean activations and quantiles, capturing the variations in neuron activations across languages. Finally, Table 7 details the full language neuron fine-tuning results, extending Table 3, comparing zero-shot performance with fine-tuning on different language neuron setups, and evaluating test-time interventions across multiple configurations.

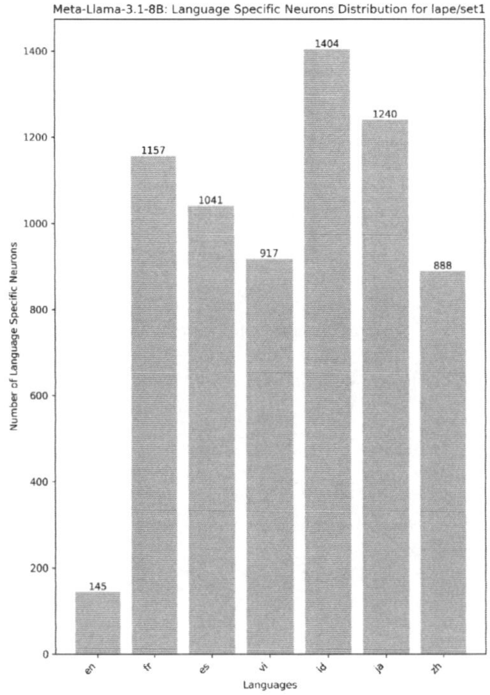

Figure 2: Llama 3.1: Number of language neurons assigned per language for LAPE in a set of languages $\{en, es, fr, vi, id, zh, ja\}$.

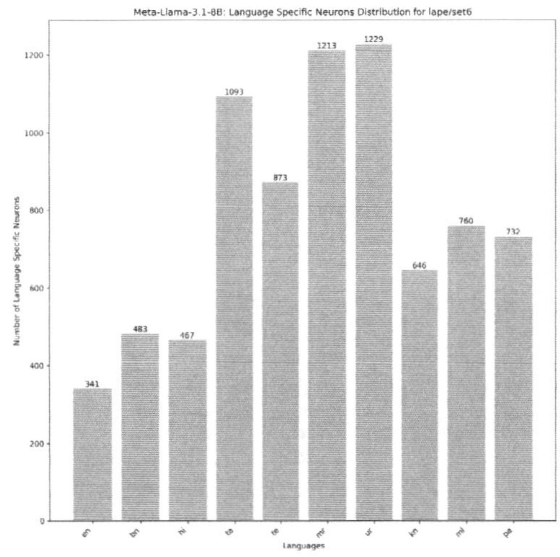

Figure 3: Llama 3.1: Number of language neurons assigned per language for LAPE in a set of languages $\{en, bn, hi, ur, mr, pa, ta, te, ml, kn\}$.

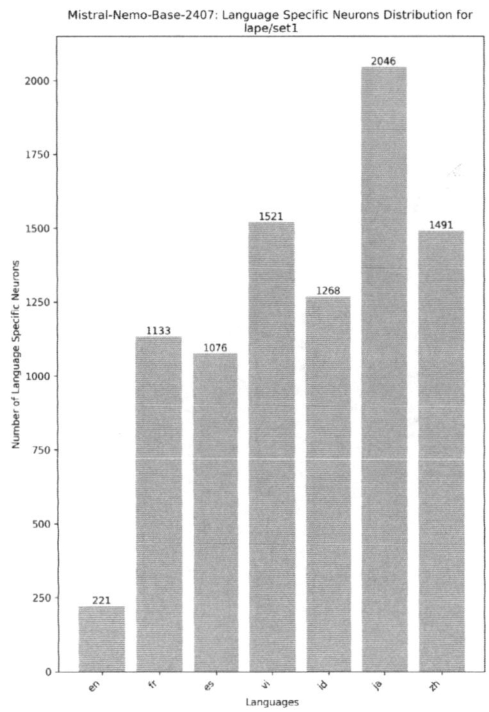

Figure 4: Mistral Nemo: Number of language neurons assigned per language for LAPE in a set of languages $\{en, es, fr, vi, id, zh, ja\}$.

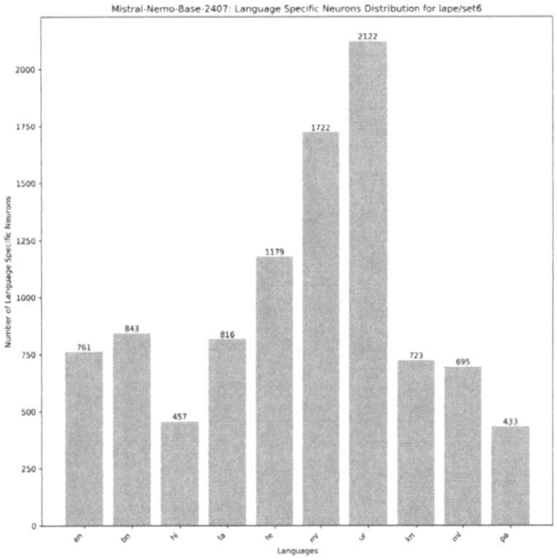

Figure 5: Mistral Nemo: Number of language neurons assigned per language for LAPE in a set of languages {*en,bn,hi,ur,mr,pa,ta, te, ml, kn*}.

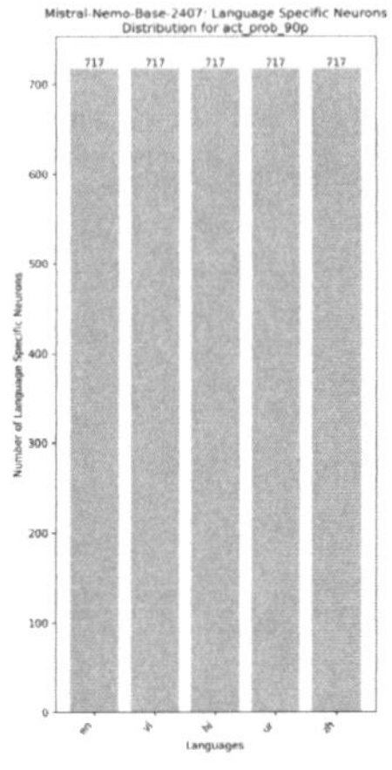

Figure 7: Mistral Nemo: Number of language neurons assigned per language for Activation Probability 90p which is same for all the languages.

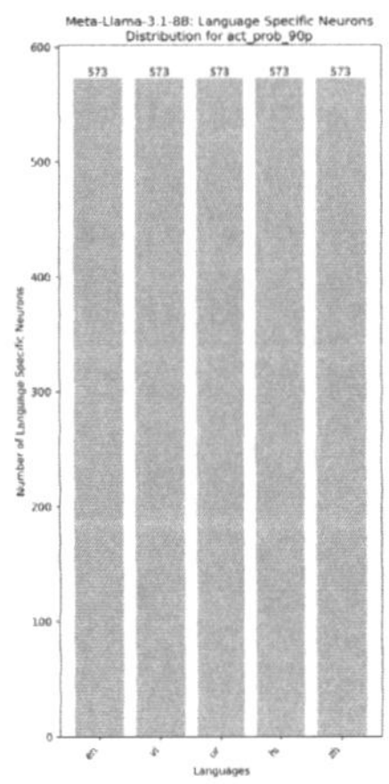

Figure 6: Llama 3.1: Number of language neurons assigned per language for Activation Probability 90p which is same for all the languages.

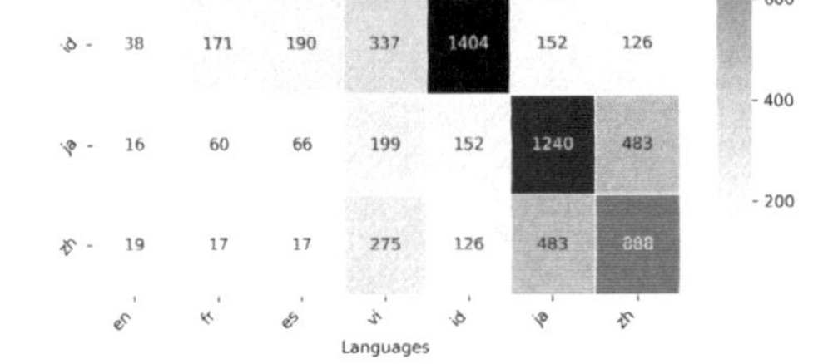

Figure 8: Llama 3.1: Language neuron overlap between languages using LAPE in a set of languages {*en,es,fr,vi,id,zh,ja*}.

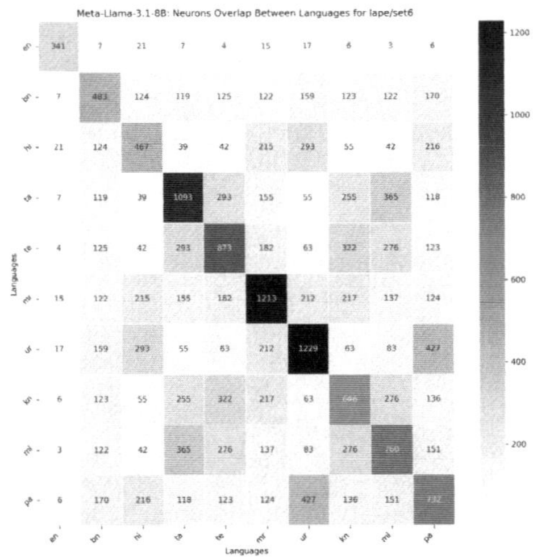

Figure 9: Llama 3.1: Language neuron overlap between languages using LAPE in a set of languages {*en,bn,hi,ur,mr,pa,ta, te, ml, kn*}.

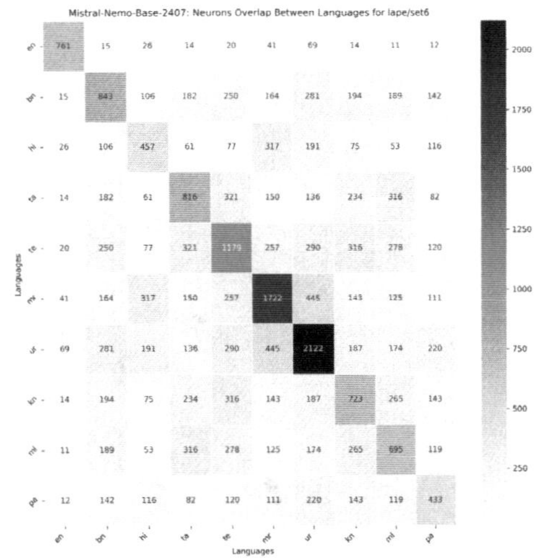

Figure 11: Mistral Nemo: Language neuron overlap between languages using LAPE in a set of languages {*en,bn,hi,ur,mr,pa,ta, te, ml, kn*}.

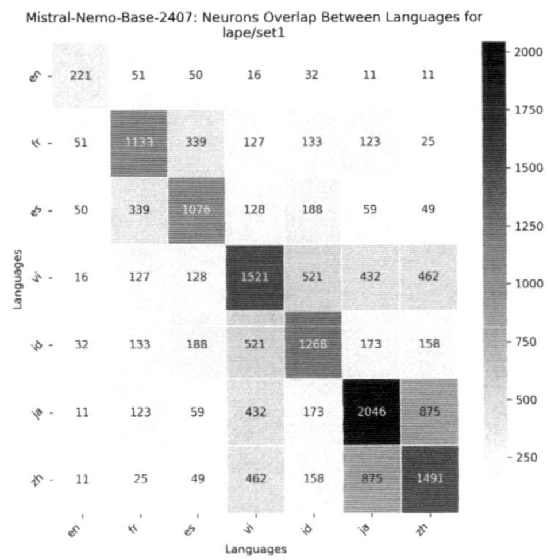

Figure 10: Mistral Nemo: Language neuron overlap between languages using LAPE in a set of languages {*en,es,fr,vi,id,zh,ja*}.

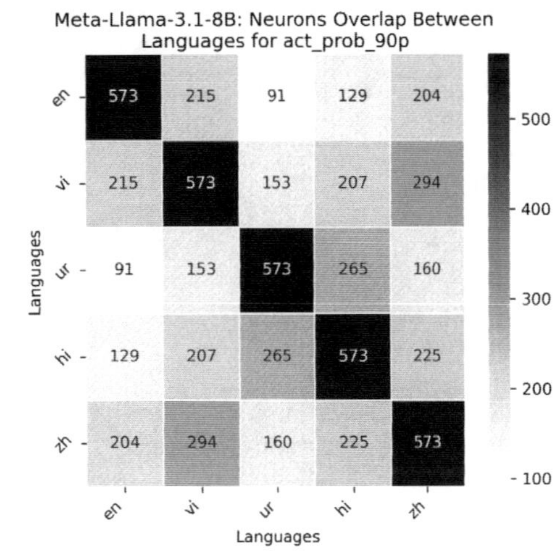

Figure 12: Llama 3.1: Language neuron overlap between languages using Activation Probability 90p.

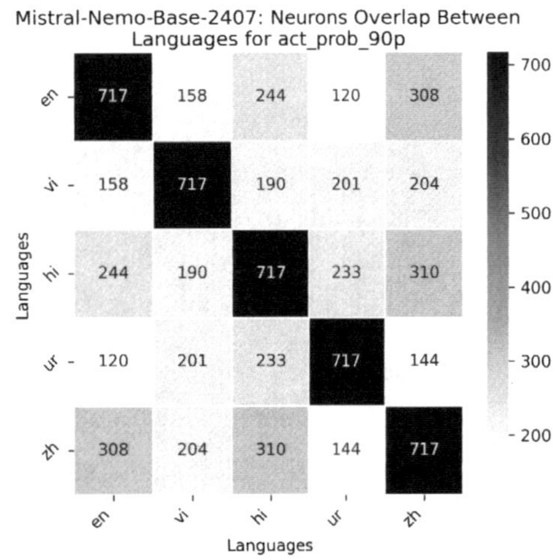

Figure 13: Mistral Nemo: Language neuron overlap between languages using Activation Probability 90p.

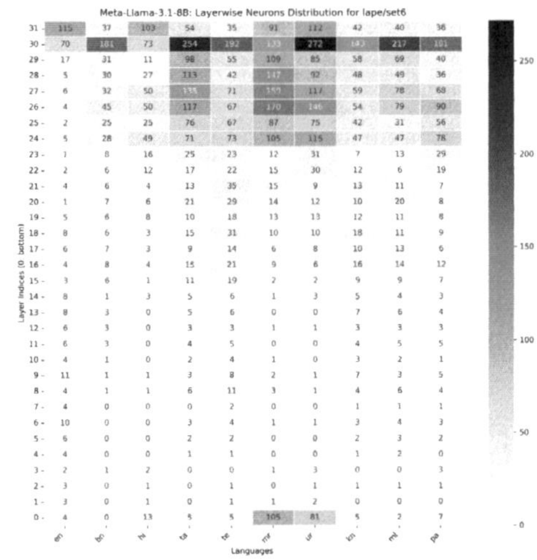

Figure 15: Llama 3.1: Layer-wise distribution of language neurons for LAPE in a set of languages {*en,bn,hi,ur,mr,pa,ta, te, ml, kn*}.

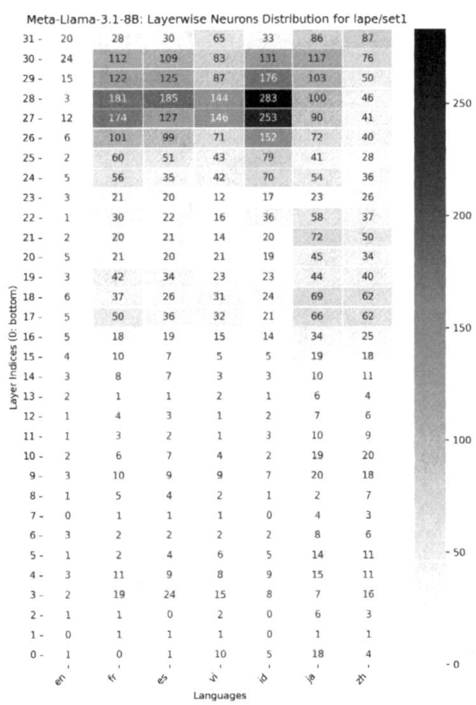

Figure 14: Llama 3.1: Layer-wise distribution of language neurons for LAPE in a set of languages {*en,es,fr,vi,id,zh,ja*}.

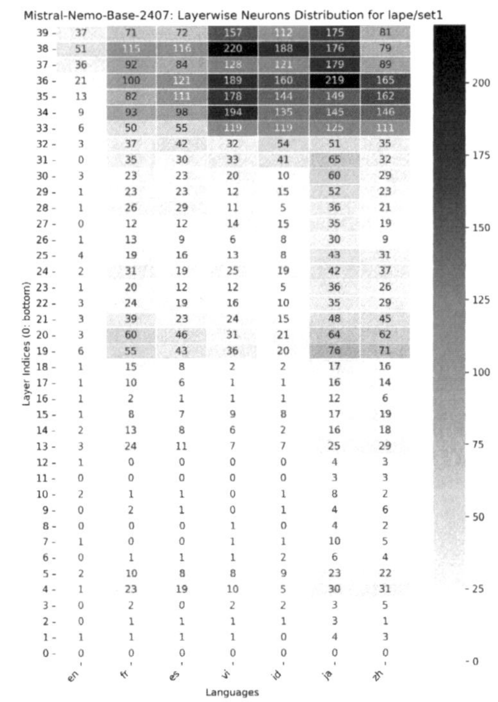

Figure 16: Mistral Nemo: Layer-wise distribution of language neurons for LAPE in a set of languages {*en,es,fr,vi,id,zh,ja*}.

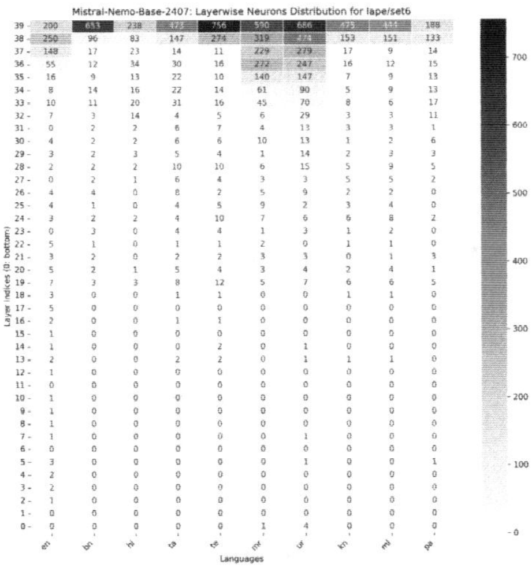

Figure 17: Mistral Nemo: Layer-wise distribution of language neurons for LAPE in a set of languages {*en,bn,hi,ur,mr,pa,ta, te, ml, kn*}.

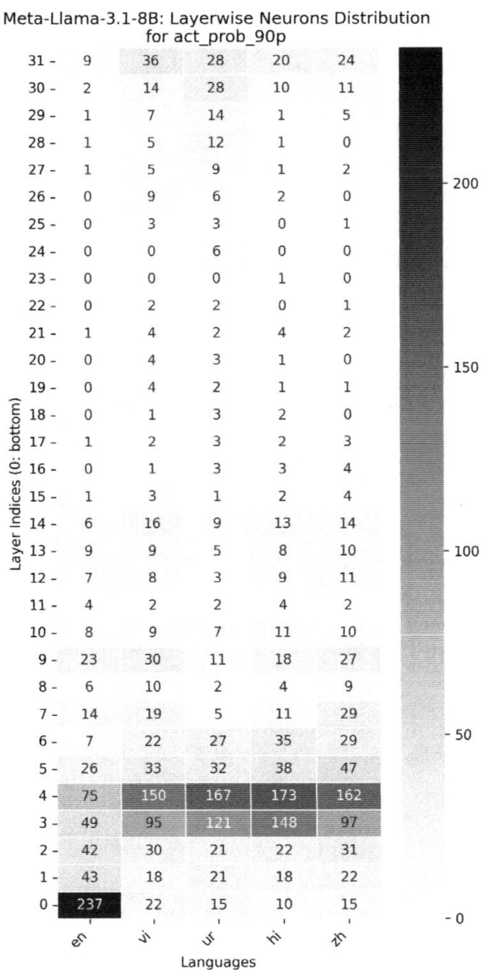

Figure 18: Llama 3.1: Layer-wise distribution of language neurons for Activation Probability 90p.

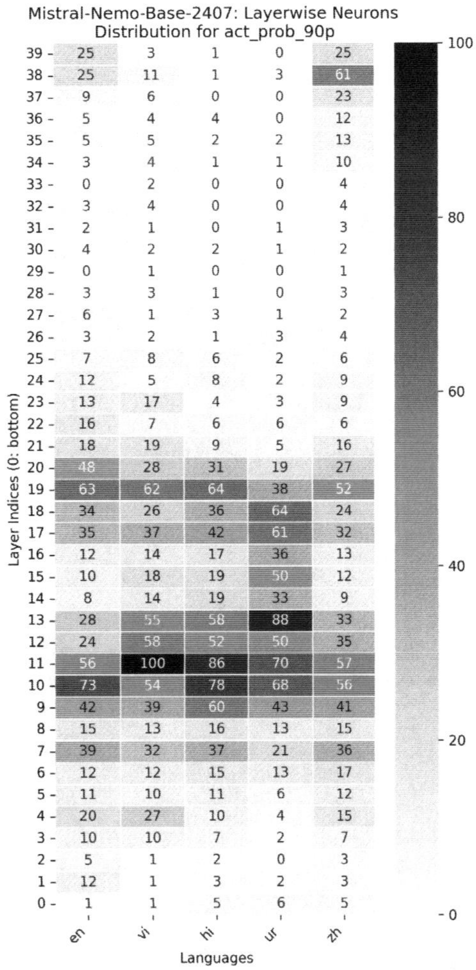

Figure 19: Mistral Nemo: Layer-wise distribution of language neurons for Activation Probability 90p.

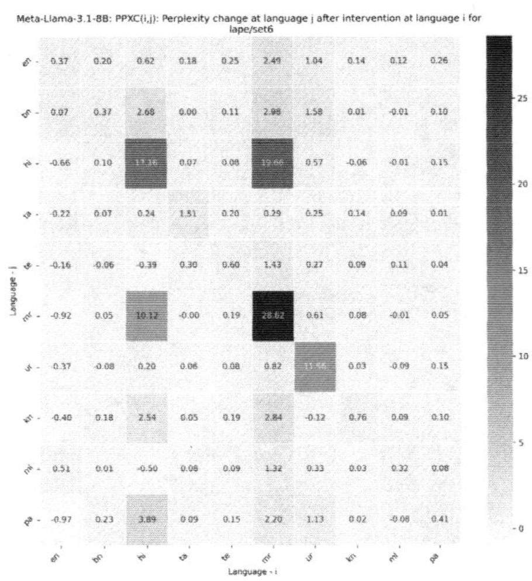

Figure 20: Llama 3.1: Perplexity change for LAPE in a set of languages {*en,bn,hi,ur,mr,pa,ta, te, ml, kn*} (on 0.1 Million tokens).

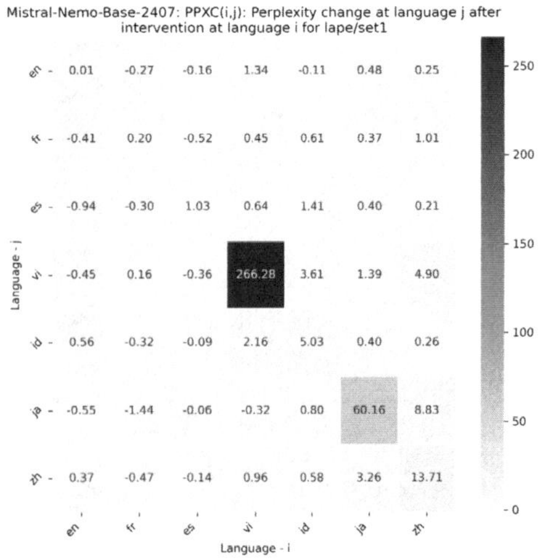

Figure 21: Mistral Nemo: Perplexity change for LAPE in a set of languages $\{en, es, fr, vi, id, zh, ja\}$ (on 0.1 Million tokens).

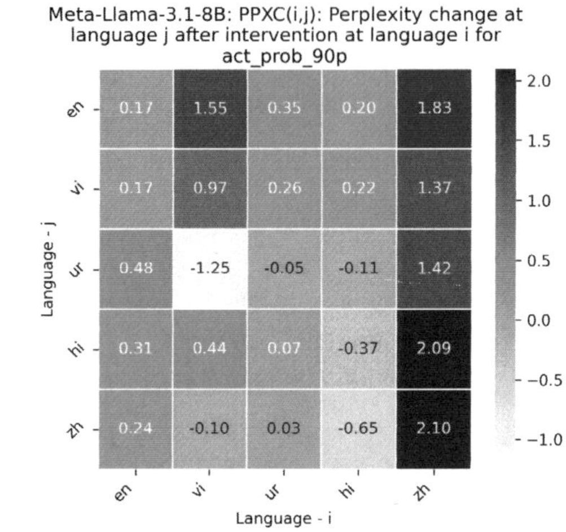

Figure 23: Llama 3.1: Perplexity change for Activation Probability 90p (on 0.1 Million tokens).

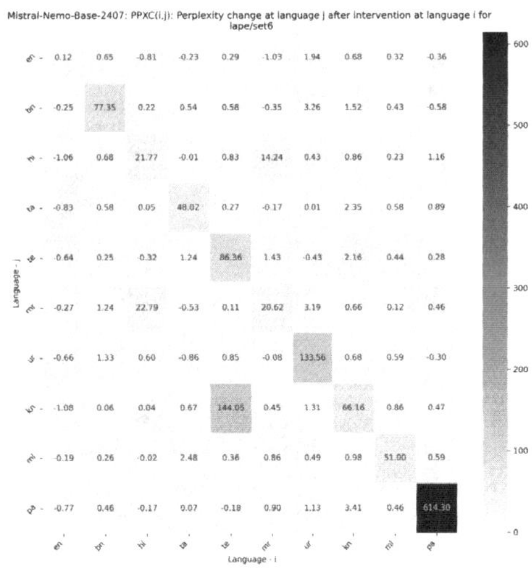

Figure 22: Mistral Nemo: Perplexity change for LAPE in a set of languages $\{en, bn, hi, ur, mr, pa, ta, te, ml, kn\}$ (on 0.1 Million tokens).

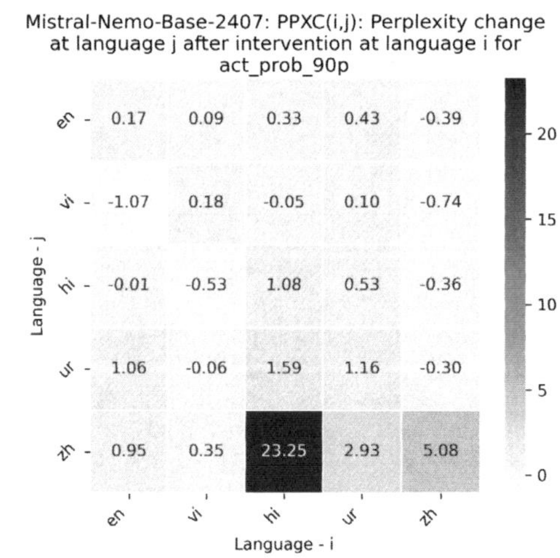

Figure 24: Mistral Nemo: Perplexity change for Activation Probability 90p (on 0.1 Million tokens).

Model & Method	Eval Lang	No Int	Int μ	Int P75	Int P90	Int P95	Int 0	Int P5	Int P10	Int P25
Llama 3.1	vi	**80.5**	79.5	79.1	79.0	78.9	79.8	73.6	77.7	**80.5**
+	hi	75.0	**75.2**	74.9	74.9	75.0	74.4	74.8	75.1	74.9
LAPE	ur	70.0	**70.4**	70.2	69.3	69.0	68.5	68.6	68.7	69.7
Llama 3.1	vi	**80.5**	78.2	78.9	79.3	79.5	79.0	76.5	77.4	78.0
+	hi	**75.0**	74.1	72.6	71.8	71.2	73.7	75.0	74.6	74.2
Act Prob 90p	ur	**70.0**	69.7	69.7	69.3	68.7	69.6	69.4	69.5	69.5
Mistral Nemo	vi	80.5	80.4	80.5	**80.6**	80.5	79.2	**80.6**	80.5	80.3
+	hi	**76.1**	69.8	67.8	66.9	66.6	74.9	73.0	72.4	71.0
LAPE	ur	66.8	66.5	67.2	67.0	66.8	**66.9**	65.8	65.4	65.7
Mistral Nemo	vi	80.5	67.4	79.0	**81.1**	**81.1**	79.8	37.4	40.7	47.8
+	hi	**76.1**	72.2	73.7	74.5	74.4	74.5	62.4	66.3	69.3
Act Prob 90p	ur	**66.8**	65.9	64.0	61.3	59.7	66.4	54.6	61.6	65.0

Table 4: Full XNLI performance results, including additional statistical interventions. This table extends Table 1 by incorporating multiple activation percentile-based interventions, including P75, P90, P95, P5, P10, and P25, alongside the mean and zero activation interventions.

Model & Method	Eval Lang	No Int	Int μ	Int P75	Int P90	Int P95	Int 0	Int P5	Int P10	Int P25
Llama 3.1	vi	41 (73.5)	40 (72.9)	36 (76.7)	31 (69.5)	28 (66.8)	32 (69.2)	4 (35.8)	10 (43.2)	39 (71.5)
+	hi	38 (64.1)	40 (65.5)	38 (66.4)	36 (65.4)	36 (66.3)	23 (49.9)	38 (62.8)	37 (62.8)	39 (65.3)
LAPE	zh	56 (77.5)	10 (62.8)	3 (58.1)	3 (56.1)	4 (52.9)	33 (63.2)	20 (49.1)	33 (63.2)	22 (67.8)
Llama 3.1	vi	41 (73.6)	39 (73.0)	26 (65.8)	23 (64.9)	24 (64.8)	42 (73.8)	33 (67.8)	36 (70.3)	39 (72.0)
+	hi	38 (64.1)	34 (60.7)	35 (62.3)	36 (62.8)	32 (61.9)	38 (62.9)	23 (54.9)	31 (58.6)	35 (60.7)
Act Prob 90p	zh	56 (77.5)	61 (80.7)	59 (79.5)	56 (78.8)	56 (78.4)	55 (78.5)	40 (61.7)	50 (73.6)	56 (79.3)
Mistral Nemo	vi	39 (74.6)	42 (76.8)	40 (76.4)	40 (75.0)	39 (73.6)	13 (45.0)	10 (40.4)	11 (41.2)	37 (73.3)
+	hi	38 (66.9)	35 (65.9)	38 (67.1)	37 (66.6)	34 (66.5)	22 (51.7)	36 (65.8)	36 (66.1)	36 (67.1)
LAPE	zh	47 (74.9)	24 (74.0)	4 (65.6)	0 (61.6)	0 (59.3)	14 (53.3)	1 (33.6)	24 (68.9)	35 (77.0)
Mistral Nemo	vi	39 (74.6)	11 (43.3)	26 (62.8)	29 (63.9)	15 (48.5)	39 (74.5)	0 (3.8)	0 (6.5)	2 (12.9)
+	hi	38 (66.9)	26 (54.4)	34 (65.1)	37 (68.9)	37 (68.7)	33 (63.8)	0 (6.0)	0 (11.9)	12 (35.2)
Act Prob 90p	zh	47 (74.9)	46 (77.4)	26 (69.9)	20 (59.8)	15 (54.9)	48 (76.2)	0 (8.5)	0 (17.0)	9 (45.6)

Table 5: Full XQuAD performance results, with exact match (EM) and F1 scores across various interventions. This table builds upon Table 2, expanding the analysis with additional intervention strategies. The results further validate the findings on test-time interventions and their impact on cross-lingual task performance.

Model	Lang	Act μ	Act P75	Act P90	Act P95	Act P5	Act P10	Act P25
Llama 3.1	en	-0.2621	-0.0493	0.1693	0.3106	-0.7943	-0.6801	-0.4892
	vi	-0.2599	-0.049	0.1648	0.3012	-0.782	-0.6709	-0.4841
	hi	-0.2728	-0.0648	0.144	0.2784	-0.7893	-0.6788	-0.4934
	ur	-0.254	-0.0498	0.1521	0.2804	-0.7604	-0.6511	-0.4684
	zh	-0.2603	-0.0505	0.1611	0.2958	-0.7797	-0.6689	-0.4826
Mistral Nemo	en	-0.3938	-0.0798	0.2477	0.4629	-1.1888	-1.0149	-0.7294
	vi	-0.399	-0.0807	0.2454	0.4564	-1.1975	-1.0237	-0.737
	hi	-0.4265	-0.1147	0.2053	0.4133	-1.2092	-1.0392	-0.7588
	ur	-0.397	-0.0881	0.2252	0.4279	-1.1722	-1.0029	-0.7238
	zh	-0.3962	-0.0715	0.2568	0.4678	-1.2088	-1.032	-0.7388

Table 6: Activation statistics for Llama 3.1 and Mistral Nemo across different languages for Wikipedia dataset. It provides an in-depth analysis of activation values, including mean activation values and key quantiles (P75, P90, P95, P5, P10, P25).

FTL	EL	No Int	Int μ	Int P90	Int 0	Int P10
Llama 3.1 with LAPE						
en	vi	**80.2**	79.6	78.5	79.2	78.0
vi	vi	**80.1**	79.5	78.6	79.2	78.0
en+vi	vi	**80.1**	79.4	78.5	79.1	78.0
en	hi	**74.9**	74.6	74.6	74.1	74.6
hi	hi	**74.9**	74.6	74.5	74.3	74.6
en+hi	hi	**74.9**	74.5	74.5	74.3	74.7
en	ur	69.8	**70.4**	69.6	70.2	69.0
ur	ur	**69.8**	70.5	69.5	70.4	69.1
en+ur	ur	70.0	**70.6**	69.5	70.3	68.9
Llama 3.1 with Act Prob 90p						
en	vi	**80.3**	78.0	79.1	78.5	77.5
vi	vi	**80.1**	78.0	79.0	78.7	77.4
en+vi	vi	**80.1**	78.0	78.9	78.8	77.4
en	hi	**74.9**	73.9	72.1	73.3	74.5
hi	hi	**74.9**	73.8	72.1	73.9	74.6
en+hi	hi	**74.9**	73.7	72.1	73.8	74.6
en	ur	69.9	**70.1**	69.4	70.0	69.5
ur	ur	69.9	70.0	69.4	**70.1**	69.5
en+ur	ur	69.8	69.9	69.3	**70.1**	69.6

Table 7: Full language neuron fine-tuning results for XNLI. This table extends Table 3, presenting fine-tuning experiments where language-specific neurons are updated in different configurations. It includes results for models fine-tuned on the source language alone, the target language alone, and both together, with evaluation of test-time interventions across multiple setups.

Model	FTL	EL	No Int
Llama 3.1	rand	vi	80.1
Llama 3.1	rand	hi	74.8
Llama 3.1	rand	ur	69.8
Mistral Nemo	rand	vi	80.4
Mistral Nemo	rand	vi	75.6
Mistral Nemo	rand	ur	65.5

Table 8: Random neuron fine-tuning results for Llama 3.1 and Mistral Nemo. The table reports zero-shot performance without intervention (No Int) after fine-tuning randomly selected 10 neurons per layers instead of language-specific neurons.

Monte Carlo Sampling for Analyzing In-Context Examples

Stephanie Schoch and **Yangfeng Ji**
Department of Computer Science
University of Virginia
Charlottesville, VA 22904
{sns2gr,yangfeng}@virginia.edu

Abstract

Prior works have shown that in-context learning is brittle to presentation factors such as the order, number, and choice of selected examples. However, ablation-based guidance on selecting the number of examples may ignore the interplay between different presentation factors. In this work we develop a Monte Carlo sampling-based method to study the impact of number of examples while explicitly accounting for effects from order and selected examples. We find that previous guidance on how many in-context examples to select does not always generalize across different sets of selected examples and orderings, and whether one-shot settings outperform zero-shot settings is highly dependent on the selected example. Additionally, inspired by data valuation, we apply our sampling method to in-context example selection to select examples that perform well across different orderings. We find a negative result, that while performance is robust to ordering and number of examples, there is an unexpected performance degradation compared to random sampling.

1 Introduction

In-context learning is an emergent ability of LLMs (Wei et al., 2022; Brown et al., 2020b) where an LLM learns to perform an unseen task by seeing a number of demonstrations in the context window (Brown et al., 2020a). While in-context learning has shown significant potential as a way to extract relevant information from an LLM and align the model with user expectations, it has also exhibited brittleness to an assortment of factors. For example, model performance when learning in-context is sensitive to which examples are selected (Rubin et al., 2022; Liu et al., 2022; Wu et al., 2023; Ye et al., 2023) as well as their orderings (Lu et al., 2022; Chen et al., 2023b; Liu et al., 2022; Chang and Jia, 2023; Guo et al., 2024; Wu et al., 2023).

Another important parameter, the number of examples, has received comparably little attention. Prior works have suggested that one-shot settings outperform zero-shot settings even when a random label is used (Min et al., 2022). Additional ablations have guided this parameter by citing performance plateaus at set numbers of examples (Wang et al., 2024; Min et al., 2022; Wu et al., 2023). However, it is unclear whether this guidance holds when accounting for other sensitive factors such as different orderings and selected examples.

Previous work on data valuation has shown the efficacy of applying Monte Carlo sampling to evaluate datum contributions under different permutations in fine-tuning settings (Ghorbani and Zou, 2019; Schoch et al., 2023). Inspired by this, we develop a Monte Carlo sampling-based method to investigate the impact of number of examples while using permutations to account for order and selection of in-context examples.

Specifically, we utilize Monte Carlo sampling and analyze performance with the addition of each exemplar. We find that performance plateaus at previously suggested numbers of examples do not consistently generalize under different permutations. Further, we find that one-shot performance may be more sensitive to the selected example than previously recognized (Min et al., 2022; Brown et al., 2020b) and the guidance of one-shot outperforming zero-shot is dependent on the selected example. Finally, we find that using Monte Carlo sampling to select in-context examples may increase robustness to effects from ordering and selected examples, but unexpectedly, does not lead to performance improvements over random sampling.

2 Related work

In-context learning In many prior works investigating in-context learning sensitivity to ordering and selected examples (see Appendix A for de-

The Sixth Workshop on Insights from Negative Results in NLP, pages 63–78
May 4, 2025

scription of in-context learning), a fixed number of examples are used (Zhang et al., 2022b; Lu et al., 2022; Min et al., 2022), with common guidance from prior ablations stating performance plateaus around $k = 4$ (Wang et al., 2024) and $k = 8$ examples (Min et al., 2022; Wu et al., 2023). Recent work has looked at the how the number of examples impacts performance on chain-of-thought reasoning benchmarks (Chen et al., 2023a) and suggested that fewer examples may be needed, yet it is otherwise unclear the effect of number of demonstrations on other tasks and prompting frameworks, particularly when controlling for order and selected examples.

Monte Carlo sampling Monte Carlo sampling has been widely adopted in the data valuation literature to provide unbiased approximations of the Shapley value (Ghorbani and Zou, 2019), based on prior work on Monte Carlo methods for Shapley value approximation (Mann and Shapley, 1962; Castro et al., 2009; Maleki et al., 2013) (see Appendix A for additional details). Recent works have also applied principles from data valuation to in-context learning example selection and ordering (Guo et al., 2024; Chang and Jia, 2023; Nguyen and Wong, 2023). While in data valuation, Monte Carlo sampling methods are used to calculate the marginal contribution of each data point averaged over a number of permutations, our motivation differs. In our setting, we are motivated by the utility of Monte Carlo sampling to provide an unbiased estimate of the influence of number of examples on in-context learning performance by reducing influence of ordering and selected examples.

3 Method

To study the effect of the number of examples, we aim to reduce the influence of ordering and selected examples as confounding factors. While averaging across trials in previous work helps reduce the influence of selected examples, it does not account for different orderings. Additionally, prior work on ordering only addresses up to $k = 4$ (Lu et al., 2022) as the possible permutations increase exponentially with respect to k. This motivates the use of Monte Carlo sampling with incremental exemplar additions as 1) the use of permutations reduces the influence of ordering, and 2) the averaging across multiple trials reduces the influence of selected examples. We explain this as well as our method in detail below.

Algorithm 1: Monte Carlo Sampling Method

Input: Training data $D_{trn} = \{1, ..., n\}$, evaluation data $D_{tst} = \{1, ..., m\}$, LLM $\mathcal{M}$, performance metric $V_{\mathcal{M}}$, parameters: K (# examples), P (# permutations)
Output: Average performance $\mu(V_{\mathcal{M}})$ for $k = \{0, ..., K\}$ for one subset S^K
Initialize $\mu_k = 0$ for $k = 0, ..., K$
Randomly sample subset S^K from D_{trn}
for $p \in \{1, ..., P\}$ **do**
    π^p: Random permutation of S^K
    for $k \in \{0, ..., K\}$ **do**
        $\mu_k \leftarrow \mu_k + V_{\mathcal{M}}(S[0:k]_{\pi})$
    end for
end for
for $k \in \{0, ..., K\}$ **do**
    $\mu_k \leftarrow \frac{1}{P}\mu_k$
end for

Consider a training dataset $D_{trn} = \{(x_i, y_i)\}_{i=1}^{n}$ that contains n training instances. Given a fixed test set D_{tst}, we aim to draw k exemplars from D_{trn} and test model performance on D_{tst}. We let $S_{\pi}^{k} \subseteq D_{trn}$ denote a subset with some ordering π and cardinality k, where $k \leq n$. Additionally, we let $V_{\mathcal{M}}$ denote the predictive performance of a model $\mathcal{M}$, e.g., prediction accuracy.

For each $k \in \{1, 2, ..., K\}$, the set of possible subsets $S^k = \{S_{(i)}^{k}\}_{i=1}^{{}_nC_k}$. The expected model performance for any given $S_{(i)}^{k}$ can be defined as:

$$E_{\pi \sim \Pi}[V_{\mathcal{M}}(S_{\pi(i)}^{k})] \quad (1)$$

where $V_{\mathcal{M}}(S_{\pi}^{k})$ is the performance of model $\mathcal{M}$ using S_{π}^{k} and Π is the uniform distribution over all $k!$ permutations of $S_{(i)}^{k}$.

For each k, exhaustively permuting all ${}_nC_k$ subsets S^k, and averaging over the expected values would give us the expected value for each number of exemplars. In practice, however, this is computationally infeasible. Instead, we utilize Monte Carlo sampling to approximate this value.

Specifically, we utilize the Monte Carlo sampling method adapted from Ghorbani and Zou (2019). First, we define K as the maximum exemplars we aim to use. Next, we sample S^K from D_{trn}. For a predefined number of permutations of S^K, we iteratively scan from the first element to the final element, computing the model perfor-

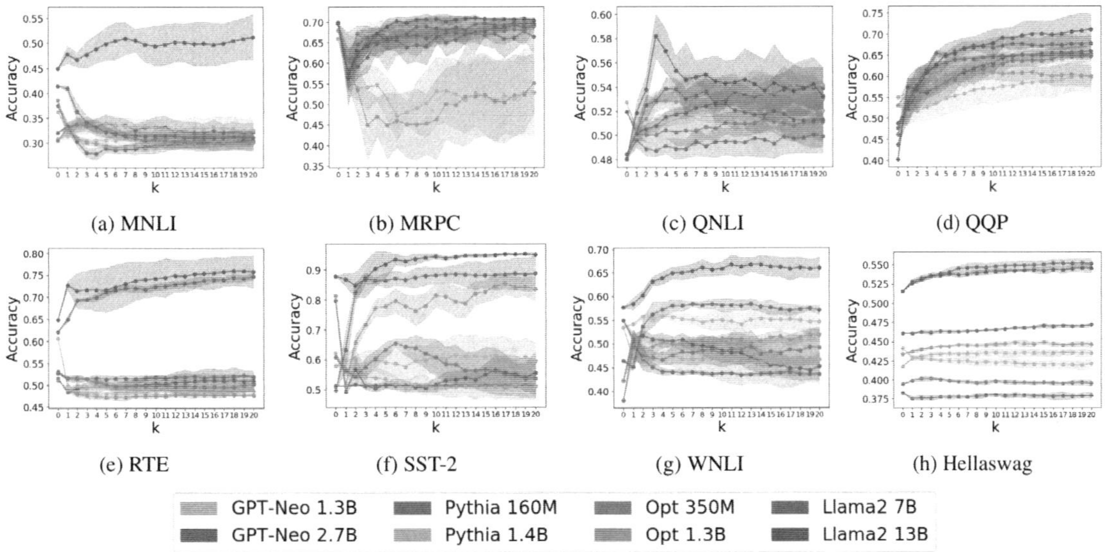

Figure 1: In-context performance for each dataset and model. Results show the average of 20 permutations at each step k in the proposed Monte Carlo sampling method. Shaded regions show standard deviation of 5 trials.

mance at each step. We average the performance for each k across p permutations. We provide the pseudo-code in algorithm 1. In practice, we perform this procedure over multiple trials, resampling S^K for each trial and averaging over the result. In our experiments, we use 5 trials and $p = 20$ permutations.

In addition to the computational speedup achievable by limiting the number of permutations, the primary benefit of our approach is that is circumvents the need to resample at each k. As we cannot exhaustively permute each S^k, if we resample for each k, there are $\frac{n!}{(n-k-1)!}$ possible permutations preceding k, each of which could produce differing downstream performance $V_{\mathcal{M}}(S^{k-1}_{\pi_{k-1}})$ due to the impact of S^{k-1} and π_{k-1} (selected examples and ordering, respectively). By sampling in this manner, we effectively eliminate the influence of $k-1$ in understanding performance at k.

4 Experiment setup

Detailed descriptions of our setup can be found in Appendix B.

Models We experiment with 8 models in total, listed in Table 1. The selected models vary in size from 160M to 13B and represent four distinct families: Pythia (Biderman et al., 2023), OPT (Zhang et al., 2022a), GPT-Neo (Black et al., 2021), and Llama2 (Touvron et al., 2023).

Datasets We use 8 datasets in our experiments across a diverse range of tasks previously represented in in-context learning analysis. Specifically, we perform experiments on natural language inference (MNLI, QNLI, WNLI), sentiment analysis (SST-2), commonsense reasoning (Hellaswag), paraphrase detection (MRPC, QQP), and textual entailment (RTE).

Sampling and Aggregation Procedure For each trial, we randomly sample 20 in-context examples from the training set. We perform 20 Monte Carlo permutations. Within each permutation, we iterate from the first example to the last, computing the accuracy on the validation set at each step. Using this procedure, we perform 5 trials for each experiment. In aggregate, we perform 100 permutations with each model and dataset combination.

5 Results

5.1 Analyzing Number of Examples

We plot the performance of each model across $k = \{1, 2, ..., 20\}$ examples, where each step represents the addition of one in-context example from the Monte Carlo permutation. In line with common practice of reporting across multiple trials with standard deviation information, our results are averaged over 5 trials, controlling for selected examples and ordering effects. Results are reported in Figure 1.

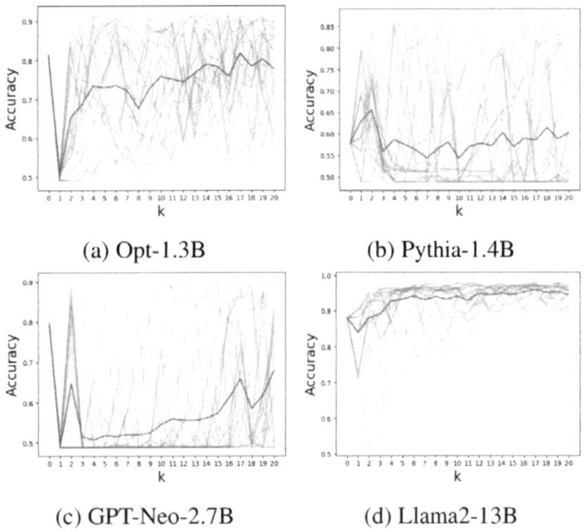

(a) Opt-1.3B (b) Pythia-1.4B

(c) GPT-Neo-2.7B (d) Llama2-13B

Figure 2: Results on SST-2. Blue lines represent individual permutations and red line indicates average across all permutations within one trial.

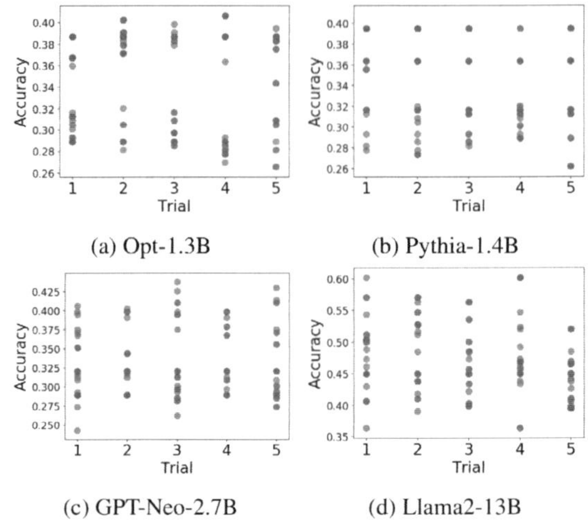

(a) Opt-1.3B (b) Pythia-1.4B

(c) GPT-Neo-2.7B (d) Llama2-13B

Figure 3: One-shot MNLI performance across 5 trials. Each blue point represents the accuracy using the first exemplar in a permutation. Red points indicate zero-shot performance. Results show that zero-shot settings can outperform one-shot settings, dependent upon the selected example.

Observed from the averaged results, our results align with ablations in prior work (Wu et al., 2023; Min et al., 2022). Specifically, much of the performance improvement across models and datasets occurs within the first 8 in-context examples, where performance then begins to plateau and only marginally increase. At face value, this result shows that prior recommendations with respect to the number of examples to use are not influenced by ordering effects as we had hypothesized prior to designing our sampling method.

Does performance consistently plateau at set numbers of exemplars? When viewing the results from individual permutations, we find that the performance plateaus by $k = 4$ (Wang et al., 2024) and $k = 8$ (Min et al., 2022; Wu et al., 2023) examples are not observable within individual permutations. On the contrary, we continue to observe erratic performance changes up through $k = 20$ examples. This suggests the previously observed plateaus on averaged results, both in prior work and recreated in Figure 1, may mask significant performance fluctuations, and the best performance within a selected example set may occur anywhere from $k = \{1, 2, ...20\}$. Additionally, we observe that in some permutations, there is a performance drop at $k = 1$. We investigate this further in the following section.

Is one example better than none? Prior work has suggested that one demonstration outperforms no demonstrations even when a random label is used (Min et al., 2022). Other work has suggested some dependence on the dataset and model (Xie et al., 2022; Brown et al., 2020b). However, our results indicate that the performance of zero-shot vs. few-shot settings may be dependent on the selected example, regardless of dataset and model. To illustrate this, in Figure 6, we plot the one-shot performance of each permutation across all 5 trials on the MNLI dataset using each model, with the zero-shot performance of the model indicated in red.

In contradiction to prior work, our results across nearly all models and datasets (see Appendix C) indicate that performance in one-shot settings can vary between significant performance improvements and significant performance degradation, depending on the selected example. This contradiction raises the question of what qualities of in-context examples can lead to such significant performance degradation in one-shot settings, and whether these have any impact when used within a k-shot setting.

Our analysis in one-shot settings across different permutations indicates that one-shot performance is more sensitive to the selected example than previously thought.

5.2 Exemplar Selection

We are interested in whether we can apply our sampling method to selecting in-context examples. Using our sampling method, each exemplar appears at

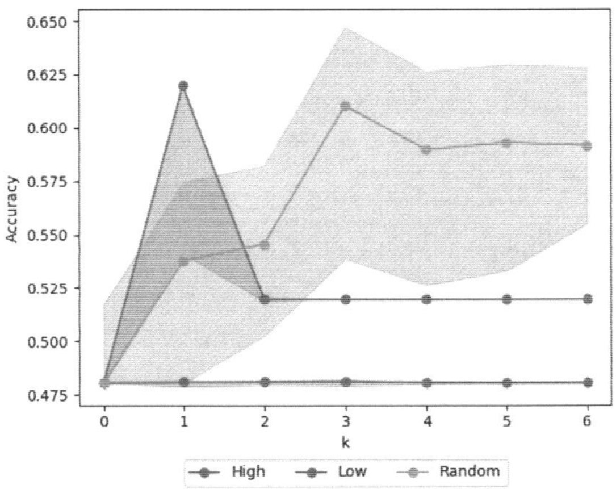

Figure 4: Performance with Llama2-13B on QNLI dataset, using in-context subsets containing the highest-performing and lowest-performing data points on average from subsection 5.1, along with a random baseline. Results represent 20 permutations, with standard deviation displayed as the shaded region for each line.

different k's under different permutations. Therefore, we are effectively averaging out different orderings and k's. It follows that we would expect exemplars associated with high average accuracy within different permutations to be associated with higher model performance overall, while being robust across orderings and different k's Further, we would expect exemplars with low average accuracies to consistently lead to poor performance.

Given the token limitations of context windows and computational time associated with increasing k, to increase the example candidate set, we use Z-score as a means to compare examples across trials. This allows us to limit context to $k = 20$ while increasing the overall candidate set and accounting for the impact of using different selected examples in each trial. We perform the sampling procedure described in section 3 with Llama2-13B on QNLI and perform the following calculation.

For a given trial t, we compute the average accuracy associated with each example e, denoted μ_e. We then take the mean over all example averages in the trial, $\mu_t = \frac{1}{k}\Sigma_{e=1}^{k}\mu_e$ with standard deviation $\sigma_t = \sqrt{\frac{\Sigma_{e=1}^{k}(\mu_e - \mu_t)}{k}}$. Finally, we compute the Z-score for each example in the trial, where $Z = \frac{\mu_e - \mu_t}{\sigma_t}$ After computing scores for all trials, we identify points with a Z-score $Z > 1 \vee Z < 1$, and select the 6 examples with the highest and lowest scores as our *high* and *low* set, respectively. We report results using each set, as well as a random baseline for in-context learning in Figure 4 using the same sampling procedure as in subsection 5.1.

When using points identified via Monte Carlo sampling as consistently high or low performing, we see a greater robustness to ordering sensitivity across k's, as evidenced by the minimal variance exhibited by these subsets. This is contrasted with the random baseline which exhibits high variance across different k's and orderings.

Interestingly, whereas our experiments in section 5.1 showed numerous instances where one-shot performance was worse than zero-shot performance, we do not observe this occurring with the lowest average performing data points. Rather, we see performance maintained at a zero-shot level. Further, while high-performing examples consistently performs above zero-shot accuracy and exhibit greater stability over varying k across permutations, the random selection exhibited the highest performance for $k > 1$. This was an unexpected result: using our Monte Carlo-based selection method led to more robust performance across k examples, but it resulted in an overall performance decrease compared to random sampling.

Our results when selecting in-context examples that on average had high or low scores across Monte Carlo permutations indicate that subsets comprised of points at each end of the spectrum exhibit lower sensitivity to ordering and number of demonstrations. While this may be promising in terms of identifying methods to increase robustness of in-context learning performance, the random selection baseline exhibited both higher overall performance and higher variance across orderings and number of examples. This raises the question of whether there is an existing performance vs. robustness tradeoff, and of what qualities contribute to example deviation from the mean performance, as well as how methods can identify examples that possess these qualities that also lead to higher performance gains.

6 Conclusion

In this work, we proposed a Monte Carlo-based sampling method to investigate previous guidance regarding number of examples to use and one- vs. zero-shot settings. We further investigated whether this method could be used to select in-context examples, finding a performance vs. robustness tradeoff.

7 Limitations

Our results are reported on models up to 13B parameters due to constraints posed by our available computational resources. We acknowledge this as a limitation, however, as our results are consistent across the model sizes we utilized, we believe our results should generalize to larger models.

Acknowledgments

We thank the reviewers for their helpful feedback. This research was supported in part by NSF III #2007492.

References

Stella Biderman, Hailey Schoelkopf, Quentin Gregory Anthony, Herbie Bradley, Kyle O'Brien, Eric Hallahan, Mohammad Aflah Khan, Shivanshu Purohit, USVSN Sai Prashanth, Edward Raff, et al. 2023. Pythia: A suite for analyzing large language models across training and scaling. In *International Conference on Machine Learning*, pages 2397–2430. PMLR.

Sid Black, Leo Gao, Phil Wang, Connor Leahy, and Stella Biderman. 2021. GPT-Neo: Large Scale Autoregressive Language Modeling with Mesh-Tensorflow.

Tom Brown, Benjamin Mann, Nick Ryder, Melanie Subbiah, Jared D Kaplan, Prafulla Dhariwal, Arvind Neelakantan, Pranav Shyam, Girish Sastry, Amanda Askell, Sandhini Agarwal, Ariel Herbert-Voss, Gretchen Krueger, Tom Henighan, Rewon Child, Aditya Ramesh, Daniel Ziegler, Jeffrey Wu, Clemens Winter, Chris Hesse, Mark Chen, Eric Sigler, Mateusz Litwin, Scott Gray, Benjamin Chess, Jack Clark, Christopher Berner, Sam McCandlish, Alec Radford, Ilya Sutskever, and Dario Amodei. 2020a. Language models are few-shot learners. In *Advances in Neural Information Processing Systems*, volume 33, pages 1877–1901. Curran Associates, Inc.

Tom Brown, Benjamin Mann, Nick Ryder, Melanie Subbiah, Jared D Kaplan, Prafulla Dhariwal, Arvind Neelakantan, Pranav Shyam, Girish Sastry, Amanda Askell, et al. 2020b. Language models are few-shot learners. *Advances in neural information processing systems*, 33:1877–1901.

Javier Castro, Daniel Gómez, and Juan Tejada. 2009. Polynomial calculation of the shapley value based on sampling. *Computers & Operations Research*, 36(5):1726–1730.

Ting-Yun Chang and Robin Jia. 2023. Data curation alone can stabilize in-context learning. In *Proceedings of the 61st Annual Meeting of the Association for Computational Linguistics (Volume 1: Long Papers)*, pages 8123–8144, Toronto, Canada. Association for Computational Linguistics.

Jiuhai Chen, Lichang Chen, Chen Zhu, and Tianyi Zhou. 2023a. How many demonstrations do you need for in-context learning? In *Findings of the Association for Computational Linguistics: EMNLP 2023*, pages 11149–11159, Singapore. Association for Computational Linguistics.

Yanda Chen, Chen Zhao, Zhou Yu, Kathleen McKeown, and He He. 2023b. On the relation between sensitivity and accuracy in in-context learning. In *Findings of the Association for Computational Linguistics: EMNLP 2023*, pages 155–167, Singapore. Association for Computational Linguistics.

William Dolan, Chris Quirk, Chris Brockett, and Bill Dolan. 2004. Unsupervised construction of large paraphrase corpora: Exploiting massively parallel news sources.

Leo Gao, Jonathan Tow, Baber Abbasi, Stella Biderman, Sid Black, Anthony DiPofi, Charles Foster, Laurence Golding, Jeffrey Hsu, Alain Le Noac'h, Haonan Li, Kyle McDonell, Niklas Muennighoff, Chris Ociepa, Jason Phang, Laria Reynolds, Hailey Schoelkopf, Aviya Skowron, Lintang Sutawika, Eric Tang, Anish Thite, Ben Wang, Kevin Wang, and Andy Zou. 2023. A framework for few-shot language model evaluation.

Amirata Ghorbani and James Zou. 2019. Data shapley: Equitable valuation of data for machine learning. In *Proceedings of the 36th International Conference on Machine Learning*, volume 97 of *Proceedings of Machine Learning Research*, pages 2242–2251. PMLR.

Qi Guo, Leiyu Wang, Yidong Wang, Wei Ye, and Shikun Zhang. 2024. What makes a good order of examples in in-context learning. In *Findings of the Association for Computational Linguistics: ACL 2024*, pages 14892–14904, Bangkok, Thailand. Association for Computational Linguistics.

Hector J Levesque, Ernest Davis, and Leora Morgenstern. 2011. The Winograd schema challenge. In *AAAI Spring Symposium: Logical Formalizations of Commonsense Reasoning*, volume 46, page 47.

Quentin Lhoest, Albert Villanova del Moral, Yacine Jernite, Abhishek Thakur, Patrick von Platen, Suraj Patil, Julien Chaumond, Mariama Drame, Julien Plu, Lewis Tunstall, Joe Davison, Mario Šaško, Gunjan Chhablani, Bhavitvya Malik, Simon Brandeis, Teven Le Scao, Victor Sanh, Canwen Xu, Nicolas Patry, Angelina McMillan-Major, Philipp Schmid, Sylvain Gugger, Clément Delangue, Théo Matussière, Lysandre Debut, Stas Bekman, Pierric Cistac, Thibault Goehringer, Victor Mustar, François Lagunas, Alexander Rush, and Thomas Wolf. 2021. Datasets: A community library for natural language processing. In *Proceedings of the 2021 Conference on Empirical Methods in Natural Language Processing: System Demonstrations*, pages 175–184, Online and Punta Cana, Dominican Republic. Association for Computational Linguistics.

Jiachang Liu, Dinghan Shen, Yizhe Zhang, Bill Dolan, Lawrence Carin, and Weizhu Chen. 2022. What makes good in-context examples for GPT-3? In *Proceedings of Deep Learning Inside Out (DeeLIO 2022): The 3rd Workshop on Knowledge Extraction and Integration for Deep Learning Architectures*, pages 100–114, Dublin, Ireland and Online. Association for Computational Linguistics.

Yao Lu, Max Bartolo, Alastair Moore, Sebastian Riedel, and Pontus Stenetorp. 2022. Fantastically ordered prompts and where to find them: Overcoming few-shot prompt order sensitivity. In *Proceedings of the 60th Annual Meeting of the Association for Computational Linguistics (Volume 1: Long Papers)*, pages 8086–8098, Dublin, Ireland. Association for Computational Linguistics.

Sasan Maleki, Long Tran-Thanh, Greg Hines, Talal Rahwan, and Alex Rogers. 2013. Bounding the estimation error of sampling-based shapley value approximation with/without stratifying. *CoRR, abs/1306.4265*, 2(1).

Irwin Mann and Lloyd S Shapley. 1962. Values of large games. 6: Evaluating the electoral college exactly. *RAND Corp., Santa Monica, CA, USA, Tech. Rep. RM-3158-PR*.

Sewon Min, Xinxi Lyu, Ari Holtzman, Mikel Artetxe, Mike Lewis, Hannaneh Hajishirzi, and Luke Zettlemoyer. 2022. Rethinking the role of demonstrations: What makes in-context learning work? In *Proceedings of the 2022 Conference on Empirical Methods in Natural Language Processing*, pages 11048–11064, Abu Dhabi, United Arab Emirates. Association for Computational Linguistics.

Tai Nguyen and Eric Wong. 2023. In-context example selection with influences. *arXiv preprint arXiv:2302.11042*.

Quora. 2017. [link].

Ohad Rubin, Jonathan Herzig, and Jonathan Berant. 2022. Learning to retrieve prompts for in-context learning. In *Proceedings of the 2022 Conference of the North American Chapter of the Association for Computational Linguistics: Human Language Technologies*, pages 2655–2671, Seattle, United States. Association for Computational Linguistics.

Stephanie Schoch, Ritwick Mishra, and Yangfeng Ji. 2023. Data selection for fine-tuning large language models using transferred shapley values. In *Proceedings of the 61st Annual Meeting of the Association for Computational Linguistics (Volume 4: Student Research Workshop)*, pages 266–275.

Richard Socher, Alex Perelygin, Jean Wu, Jason Chuang, Christopher D Manning, Andrew Y Ng, and Christopher Potts. 2013. Recursive deep models for semantic compositionality over a sentiment treebank. In *Proceedings of the 2013 conference on empirical methods in natural language processing*, pages 1631–1642.

Hugo Touvron, Thibaut Lavril, Gautier Izacard, Xavier Martinet, Marie-Anne Lachaux, Timothée Lacroix, Baptiste Rozière, Naman Goyal, Eric Hambro, Faisal Azhar, et al. 2023. Llama: Open and efficient foundation language models. *arXiv preprint arXiv:2302.13971*.

Alex Wang, Amanpreet Singh, Julian Michael, Felix Hill, Omer Levy, and Samuel Bowman. 2018. GLUE: A multi-task benchmark and analysis platform for natural language understanding. In *Proceedings of the 2018 EMNLP Workshop BlackboxNLP: Analyzing and Interpreting Neural Networks for NLP*, pages 353–355, Brussels, Belgium. Association for Computational Linguistics.

Liang Wang, Nan Yang, and Furu Wei. 2024. Learning to retrieve in-context examples for large language models. In *Proceedings of the 18th Conference of the European Chapter of the Association for Computational Linguistics (Volume 1: Long Papers)*, pages 1752–1767, St. Julian's, Malta. Association for Computational Linguistics.

Jason Wei, Yi Tay, Rishi Bommasani, Colin Raffel, Barret Zoph, Sebastian Borgeaud, Dani Yogatama, Maarten Bosma, Denny Zhou, Donald Metzler, Ed H. Chi, Tatsunori Hashimoto, Oriol Vinyals, Percy Liang, Jeff Dean, and William Fedus. 2022. Emergent abilities of large language models. *Transactions on Machine Learning Research*. Survey Certification.

Adina Williams, Nikita Nangia, and Samuel Bowman. 2018. A broad-coverage challenge corpus for sentence understanding through inference. In *Proceedings of the 2018 Conference of the North American Chapter of the Association for Computational Linguistics: Human Language Technologies, Volume 1 (Long Papers)*, pages 1112–1122.

Zhiyong Wu, Yaoxiang Wang, Jiacheng Ye, and Lingpeng Kong. 2023. Self-adaptive in-context learning: An information compression perspective for in-context example selection and ordering. In *Proceedings of the 61st Annual Meeting of the Association for Computational Linguistics (Volume 1: Long Papers)*, pages 1423–1436, Toronto, Canada. Association for Computational Linguistics.

Sang Michael Xie, Aditi Raghunathan, Percy Liang, and Tengyu Ma. 2022. An explanation of in-context learning as implicit bayesian inference. In *International Conference on Learning Representations*.

Jiacheng Ye, Zhiyong Wu, Jiangtao Feng, Tao Yu, and Lingpeng Kong. 2023. Compositional exemplars for in-context learning. In *Proceedings of the 40th International Conference on Machine Learning*, volume 202 of *Proceedings of Machine Learning Research*, pages 39818–39833. PMLR.

Rowan Zellers, Ari Holtzman, Yonatan Bisk, Ali Farhadi, and Yejin Choi. 2019. Hellaswag: Can a machine really finish your sentence? In *Proceedings of the 57th Annual Meeting of the Association for Computational Linguistics*, pages 4791–4800.

Susan Zhang, Stephen Roller, Naman Goyal, Mikel Artetxe, Moya Chen, Shuohui Chen, Christopher Dewan, Mona Diab, Xian Li, Xi Victoria Lin, et al. 2022a. Opt: Open pre-trained transformer language models. *arXiv preprint arXiv:2205.01068*.

Yiming Zhang, Shi Feng, and Chenhao Tan. 2022b. Active example selection for in-context learning. In *Proceedings of the 2022 Conference on Empirical Methods in Natural Language Processing*, pages 9134–9148, Abu Dhabi, United Arab Emirates. Association for Computational Linguistics.

Model	Parameters
Pythia (Biderman et al., 2023)	160M 1.4B
OPT (Zhang et al., 2022a)	350M 1.3B
GPT-Neo (Black et al., 2021)	1.3B 2.7B
LLaMa2 (Touvron et al., 2023)	7B 13B

Table 1: Models used in our experiments. We select a range of different model families and parameter sizes. Parameter range is upper bounded based on available compute.

A Additional Background

In-Context Learning: In-context learning enables pre-trained models to learn an unseen task using a set of exemplars concatenated in the context window. Formally, given a test example x, in-context learning concatenates K demonstration examples to the task instruction I, where $S = \{x_{\pi(i)}, y_{\pi i}\}_{i=1}^{K}$ denotes the example set given some order π.

Monte Carlo Sampling: Within the context of data valuation, the underlying idea of Monte Carlo sampling is to sample random permutations of the data points and iterate from the first to last element in each permutation. Specifically, for p Monte Carlo iterations, a dataset D is randomly permuted. Following, these methods scan from the first element of the permutation to the last element of the permutation and compute the performance of the model at each timestep. In data valuation, Monte Carlo sampling methods are used to calculate the marginal contribution of each data point averaged over a number of permutations.

B Experiment Setup Details

We adapt the Language Model Evaluation Harness package (Gao et al., 2023) to conduct our experiments. All experiments use the package's default prompts for each dataset.

Details on models and datasets used can be found in Table 1 and Table 2, respectively.

Notably, the upper bound of the parameter range for models is due to our resource constraint, as each experiment is run using a single NVIDIA A100

Dataset	Task	#Train	#Val	#Classes
MNLI (Williams et al., 2018)	Natural Language Inference	393k	9.82k	3
MRPC (Dolan et al., 2004)	Paraphrase Detection	3.67k	408	2
QNLI (Wang et al., 2018)	Natural Language Inference	105k	5.46k	2
QQP (Quora, 2017)	Paraphrase Detection	364k	40.4k	2
RTE [1]	Textual Entailment	2.49k	277	2
SST-2 (Socher et al., 2013)	Sentiment Analysis	67.3k	872	2
WNLI (Levesque et al., 2011)	Natural Language Inference	635	71	2
Hellaswag (Zellers et al., 2019)	Commonsense Reasoning	39.9k	10k	4

Table 2: Datasets used in our experiments. We use the distributions available from Huggingface (Lhoest et al., 2021), and use the respective validation sets to measure performance.

GPU.

For each dataset, we utilize the splits available from Huggingface. As the GLUE benchmark datasets do not have labeled test sets, we use the validation sets for evaluation. Additionally, as we are performing inference after the addition of every example within each permutation, we follow a protocol from prior work and sub-sample 256 instances from the validation set to control inference overhead (Lu et al., 2022).

C Additional results

This appendix contains:

- Additional scatter plots (section 5.1)
- Single trial averages overlaying individual permutations (section 5.1)

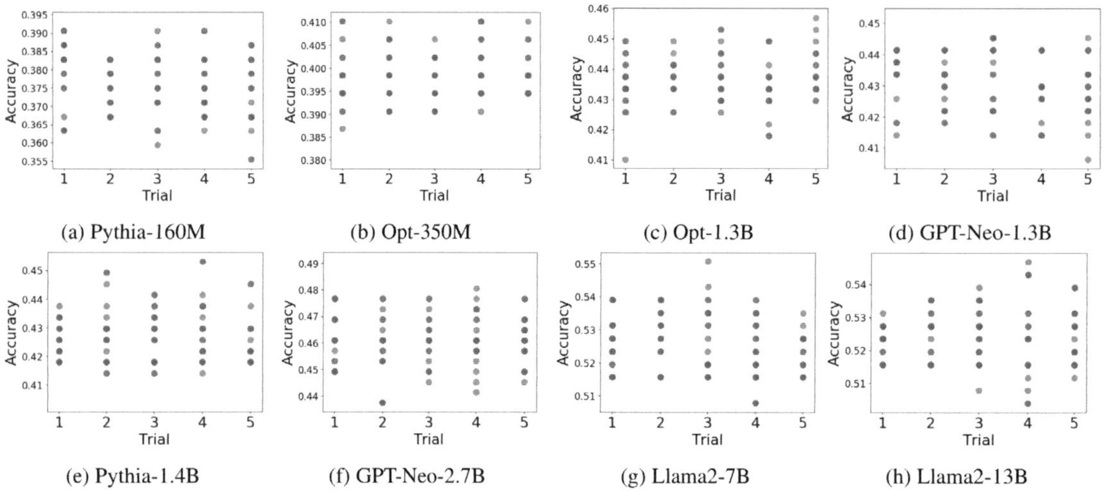

(a) Pythia-160M (b) Opt-350M (c) Opt-1.3B (d) GPT-Neo-1.3B

(e) Pythia-1.4B (f) GPT-Neo-2.7B (g) Llama2-7B (h) Llama2-13B

Figure 5: One-shot in-context learning performance on the Hellaswag dataset across 5 trials.

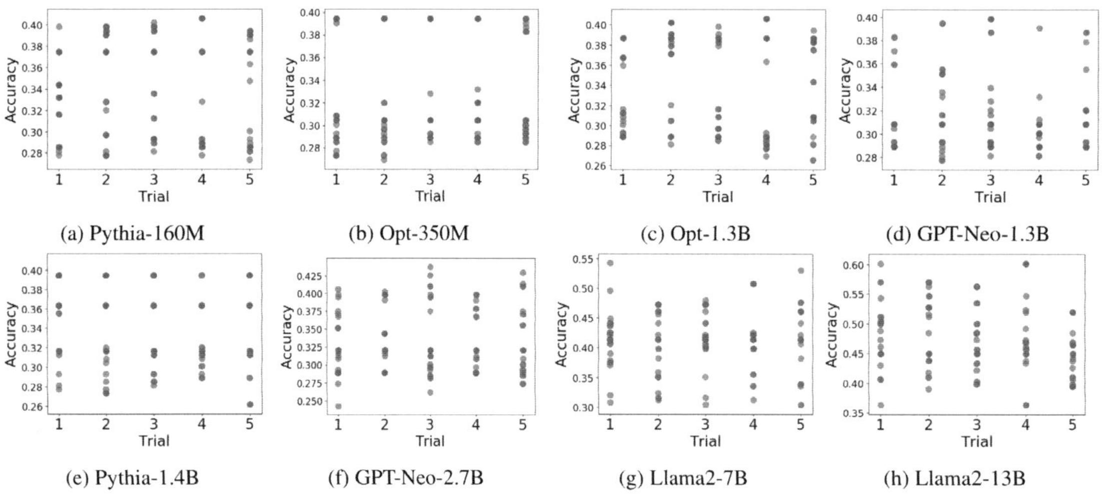

(a) Pythia-160M (b) Opt-350M (c) Opt-1.3B (d) GPT-Neo-1.3B

(e) Pythia-1.4B (f) GPT-Neo-2.7B (g) Llama2-7B (h) Llama2-13B

Figure 6: One-shot in-context learning performance on the MNLI dataset across 5 trials. Each blue point represents the accuracy using the first in-context example of a permutation, with 20 permutations per trial. The red points indicate the zero-shot performance of the model. Results indicate that zero-shot settings can outperform one-shot settings, dependent upon the selected in-context example.

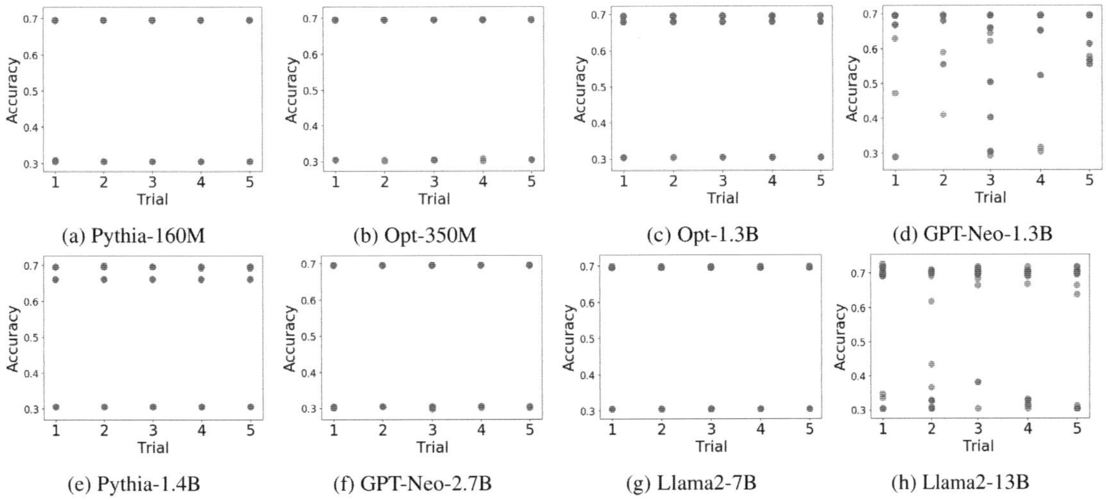

(a) Pythia-160M (b) Opt-350M (c) Opt-1.3B (d) GPT-Neo-1.3B

(e) Pythia-1.4B (f) GPT-Neo-2.7B (g) Llama2-7B (h) Llama2-13B

Figure 7: One-shot in-context learning performance on the MRPC dataset across 5 trials.

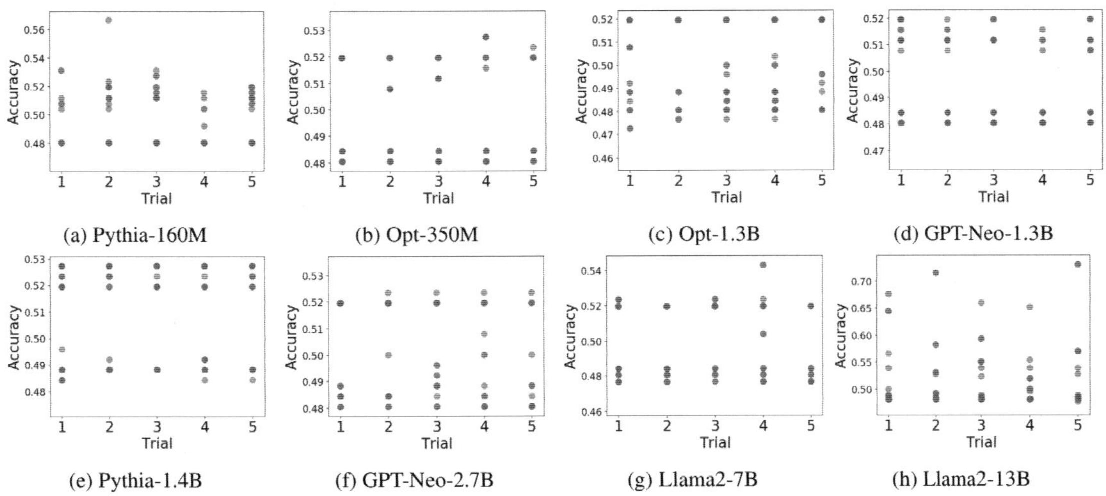

(a) Pythia-160M (b) Opt-350M (c) Opt-1.3B (d) GPT-Neo-1.3B

(e) Pythia-1.4B (f) GPT-Neo-2.7B (g) Llama2-7B (h) Llama2-13B

Figure 8: One-shot in-context learning performance on the QNLI dataset across 5 trials.

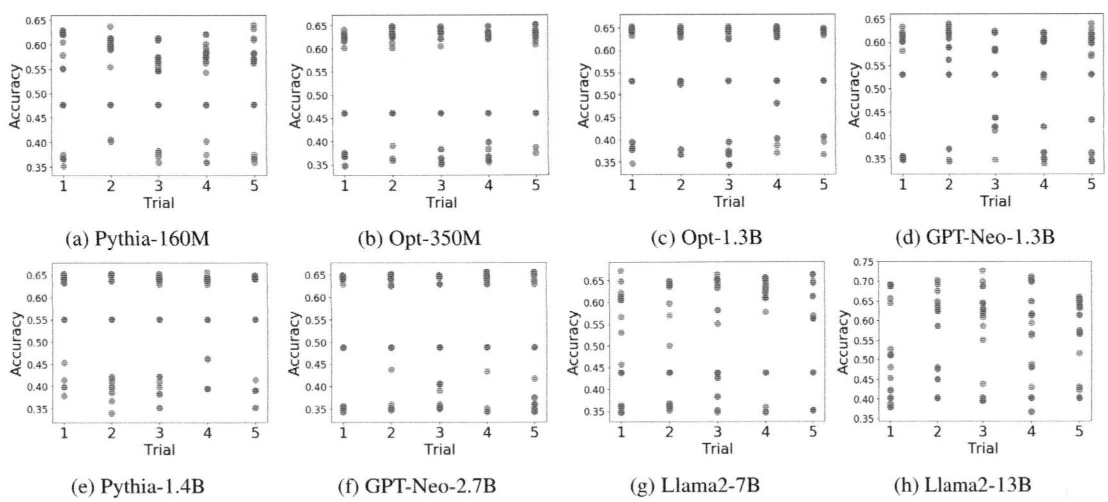

(a) Pythia-160M (b) Opt-350M (c) Opt-1.3B (d) GPT-Neo-1.3B

(e) Pythia-1.4B (f) GPT-Neo-2.7B (g) Llama2-7B (h) Llama2-13B

Figure 9: One-shot in-context learning performance on the QQP dataset across 5 trials.

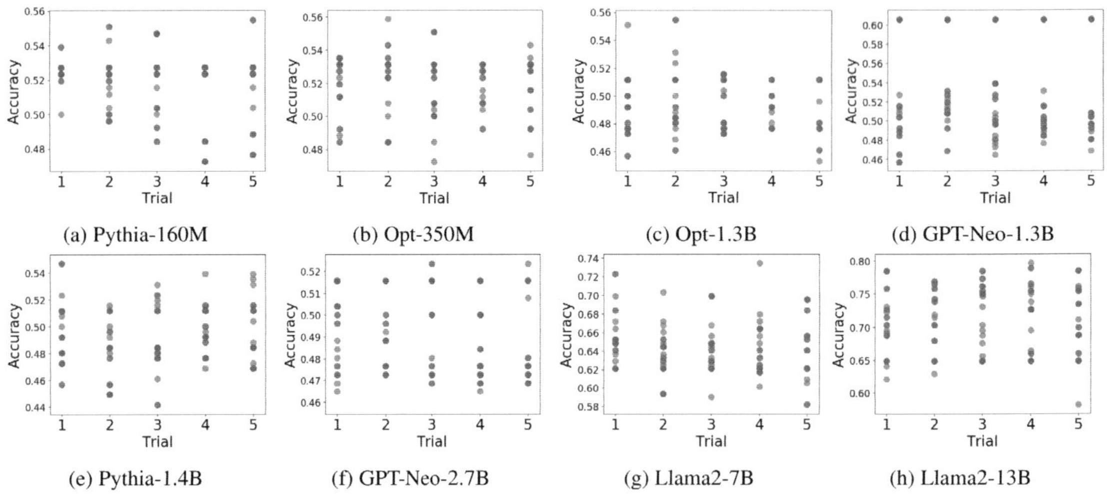

(a) Pythia-160M (b) Opt-350M (c) Opt-1.3B (d) GPT-Neo-1.3B

(e) Pythia-1.4B (f) GPT-Neo-2.7B (g) Llama2-7B (h) Llama2-13B

Figure 10: One-shot in-context learning performance on the RTE dataset across 5 trials.

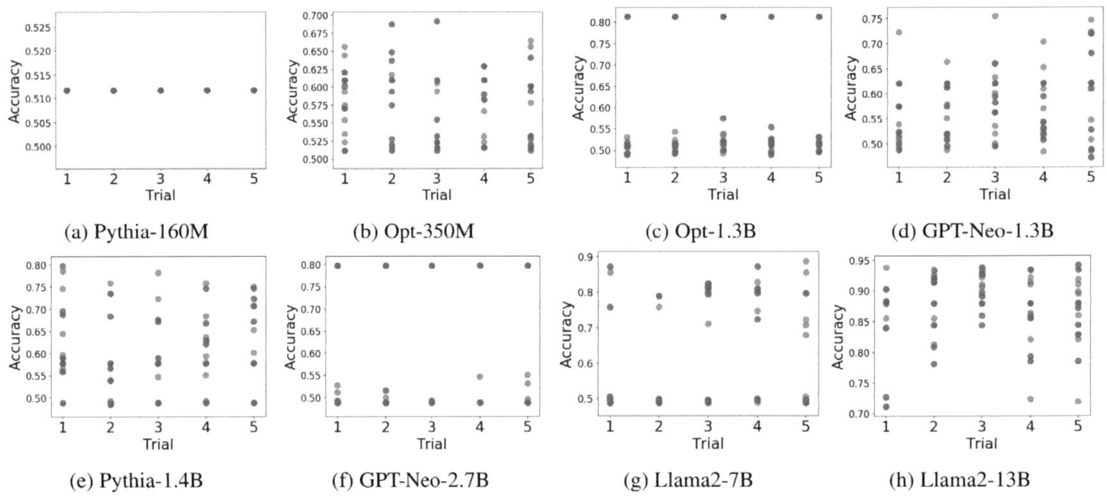

(a) Pythia-160M (b) Opt-350M (c) Opt-1.3B (d) GPT-Neo-1.3B

(e) Pythia-1.4B (f) GPT-Neo-2.7B (g) Llama2-7B (h) Llama2-13B

Figure 11: One-shot in-context learning performance on the SST-2 dataset across 5 trials.

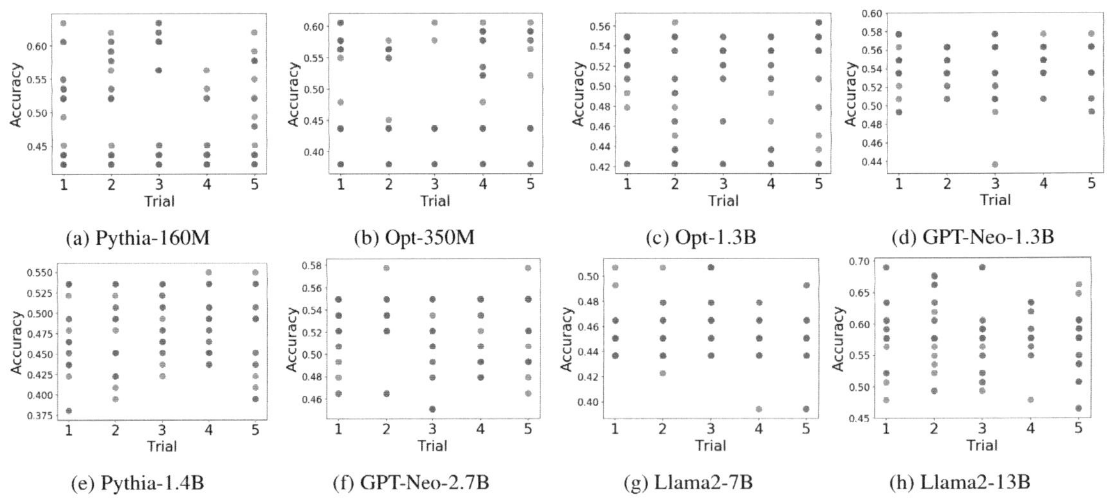

(a) Pythia-160M (b) Opt-350M (c) Opt-1.3B (d) GPT-Neo-1.3B

(e) Pythia-1.4B (f) GPT-Neo-2.7B (g) Llama2-7B (h) Llama2-13B

Figure 12: One-shot in-context learning performance on the WNLI dataset across 5 trials.

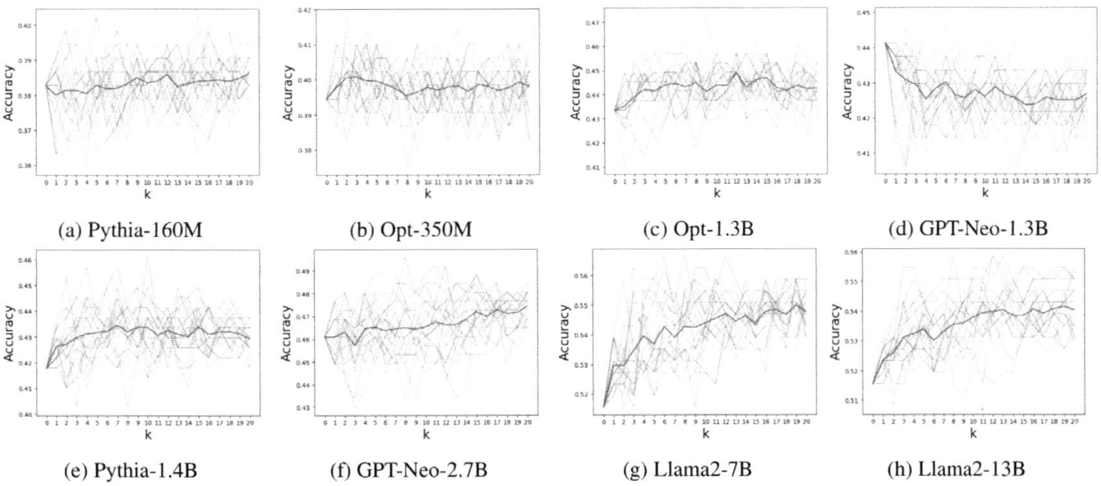

(a) Pythia-160M (b) Opt-350M (c) Opt-1.3B (d) GPT-Neo-1.3B

(e) Pythia-1.4B (f) GPT-Neo-2.7B (g) Llama2-7B (h) Llama2-13B

Figure 13: Performance of each model on Hellaswag dataset. In each plot, the red line indicates the averages of all permutations for one trial, overlaying blue lines for individual permutations.

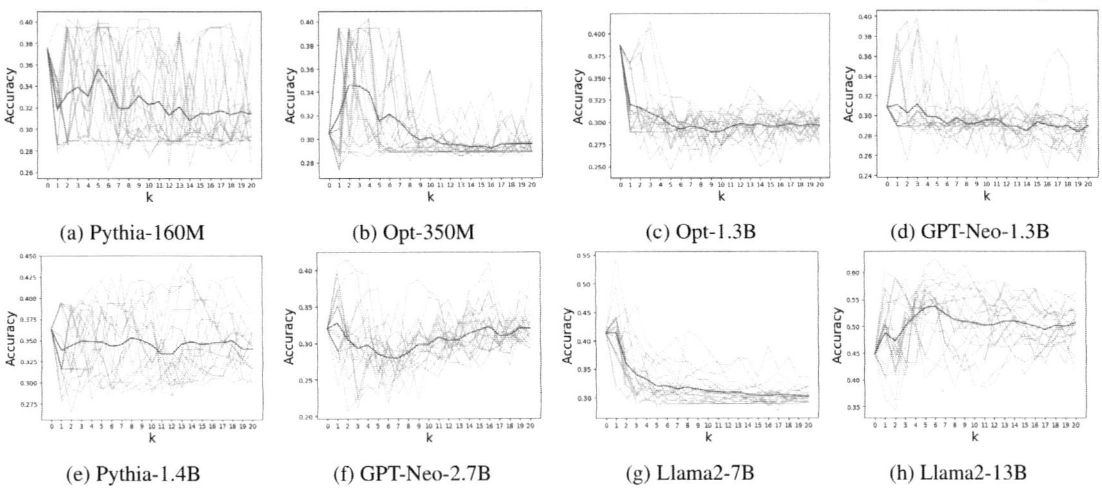

(a) Pythia-160M (b) Opt-350M (c) Opt-1.3B (d) GPT-Neo-1.3B

(e) Pythia-1.4B (f) GPT-Neo-2.7B (g) Llama2-7B (h) Llama2-13B

Figure 14: Performance of each model on MNLI dataset. In each plot, the red line indicates the averages of all permutations for one trial, overlaying blue lines for individual permutations.

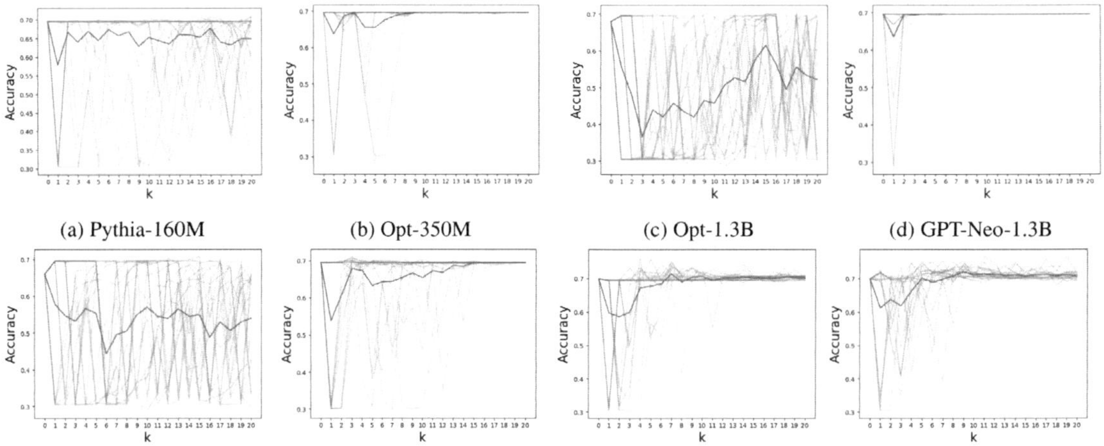

(a) Pythia-160M (b) Opt-350M (c) Opt-1.3B (d) GPT-Neo-1.3B

(e) Pythia-1.4B (f) GPT-Neo-2.7B (g) Llama2-7B (h) Llama2-13B

Figure 15: Performance of each model on MRPC dataset. In each plot, the red line indicates the averages of all permutations for one trial, overlaying blue lines for individual permutations.

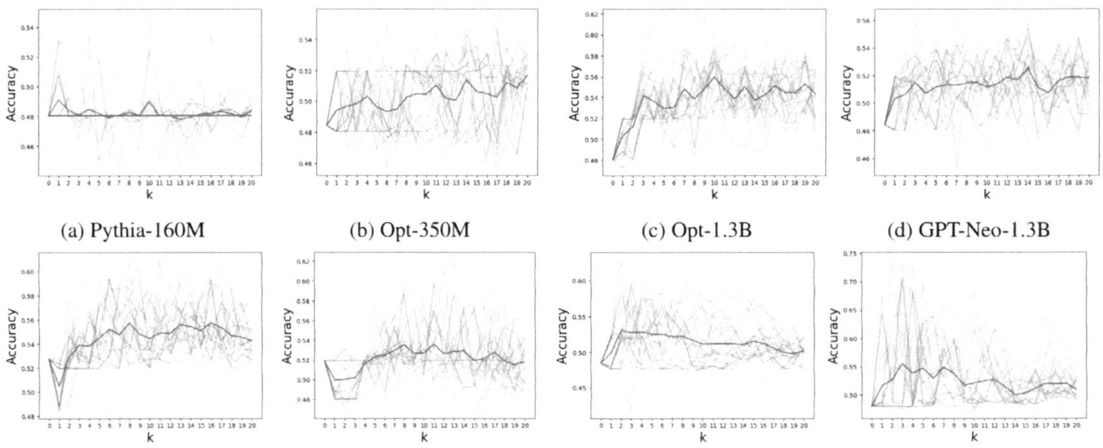

(a) Pythia-160M (b) Opt-350M (c) Opt-1.3B (d) GPT-Neo-1.3B

(e) Pythia-1.4B (f) GPT-Neo-2.7B (g) Llama2-7B (h) Llama2-13B

Figure 16: Performance of each model on QNLI dataset. In each plot, the red line indicates the averages of all permutations for one trial, overlaying blue lines for individual permutations.

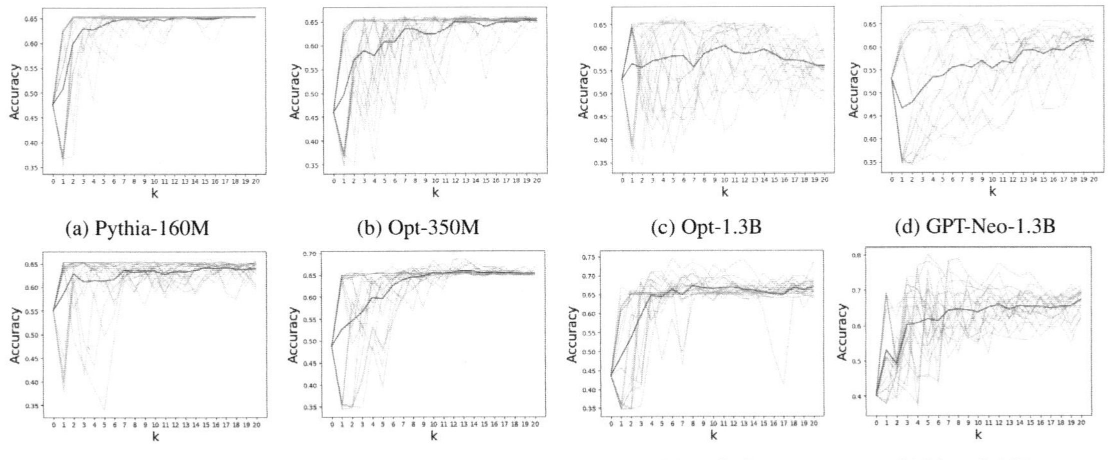

(a) Pythia-160M (b) Opt-350M (c) Opt-1.3B (d) GPT-Neo-1.3B

(e) Pythia-1.4B (f) GPT-Neo-2.7B (g) Llama2-7B (h) Llama2-13B

Figure 17: Performance of each model on QQP dataset. In each plot, the red line indicates the averages of all permutations for one trial, overlaying blue lines for individual permutations.

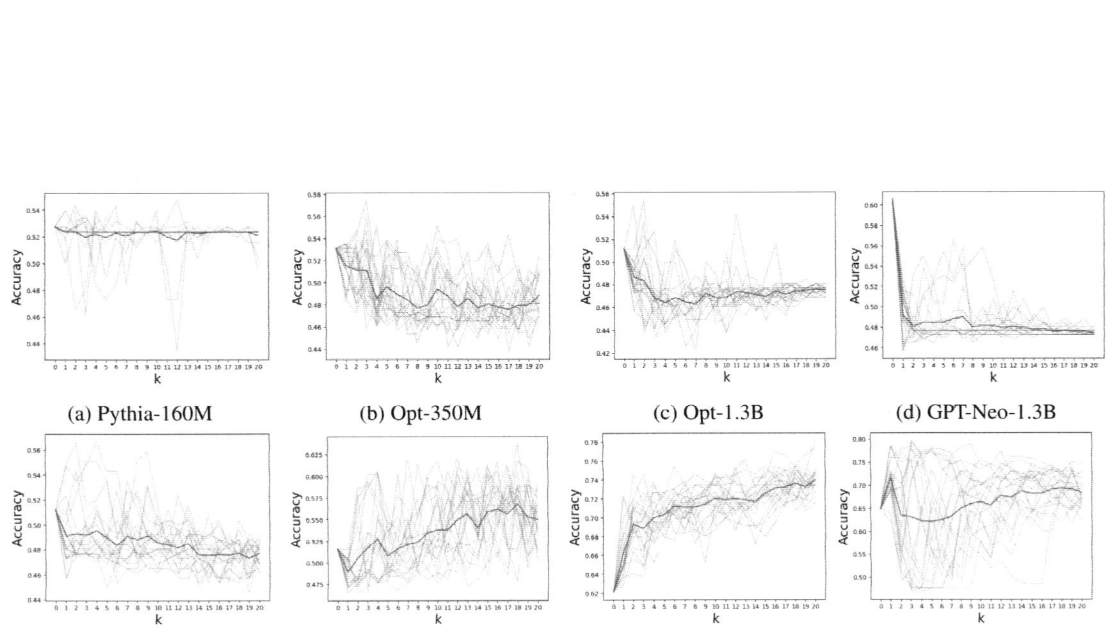

(a) Pythia-160M (b) Opt-350M (c) Opt-1.3B (d) GPT-Neo-1.3B

(e) Pythia-1.4B (f) GPT-Neo-2.7B (g) Llama2-7B (h) Llama2-13B

Figure 18: Performance of each model on RTE dataset. In each plot, the red line indicates the averages of all permutations for one trial, overlaying blue lines for individual permutations.

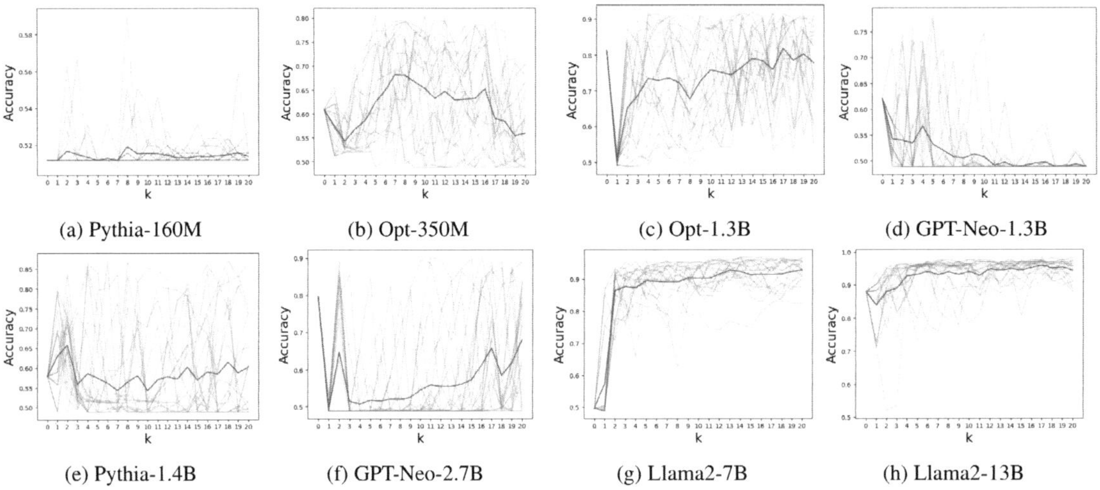

(a) Pythia-160M (b) Opt-350M (c) Opt-1.3B (d) GPT-Neo-1.3B

(e) Pythia-1.4B (f) GPT-Neo-2.7B (g) Llama2-7B (h) Llama2-13B

Figure 19: Performance of each model on SST-2 dataset. In each plot, the red line indicates the averages of all permutations for one trial, overlaying blue lines for individual permutations.

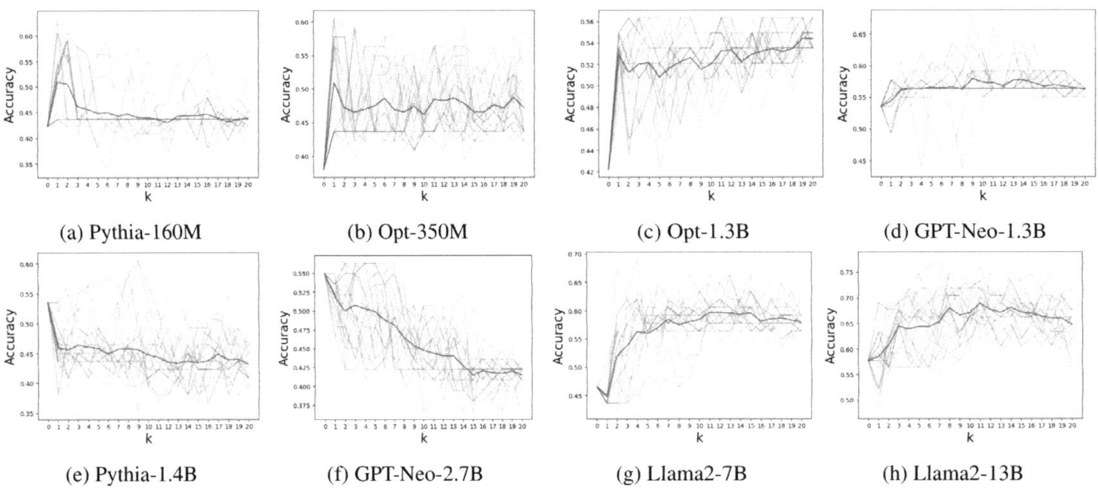

(a) Pythia-160M (b) Opt-350M (c) Opt-1.3B (d) GPT-Neo-1.3B

(e) Pythia-1.4B (f) GPT-Neo-2.7B (g) Llama2-7B (h) Llama2-13B

Figure 20: Performance of each model on WNLI dataset. In each plot, the red line indicates the averages of all permutations for one trial, overlaying blue lines for individual permutations.

Does Training on Synthetic Data Make Models Less Robust?

Lingze Zhang and **Ellie Pavlick**
Brown University
{lingze_zhang, ellie_pavlick}@brown.edu

Abstract

An increasingly common practice is to train large language models (LLMs) using synthetic data. Often this synthetic data is produced by the same or similar LLMs as those it is being used to train. This raises the question of whether the synthetic data might in fact exacerbate certain "blindspots" by reinforcing heuristics that the LLM already encodes. In this paper, we conduct simulated experiments on the natural language inference (NLI) task with Llama-2-7B-hf models. We use MultiNLI as the general task and HANS, a targeted evaluation set designed to measure the presence of specific heuristic strategies for NLI, as our "blindspot" task. Our goal is to determine whether performance disparities between the general and blind spot tasks emerge. Our results indicate that synthetic data does not reinforce blindspots in the way we expected. Specifically, we see that, while fine-tuning with synthetic data doesn't necessarily reduce the use of the heuristic, it also does not make it worse as we hypothesized. [1]

1 Introduction and Related Work

Constructing a dataset for a specific task in natural language processing can be costly in terms of time and labor. An increasingly common approach to solve this problem is to take advantage of large language models (LLMs) to generate training data. It's simple to fine-tune an LLM or just use in-context learning to generate huge amounts of training data with a relatively small number of demonstrations. However, how effective the model-written datasets are for different tasks is still an open question.

Model-generated training data is widely used in different domains like image classification (Besnier et al., 2020; Gowal et al., 2021), visual language concepts understanding (Cascante-Bonilla et al., 2023) and medical image understanding (Fernandez et al., 2022). In many NLP tasks, such as commonsense reasoning (Yang et al., 2020), question-answering (Bartolo et al., 2021; Paranjape et al., 2022), sycophancy reduction (Wei et al., 2024), cultural debiasing (Li et al., 2024a,b) and general instruction alignment (Wang et al., 2023), synthetic data created with generative models are utilized in model training. In cases where there are limited sources for model training, synthetic data would greatly benefit the performance of finetuned model. High-quality model-written datasets may also be used for evaluations. Perez et al. (2023) created 154 evaluation datasets and discovered inverse scaling of language models in some scenarios.

However, synthetic data may also be harmful. Shumailov et al. (2024) found that language models may collapse if recursively finetuned with generated text. Such degradation has also been discovered in image generation tasks (Alemohammad et al., 2024). The use of synthetic data is also criticized from the perspective of ethics and social impact (Susser and Seeman, 2024). There's a series of research about what bias is manifested in synthetic data and how the performance in specific tasks is affected. For example, gender stereotype is a common kind of bias amplified in data generated by language models (Kirk et al., 2021; Kotek et al., 2023a). Li et al. (2023) investigated the text classification task and showed that subjectivity is a matter affecting the performance of models trained with synthetic data. Bisbee et al. (2024) found less variation in ChatGPT responses than in the real ANES survey. Similarly, a study from Chen et al. (2024) indicates that the uniform format of synthetic data can lead to pattern overfitting and thus harm the instruction-following capabilities of the model trained with it. Seddik et al. (2024) reveals that the recursive training loop makes the tails of the original distribution disappear and makes the model forget the real distribution from a statistical

[1] Our code is available at https://github.com/untakenJ/synthetic-data-blindspot.

The Sixth Workshop on Insights from Negative Results in NLP, pages 79–85
May 4, 2025 ©2025 Association for Computational Linguistics

perspective.

One particular way in which synthetic data might be harmful is if it reinforces ungeneralizable heuristics. It is well know that LLMs often rely on features that perform well on the training set but do not necessarily generalize as we would like, for example, relying on gender bias (Kotek et al., 2023b), word-overlap bias in NLI (Rajaee et al., 2022), or exhibiting a preference toward longer responses in text generation (Singhal et al., 2024). We refer to these types of heuristics as *blindspots*.

In this work, we hypothesize that, because synthetic data less diverse than the original training data (Whitney and Norman, 2024), it is more likely to have blindspots and thus that fine-tuning on model-generated data will exacerbate these blindspots in the tuned model. In particular, we hypothesize that the synthetic data will encode the heuristic to a larger extent than naturally occurring data would, and thus that fine-tuning on synthetic data will lead the model to more strongly favor the heuristic. This weakness would be revealed in data that specifically is designed to test whether models are using the heuristic, as models trained on synthetic data might still show improved performance on generic test sets on which the heuristic performs well.

As a case study, we focus on the natural language inference (NLI) task evaluated with the MultiNLI dataset (Williams et al., 2018). The MultiNLI dataset covers general examples collected from various sources, but models trained on MultiNLI may tend to make judgments based on superficial syntactic properties and perform badly on HANS, an adversarial dataset created with syntactic heuristics (McCoy et al., 2019). The HANS task can be regarded as a measure of the model's "blindspot".

Our expected result is that finetuning an NLI model with synthetic MultiNLI-like data will reduce its performance on HANS while improving its performance on the MultiNLI test set. However, we observed that this is not a consistent pattern under various settings of starting point model and size of synthetic dataset, though some biases do exist in the synthetic dataset. Our hypothesis is thus not fully supported by the experimental results. We have nonetheless discovered different patterns of performance change on both test sets in different scenarios. We hope the discovered insights will foster novel research ideas in understanding model degradation with synthetic training data and advancing fairness and robustness of language models.

2 Methods

2.1 Overview

We assume a **t**ask model T and a **g**enerator model G. T can be a model for any kind of NLP tasks, and G is a language model used to generate training examples for T. Let $\mathcal{X}_T$ denote the set of all possible input of model T. The existence of a blindspot means that there's a non-random subset $\widetilde{\mathcal{X}_T} \subseteq \mathcal{X}_T$ on which the model T performs worse than on $\mathcal{X}_T$ in general. Let $\mathcal{D}^G$ denote the synthetic dataset generated by G, and $T^{\mathcal{D}^G}$ denote the model fine-tuned on $\mathcal{D}^G$. Our hypothesis is that $T^{\mathcal{D}^G}$ will perform worse than T on $\widetilde{\mathcal{X}_T}$, but better than T on $\mathcal{X}_T$.

2.2 Tasks, Models and Datasets

2.2.1 Tasks

In this study, we focus on the natural language inference (NLI) task. An input example of this task contains a premise sentence, a hypothesis sentence, and a label indicating the relationship between the two sentences. The label can be one of $\{entailment, neutral, contradictory\}$.

2.2.2 Models and Input

Our experiments are based on the Llama-2-7B-hf model (Touvron et al., 2023). We fine-tuned a Llama-2 model with a classification head on top with MultiNLI as the task model T. The input sequence is constructed with the template

> *Please indicate the relationship between the premise and the hypothesis with entailment, neutral or contradiction. Premise: <premise> Hypothesis: <hypothesis> The relationship between premise and hypothesis is*

and the classification is based on the embedding of the last token in the input sequence. Our generator G is also a Llama-2-7B-hf model fine-tuned with MultiNLI. It's tuned to generate examples in the form of

> *This is an example where the relationship between the premise and the hypothesis is <label>. Premise: <premise> Hypothesis: <hypothesis> – This is the end of the example.*

The label is put before the premise and the hypothesis for more flexible control of generated labels.

2.2.3 Datasets

We use MultiNLI (Williams et al., 2018) as a measure of the models performance on NLI in general. The original task model T and generator G are both Llama-2-7B-hf models finetuned on MultiNLI. To measure the presence of the "blindspot", we use HANS (McCoy et al., 2019). HANS is an NLI dataset created adversarially with three heuristics: the lexical overlap heuristic, the subsequence heuristic, and the constituent heuristic. Poor performance on HANS indicates that the model is likely using these heuristics to solve the NLI task.

When training the task model T, we used the training set of MultiNLI as the training data, with 750 examples (250 for each label) excluded as the dev set. HANS is not used in training at all, but the results on its test set are reported. The maximum training set size for T is 391,722.

Note that there are only two labels in HANS (because of how the dataset is constructed): *entailment* and *non-entailment*. In our experiments, the base task model and generator are fine-tuned with three labels of MultiNLI. When testing on HANS, predicted labels *neutral* and *contradictory* are both regarded as *non-entailment*.

2.3 Experiments

2.3.1 Basic Setting

In our experiment pipeline, we first fine-tuned a classifier model T with the MultiNLI training set from the pretrained Llama-2-7B-hf model with a classification head. Then we fine-tuned another Llama-2-7B-hf model as the generator G, also with the MultiNLI training set. After training G, we generated a dataset $\mathcal{D}^G$ with it and used $\mathcal{D}^G$ to further fine-tune T to obtain the further tuned model $T^{\mathcal{D}^G}$. We varied T (by changing the number of MultiNLI examples used for the initial fine-tuning) and $\mathcal{D}^G$ for different settings.

2.3.2 Starting Models

The initial task model T is fine-tuned with data from the original MultiNLI dataset. In order to simulate task models in different stages, we trained 6 starting models with training set sizes of 0 (meaning the official pretrained model with a random classification head), 5000, 10000, 20000, 100000, and 391722.

2.3.3 Synthetic Datasets

The synthetic data examples are all generated by a Llama-2-7B-hf model G fine-tuned with the MultiNLI training set for 1 epoch. The generator model is fine-tuned to generate text in the specific format aforementioned with the following prompt:

> *This is an example where the relationship between the premise and the hypothesis is <label>*

We kept the generated examples in which the premise and the hypothesis can be extracted with a regular expression without further filtering.

We generated 1,819,813 examples, which is more than necessary for the training. We sampled two kinds of synthetic datasets: uniformly random sampled datasets and showcasing datasets with a stronger bias. We took the lexical overlap (LO) heuristic addressed in the HANS dataset as an example. Lexical overlap means all the words in the hypothesis appear in the premise.

Based on the availability of synthetic data, we constructed synthetic training sets of three sizes: 73080, 36040, and 18020. In each synthetic set, there are equal numbers of examples with each label. The random synthetic dataset (marked as *Synthetic*) is uniformly sampled for each label, and the more strongly biased dataset (*Biased Synthetic*) is sampled to make sure all entailment examples follow the lexical overlap heuristic and all other examples do not. We also included baseline datasets sampled from the original MultiNLI training set of the same sizes, marked as *Original*. The datasets used in the experiment can be represented as $\{73080, 36040, 18020\} \times \{Original, Synthetic, Biased\ Synthetic\}$.

2.3.4 Test Sets

We report our results on three test sets: the MultiNLI Matched test set, the HANS test set, and the subset of the HANS test set with lexical overlap and a non-entailment label, which reflects the model's performance specifically on the blind spot. In addition to the augmented model with different training sets, we also report the classification performance of each starting model.

3 Results

Our main results are reported in Figure 1. Each subplot corresponds to a different starting model T. When starting with undertrained task models, further fine-tuning with synthetic data will improve the performance on the MultiNLI Matched test set. The amount of improvement is on par with

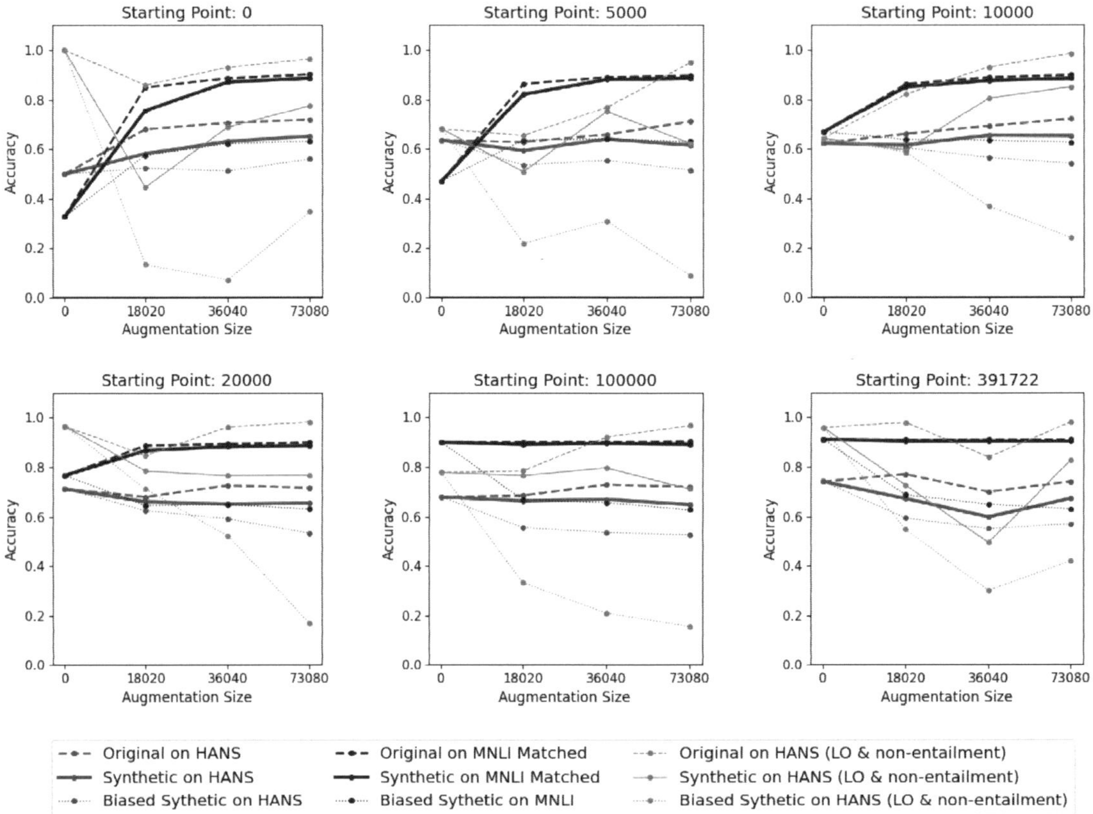

Figure 1: Augmented model performance under different settings.

the model fine-tuned with original MultiNLI training data if the training set size is large enough. For relatively well-established starting models, neither fine-tuning with original nor synthetic data would significantly improve the performance of MultiNLI.

The performance on the HANS test set is trickier. The hypothesized trend , in which the performance of HANS goes down while the performance of MultiNLI goes up, only happens in for the 20K starting point. We also see a fairly sizable drop in HANS performance for the 392K starting point, but the curve is not monotonic and thus it is inconclusive. Overall, under most settings, further fine-tuning with original MultiNLI data would always benefit more or harm less on HANS performance than synthetic data. The gap does exist, but may not be as serious as expected.

As a sanity check, we also trained the model with the biased synthetic dataset in which all examples with lexical overlap are labeled entailment, and no example with neural or contradiction label satisfies the lexical overlap heuristic. As expected, such models perform worst in almost all tests, with the accuracy on the HANS subset of lexical overlap heuristic and non-entailment label dropping significantly towards zero over training. This indicates that a very biased synthetic dataset could exacerbate blindspots as expected, and thus implies that true synthetic data does not overrepresent the heuristic as much as hypothesized.

4 Conclusion

From the simulated experiments, we observed that while training the task model with synthetic data contributes to the performance on the general tasks almost equally compared with training with the original data, the contribution gap on the "more difficult" blindspot task does exist. Under some settings, there's a dispersion where the accuracy on the blindspot task goes down while the general task accuracy goes up, but this is not a consistent tendency. Reinforcement of bias while training may happen, but this would probably not cause significant issues if we just use the unfiltered synthetic data for training.

Limitations

Dataset	Label	Count	# LO	% LO	% S:O
	Ent.	631992	24360	3.854	2.352
Syn.	Neu.	562822	690	0.123	2.320
	Con.	624999	1504	0.241	1.827
	Ent.	130541	2139	1.639	-
Orig.	Neu.	130573	69	0.053	-
	Con.	130608	172	0.132	-

Table 1: Statistics of examples with lexical overlap in original and synthetic data. There are generally more cases in synthetic data, and the correlation between lexical overlap and the entailment label is reinforced.

We need to note that the study with MultiNLI and HANS is a case study addressing the issue of bias reinforcement when training models with synthetic data. It's still an open question whether the results about the biases we are studying are generalizable to other cases. According to Table 1, lexical overlap is more common in the synthetic dataset than in MulitNLI for all labels, which may indicate that synthetic data is less diverse. However, the correlation between lexical overlap and entailment label is just slightly stronger. Different kinds of bias can emerge in very different ways in synthetic data, and this makes it challenging to evaluate the effect of training models with synthetic data holistically.

Our design choices about the experiments may also be arbitrary. The task model we choose is the Llama-2-7B-hf model with a classification head. The pretrained Llama model is a relatively strong model, while the initialization of the classification head is random. Whether jointly training these parts is a reasonable choice is still arguable. Moreover, the two-step approach of model training is also not the only choice. It's also common to mix the original and synthetic data in different ratios and train the model with the mixed dataset in one run. Varying the experiment design is also necessary for further validations about the findings in this study.

Another notable point is that pretrained large language models, such as Llama, encode a wealth of world knowledge. Many potential biases may have been mitigated during training, particularly for models deployed in real-world applications, which are typically much larger and more powerful than the fine-tuned Llama-2-7B-hf generator used in our study. On the other hand, human-created or audited data are not inherently free from implicit biases. The more concentrated distribution and reduced diversity of synthetic data might reinforce biases in certain blindspot scenarios. However, the rich world knowledge embedded in the generator model can also address some biases, potentially outperforming humans in certain cases and contributing positively to bias mitigation. A critical direction for future research is to disentangle these two effects and assess the significance of each, thereby enhancing our understanding of the impact of training models with synthetic data.

References

Sina Alemohammad, Josue Casco-Rodriguez, Lorenzo Luzi, Ahmed Imtiaz Humayun, Hossein Babaei, Daniel LeJeune, Ali Siahkoohi, and Richard Baraniuk. 2024. Self-consuming generative models go MAD. In *The Twelfth International Conference on Learning Representations*.

Max Bartolo, Tristan Thrush, Robin Jia, Sebastian Riedel, Pontus Stenetorp, and Douwe Kiela. 2021. Improving question answering model robustness with synthetic adversarial data generation. In *Proceedings of the 2021 Conference on Empirical Methods in Natural Language Processing*, pages 8830–8848, Online and Punta Cana, Dominican Republic. Association for Computational Linguistics.

Victor Besnier, Himalaya Jain, Andrei Bursuc, Matthieu Cord, and Patrick Pérez. 2020. This dataset does not exist: Training models from generated images. In *ICASSP 2020 - 2020 IEEE International Conference on Acoustics, Speech and Signal Processing (ICASSP)*, pages 1–5.

James Bisbee, Joshua D Clinton, Cassy Dorff, Brenton Kenkel, and Jennifer M Larson. 2024. Synthetic replacements for human survey data? the perils of large language models. *Political Analysis*, pages 401–416.

Paola Cascante-Bonilla, Khaled Shehada, James Seale Smith, Sivan Doveh, Donghyun Kim, Rameswar Panda, Gul Varol, Aude Oliva, Vicente Ordonez, Rogerio Feris, et al. 2023. Going beyond nouns with vision & language models using synthetic data. In *Proceedings of the IEEE/CVF International Conference on Computer Vision*, pages 20155–20165.

Jie Chen, Yupeng Zhang, Bingning Wang, Xin Zhao, Ji-Rong Wen, and Weipeng Chen. 2024. Unveiling the flaws: Exploring imperfections in synthetic data and mitigation strategies for large language models. In *Findings of the Association for Computational Linguistics: EMNLP 2024*, pages 14855–14865, Miami, Florida, USA. Association for Computational Linguistics.

Virginia Fernandez, Walter Hugo Lopez Pinaya, Pedro Borges, Petru-Daniel Tudosiu, Mark S Graham, Tom Vercauteren, and M Jorge Cardoso. 2022. Can segmentation models be trained with fully synthetically generated data? In *International Workshop on Simulation and Synthesis in Medical Imaging*, pages 79–90. Springer.

Sven Gowal, Sylvestre-Alvise Rebuffi, Olivia Wiles, Florian Stimberg, Dan Andrei Calian, and Timothy A Mann. 2021. Improving robustness using generated data. *Advances in Neural Information Processing Systems*, 34:4218–4233.

Hannah Rose Kirk, Yennie Jun, Filippo Volpin, Haider Iqbal, Elias Benussi, Frederic Dreyer, Aleksandar Shtedritski, and Yuki Asano. 2021. Bias out-of-the-box: An empirical analysis of intersectional occupational biases in popular generative language models. *Advances in neural information processing systems*, 34:2611–2624.

Hadas Kotek, Rikker Dockum, and David Sun. 2023a. Gender bias and stereotypes in large language models. In *Proceedings of the ACM collective intelligence conference*, pages 12–24.

Hadas Kotek, Rikker Dockum, and David Sun. 2023b. Gender bias and stereotypes in large language models. In *Proceedings of The ACM Collective Intelligence Conference*, CI '23, page 12–24, New York, NY, USA. Association for Computing Machinery.

Cheng Li, Mengzhou Chen, Jindong Wang, Sunayana Sitaram, and Xing Xie. 2024a. Culturellm: Incorporating cultural differences into large language models. *Preprint*, arXiv:2402.10946.

Cheng Li, Damien Teney, Linyi Yang, Qingsong Wen, Xing Xie, and Jindong Wang. 2024b. Culturepark: Boosting cross-cultural understanding in large language models. *Preprint*, arXiv:2405.15145.

Zhuoyan Li, Hangxiao Zhu, Zhuoran Lu, and Ming Yin. 2023. Synthetic data generation with large language models for text classification: Potential and limitations. In *Proceedings of the 2023 Conference on Empirical Methods in Natural Language Processing*, pages 10443–10461, Singapore. Association for Computational Linguistics.

Tom McCoy, Ellie Pavlick, and Tal Linzen. 2019. Right for the wrong reasons: Diagnosing syntactic heuristics in natural language inference. In *Proceedings of the 57th Annual Meeting of the Association for Computational Linguistics*, pages 3428–3448, Florence, Italy. Association for Computational Linguistics.

Bhargavi Paranjape, Matthew Lamm, and Ian Tenney. 2022. Retrieval-guided counterfactual generation for QA. In *Proceedings of the 60th Annual Meeting of the Association for Computational Linguistics (Volume 1: Long Papers)*, pages 1670–1686, Dublin, Ireland. Association for Computational Linguistics.

Ethan Perez, Sam Ringer, Kamile Lukosiute, Karina Nguyen, Edwin Chen, Scott Heiner, Craig Pettit, Catherine Olsson, Sandipan Kundu, Saurav Kadavath, Andy Jones, Anna Chen, Benjamin Mann, Brian Israel, Bryan Seethor, Cameron McKinnon, Christopher Olah, Da Yan, Daniela Amodei, Dario Amodei, Dawn Drain, Dustin Li, Eli Tran-Johnson, Guro Khundadze, Jackson Kernion, James Landis, Jamie Kerr, Jared Mueller, Jeeyoon Hyun, Joshua Landau, Kamal Ndousse, Landon Goldberg, Liane Lovitt, Martin Lucas, Michael Sellitto, Miranda Zhang, Neerav Kingsland, Nelson Elhage, Nicholas Joseph, Noemi Mercado, Nova DasSarma, Oliver Rausch, Robin Larson, Sam McCandlish, Scott Johnston, Shauna Kravec, Sheer El Showk, Tamera Lanham, Timothy Telleen-Lawton, Tom Brown, Tom Henighan, Tristan Hume, Yuntao Bai, Zac Hatfield-Dodds, Jack Clark, Samuel R. Bowman, Amanda Askell, Roger Grosse, Danny Hernandez, Deep Ganguli, Evan Hubinger, Nicholas Schiefer, and Jared Kaplan. 2023. Discovering language model behaviors with model-written evaluations. In *Findings of the Association for Computational Linguistics: ACL 2023*, pages 13387–13434, Toronto, Canada. Association for Computational Linguistics.

Sara Rajaee, Yadollah Yaghoobzadeh, and Mohammad Taher Pilehvar. 2022. Looking at the overlooked: An analysis on the word-overlap bias in natural language inference. In *Proceedings of the 2022 Conference on Empirical Methods in Natural Language Processing*, pages 10605–10616, Abu Dhabi, United Arab Emirates. Association for Computational Linguistics.

Mohamed El Amine Seddik, Suei-Wen Chen, Soufiane Hayou, Pierre Youssef, and Merouane Abdelkader DEBBAH. 2024. How bad is training on synthetic data? a statistical analysis of language model collapse. In *First Conference on Language Modeling*.

Ilia Shumailov, Zakhar Shumaylov, Yiren Zhao, Nicolas Papernot, Ross Anderson, and Yarin Gal. 2024. Ai models collapse when trained on recursively generated data. *Nature*, 631(8022):755–759.

Prasann Singhal, Tanya Goyal, Jiacheng Xu, and Greg Durrett. 2024. A long way to go: Investigating length correlations in RLHF. In *First Conference on Language Modeling*.

Daniel Susser and Jeremy Seeman. 2024. Critical provocations for synthetic data. *Surveillance and Society*, 22(4):453–459.

Hugo Touvron, Louis Martin, Kevin Stone, Peter Albert, Amjad Almahairi, Yasmine Babaei, Nikolay Bashlykov, Soumya Batra, Prajjwal Bhargava, Shruti Bhosale, et al. 2023. Llama 2: Open foundation and fine-tuned chat models. *arXiv preprint arXiv:2307.09288*.

Yizhong Wang, Yeganeh Kordi, Swaroop Mishra, Alisa Liu, Noah A. Smith, Daniel Khashabi, and Hannaneh Hajishirzi. 2023. Self-instruct: Aligning language models with self-generated instructions. In *Proceedings of the 61st Annual Meeting of the Association for Computational Linguistics (Volume 1: Long Papers)*, pages 13484–13508, Toronto, Canada. Association for Computational Linguistics.

Jerry Wei, Da Huang, Yifeng Lu, Denny Zhou, and Quoc V. Le. 2024. Simple synthetic data reduces sycophancy in large language models. *Preprint*, arXiv:2308.03958.

Cedric Deslandes Whitney and Justin Norman. 2024. Real risks of fake data: Synthetic data, diversity-washing and consent circumvention. In *The 2024 ACM Conference on Fairness, Accountability, and Transparency*, pages 1733–1744.

Adina Williams, Nikita Nangia, and Samuel Bowman. 2018. A broad-coverage challenge corpus for sentence understanding through inference. In *Proceedings of the 2018 Conference of the North American Chapter of the Association for Computational Linguistics: Human Language Technologies, Volume 1 (Long Papers)*, pages 1112–1122, New Orleans, Louisiana. Association for Computational Linguistics.

Yiben Yang, Chaitanya Malaviya, Jared Fernandez, Swabha Swayamdipta, Ronan Le Bras, Ji-Ping Wang, Chandra Bhagavatula, Yejin Choi, and Doug Downey. 2020. Generative data augmentation for commonsense reasoning. In *Findings of the Association for Computational Linguistics: EMNLP 2020*, pages 1008–1025, Online. Association for Computational Linguistics.

Bridging the Faithfulness Gap in Prototypical Models

Andrew Koulogeorge[♠,*]
akouloge@andrew.cmu.edu

Sean Xie[†,*]
sean.xie.gr@dartmouth.edu

Saeed Hassanpour [†,‡]
saeed.hassanpour@dartmouth.edu

Soroush Vosoughi [†]
soroush.vosoughi@dartmouth.edu

♠ Department of Computer Science, Carnegie Mellon University
†Department of Computer Science, ‡Department of Biomedical Data Science, Dartmouth College
* indicates equal contribution.

Abstract

Prototypical Network-based Language Models (PNLMs) have been introduced as a novel approach for enhancing interpretability in deep learning models for Natural Language Processing (NLP). In this work, we show that, despite the transparency afforded by their case-based reasoning architecture, current PNLMs are, in fact, not faithful, i.e. their explanations do not accurately reflect the underlying model's reasoning process. By adopting an axiomatic approach grounded in the seminal works' definition of faithfulness, we identify two specific points in the architecture of PNLMs where unfaithfulness may occur. To address this, we introduce `Faithful Alignment (FA)`, a two-part framework that ensures the faithfulness of PNLMs' explanations. We then demonstrate that `FA` achieves this goal without compromising model performance across downstream tasks and ablation studies.

1 Introduction

In recent years, deep learning-based language models have drastically enhanced performance across various NLP tasks (Vaswani et al., 2017; Radford et al., 2021). Despite their high predictive accuracy, these models remain opaque, meaning their decision-making processes are not easily understandable to humans. Consequently, numerous Explainable AI (XAI) techniques have been developed to interpret model decisions for end users (Ribeiro et al., 2016b; Lundberg and Lee, 2017; Shrikumar et al., 2019). A recent advancement in the XAI domain is the use of prototypical networks for interpretability. Originally introduced for few-shot learning (Snell et al., 2017), prototypical networks offer a unique advantage in interpretability due to their case-based reasoning architecture. Although initially adapted for increased interpretability in Computer Vision (CV) tasks (Chen et al., 2019; Hase et al., 2019; Ma et al., 2023), several recent works in NLP have begun to develop similar prototypical-based models to enhance interpretability in NLP contexts (Xie et al., 2023; Das et al., 2022; Van Aken et al., 2022; Friedrich et al., 2022). Despite their application in a wide range of tasks from propaganda detection (Das et al., 2022) to ICD-9 diagnosis prediction (Van Aken et al., 2022), the *faithfulness*[1] of PNLMs remains unexamined. Faithfulness is a necessary condition for any deployed machine learning model since unfaithful model explanations can lead to dangerous outcomes such as leading a user to trust a model's *incorrect* prediction simply because its explanation looks convincing (Rudin, 2018; Bansal et al., 2021; Lyu et al., 2024).

In this work, we assess the faithfulness of PNLMs using axioms from seminal interpretability studies (Chen et al., 2019) and identify two key flaws in state-of-the-art PNLM architectures (Xie et al., 2023; Das et al., 2022; Van Aken et al., 2022) that result in explanations of current PNLMs to be **unfaithful** (see Figure 1). To address these shortcomings, we propose `Faithful Alignment`, a two-part framework designed to ensure faithful prototypical model explanations. Our contributions are as follows:

1. We define reasoning in prototypical models as comprising (1) class connections in the final linear layer and (2) the similarity between the encoded test example and the learned prototypes in prototypical space. Through this lens, we identify two areas in the existing PNLMs' workflow where their provided explanations deviate from model reasoning and thus are unfaithful.

2. We propose a solution in the form of the `Faithful Alignment` framework (hence-

[1]For additional details on PNLMs, interpretability and faithfulness, we refer the reader to §A

The Sixth Workshop on Insights from Negative Results in NLP, pages 86–99

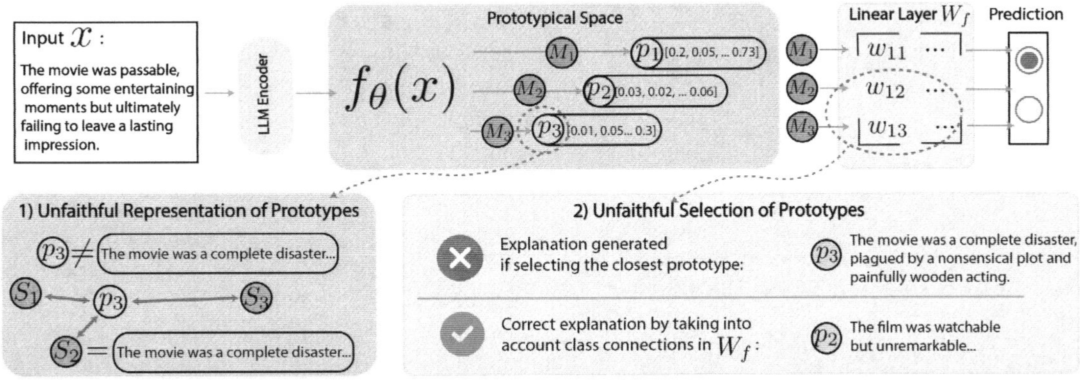

Figure 1: General work flow of Prototypical Network-based Language Models (PNLM). $f_\theta(x)$ is the compressed encoding of the input at test time. p_i is the ith learned prototype and S_i is the compressed encoding of the ith training example. Red circles indicate architectural flaws which can lead to unfaithful explanations: 1) Unfaithful explanations may result from a prototype vector being misrepresented by text from another latent encoding. 2) Unfaithful explanations may result from the wrong prototype being selected as most influential on prediction.

force abbreviated as FA), which addresses the aforementioned faithfulness issues in PNLMs.

3. We empirically validate that our solution for faithfulness in PNLMs does not significantly degrade performance across a wide range of PNLM architectures and tasks (§4). We conduct additional ablation studies to demonstrate the robustness of our framework (§E).

2 Unfaithfulness in Prototypical Networks

We briefly outline the PNLM workflow before describing two architectural shortcomings that lead to unfaithfulness. Let f_θ be a language model (e.g., BERT) such that $f_\theta : \mathbb{R}^{L\times d} \rightarrow \mathbb{R}^H$ where f_θ maps x, a sequence of L embedded tokens, to a compressed hidden representation $f_\theta(x) \in \mathbb{R}^H$. Through specialized training objectives, the PNLM learns $P = \{p_j\}_{j=1}^m$, a set of m prototypes where $p_j \in \mathbb{R}^H$. During inference, the PNLM feeds $f_\theta(x)$ into the prototypical space to obtain $M \in \mathbb{R}^m$ where M_j is the similarity between $f_\theta(x)$ and p_j. These similarities in M are then either passed through a final linear layer $W_f \in \mathbb{R}^{C\times m}$ to produce logits for prediction[2] (Das et al., 2022; Xie et al., 2023) or are used directly to obtain a prediction (Van Aken et al., 2022). This architecture enables PNLMs to generate textual explanations by (a) identifying the most influential prototypes for prediction and (b) extracting textual representation from those prototypes. In the following subsections, we analyze the unfaithfulness of existing PNLMs through the lenses of (a) and (b).

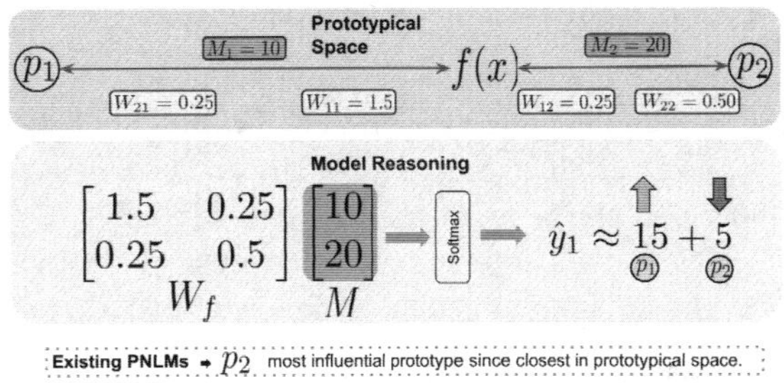

Figure 2: Example of how existing PNLMs are susceptible to incorrectly identifying the most influential prototypes. The prototype with the largest influence on prediction is p_1 due to W_{11}'s large magnitude, despite p_2 being closest to $f_\theta(x)$ in the prototypical space. Since existing PNLM's derive their explanations from prototypes chosen solely based on distance in the prototypical space, existing works would incorrectly identify p_2 as most influential on prediction.

2.1 Unfaithful Selection of Prototypes

First, we investigate how existing PNLMs can exhibit unfaithfulness when selecting the most influential prototypes. Despite Xie et al. (2023) and Das et al. (2022) claiming to use the most influential prototypes when deriving their explanations, both *only* consider proximity in the prototypical space when ranking prototype influence. **By neglecting the impact of W_f on prediction, previous works do not capture the full reasoning pro-**

[2] Similarity calculation and training objectives for existing PNLMs vary. For details, please refer to §C.2

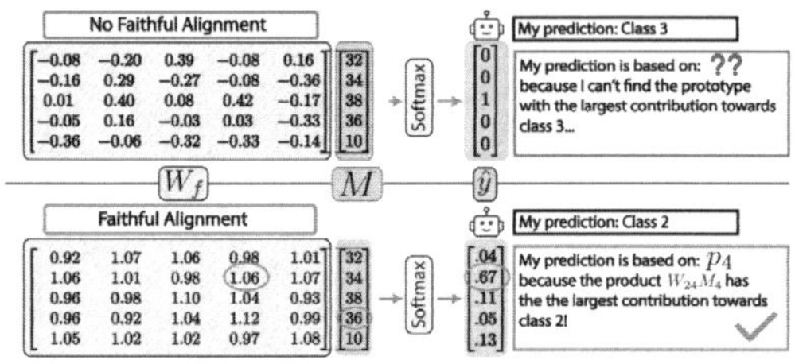

Figure 3: Empirical Demonstration of Faithful Retrieval with ProtoTex model on SST5 with 5 prototypes. (Top) without FR, negative reasoning in W_f clouds the model's ability to discern the most influential prototype. (Bottom) After FR, the PNLM is able to unambiguously determine the most influential prototype.

cess of PNLMs and thus are prone to unfaithful explanations (We show such an example in Figure 2). In this section, we eliminate the ambiguity surrounding reasoning for PNLMs by defining it *directly* based on the computations that dictate model output. The output logit of class c is calculated as:

$$\hat{y_c} = \sum_{j=1}^{m} W_{cj} M_j \tag{1}$$

where the product $W_{cj}M_j$ is the *total* contribution of the jth prototype on predicting the cth class. Because similarity measures are multiplied by W_f to obtain logits, **the reasoning process of PNLMs is the combined effect of distance calculation and weighted product in the final layer**. Since faithfulness is defined as the extent to which explanations accurately reflect a model's reasoning process (Jacovi and Goldberg, 2020), and W_f directly affects model prediction, current PNLMs that neglect the impact of W_f when generating the most influential prototypes are **unfaithful.** In this work, we contend that to accurately represent model reasoning, PNLMs (and Prototypical Networks at large) *must* generate their explanations using both the similarity between the example $f_\theta(x)$ and prototype p_j, along with the $W_{cj} \in W$ weighting their distance[3]. Moreover, current PNLM architectures (Das et al., 2022; Xie et al., 2023) permit negative parameters in W_f which leads the model to utilize negative reasoning, thus obscuring the determination of the prototype that contributed most significantly to model output. Specifically, the model may predict a particular class because it's confident the example *does not* belong to other classes. In Figure 3 (Top), we show an instance of how negative parameters in W_f create ambiguity in identifying the most contributing prototype *even when accounting for the combined effects of similarity measures M and their weights W_f.*

2.2 Unfaithful Representation of Prototypes

Second, unfaithfulness can occur in PNLMs when prototypes are represented by text that inaccurately reflects model reasoning. Let D be the training data set and $S = \{f_\theta(x_i) \mid \forall\, x_i \in D\}$ be the set of encoded training data where we denote $S_i = f_\theta(x_i)$. Since each prototype $p_j \in P$ is a learned, dense vector in $\mathbb{R}^H$, there does not exist a direct, human-interpretable textual representation of p_j. In order to render these inherently opaque prototypes understandable to humans, existing PNLMs represent their prototypes using the text of the most similar [4] encoded training example S_i. More formally, a PNLM obtains a human-readable textual representation for prototype p_j via the following assignation:

$$\text{Text of } [p_j] \leftarrow \text{Text of} \left[\arg\min_{S_i} \|S_i - p_j\|_2^2 \right] \tag{2}$$

where Text of $[S_i]$ is the raw text associated with the embedded token sequence x_i. We illustrate this process in Figure 4 (Left). Since prototypes are represented by S_i, which does not partake in *any* of the model's computation, explanations utilizing S_i do not accurately reflect model reasoning and are therefore unfaithful (Jacovi and Goldberg, 2020). We empirically evaluate this imprecision in explanations as the *faithfulness gap* in Figure 4 (Right). If current PNLMs are indeed *inherently faithful* as they claim to be, our experiments should reveal the textual representations (S_i) to align with the parameters involved in computation, i.e. there should be no difference between each textual encoding S_i and p_j (green box). Nonetheless, our experiments in Figure 4 show that there exists a non-zero faithfulness gap for every prototype in SOTA PNLM architectures (Das et al., 2022; Xie et al., 2023).

3 Solution: Faithful Alignment

In this section we describe Faithful Alignment (FA), a two-part solution consisting of Faithful Retrieval (FR) and Faithful Projection (FP).

[3]Note that for (Van Aken et al., 2022) $W_f = I$

[4]The most similar example is defined as the minimum L_2 distance in the prototypical space

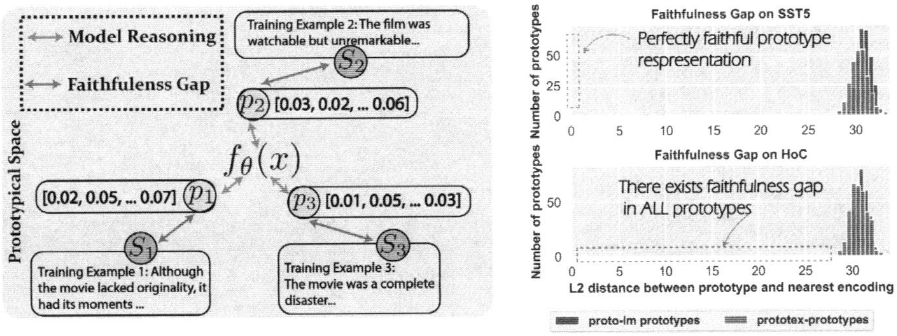

Figure 4: (Left) Faithfulness Gap in the Prototypical Space for PNLMs. The distance between a test time example $f(x)$ and the learned prototypes p_j influences the model's prediction, yet the model's explanations for p_j are derived from S_i which *does not* participate in the computation of the output. (Right) Faithfulness gap evaluated for `proto-lm` and `ProtoTex` on two datasets (SST5 and HoC). For each learned prototype p_j, we compute the L_2 distance to the encoding of its assigned textual representation. The green box indicates prototype representations that would be perfectly faithful i.e. 0 faithfulness gap. The red box highlights the fact that there exists a faithfulness gap for all prototypes in both models, empirically demonstrating the misalignment between model reasoning and model explanations.

3.1 `Faithful Retrieval`

To enable PNLMs to faithfully select prototypes for explanations, we propose the following two constraints, which, together, form `Faithful Retrieval`:

- If k textual explanations are provided by a PNLM, the k prototypes must be retrieved via:

$$\arg\max_{j} {}_k \{W_{\hat{c}j} M_j \mid \forall j \in [m]\} \quad (3)$$

  where $W_{\hat{c}l}$ represents the class connection between the output class $\hat{c}$ and prototype j. More concretely, suppose that the predicted class is $\hat{c}$. `FR` then selects top k most influential prototypes computing all m weight/distance pairs $W_{\hat{c}j} M_j$ and returning prototypes at the largest k pairs' indices.

- All class connections in W_f that weigh incoming similarity measures must be positive

$$\{W_{cj} > 0 \mid \forall j \in [m], \forall c \in C\} \quad (4)$$

Equation 3 ensures that prototypes' influence takes into account both similarity M and weights W_f. Equation 4 prevents PNLM from utilizing negative reasoning in the final layer which obstructs the identification of the most influential prototype. In Figure 3 (bottom), we show an example where the application of `FR` allows us to unambiguously determine the top k most influential prototypes by directly comparing their contributions ($W_{cj} M_j$) towards the output. Together, Equations 3 and 4 formalize the procedure for robust prototype selection, a crucial detail neglected by the works of Das et al. (2022) and Xie et al. (2023) that lead to unfaithfulness.

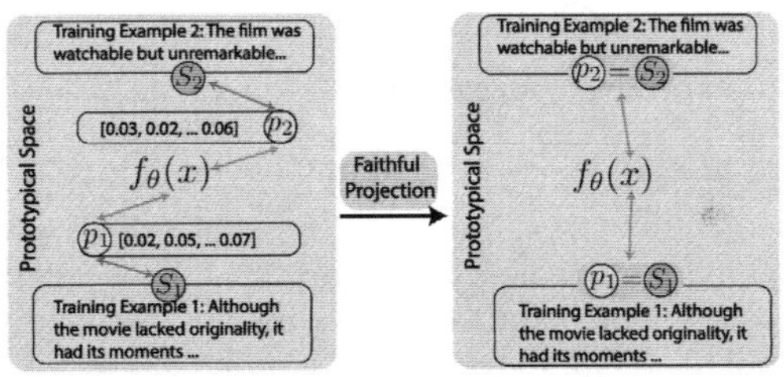

Figure 5: Illustration of Faithful Projection's effect in the prototypical space. `FP` aligns the PNLM's reasoning and explanations by forcing each prototype to become exactly equal to an encoded training example.

3.2 `Faithful Projection`

To ensure that PNLM explanations participate in the models computation, we propose Faithful Projection (FP) which endows each prototype with an encoding from the training dataset. More formally, let $S_i \in S$ be the encoding of a known example in D. For each prototype in the prototypical layer, we perform the following projection after training:

$$p_j = \arg\min_{S_i} \|S_i - p_j\|_2^2 \quad \forall\, j \in [m] \quad (5)$$

`FP` closes the faithfulness gap by forcing each

PNLM	Base LLM	SST2	SST5	QNLI	RTE	HoC	AVg Gain/Loss (per PNLM)
Proto-lm + (FA) / Proto-lm	BERT-base	**90.8/90.0**	50.3/53.2	**85.9/85.8**	67.5/68.6	**94.0/84.3**	+0.72
	RoBERTa-large	**92.4/92.3**	47.4/52.9	**87.9/87.8**	**62.8/62.1**	–	
	BART-large	92.2/92.4	55.8/54.8	**89.0/89.0**	74.7/75.1	–	
	ELECTRA	**93.3/90.1**	**50.1/47.3**	**91.0/90.1**	**74.8/74.7**	**54.3/49.9***	
	Llama-2-7b	**93.6/91.2**	47.7/48.3	**92.2/91.3**	**80.3/80.0**	36.7/36.9*	
ProtoTex + (FA) / ProtoTex	BERT-base	**91.1/90.8**	48.7/50.5	82.0/90.3	53.0/66.7	89.3/95.3	-2.94
	RoBERTa-large	92.3/94.0	**46.7/44.4**	83.5/92.3	52.7/60.0	–	
	BART-large	94.6/95.9	51.3/52.2	88.9/93.2	63.1/77.6	–	
	ELECTRA	**95.0/94.8**	47.6/49.2	**92.3/92.2**	72.2/73.2	52.1/51.0*	
	Llama-2-7b	**94.3/94.3**	43.0/44.3	93.5/93.6	**81.3/81.0**	32.5/36.0*	
ProtoPatient + (FA) / ProtoPatient	BERT-base	**91.7/91.7**	**52.1/51.0**	**82.8/82.7**	**67.5/64.2**	**94.5/93.0**	+0.64
	RoBERTa-large	**91.5/91.4**	53.7/54.0	**84.2/84.2**	**76.5/72.9**	–	
	BART-large	**90.8/90.8**	49.7/53.8	**87.4/87.4**	**77.6/73.3**	–	
Avg Gain/Loss (per task):		**+0.30**	-0.91	-1.48	-1.95	**+1.47**	

Table 1: Performance of FA on NLP tasks and across PNLM architectures. **Bolded** numbers indicate scenarios where the FA-applied PNLM achieved performance that is higher than or equivalent to the regular PNLM. Overall, we observe that FA-applied models experience only minor decreases in accuracy. Results with * are obtained from PNLMs with a base LM that was *not* finetuned on the task (HoC), hence relatively lower performance. We note that, even in these cases, applying FA did not significantly degrade the performance of the PNLM.

prototype to become an encoding from the training dataset. Figure. 5 provides an illustration of this process. After FP, textual representations now directly reflect the parameters contributing to modeling reasoning. Thus, FP not only allows us to map a continuous prototype tensor onto discrete words for human comprehension but also align PNLMs' prototype-based explanations completely with model reasoning.

4 Effect of FA on Downstream Tasks

Because FA makes PNLM architectures mechanically faithful, it is important to examine its impact on model performance. Specifically, we conduct experiments to compare the performance of PNLMs without FA against FA-applied PNLMs. In Table 1, we verify that FA does not degrade accuracy on downstream tasks on a wide range of PNLM architectures (§C.2), base LLM encoders and NLP tasks (§C.1) . Our experimental results indicate that FA-applied models performs well overall, with only minor reductions in performance across NLP tasks. To further demonstrate the robustness of FA, we also conduct ablation studies in §E. We believe the robust performance of FA shows its promise as a framework for ensuring faithfulness for prototypical networks while maintaining performance.

5 Conclusion

In this work, we build on foundational ideas in XAI, interpretability, and faithfulness to identify two key shortcomings of existing PNLMs that cause their explanations to be unfaithful: 1) the selection of incorrect prototypes for explanation, and 2) the misrepresentation of prototypes in model reasoning. To address these issues, we introduce a faithfulness-ensuring framework, FA, and validate its robustness through extensive experiments. We believe our contribution bridges a crucial gap in the current understanding of faithfulness in the context of prototypical models. We hope future prototypical networks can leverage our framework to prevent unfaithful explanations.

6 Limitations

We outline several limitations of our work below:

- Despite the improvements made to the faithfulness of PNLMs through FA, they still remain dependent on an underlying language model to convert text into a semantic space. Consequently, the interpretability of PNLMs is still constrained by the interpretability of the foundational language model.
- Additionally, while the case-based reasoning of FA-applied PNLM explanations is faithful, the cases used for explanation are restricted to examples from the training set. This limit on the *expressiveness* of the interpretability of PNLMs is an area that warrants further research and exploration.
- Moreover, a significant issue affecting the faithfulness of current PNLMs is that LLM embeddings cannot be directly translated back into discrete words. Making progress in this research area will not only resolve a key unfaithfulness issue addressed by our framework

but will also greatly benefit the field of interpretability as a whole.

7 Ethics Statement

All datasets used in our experiments are publicly available datasets. None of the experimental data directly utilized and/or collected in our experiments is related to identifiable individuals, ensuring that all data remains anonymous by nature. We conducted our experiments with a focus on transparency and reproducibility. Any potential limitations of our experiments are thoroughly analyzed and discussed.

8 Acknowledgements

This research was supported in part by grants from the US National Library of Medicine (R01LM012837 & R01LM013833), the US National Cancer Institute (R01CA249758), the US National Science Foundation (NSF Award 2242072), and the John Templeton Foundation. The authors extend their sincerest gratitude to Andrew Brennan, Yiren Jian, Alex DeJournett, Alan Sun and Jeffrey Jiang for their help and support during the research process. Additionally, the authors would also like to thank Akira Toriyama, who passed away during the preparation of this work. Toriyama's art touched countless lives, including our own, inspiring many to face life's challenges with courage and determination.

References

Abien Fred Agarap. 2018. Deep learning using rectified linear units (relu). *arXiv preprint arXiv:1803.08375*.

Pepa Atanasova, Jakob Grue Simonsen, Christina Lioma, and Isabelle Augenstein. 2020. A diagnostic study of explainability techniques for text classification. *arXiv preprint arXiv:2009.13295*.

Simon Baker, Ilona Silins, Yufan Guo, Imran Ali, Johan Högberg, Ulla Stenius, and Anna Korhonen. 2015. Automatic semantic classification of scientific literature according to the hallmarks of cancer. *Bioinformatics*, 32(3):432–440.

Gagan Bansal, Tongshuang Wu, Joyce Zhou, Raymond Fok, Besmira Nushi, Ece Kamar, Marco Tulio Ribeiro, and Daniel Weld. 2021. Does the whole exceed its parts? the effect of ai explanations on complementary team performance. In *Proceedings of the 2021 CHI Conference on Human Factors in Computing Systems*, CHI '21, New York, NY, USA. Association for Computing Machinery.

Rich Caruana, Yin Lou, Johannes Gehrke, Paul Koch, Marc Sturm, and Noemie Elhadad. 2015. Intelligible models for healthcare: Predicting pneumonia risk and hospital 30-day readmission. In *Proceedings of the 21th ACM SIGKDD international conference on knowledge discovery and data mining*, pages 1721–1730.

Diogo V Carvalho, Eduardo M Pereira, and Jaime S Cardoso. 2019. Machine learning interpretability: A survey on methods and metrics. *Electronics*, 8(8):832.

Aaron Chan, Maziar Sanjabi, Lambert Mathias, Liang Tan, Shaoliang Nie, Xiaochang Peng, Xiang Ren, and Hamed Firooz. 2022. Unirex: A unified learning framework for language model rationale extraction. In *International Conference on Machine Learning*.

Chaofan Chen, Oscar Li, Daniel Tao, Alina Barnett, Cynthia Rudin, and Jonathan K Su. 2019. This looks like that: deep learning for interpretable image recognition. *Advances in neural information processing systems*, 32.

Kevin Clark, Minh-Thang Luong, Quoc V Le, and Christopher D Manning. 2020. Electra: Pre-training text encoders as discriminators rather than generators. *arXiv preprint arXiv:2003.10555*.

Ido Dagan, Oren Glickman, and Bernardo Magnini. 2005. The pascal recognising textual entailment challenge. In *Machine learning challenges workshop*, pages 177–190. Springer.

Anubrata Das, Chitrank Gupta, Venelin Kovatchev, Matthew Lease, and Junyi Jessy Li. 2022. Prototex: Explaining model decisions with prototype tensors. *arXiv preprint arXiv:2204.05426*.

Jacob Devlin, Ming-Wei Chang, Kenton Lee, and Kristina Toutanova. 2018. Bert: Pre-training of deep bidirectional transformers for language understanding. *arXiv preprint arXiv:1810.04805*.

Jay DeYoung, Sarthak Jain, Nazneen Fatema Rajani, Eric Lehman, Caiming Xiong, Richard Socher, and Byron C. Wallace. 2020. Eraser: A benchmark to evaluate rationalized nlp models.

Finale Doshi-Velez and Been Kim. 2017. Towards a rigorous science of interpretable machine learning. *arXiv preprint arXiv:1702.08608*.

Radwa ElShawi, Youssef Sherif, Mouaz Al-Mallah, and Sherif Sakr. 2021. Interpretability in healthcare: A comparative study of local machine learning interpretability techniques. *Computational Intelligence*, 37(4):1633–1650.

Felix Friedrich, Patrick Schramowski, Christopher Tauchmann, and Kristian Kersting. 2022. Interactively providing explanations for transformer language models.

Tianyu Gao, Xu Han, Zhiyuan Liu, and Maosong Sun. 2019. Hybrid attention-based prototypical networks for noisy few-shot relation classification. In *Proceedings of the AAAI Conference on Artificial Intelligence*, volume 33, pages 6407–6414.

Peter Hase, Chaofan Chen, Oscar Li, and Cynthia Rudin. 2019. Interpretable image recognition with hierarchical prototypes. In *Proceedings of the AAAI Conference on Human Computation and Crowdsourcing*, volume 7, pages 32–40.

Qihan Huang, Mengqi Xue, Wenqi Huang, Haofei Zhang, Jie Song, Yongcheng Jing, and Mingli Song. 2023. Evaluation and improvement of interpretability for self-explainable part-prototype networks. In *Proceedings of the IEEE/CVF International Conference on Computer Vision*, pages 2011–2020.

Alon Jacovi and Yoav Goldberg. 2020. Towards faithfully interpretable nlp systems: How should we define and evaluate faithfulness? *arXiv preprint arXiv:2004.03685*.

Zhong Ji, Xingliang Chai, Yunlong Yu, Yanwei Pang, and Zhongfei Zhang. 2020. Improved prototypical networks for few-shot learning. *Pattern Recognition Letters*, 140:81–87.

José Jiménez-Luna, Francesca Grisoni, and Gisbert Schneider. 2020. Drug discovery with explainable artificial intelligence. *Nature Machine Intelligence*, 2(10):573–584.

Mike Lewis, Yinhan Liu, Naman Goyal, Marjan Ghazvininejad, Abdelrahman Mohamed, Omer Levy, Ves Stoyanov, and Luke Zettlemoyer. 2019. Bart: Denoising sequence-to-sequence pre-training for natural language generation, translation, and comprehension. *arXiv preprint arXiv:1910.13461*.

Zachary C Lipton. 2018. The mythos of model interpretability: In machine learning, the concept of interpretability is both important and slippery. *Queue*, 16(3):31–57.

Yinhan Liu, Myle Ott, Naman Goyal, Jingfei Du, Mandar Joshi, Danqi Chen, Omer Levy, Mike Lewis, Luke Zettlemoyer, and Veselin Stoyanov. 2019. Roberta: A robustly optimized bert pretraining approach. *arXiv preprint arXiv:1907.11692*.

Scott Lundberg and Su-In Lee. 2017. A unified approach to interpreting model predictions.

Qing Lyu, Marianna Apidianaki, and Chris Callison-Burch. 2024. Towards Faithful Model Explanation in NLP: A Survey. *Computational Linguistics*, pages 1–67.

Chiyu Ma, Brandon Zhao, Chaofan Chen, and Cynthia Rudin. 2023. This looks like those: Illuminating prototypical concepts using multiple visualizations.

Andrew L. Maas, Raymond E. Daly, Peter T. Pham, Dan Huang, Andrew Y. Ng, and Christopher Potts. 2011. Learning word vectors for sentiment analysis. In *Proceedings of the 49th Annual Meeting of the Association for Computational Linguistics: Human Language Technologies*, pages 142–150, Portland, Oregon, USA. Association for Computational Linguistics.

Ibrahim Naji. 2012. TSATC: Twitter Sentiment Analysis Training Corpus. In *thinknook*.

Alec Radford, Jong Wook Kim, Chris Hallacy, Aditya Ramesh, Gabriel Goh, Sandhini Agarwal, Girish Sastry, Amanda Askell, Pamela Mishkin, Jack Clark, Gretchen Krueger, and Ilya Sutskever. 2021. Learning transferable visual models from natural language supervision.

Marco Tulio Ribeiro, Sameer Singh, and Carlos Guestrin. 2016a. " why should i trust you?" explaining the predictions of any classifier. In *Proceedings of the 22nd ACM SIGKDD international conference on knowledge discovery and data mining*, pages 1135–1144.

Marco Tulio Ribeiro, Sameer Singh, and Carlos Guestrin. 2016b. "why should i trust you?": Explaining the predictions of any classifier.

Cynthia Rudin. 2018. Please stop explaining black box models for high stakes decisions. *Stat*, 1050(26):457.

Avanti Shrikumar, Peyton Greenside, and Anshul Kundaje. 2019. Learning important features through propagating activation differences.

Jake Snell, Kevin Swersky, and Richard S. Zemel. 2017. Prototypical networks for few-shot learning.

Richard Socher, Alex Perelygin, Jean Wu, Jason Chuang, Christopher D. Manning, Andrew Ng, and Christopher Potts. 2013. Recursive deep models for semantic compositionality over a sentiment treebank. In *Proceedings of the 2013 Conference on Empirical Methods in Natural Language Processing*, pages 1631–1642, Seattle, Washington, USA. Association for Computational Linguistics.

Shengli Sun, Qingfeng Sun, Kevin Zhou, and Tengchao Lv. 2019. Hierarchical attention prototypical networks for few-shot text classification. In *Proceedings of the 2019 conference on empirical methods in natural language processing and the 9th international joint conference on natural language processing (EMNLP-IJCNLP)*, pages 476–485.

Hugo Touvron, Louis Martin, Kevin Stone, Peter Albert, Amjad Almahairi, Yasmine Babaei, Nikolay Bashlykov, Soumya Batra, Prajjwal Bhargava, Shruti Bhosale, et al. 2023. Llama 2: Open foundation and fine-tuned chat models. *arXiv preprint arXiv:2307.09288*.

Betty Van Aken, Jens-Michalis Papaioannou, Marcel G Naik, Georgios Eleftheriadis, Wolfgang Nejdl, Felix A Gers, and Alexander Löser. 2022. This patient looks like that patient: Prototypical networks for interpretable diagnosis prediction from clinical text. *arXiv preprint arXiv:2210.08500*.

Ashish Vaswani, Noam Shazeer, Niki Parmar, Jakob Uszkoreit, Llion Jones, Aidan N. Gomez, Lukasz Kaiser, and Illia Polosukhin. 2017. Attention is all you need.

Alex Wang, Amanpreet Singh, Julian Michael, Felix Hill, Omer Levy, and Samuel R Bowman. 2018. Glue: A multi-task benchmark and analysis platform for natural language understanding. *arXiv preprint arXiv:1804.07461*.

Sean Xie, Soroush Vosoughi, and Saeed Hassanpour. 2023. Proto-lm: A prototypical network-based framework for built-in interpretability in large language models. *arXiv preprint arXiv:2311.01732*.

Sean Xie, Soroush Vosoughi, and Saeed Hassanpour. 2024. Ivra: A framework to enhance attention-based explanations for language models with interpretability-driven training. In *Proceedings of the 7th BlackboxNLP Workshop: Analyzing and Interpreting Neural Networks for NLP*, pages 431–451.

A Additional Related Works and Background

A.1 Prototypical Networks and Interpretability

Prototypical networks (Snell et al., 2017) originated as a type of few-shot learning model designed to classify new examples by comparing them to class prototypes obtained via averaging instances of each class in an embedding space (Ji et al., 2020). The transparency of prototypical models and their intuitive case-based reasoning process led to their adoption to interpret deep neural networks (Gao et al., 2019; Sun et al., 2019; Chen et al., 2019; Hase et al., 2019). Continued development in XAI has revealed the multi-facetedness of the field of interpretability (Doshi-Velez and Kim, 2017; Lipton, 2018). There now exists various different aspects in interpretability such as "plausibility" (how convincing explanations are to humans (Jacovi and Goldberg, 2020; ElShawi et al., 2021; Chan et al., 2022)), or "consistency" (similarity between explanations for similar inputs) (Carvalho et al., 2019; Atanasova et al., 2020; Xie et al., 2024). In this work, we focus on the criterion of ***faithfulness***, which is qualitatively described as how accurately a model's reasoning process is reflected in its explanations (Ribeiro et al., 2016a; Jacovi and Goldberg, 2020; Lyu et al., 2024). Recent research has shown that ***faithfulness*** has emerged as a crucial interpretability criterion since unfaithful explanations pose risks in high-stakes areas. (Caruana et al., 2015; Rudin, 2018; Jiménez-Luna et al., 2020).

A.2 Existing Techniques for Measuring Faithfulness and Pitfalls

A plethora of techniques have emerged to evaluate the faithfulness of model explanations. These techniques include Axiomatic Evaluation (prove unfaithfulness by showing necessary faithfulness assumptions are violated), Simulatability (using model explainations to predict model outputs), Perturbation Methods (stability of explanation under input perturbation), and others. (Lyu et al., 2024). **Unfortunately, no definitive measure of faithfulness exists in the XAI community** and evaluation metrics are often not directly comparable with each other and yield inconsistent results, making it difficult to objectively assess progress. (Lyu et al., 2024). Regarding the interpretability of prototypical networks, works that quantify model faithfulness have done so on a token/pixel level on the input text/image[5]. For example, Huang et al. 2023 defines Inconsistency and Instability to understand variations in the pixel attribution map on top of the test-time example, and Van Aken et al. 2022 applies the benchmark established by Atanasova et al. 2020 to quantify the faithfulness of highlighted input tokens compared to post-hoc methods. While these metrics are significant in their own right, they do not capture the faithfulness of explanations generated on the example level from the prototype itself (training image patches in CV, training text examples in NLP). Specifically, they ignore the question of whether or not the prototype was accurately *identified* or *represented* in the first place. On the whole, existing faithfulness metrics fall short in measuring the faithfulness of prototypical networks effectively. We will show in §2 that prototypical networks, even those asserting to be faithful by design suffer from underlying faithfulness issues.

A.3 Axiomatic Evaluation of Faithfulness in Prototypical Networks

On gauging the faithfulness of prototypical networks, the seminal work of Chen et al. 2019 took an axiomatic approach in their evaluation strategy.

[5]The work of Xie et al. (2023) attempted to extend existing faithfulness metrics to the example level , but we believe these metrics were applied incorrectly. We delve into details in §F

Chen et al. 2019 emphasized that their architecture is faithful by design by establishing a direct connection between their generated explanations and the computations driving predictions. When adapting prototypical networks to NLP, similar mechanical arguments were made to assert model faithfulness, but **without** the necessary architectural design to support these claims. In this work, we aim to expose the faithfulness shortcomings in current PNLM architectures by leveraging the same axiomatic analysis employed by (Chen et al., 2019). Specifically, recent works (Das et al., 2022; Van Aken et al., 2022; Xie et al., 2023) on PNLM have failed to align prototypes with latent training examples and has neglected prototype influence on prediction when generating explanations. For further discussion on our evaluation of faithfulness, see §F.

B Proto-lm Faux Faithfulness

As noted in the related works section, Xie et al. 2023 is the only work to our knowledge that claim's PNLM's are faithful on the example level. In this section, we outline why we believe the faithfulness experiments in Xie et al. 2023 were faulty and resulted in a false sense of model faithfulness.

Xie et al. 2023 extends the perturbation based metrics introduced in DeYoung et al. 2020, Comprehensiveness and Sufficiency, to claim the faithfulness of their PNLMs explanations. In the original work, DeYoung et al. 2020 defined these metrics with respect to a model's explanations (or "rationals", as they refereed to them) which are highlighted input tokens. Let x_i be the original input text sequence, r_i be the models explanation, and $m(x_i)_j$ be the original prediction provided by a model m for class j. The Comprehensiveness and Sufficiency of the models explanation r_i are numerically defined by:

$$\text{Comprehensiveness} = m(x_i)_j - m(x_i/r_i)_j \quad (6)$$

$$\text{Sufficiency} = m(x_i)_j - m(r_i)_j \quad (7)$$

See Figure 6 for an illustration of how Comprehensiveness and Sufficiency are computed as defined in DeYoung et al. 2020. Intuitively, these metrics are measuring how the model's performance changes when the model's explanation is taken away and when only the explanation is available to the model, allowing us to quantify how much the model is leveraging its explanations for its predictions. For more detail, see the original work. (DeYoung et al., 2020)

Xie et al. 2023 extends these metrics to prototypical networks by treating PNLM prototypes as rationales, which were previously considered to be highlighted tokens from the input text r_i. Comprehensiveness and Sufficiency were then computed based on analyzing the model's prediction change when removing/retaining prototypes from the last layer during inference following the same Equations as 6 and 7.

As demonstrated in this work, without FA, prototypes in PNLMs (like Proto-lm) are not utilized for generating model explanations; instead, the nearest training encoding to the prototype is used. The explanations for existing PNLMs without FA is the text associated with the nearest training encoding S_i to each prototype, yet S_i appears nowhere in Xie et al. 2023's faithfulness experiments.

We illustrate the faithfulness gap between the tensors PNLMs reason with and the tensors PNLMs generate explanations with in Figure 4. From the Faithfulness Gap, its clear that the experiments conducted in Xie et al. 2023 did not incorporate the PNLM's explanation in the experimentation at all, leading Sufficiency and Comprehensiveness to fail to quantify the faithfulness of the PNLM's explanations and ultimately lead to a false sense of the model's faithfulness.

We note that if FA was applied to Proto-lm, aligning the prototypes with latent training examples, the efficacy of Comprehensiveness and Sufficiency measuring the faithfulness of the model's explanations would be restored since then the prototypes would be faithfully interpretable as the model's explanations. We excluded this experiment comparing Comprehensiveness and Sufficiency before and after applying FA to a PNLM since the results obtained in the former case are meaningless- without FA, the PNLM explanations are derived from S_i, which does not participate in the original experimentation from Xie et al. 2023 at all.

C Experimental Details

C.1 Datasets and Tasks

The datasets and tasks in our experiments in Table. 1 include sentiment classification (Socher et al., 2013) , natural language inference(Wang et al., 2018), entailment recognition (Dagan et al., 2005),

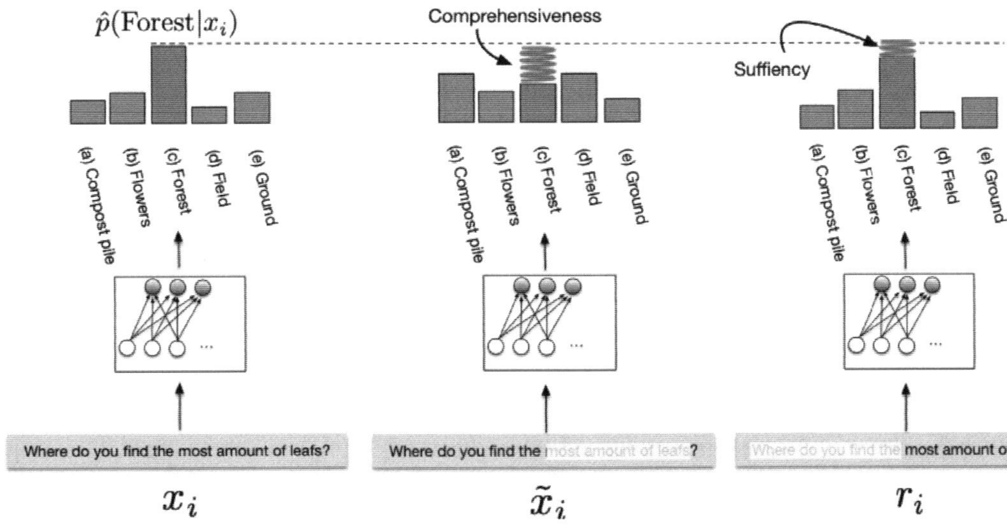

Figure 6: An illustration of how Comprehensiveness and Sufficiency are computed based on an input text sequence x_i and the models explanation, which is a highlighted sequence of input tokens, r_i. Figure from (DeYoung et al., 2020)

and cancer type classification (Baker et al., 2015). We use BERT (Devlin et al., 2018), RoBERTa (Liu et al., 2019), BART (Lewis et al., 2019), ELECTRA (Clark et al., 2020) and Llama-2 (Touvron et al., 2023) as base models upon which we implement PNLM architectures described in the following section.

C.2 PNLM Architecture Description

In this section we provide brief descriptions of the following three PNLMs architectures pertinent to our experiments in §4.

C.2.1 Proto-lm

Let P denote the set of its prototypes, `proto-lm` (Xie et al., 2023) utilizes $|P| = N$ prototypes that are evenly distributed between C classes i.e. each prototype is assigned a class $c \in C$, with each class c having $\frac{N}{C}$ prototypes. To obtain $f_\theta(x_i)$, `proto-lm` leverages a token-attention layer that takes $x_i \in \mathbb{R}^{L \times d}$ to $f_\theta(x_i) \in \mathbb{R}^H$. Similarities measures M in `protolm` are obtained via taking the inverse L2 distance between the prototypical encoding $f_\theta(x_i)$ and $p \in P$. During training `proto-lm` seeks to minimize a cohesion loss term $\mathscr{L}_{coh}$ and maximize a separation loss term $\mathscr{L}_{sep}$. Let K be an integer hyperparameter, p_j be a prototype, and P_{y_i} represent all prototypes in P that belong to class y_i, the cohesion and separation loss terms in `proto-lm` are defined respectively:

$$\mathscr{L}_{coh} = \frac{1}{K} \cdot \sum_{\forall j: p_j \in P_{y_i}} \max_K \|S_i - p_j\|_2^2 \quad (8)$$

$$\mathscr{L}_{sep} = -\frac{1}{K} \cdot \sum_{\forall j: p_j \notin P_{y_i}} \min_K \|S_i - p_j\|_2^2 \quad (9)$$

During training, `proto-lm` incorporates the above two loss terms along with standard cross entropy loss into its training objective. The architecture of `proto-lm` utilizes class connections with preset directions. Specifically, let j_c indicate the class assigned to prototype j, all class connections in W_f between class c' and prototypes that have $j_c = c'$ are positive and class connections between class c' and prototypes with class $j_c \in \{C \setminus c'\}$ are negative. i.e.

$$W_{\{j, j_c\}} \geq 0 \;\; \forall j \;\; \text{s.t.} \;\; j_c = c' \quad (10)$$

$$W_{\{j, j_c\}} \leq 0 \;\; \forall j \;\; \text{s.t.} \;\; j_c \neq c' \quad (11)$$

When applying `FR` to `proto-lm`, we set all class connections between prototype j and classes $c \in \{C \setminus c'\}$ to 0. Formally, we perform the following update after training, let $jc \in C$:

$$W_{\{j, j_c\}} \leftarrow 0 \;\; \forall j \;\; \text{s.t.} \;\; j_c \neq c' \quad (12)$$

When applying `FP` on `proto-lm`, all encodings projected are restricted to encodings from the same class as each prototype.

PNLM	Base LLM	SST2	SST5	QNLI	RTE	HoC
Proto-lm + (FA) / Proto-lm	BERT-base	3e-6/64/1000	3e-6/16/200	3e-5/16/800	3e-5/16/200	3e-6/32/1100
	RoBERTa-large	3e-5/64/1000	3e-5/64/200	3e-5/16/800	3e-6/16/200	–
	BART-large	3e-5/64/1000	3e-5/64/200	3e-5/16/800	3e-5/16/200	–
	ELECTRA	3e-6/32/1000	3e-6/32/200	3e-5/16/800	3e-6/16/200	3e-6/32/200
	Llama-2-7b	3e-6/16/400	3e-6/16/200	3e-6/16/400	3e-6/16/200	3e-6/16/200
ProtoTex + (FA) / ProtoTex	BERT-base	3e-5/64/200	3e-5/64/200	3e-5/16/200	3e-5/16/200	3e-7/64/220
	RoBERTa-large	3e-5/64/200	3e-5/64/200	3e-5/16/200	3e-6/16/200	–
	BART-large	3e-5/64/200	3e-5/64/200	3e-5/16/200	3e-5/16/200	–
	ELECTRA	3e-6/32/1000	3e-6/32/200	3e-5/16/800	3e-6/16/200	3e-6/32/200
	Llama-2-7b	3e-6/16/400	3e-6/16/200	3e-6/16/400	3e-6/16/200	3e-6/16/200
ProtoPatient + (FA)	BERT-base	3e-5/64/5	3e-5/64/5	3e-5/64/2	3e-5/64/2	3e-5/32/11
	RoBERTa-large	3e-5/64/5	3e-5/64/5	3e-5/64/2	3e-5/64/2	–
	BART-large	3e-5/64/5	3e-6/64/5	3e-6/64/2	3e-5/64/2	–

Table 2: Hyperparameters of models whose accuracies are reported in Table. 1. The numbers reported in each cell correspond to **learning rate/batch size/number of prototypes** For `proto-lm`, $\lambda = 0.5, \lambda_1 = 0.25, \lambda_2 = 0.25$. For `prototex`, $\lambda_1 = \lambda_2 = \frac{1}{3}$.

C.2.2 ProtoTex

`ProtoTex` (Das et al., 2022) is a PNLM that does not utilize class-assigned prototypes. The N prototypes in `ProtoTex` and their class connections in W_f are freely learned. In addition, calculation of prototypical encodings in `ProtoTex` do not involve token attention as in the case of `proto-lm` and `ProtoPatient`. In our implementation, we chose to use prototypes of dimension $\mathbb{R}^H$ because it led to the highest performance across tasks. Since the output of base LLMs is in dimension $\mathbb{R}^{L\times H}$, we took the mean along the token dimension when calculating encodings $f_\theta(x_i)$.

Similarity measures M in `ProtoTex` are the raw L2 distances between prototypes and $f_\theta(x_i)$. The training objective of `ProtoTex` is similar to `proto-lm`. Specifically, during training, in addition to minimizing cross entropy, `ProtoTex` seeks to minimize distance between prototypes and at least one encoded input.

$$\mathscr{L}_{p1} = \frac{1}{M} \cdot \sum_{j=1}^{M} \min_{i=1,n} \|p_j - S_i\|_2^2 \tag{13}$$

as well as minimizng distance between encoded input and at least one prototype

$$\mathscr{L}_{p2} = \frac{1}{n} \cdot \sum_{i=1}^{n} \min_{j=1,M} \|S_i - p_j\|_2^2 \tag{14}$$

Because there are no predetermined negative class connections in W_f, when applying `FR` we remove negative reasoning from `ProtoTex` by applying the ReLU (Agarap, 2018) activation function on weights in W_f during each forward pass i.e.

$$W_{jc} = \max\{W_{jc}, 0\} \quad \forall j \in [m], \ \forall c \in C \tag{15}$$

C.2.3 ProtoTex

`ProtoTex` (Das et al., 2022) is a PNLM that does not utilize class-assigned prototypes. The N prototypes in `ProtoTex` and their class connections in W_f are freely learned. In addition, calculation of prototypical encodings in `ProtoTex` do not involve token attention as in the case of `proto-lm` and `ProtoPatient`. In our implementation, we chose to use prototypes of dimension $\mathbb{R}^H$ because it led to the highest performance across tasks. Since the output of base LLMs is in dimension $\mathbb{R}^{L\times H}$, we took the mean along the token dimension when calculating encodings $f_\theta(x_i)$.

C.3 ProtoPatient

The PNLM of `ProtoPatient` (Van Aken et al., 2022) utilizes 1 prototype per class $c \in C$. Prototypical encoding calculation utilize both a dimension reduction layer as well as a label-wise attention layer. For each input x_i, the dimension reduction layer reduces the output dimension H of the base LLM to $\frac{H}{3}$ and the label-wise attention collapses the L dimension to produce $f_\theta(x_i) \in \mathbb{R}^{\frac{H}{3}}$. Similarity measures M in `ProtoPatient` are the *negative* of raw L2 distance measures between $f_\theta(x_i)$ and prototypes. In addition, `ProtoPatient` does not utilize class connections and instead produces output logits via taking the sigmoid of M.

Similarity measures M in `ProtoPatient` are the *negative* of raw L2 distance measures between $f_\theta(x_i)$ and prototypes. In addition, `ProtoPatient` does not utilize class connections and instead produces output logits via taking the sigmoid of M. The training objective of `ProtoPatient` consists of a single cross entropy term defined as follows

$$\mathscr{L} = \sum_{p \in P} \sum_{c \in C} \mathsf{BCE}(\hat{y}_{pc}, y_{pc}) \tag{16}$$

where $\hat{y}_{pc}$ is the output of prototype p for class c and $y_{pc} \in 0, 1$ is the ground truth. We note here that `ProtoPatient` initializes its prototypes with the average encoding examples from the prototypes' respective classes before training for the BCE objective in eq. 16.

We empirically found that ProtoPatient has a smaller faithfulness gap than Proto-lm and ProtoTEx, and we hypothesize this is due to (1) the objective function not directly optimizing for prototype clustering/separation and (2) the prototype initialization to latent training encoding of examples from the same class as the prototype. While ProtoPatient is still structurally vulnerable to faithfulness issues since their explanations (encoded training examples) don't impact predictions, it is our belief that Proto-Patient is more faithful than Proto-lm and ProtoTEx since Proto-Patient has a smaller faithfulness gap, i.e, the predictions and explanations are more aligned in the latent space.

D Hyperparameters and Compute Resources

Our compute resources consist of 4× RTX 6000, 4× RTX 4500 and 4× RTX 3090. In Table. 2 below, we describe the hyperparameter setup (learning rate, batch size and the number of prototypes) we used to obtain results in Table 1. We ran all models for a maximum of 15 epochs and report performance from the best iteration of the model during training. The running time of no individual experiment in Table. 2 exceeded 5 hours.

E Additional Experiments

E.1 Size of Projection Dataset

Although we have shown in earlier sections that FA can achieve competitive results on a wide range of tasks, it is important to consider whether the amount of training data used during projection impacts performance. Specifically, what happens if we use only a *subset* of the training data to faithfully project prototypes during FA? To investigate this, we conduct experiments by applying FA with varying sizes of training datasets. Specifically, we trained 8 `proto-lm` models on SST2, SST5, and HoC ($C = 2$, $C = 5$ and $C = 11$, respectively) with prototype counts that are multiples of C, totaling $|\{1, 2, 5, 10, 20, 40, 80, 100\} \times \{2, 5, 11\}| = 24$ models. We then apply FA to each model with different amount of training data and calculate the change in accuracy. In Figure 7, we show the gain/loss in accuracy averaged across the three tasks. We find that, when the number of prototypes in the PNLM is large but the training data for projection is limited, performance generally drops significantly. We reason that this is because prototypical features are derived from a shared, small sample, thus reducing prototype uniqueness (Das et al., 2022). On the other hand, this issue does not arise with large amount of projection data and fewer prototypes, as the prototypes can leverage features from the most apt sample encodings. Interestingly, when both the number of prototypes and training data size are small, we observe notable performance improvements, as FA helps the few prototypes capture the most important features. Overall, our experiments show that FA-applied models maintain performance with sufficient training data, but selecting the right number of prototypes is crucial if one wishes to reduce the amount of training data used during FA.

E.2 Generalizability of FA

Given that the FP component of FA restricts prototypical features to encodings of samples within a specific dataset, it is reasonable to expect that FA-applied PNLMs is prone to overfitting. To explore the generalizability of faithfully-aligned prototypes, we apply FA to a trained PNLM on the SST2 dataset and observe how well it performs when classifying examples from two *other* sentiment classification datasets: IMDb movie reviews (Maas et al., 2011) and the Twitter Sentiment Analysis Training Corpus (Naji, 2012). In Fig. 8, we present the zero-shot accuracy (on IMDb and TSATC) of PNLMs that were trained on SST2 and were also applied FA using the SST2 dataset in red. For comparison, we also show the zero-shot accuracy of PNLMs that were trained on SST2 but *without* applying FA in yellow. We find that, in zero-shot settings, FA-applied PNLMs are able to outperform

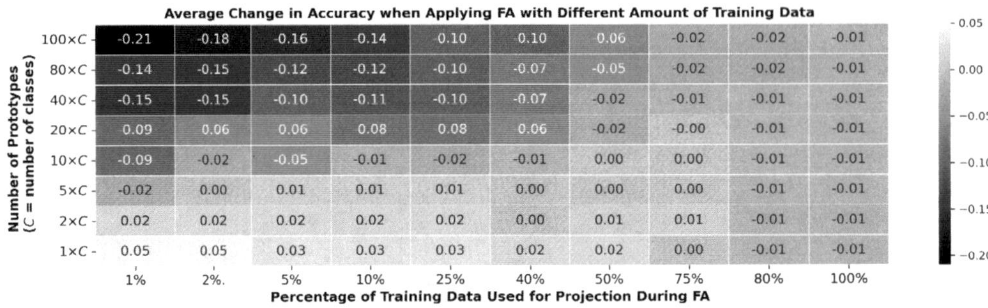

Figure 7: Change in accuracy of `Proto-lm` models after applying FA with different amount of training data. Results obtained are the average across SST2, SST5 and HoC. `Proto-lm` models have prototypes counts that are multiples of C which is the number of classes in each dataset, with $C = 2$ for SST2, $C = 5$ for SST5 and $C = 11$ for HoC.

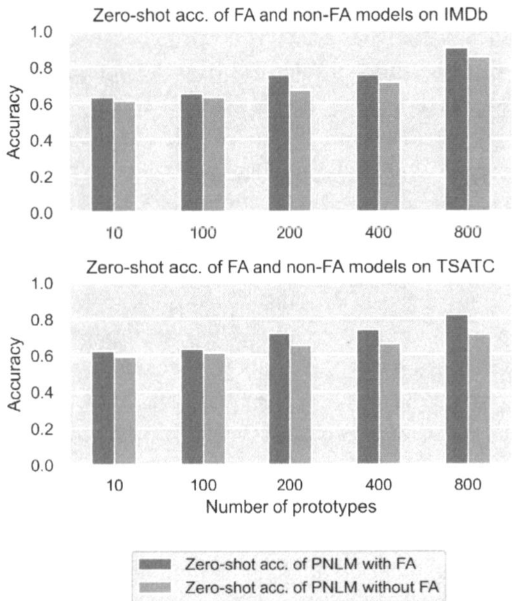

Figure 8: Model accuracy on IMDb and TSATC. red bars represent the accuracy of a zero-shot PNLM with FA applied using examples from SST2. yellow bars represent the zero-shot accuracy of the base PNLM but without FA applied. Both models were trained on SST2.

PNLMs without FA across architectures with different number of prototypes, indicating that FA-applied PNLMs generalize well to unseen data. Furthermore, as the number of prototypes increases, the performance difference between the models with and without FA widens. We believe this is because a larger set of prototypes provides greater representational power during the FA process, resulting in a robust model that excels on various datasets.

E.3 Comparison with Case-based-reasoning Models

Another notable effect of FA projecting the learned prototypes onto training encodings is the resulting model architecture's similarity to K-Nearest-Neighbor models. We therefore conduct experiments comparing the performances of FA and KNN-based approaches under different settings. First, we build a KNN model using the encodings of a *base language model* (i.e. BERT). We then build a KNN model using the encodings (in prototypical space) of a non-FA PNLM (i.e. an instance of `proto-lm`). Finally, we build a KNN model using the encodings of a FA-applied PNLM. We compare the performance of these three case-based-reasoning models against the PNLM as well as the FA-applied PNLM on the 11-class cancer classification dataset (HoC). We present our results for PNLMs of varying prototypes in Fig. 9. We observe that with a high number of prototypes, FA allows PNLMs to outperform KNN models. Additionally, KNN-based models suffer in terms of performance when K becomes too large, unless aided by FA. This is likely because the HoC dataset has a limited number of examples per class. A large K parameter forces KNN models to use neighbors from other classes, leading to a drop in performance. FA-applied PNLMs do not have this issue because the class connections in W_f ensure that examples from the correct class receive more weight.

F Frequently Asked Questions

Where are the quantitative metrics justifying (A) that the identified PNLMs are unfaithful and (B) that FA improves these models faithfulness?

(A) We reiterate that no existing faithfulness metrics are applicable to quantify the faithfulness of

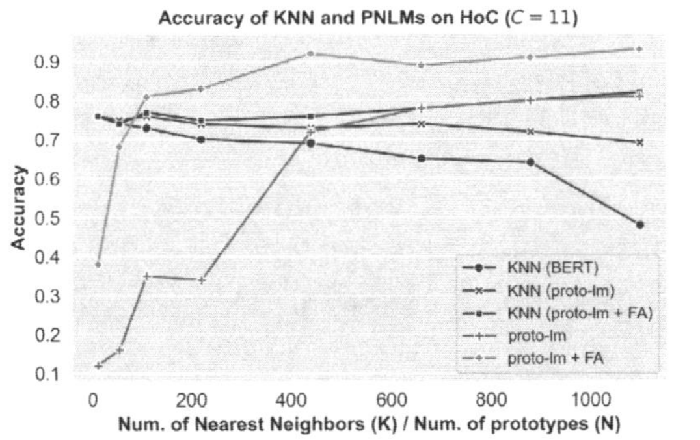

Figure 9: Accuracy of KNN-based models and FA-applied PNLMs.

Prototypical Networks on the example level. If such metrics existed, the faithfulness issues identified in this work would have been immediately identified and resolved by previous work. We believe that developing such a metric is an important area of future research and that the lack of said metric played a role in the prevalence of existing PNLM unfaithfulness.

Our claims regarding the unfaithfulness of the identified PNLMs in §2 is rooted in prototypical faithfulness principles established in (Chen et al., 2019), such as the principle that latent encoding need to be equal to prototypes in the prototypical layer, as well as the qualitative description of faithfulness, which states that for an explanation to be faithful, it must align with the reasoning process of the model. The case-based reasoning architecture of Prototypical Networks enables us to explicitly define the reasoning process of the model based on the similarity computation in P and the class connections in W_f. This framing allows us to transparently view inference as a weighted similarity (using W_f) between the encoded test-time example, $f_\theta(x)$, and prototypes $P = \{p_j\}_{j=1}^{m}$. Explanations in (Xie et al., 2023; Das et al., 2022) are chosen solely based on the similarity in P and do not consider class connections in W_f, resulting in an overt diversion with the reasoning process of the Prototypical Network and thus unfaithful explanations.

Faithful Alignment resolves both of these issues: prototypes are restored as latent training examples, adhering to (Chen et al., 2019), and prototypes are selected for explanation based on **all** the computation that effects prediction instead of just computation in P, adhering to (Jacovi and Goldberg, 2020).

Why does FA not work as well on ProtoTEx as it does on Proto-lm and Proto-Patient?

We hypothesize this is because ProtoTEx does not assign a specific class to the prototypes before learning, unlike how it's done in Proto-lm and ProtoPatient. Since projection is done to the nearest encoding in the training example, we hypothesize that there is greater risk of the prototype being projected onto a less representative training example when classes are not preassigned to prototypes. For example, if the prototype before projection was of class 3 but the training example nearest to it was of class 4, then faithful projection could more significantly affect the model's reasoning.

We remark that the performance of FA with ProtoTEx still remains competitive across a diverse set of tasks and the performance was stronger when applied using more recent models such as ELECTRA or Llama.

Why are there no experimentation with FA applied to CV models/datasets?

In short, we didn't experiment with any CV models/datasets because we are not aware of any unfaithful Prototypical Networks in CV. We experimented with the three PNLMs we identified as having architectural flaws that lead to unfaithful model explanations to demonstrate we can resolve the previously unknown faithfulness issues without sacrificing model performance. We reiterate that FA is a general framework that can ensure faithful explanations for Prototypical Networks in both CV and NLP. The techniques which comprise FA, namely FP and FR, act on the prototypical layer P and final linear layer W_f, which are present in Prototypical Networks independent of input modality.

Aligning Sizes of Intermediate Layers by LoRA Adapter for Knowledge Distillation

Takeshi Suzuki
Institute of Science Tokyo
suzuki.t.dp@m.titech.ac.jp

Hiroaki Yamada
Institute of Science Tokyo
yamada@comp.isct.ac.jp

Takenobu Tokunaga
Institute of Science Tokyo
take@c.titech.ac.jp

Abstract

Intermediate Layer Distillation (ILD) is a variant of Knowledge Distillation (KD), a method for compressing neural networks. ILD requires mapping to align the intermediate layer sizes of the teacher and student models to compute the loss function in training, while this mapping is not used during inference. This inconsistency may reduce the effectiveness of learning in intermediate layers. In this study, we propose LoRAILD, which uses LoRA adapters to eliminate the inconsistency. However, our experimental results show that LoRAILD does not outperform existing methods. Furthermore, contrary to previous studies, we observe that conventional ILD does not outperform vanilla KD. Our analysis of the distilled models' intermediate layers suggests that ILD does not improve language models' performance.

1 Introduction

The LLM's performance is rapidly improving on various natural language processing (NLP) tasks at the cost of the huge parameter size, resulting in enormous computational costs. Therefore, reducing the parameter size while retaining the model's performance is an important research topic.

Knowledge distillation (KD) (Buciluǎ et al., 2006; Hinton et al., 2015) is one of the model compression methods. KD employs two models: a teacher model and a student model. The teacher model is already trained for a specific task. The teacher's output serves as soft labels that guide the student model that mimics the teacher's behavior.

While KD usually uses the output of the teacher, intermediate layer distillation (ILD) (Romero et al., 2015) uses the information of intermediate layers as well; ILD has been claimed to be superior to the vanilla KD in previous studies (Sun et al., 2019; Passban et al., 2021; Haidar et al., 2022).

In this study, we introduce LoRAILD, which is designed to improve the conventional ILD by employing the LoRA (Hu et al., 2021) adapter in aligning sizes of intermediate layers between the teacher and the student. We evaluate the performance of LoRAILD through empirical comparisons with conventional KD baselines. In general, we find that our LoRAILD does not outperform the conventional ILD baselines, and even the conventional ILD is not necessarily superior to the vanilla KD, at least in our experimental settings.

2 Background

2.1 Knowledge Distillation

In KD (Buciluǎ et al., 2006; Hinton et al., 2015), a student model is trained using a loss function based on the difference between its output and the teacher's output, as well as a loss function calculating errors against gold labels. KD's combined loss function L is defined as (1).

$$L = \lambda L_{\mathrm{CE}} + (1 - \lambda) L_{\mathrm{KD}} \tag{1}$$

$$L_{\mathrm{KD}} = \mathrm{KL}(\mathrm{Teacher}(X), \mathrm{Student}(X)), \tag{2}$$

where L_{CE} is the cross-entropy loss, $\mathrm{KL}(\cdot,\cdot)$ is the KL divergence. $\mathrm{Teacher}(X)$ and $\mathrm{Student}(X)$ are the probability distributions obtained as outputs when X is input to the teacher and the student, respectively. In training the student, the parameters of the teacher are fixed.

2.2 Intermedite Layer Distillation

Intermediate layer distillation (ILD) (Romero et al., 2015) is a variant of KD. ILD uses not only the teacher and student outputs but also the information of their intermediate layers. ILD requires the alignment of the number of layers and layer sizes between the student and the teacher.

When the number of layers between two models differs, adjustment is necessary, which is the focal topic of past ILD research. PKD (Sun et al., 2019) heuristically selects the same number of layers from the teacher as those in the student. In

The Sixth Workshop on Insights from Negative Results in NLP, pages 100–105
May 4, 2025

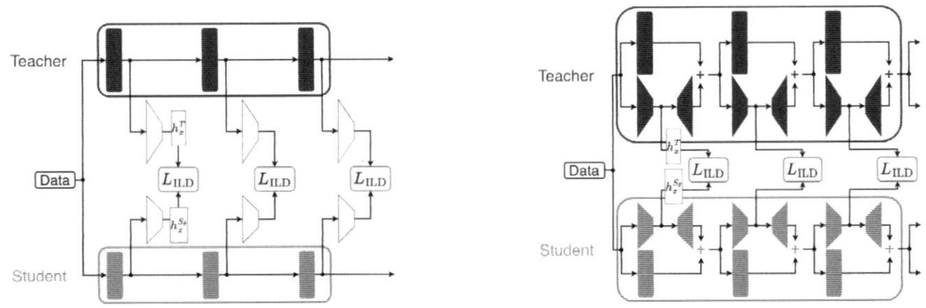

(a) Previous ILD

(b) LoRAILD

Figure 1: Overview of LoRAILD (blue: teacher, green: student, yellow: linear mapping)

PKD, the selected layers are consistent through the student training. ALP-KD (Passban et al., 2021) constructs groups of teacher layers, and each group corresponds to a layer in the student. The outputs from layers in a group are aggregated by calculating the weighted average. RAIL-KD (Haidar et al., 2022) dynamically selects layers of the teacher at random in each epoch.

When the intermediate layer size is inconsistent between the teacher and the student, the size must be aligned to compute the loss function. Previous studies (Romero et al., 2015; Haidar et al., 2022) employed some mapping methods for the alignment. FitNets (Romero et al., 2015) employed convolutional regressors, and RAIL-KD (Haidar et al., 2022) used linear layers for mapping. During student training, these mappings are trained alongside all the other parameters of the student. However, the mappings are used only in the student training phase, so the model's structure is inconsistent between training and inference.

This inconsistency might degrade the effectiveness of ILD. If only the mappings are tuned very well with a task while the intermediate layers of the student might not develop good features, removing the mappings in inference will degrade the student's performance.

3 Method

3.1 LoRAILD

To tackle the problem of structure inconsistency, we propose LoRAILD, which employs LoRA adapters replacing the conventional mappings. As LoRAILD utilizes the LoRA adapters both in the training and the inference phase by design, the discrepancy of model structure no longer exists.

LoRA (Hu et al., 2021) is one of the methods to reduce the computational cost during training by assigning two low-rank matrices of size $\mathbb{R}^{i\times r}$ and $\mathbb{R}^{r\times o}$ to a certain module in the model and only training them. i and o are the number of input and output sizes of the module to be assigned, respectively. Since low-rank matrices have the same architecture as linear mapping and the r value, which is the output size of the input-side matrix, can be set manually, we can convert the intermediate layer size of the teacher and the student into the same by setting the r properly. Thus, they can be used as a substitute for conventional linear mappings. Moreover, these matrices are used in the inference phase. Therefore, we can maintain linear mappings by using low-rank matrices. Figure 1b shows the outline of LoRAILD. In the conventional ILD, the loss is calculated using the output of a linear layer (yellow part of Figure 1a). In contrast, in LoRAILD, the loss function is calculated using the output of the input-side matrix of the LoRA adapter (trapezoidal part of Figure 1b).

The loss function is given by equation (4).

$$L_{\text{ILD}} = \frac{1}{N}\sum_{x\in batch}\left\|\frac{h_x^T}{\|h_x^T\|_2} - \frac{h_x^{S_\theta}}{\|h_x^{S_\theta}\|_2}\right\|_2^2 \quad (3)$$

$$L = \lambda_1 L_{\text{CE}} + \lambda_2 L_{\text{KD}} + \lambda_3 L_{\text{ILD}} \quad (4)$$

N is the batch size, h_x^* is the output of the input-side matrix of the LoRA adapter for x. The outputs of each layer are concatenated to compute the loss function. The T and S_θ denote the teacher and the student, respectively. The L_{CE} and L_{KD} are the same as in equation (1). This is the same as the loss function used in previous ILD methods (Sun et al., 2019; Haidar et al., 2022).

3.2 Alignment of layers

While LoRA adaptors address the size alignment issue, we still need to fill the gap between the number of layers in the teacher and the student. In this study, we employ the following three methods.

Fixed Always select the same layer during student training.

Average Allocate some layers of the teacher to each layer of the student, and average the output of the allocated layers.

Random Randomly select a layer of the teacher for each layer of the student. The sequence of the selected layers is preserved. The random selection is performed at each mini-batch (Random step) or each epoch (Random epoch).

Fixed, Average, and Random are almost the same as those used in the previous studies: PKD (Sun et al., 2019), ALP-KD (Passban et al., 2021), and RAIL-KD (Haidar et al., 2022). Unlike ALP-KD, h is simply averaged, and a weighted average is not used in the Average method.

Appendix A shows the alignment patterns between the student and teacher layers for Fixed and Average.

3.3 Curriculum Learning

LoRAILD did not perform well in our preliminary trials, where we observed that L_{ILD} decreased first and L_{CE} did not decrease well. In order to make sure L_{CE} to decrease, we introduced curriculum learning in which only L_{CE} and L_{KD} are trained first, and L_{ILD} is added to L later.

4 Experiment

4.1 Experimantal Settings

In our experiments, we use RoBERTa-large (Liu et al., 2019) for the teacher and DistilRoBERTa-base (Sanh et al., 2019) for the student. LoRA adapters are added to both models. The teacher trains only LoRA adapters, and the student trains both LoRA and the original model.

The dataset used in this experiment consists of six tasks from the GLUE (Wang et al., 2018) benchmark: CoLA, MRPC, QNLI, RTE, SST-2, and STS-B. Since the GLUE benchmark does not publish the gold labels for the test set, we use the original validation set as a test set, 10 percent of the original training set for validation, and the remaining 90 percent for training. The evaluation metrics are the Matthews correlation coefficient for CoLA, the F1 score for MRPC, the Pearson correlation coefficient for STS-B, and accuracy for the others.

Baselines are the finetuned student without KD (w/o KD), the model with normal KD (Vanilla KD), RAIL-KD (RAIL-KD$_\mathrm{c}$, RAIL-KD$_\mathrm{l}$), and the model RAIL-KD$_\mathrm{c}$ with curriculum learning (Curriculum); curriculum learning was not used in the original RAIL-KD paper (Haidar et al., 2022). In RAIL-KD$_\mathrm{l}$, L_{ILD} is computed per layer, while RAIL-KD$_\mathrm{c}$ uses concatenated intermediate outputs. The hyperparameters are listed in Appendix C.

All reported metrics are the average of five runs, and we conduct one-tailed permutation tests at a significance level of 2.5%.

4.2 Result

	CoLA	MRPC	QNLI	RTE	SST-2	STS-B
Teacher	0.594	0.884	0.947	0.798	0.959	0.912
w/o KD	0.567	<u>0.876</u>	<u>0.906</u>	0.676	0.919	0.881
Vanilla KD	0.566	<u>0.874</u>	0.912	<u>0.622</u>	0.925	0.883
RAIL-KD						
RAIL-KD$_\mathrm{c}$	0.568	**0.892**	0.916	0.658	**0.929**	0.882
RAIL-KD$_\mathrm{l}$	0.585	0.882	<u>0.907</u>	<u>0.522</u>	<u>0.907</u>	0.886
Curriculum	0.568	0.889	<u>0.912</u>	**0.677**	<u>0.928</u>	0.881
LoRAILD						
Fixed	0.565	0.880	0.912	0.651	0.922	0.880
Average	**0.596**	0.874	0.913	0.656	0.921	**0.886**
Random step	0.592	<u>0.846</u>	**0.916**	0.637	0.920	0.881
Random epoch	0.573	<u>0.886</u>	0.911	0.659	0.915	0.882

Table 1: Results on test set

Table 1 shows the result. Bold figures indicate the best performance for each task. They are significantly higher than underlined ones. None of the LoRAILD-based models showed clear improvement from the baselines. Fixed and Random epoch did not outperform previous methods in any task. Average showed the best scores in CoLA and STS-B; however, we could not confirm their statistical significance. Although Random step achieved the best score in QNLI among all the models, its improvement is subtle and not statistically distinguishable from RAIL-KD$_\mathrm{c}$. Given the little improvement in LoRAILD, the LoRA adapters in LoRAILD could not perform as we expected, and they might disturb intermediate layers' learning.

Moreover, none of the RAIL-KD models outperforms w/o KD and Vanilla KD. These results contradict the previous study's outcome; they reported that RAIL-KD (Haidar et al., 2022) outperformed w/o KD and Vanilla KD at all tasks in their

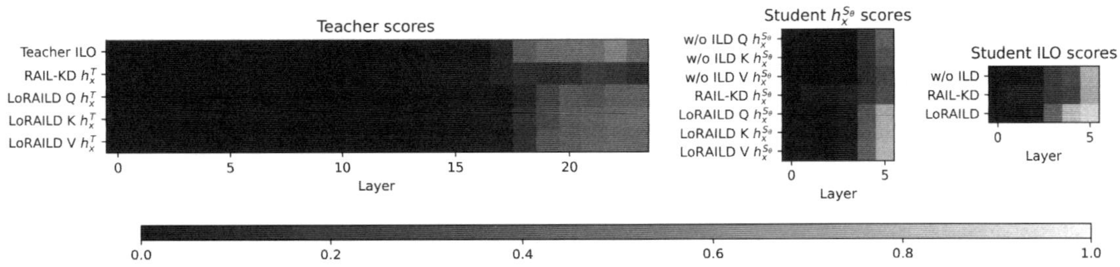

Figure 2: Clustering scores (ILO means intermediate layer output)
left: Teacher, middle: Student's $h_x^{S_\theta}$, right: Students' intermediate layer output

experiment. The lower performance of RAIL-KD than Vanilla KD aligns with our hypothesis that removing the linear mapping during inference may degrade the effectiveness of ILD.

5 Analysis

5.1 Analysis method

To examine how the intermediate layers of the models embed features in RAIL-KD and LoRAILD, we conduct a cluster analysis of features used in loss calculation and intermediate layer outputs. For both the teacher and the student of LoRAILD, RAIL-KD, and w/o ILD ($\lambda_3 = 0$), we obtain h_x^* and direct outputs from intermediate layers, where the models are fed with our training set. Note that h_x^T in this section is the value before layer alignment. We cluster the obtained vectors by k-means (MacQueen, 1967) clustering ($k = 2^1$). We use the same tasks as our experiment except for STS-B, which is regression.

We evaluate the clusters by calculating the Adjusted Rand Index (ARI) (Hubert and Arabie, 1985; Steinley, 2004) against gold clusters that are constructed according to the gold labels.

The higher ARI suggests the student acquires better representation for solving the task through the training. A higher ARI for the teacher means its intermediate layers provide more useful information to train the student.

5.2 Analysis result

Figure 2 illustrates the ARI scores. The left and middle matrices indicate the scores calculated for h_x^T and $h_x^{S_\theta}$ from the teacher and the student, respectively. The right matrix indicates the scores for the outputs from the student's intermediate layer. Each cell corresponds to an aggregated score across the tasks by averaging. In BERT, the latter layers process the semantics of sentences (Tenney et al., 2019; Jawahar et al., 2019). As the tasks used in this analysis, except for the CoLA, concern the semantics of the sentences, the latter layers play important roles in these tasks.

In the left figure, h_x^T in RAIL-KD indicates a lower score in the latter layers (≥ 18) compared to the original intermediate layer output of the teacher (Teacher ILO), suggesting information useful for the tasks is not provided to the student. On the other hand, LoRAILD scored higher in the latter layers, indicating that the teacher conveys more useful information to the student. We initially hypothesized that removing the linear mapping could degrade the performance because it also removes information learned in the linear mapping. However, we found that the linear mapping in RAIL-KD does not actually learn information about the task; rather, it degrades the quality of the teacher signal from Teacher ILO.

In the middle and right figures, RAIL-KD does not show improvement from w/o ILD in the latter layers (≥ 4), while LoRAILD successfully does.

This result indicates that our LoRAILD provides a better method to align the intermediate layers between the student and the teacher.

6 Conclusion

Our experimental result (Table 1) showed that ILD did not improve performance from Vanilla KD regardless of using the intermediate layers (LoRAILD) or not (RAIL-KD). Although our analysis revealed that our LoRAILD provided better alignment for intermediate layers, this improvement did not improve the downstream tasks. Thus, we conclude that the current ILD approach has little impact on the performance of the language model.

[1]All the tasks employed in our analysis are binary classification.

7 Limitation

Different experimental settings from the previous studies Although our experimental results report negative results not aligned with those reported in RAIL-KD (Haidar et al., 2022), our finding does not directly reject the previous results. Instead, our results suggest that ILD might not be generalizable to different settings as initially expected.

The RAIL-KD and other baselines used in our experiment employ different base models, datasets, and hyperparameters from their original ones, so our experiment does not completely replicate their original settings.

We acknowledge that our teacher models are different from the previous studies. This is because the teacher models used in the previous study are not publicly available. Also, the architecture of the teacher model we used differs from that of the previous studies because of the addition of the LoRA adapter.

As for the data set, as described in section 4.1, our dataset split is different. 90% of the GLUE train set was used as our train set, the remaining 10% of the GLUE train set as a validation set, and the original validation set as a test set.

Due to the different conditions described above, we had to perform a hyperparameter search to find the optimal values for our settings.

Scope of our experiments Our study addressed a scenario in which the intermediate layer size of the teacher and student models is different, and we always have to transform the outputs and align their sizes. Thus, the intermediate layer output from the teacher model was not directly used as the teacher signal for the student model in any of our experiments. We acknowledge that we have no conclusion for a case where the intermediate layer size is the same between the teacher and student and ILD can use the direct outputs from the teacher's intermediate layers without any alignment. That case is outside of the scope of this paper.

References

Cristian Buciluǎ, Rich Caruana, and Alexandru Niculescu-Mizil. 2006. Model compression. In Proceedings of the 12th ACM SIGKDD International Conference on Knowledge Discovery and Data Mining, KDD '06, page 535–541, New York, NY, USA. Association for Computing Machinery.

Md Akmal Haidar, Nithin Anchuri, Mehdi Rezagholizadeh, Abbas Ghaddar, Philippe Langlais, and Pascal Poupart. 2022. RAIL-KD: RAndom intermediate layer mapping for knowledge distillation. In Findings of the Association for Computational Linguistics: NAACL 2022, pages 1389–1400, Seattle, United States. Association for Computational Linguistics.

Geoffrey Hinton, Oriol Vinyals, and Jeff Dean. 2015. Distilling the Knowledge in a Neural Network. arxiv preprint, arXiv:1503.02531.

Edward J. Hu, Yelong Shen, Phillip Wallis, Zeyuan Allen-Zhu, Yuanzhi Li, Shean Wang, Lu Wang, and Weizhu Chen. 2021. LoRA: Low-Rank Adaptation of Large Language Models. arxiv preprint, arXiv:2106.09685.

Lawrence Hubert and Phipps Arabie. 1985. Comparing partitions. Journal of Classification, 2(1):193–218.

Ganesh Jawahar, Benoît Sagot, and Djamé Seddah. 2019. What does BERT learn about the structure of language? In Proceedings of the 57th Annual Meeting of the Association for Computational Linguistics, pages 3651–3657, Florence, Italy. Association for Computational Linguistics.

Yinhan Liu, Myle Ott, Naman Goyal, Jingfei Du, Mandar Joshi, Danqi Chen, Omer Levy, Mike Lewis, Luke Zettlemoyer, and Veselin Stoyanov. 2019. Roberta: A robustly optimized BERT pretraining approach. arXiv, abs/1907.11692.

J. B. MacQueen. 1967. Some methods for classification and analysis of multivariate observations. In Proc. of the fifth Berkeley Symposium on Mathematical Statistics and Probability, volume 1, pages 281–297. University of California Press.

Peyman Passban, Yimeng Wu, Mehdi Rezagholizadeh, and Qun Liu. 2021. Alp-kd: Attention-based layer projection for knowledge distillation. Proceedings of the AAAI Conference on Artificial Intelligence, 35(15):13657–13665.

Adriana Romero, Nicolas Ballas, Samira Ebrahimi Kahou, Antoine Chassang, Carlo Gatta, and Yoshua Bengio. 2015. FitNets: Hints for Thin Deep Nets. arXiv preprints, arXiv:1412.6550.

Victor Sanh, Lysandre Debut, Julien Chaumond, and Thomas Wolf. 2019. Distilbert, a distilled version of bert: smaller, faster, cheaper and lighter. arXiv, abs/1910.01108.

Douglas Steinley. 2004. Properties of the Hubert-Arabie adjusted rand index. Psychol Methods, 9(3):386–396.

Siqi Sun, Yu Cheng, Zhe Gan, and Jingjing Liu. 2019. Patient knowledge distillation for BERT model compression. In Proceedings of the 2019 Conference on Empirical Methods in Natural Language Processing and the 9th International Joint Conference on

Natural Language Processing (EMNLP-IJCNLP), pages 4323–4332, Hong Kong, China. Association for Computational Linguistics.

Ian Tenney, Dipanjan Das, and Ellie Pavlick. 2019. BERT rediscovers the classical NLP pipeline. In Proceedings of the 57th Annual Meeting of the Association for Computational Linguistics, pages 4593–4601, Florence, Italy. Association for Computational Linguistics.

Alex Wang, Amanpreet Singh, Julian Michael, Felix Hill, Omer Levy, and Samuel Bowman. 2018. GLUE: A multi-task benchmark and analysis platform for natural language understanding. In Proceedings of the 2018 EMNLP Workshop BlackboxNLP: Analyzing and Interpreting Neural Networks for NLP, pages 353–355, Brussels, Belgium. Association for Computational Linguistics.

A Alignment

Fixed Student	Fixed Teacher	Average Student	Average Teacher
0	3	0	0, 1, 2, 3
1	7	1	4, 5, 6, 7
2	11	2	8, 9, 10, 11
3	15	3	12, 13, 14, 15
4	19	4	16, 17, 18, 19
5	23	5	20, 21, 22, 23

Table 2: Alignment

Table 2 shows the alignment of the student and teacher models for the alignment methods Fixed and Average. L_{ILD} was computed using the vector of concatenated $h_x^{S_\theta}$ from layer 0 to layer 5 of the student model, and the vector of concatenated h_x^T from layers 3, 7, ..., and 23 of the teacher model.

In Average, the concatenation of averages of h_x^T from layer 0, 1, 2, and 3, ... , average of h_x^T from layer 20, 21, 22, and 23 was used to calculate L_{ILD}.

B Results on Validation Set

Table 3 shows results on validation set as well as test set.

C Hyperparameters

The hyperparameters used in the experiments are shown in Table 4. In the middle part of the table, epochs where we initiated curriculum learning are illustrated. In the curriculum learning, $(\lambda_1, \lambda_2, \lambda_3)$ is varied from the initial to the final state; only the RTE task experimented with two different final states.

	CoLA	MRPC	QNLI	RTE	SST-2	STS-B
Teacher	0.673	0.894	0.935	0.779	0.960	0.920
w/o KD	0.615	0.872	0.894	0.692	0.947	0.896
Vanilla KD	0.635	0.888	0.903	0.716	0.954	0.916
RAIL-KD						
RAIL-KD$_c$	0.625	0.902	0.905	0.716	0.954	0.917
RAIL-KD$_l$	0.633	0.899	0.899	0.597	0.952	0.916
Curriculum	**0.650**	**0.903**	**0.907**	**0.748**	0.955	**0.920**
LoRAILD						
Fixed	0.628	0.883	0.905	0.688	0.955	0.912
Average	0.637	0.871	0.904	0.717	0.954	0.919
Random step	0.633	0.848	0.904	0.680	**0.956**	0.913
Random epoch	0.627	0.888	0.904	0.726	0.955	0.912

Table 3: Result for valitation set

Learning rate	{1, 2, 5}e-{4, 5}
r (output size of mapping)	32
Epoch (Teacher model)	4
Epoch (Student model)	20
Curriculum Learning	
Tasks	Epoch to start
CoLA	5-10
MRPC	5-10
QNLI	5-10
RTE	5-10
SST-2	2-4
STS-B	2-4
States	$(\lambda_1, \lambda_2, \lambda_3)$
Initial state	$(0.5, 0.5, 0)$
Final state	$(0.333, 0.333, 0.333)$
Final state(RTE only)	$(0.5, 0, 0.5)$

Table 4: Hyperparameters

LLMs are not Zero-Shot Reasoners for Biomedical Information Extraction

Aishik Nagar[1] **Viktor Schlegel**[2,3] **Thanh-Tung Nguyen** **Hao Li**[3]
Yuping Wu[3] **Kuluhan Binici**[4] **Stefan Winkler**[4]

[1]ASUS Intelligent Cloud Services (AICS), Singapore
[2]Imperial College London, Imperial Global Singapore
[3]University of Manchester, United Kingdom
[4]National University of Singapore, Singapore
Correspondence to: v.schlegel@imperial.ac.uk

Abstract

Large Language Models (LLMs) are increasingly adopted for applications in healthcare, reaching the performance of domain experts on tasks such as question answering and document summarisation. Despite their success on these tasks, it is unclear how well LLMs perform on tasks that are traditionally pursued in the biomedical domain, such as structured information extraction. To bridge this gap, in this paper, we systematically benchmark LLM performance in Medical Classification and Named Entity Recognition (NER) tasks. We aim to disentangle the contribution of different factors to the performance, particularly the impact of LLMs' task knowledge and reasoning capabilities, their (parametric) domain knowledge, and addition of external knowledge. To this end, we evaluate various open LLMs—including BioMistral and Llama-2 models—on a diverse set of biomedical datasets, using standard prompting, Chain-of-Thought (CoT) and Self-Consistency based reasoning as well as Retrieval-Augmented Generation (RAG) with PubMed and Wikipedia corpora. Counter-intuitively, our results reveal that standard prompting consistently outperforms more complex techniques across both tasks, laying bare the limitations in the current application of CoT, self-consistency and RAG in the biomedical domain. Our findings suggest that advanced prompting methods developed for knowledge- or reasoning-intensive tasks, such as CoT or RAG, are not easily portable to biomedical tasks where precise structured outputs are required. This highlights the need for more effective integration of external knowledge and reasoning mechanisms in LLMs to enhance their performance in real-world biomedical applications.

1 Introduction

The success of Large Language Models (LLMs) is reshaping AI healthcare applications, particularly in Question Answering (Budler et al., 2023; Subramanian et al., 2024), summarization (Van Veen et al., 2024; Schlegel et al., 2023; Nagar et al., 2024), and extracting insights from unstructured patient-generated health data (Li et al., 2023). While advancements in fine-tuning and in-context learning (ICL) have improved LLM performance, these rely on readily available structured training data (Abburi et al., 2023; Zhang et al., 2024; Gutierrez et al., 2022). However, in biomedical contexts, such resources are often unavailable due to domain shifts (Hadi et al., 2023) or ad-hoc requirements —for example when researchers need to process a set of medical records to find patients satisfying inclusion criteria for a clinical trial (Jullien et al., 2023; Hadi et al., 2023) (e.g., whether they're a smoker). This limits the effectiveness of parametric knowledge improvements in LLMs, necessitating strong zero-shot capabilities for structured prediction tasks such as biomedical classification and Named Entity Recognition. Despite this, the literature currently lacks a systematic investigation of other crucial aspects of knowledge utilization in zero-shot performance of LLMs in such tasks.

In order to address this research gap, we first postulate that LLM performance in true zero-shot settings—where only task labels and their meaningful names are provided (Lampert et al., 2014)—hinges on three categories of knowledge: *(a) Parametric Knowledge*: Information embedded in model weights; *(b) Task Knowledge*: Understanding of task-specific labels and context; *(c) External Knowledge*: Additional retrieved context to supplement decision-making.

Existing research evaluating these factors in LLMs for the medical domain focus on knowledge-intensive tasks like Multiple-Choice QA (Nori et al., 2023; Subramanian et al., 2024), but their capabilities in structured prediction tasks, such as medical classification and information extraction, remain underexplored. Additionally, tech-

The Sixth Workshop on Insights from Negative Results in NLP, pages 106–120
May 4, 2025

niques like zero-shot Chain-of-Thought (CoT) reasoning (Wei et al., 2022; Wang and Zhou, 2024), self-consistency (Wang et al., 2022), and Retrieval-Augmented Generation (RAG) (Li et al., 2024) require systematic evaluation in these contexts.

Additionally, evaluations often focus on proprietary models like ChatGPT (Biswas, 2023) or GPT-4 (OpenAI, 2023), which pose challenges due to computational cost, privacy concerns, and inaccessibility for techniques like constrained decoding. Despite the growing concerns regarding reliability of LLMs in medical applications, techniques like constrained decoding which have shown promise in mitigating LLM hallucinations have not been systematically applied to medical information extraction or classification.

Thus, four key issues currently hinder progress: *(i)* Reliance on training sets and parametric knowledge for structured prediction, which may be unrealistic; *(ii)* Lack of true zero-shot evaluations for structured tasks beyond surrogate QA; *(iii)* Dependence on large-scale, proprietary LLMs, limiting practical deployment. *(iv)* Lack of a systematic analysis of impact of latest techniques such as Chain-of-thought reasoning, RAG and constrained generation in medical structured prediction tasks.

This paper systematically benchmarks LLMs in medical classification and Named Entity Recognition (NER), assessing task and external knowledge while controlling parametric knowledge. We evaluate CoT reasoning, RAG, and constrained generation, offering insights into their applicability.

First, we present the first comprehensive benchmark of task and external knowledge adaptation for LLMs in medical structured prediction tasks. **Second**, we analyze the impact of knowledge enhancement techniques, including CoT, self-consistency, RAG, and constrained generation. **Third**, we demonstrate that parametric knowledge capacity, i.e., model size, is the primary driver of zero-shot performance, highlighting the limitations and potential of current LLM architectures.

2 Related Work

We survey the existing benchmarking literature for the medical domain in the **appendix section A**, outlining the lack of studies focusing on structured prediction tasks. Furthermore, we cover recent prompting techniques that were proposed to elicit reasoning in LLMs, and augment their domain knowledge, either by better tapping into their parametric knowledge or by explicitly providing them with relevant external context. Notably, we omit approaches that rely on existence of training sets, such as few-shot prompting (Wang et al., 2023) or model fine-tuning, as one of the key challenges in the medical domain is the lack of annotated task data, due to privacy concerns over sharing medical records. Instead, as outlines in the introduction, we focus on "true" zero-shot capabilities of LLMs.

Reasoning- and Knowledge-enhancing approaches: Current work attempts to improve the performance of LLMs from different knowledge utilization perspectives. One of the obvious methods is full parameter domain-specific pretraining (Xie et al., 2024). For example, Chen et al. (2023) propose the largest medical foundation model, trained on both biomedical and clinical data, up to 70B. Bolton et al. (2024), on the other hand, believe larger LLMs are computationally expensive to run, proposing a 2.7B LLM specific for biomedical NLP tasks. When fine-tuned, the relatively small model compete with larger LLMs. In our study, we compare domain-generalist models with those adapted to the medical domain. Since full parameter tuning is costly, many works focus on domain knowledge adaptation by pretraining (Shi et al., 2024; Song et al., 2024) or instruction tuning (Willard and Louf, 2023) with adapters. Training-free approaches encompass chain-of-thought (CoT) (Wei et al., 2022; Jeong et al., 2024), self-consistency (Wang et al., 2022), and, concerned with lack of grounding resulting in hallucination, recent work introduce RAG methods (Li et al., 2024; Wang et al., 2024b; Yu et al., 2023; Munnangi et al., 2024; Wang et al., 2024a; Soong et al., 2023). However, most of these efforts have focused on performance in a particular knowledge paradigm and have lacked a systematic assessment of their performance on structured prediction, which we address in our study.

3 Methodology

Our methodology is designed to answer the following two research questions:

1. How well do Large Language Models (LLMs) perform on structured prediction tasks when provided with unstructured inputs?

2. To what extent can approaches that enhance task knowledge and external knowledge improve their performance?

To answer the first research question, we benchmark LLMs on biomedical text classification and NER datasets, focusing on the "true" zero-shot setting to evaluate models' *parametric knowledge*. This reflects real-world scenarios where annotated data is often unavailable due to ad-hoc task requirements, resource limitations and privacy constraints (Giachelle et al., 2021). This leads to what Fries et al. (2022b) describe as "dataset debt", highlighting issues like inconsistent documentation, lack of domain-specific information except generic entities and difficulties adapting datasets to niche domains. Clinicians face significant time constraints, which limit even few-shot annotations (Xia and Yetisgen-Yildiz, 2012; Wac et al., 2024; Farri et al., 2013). These factors make **fine-tuning and few-shot approaches impractical** for structured prediction tasks in the biomedical domain, **positioning zero-shot methods as a scalable solution for real-world biomedical tasks**.

To answer the second question, we compare their zero-shot performance to various methods that aim to enhance *task knowledge* and *external knowledge*, while keeping the *parametric knowledge* static.

Techniques Table 1 lists our methods. We use VANILLA prompting as the baseline, and enhance it with advanced approaches: chain-of-thought (CoT) (Wei et al., 2022) and self-consistency (SC) (Wang et al., 2022), along with retrieval-augmented generation (RAG) (Lewis et al., 2020) that leverages FAISS with PubMed abstracts and Wikipedia articles, embedding documents via `all-MiniLM-L6-v2` (Reimers and Gurevych, 2019). We also apply constrained decoding (Willard and Louf, 2023) to enforce structured outputs. For NER, we adopt a two-stage approach: Stage 1 assigns generic entity labels (e.g., "Bodypart"), and Stage 2 refines them to fine-grained labels. Self-consistency is employed in both tasks to aggregate multiple reasoning paths via majority voting.

Complete details of our datasets, techniques and methods are described in Appendix D.

4 Evaluation Results

The complete table of results is provided in table 2. We give an overview of our findings followed by a deeper analysis of the evaluated techniques.

4.1 Overview of results

	Technique	CLS	NER	
		F1	F1-S	F1-L
BioMistral-7B	VANILLA	36.5	3.3	2.2
	CoT	31.3	1.5	1.3
	SC-CoT	20.5	0.8	0.4
	CoT-RAG-P	14.7	1.6	1.2
	CoT-RAG-W	15.5	1.3	1.0
	SC-CoT-RAG-P	19.2	0.5	0.4
	SC-CoT-RAG-W	21.6	0.4	0.3
Llama-2-70B	VANILLA	40.3	8.6	5.8
	CoT	35.9	10.3	7.3
	SC-CoT	28.0	9.1	5.4
	CoT-RAG-P	16.5	9.9	7.1
	CoT-RAG-W	15.7	10.6	7.2
	SC-CoT-RAG-P	27.2	9.0	5.4
	SC-CoT-RAG-W	26.6	9.1	5.3
Llama-2-7B	VANILLA	34.9	6.5	5.2
	CoT	30.6	4.9	2.5
	SC-CoT	24.6	5.1	3.0
	CoT-RAG-P	14.3	4.6	2.3
	CoT-RAG-W	14.5	4.2	1.7
	SC-CoT-RAG-P	25.5	5.7	2.9
	SC-CoT-RAG-W	11.1	5.6	3.2

Table 2: Performance of each model and technique combination across Classification and NER datasets. For classification, we report Micro-F1 and for NER we report both Span-Identification Micro-F1 performance as well as full Micro-F1 performance, including recognizing correct types.

Reasoning and knowledge-enhancing techniques do not improve performance. Figures 1 and 2 compare the best-performing techniques for classification and NER. Surprisingly, Table 2 in the Appendix shows that Standard Prompting consistently achieves the highest average F1 scores across models: BioMistral-7B (36.48%), Llama-2-70B-Chat-AWQ (40.34%), and Llama-2-7b-chat-hf (34.92%). This suggests that for structured prediction tasks, complex reasoning techniques like CoT or RAG do not outperform Standard Prompting.

For NER, Standard Prompting remains effective, but performance varies across models and datasets. Scores are significantly lower than typical F1 scores in biomedical NER benchmarks such as NCBI disease corpus (Doğan et al., 2014;

Technique	Details	Comments
VANILLA	Standard prompting.	Baseline for all tasks.
CHAIN-OF-THOUGHT (CoT) (Wei et al., 2022)	Chain-of-thought reasoning.	Effective for QA and logical reasoning. For NER, adapted into a two-stage approach where generic entity names are first induced (e.g., *Bodypart*), followed by fine-grained labeling.
SELF-CONSISTENCY (SC) (Wang et al., 2022)	Majority voting across sampled reasoning paths.	Applied in both stages of the two-stage NER approach.
RETRIEVAL-AUGMENTED-GENERATION (RAG) (Lewis et al., 2020)	Retrieval-augmented generation using FAISS (Douze et al., 2024).	Used PubMed (Sanyal et al., 2021) and Wikipedia as corpora. PubMed improved performance; Wikipedia degraded performance for medical QA (Xiong et al., 2024).
CONSTRAINED DECODING (Willard and Louf, 2023)	Restricted outputs to ensure structured extraction.	Avoided hallucinations. Ensured span and label consistency in NER tasks.

Table 1: Techniques Summary with Comments and Details. Complete details can be found in Appendix D.

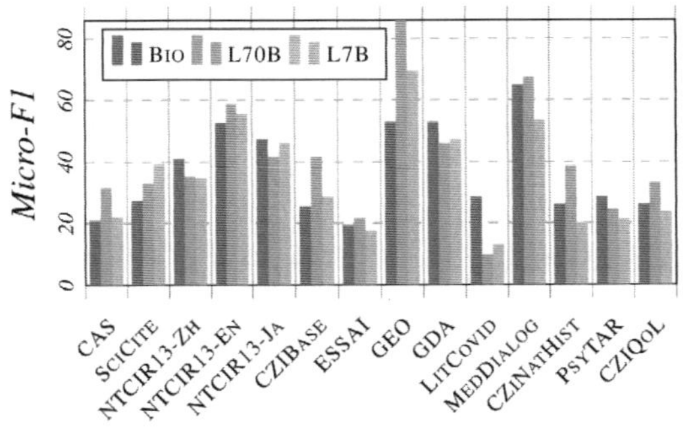

Figure 1: Best-performing *Standard Prompting* method for BioMistral 7B, Llama-70B and Llama-7B for all classification tasks.

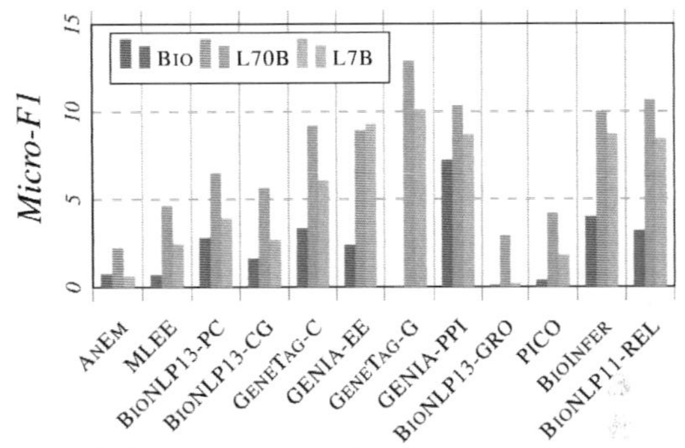

Figure 2: Best-performing *Standard Prompting* method for BioMistral 7B, Llama-70B and Llama-7B for all NER tasks.

Krallinger et al., 2015) and CHEMDNER, where specialized models achieve up to 0.90 Span F1 scores (Kocaman and Talby, 2021; Zhou et al., 2023). However, similar to our findings, zero-shot NER scores tend to be low, even in general domains (Shen et al., 2021) and when providing label descriptions (Picco et al., 2024).

The likely reason for poor performance is that these approaches excel in knowledge- and reasoning-intensive tasks like Question Answering (Nori et al., 2023) or Mathematical Reasoning (Wang and Zhou, 2024; Wang et al., 2022; Li et al., 2024), but structured prediction tasks require understanding task semantics over generic reasoning. These tasks rely less on broad knowledge from biomedical papers or Wikipedia and more on domain-specific application within the given input. Effective models must handle specialized vocabulary, jargon, acronyms, and synonyms varying across subfields (Kim et al., 2007; Zheng et al., 2018; Jiang and Xu, 2024). They must also resolve ambiguity, polysemy, and syntactic nuances in biomedical concepts, which the LLMs to not have been able to capture.

Scale drives improvements. Consistent with prior findings, the 70B model shows notable gains over the 7B model (5.4% for classification, 2.2% for NER Span F1). The largest performance gap appears when using SC with COT and RAG (Wikipedia), where the 70B model surpasses the 7B model by 15.45%. This suggests the larger model excels at leveraging external knowledge when paired with SC and chain-of-thought prompting. The 70B model's greater capacity is particularly beneficial for handling complex reasoning and knowledge integration (Wei et al., 2022). This is further supported by its 10.91% improvement when SC is added to Wikipedia-based RAG, helping mitigate performance drops from irrelevant external information. Unlike classification tasks, where Standard Prompting performed best, NER performance remains stable with advanced prompting techniques, especially in larger models like Llama-2-70B, likely due to the inherent lack of epistemic certainty in NER outputs.

4.2 Detailed Comparison of Prompting Techniques

CoT and SC underperform without sufficient parametric knowledge. For BioMistral-7B, SC-

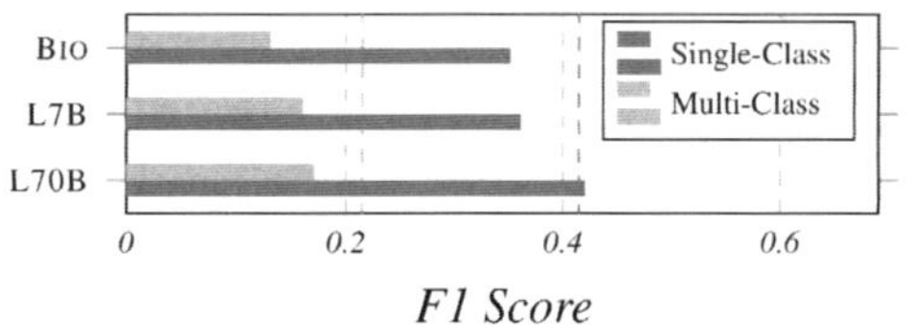

Figure 3: Performance comparison for **Bio**Mistral 7B, Llama**7B** and Llama**70B** on single- and multi-label datasets, with random guess baselines of 0.415 and 0.215, respectively.

CoT prompts reduce classification performance by about 16%. One reason may be that domain-specific pre-training, while enhancing performance on specialized biomedical tasks, can limit the model's general adaptability(Brokman and Kavuluru, 2024). Similar to RAG, SC does not consistently improve NER. While SC aims to generate multiple reasoning paths and select the most consistent one, it may introduce errors when the model's epistemic certainty in its outputs is low, leading to performance drops. For NER, combining CoT and SC with RAG (Wikipedia) produces the largest performance gap between 70B and 7B models, suggesting that larger models use external knowledge and complex reasoning more effectively when parametric knowledge is limited.

RAG does not help information extraction. Although RAG can improve QA tasks by retrieving relevant facts (Xiong et al., 2024), it seems less useful for classification and information extraction, where irrelevant information misleads the model, creating additional complexity. This results in a drop in classification accuracy, dropping 16.91% with PubMed Corpora and 16.47% with Wikipedia compared to the best classification method.

SC helps filter noise for RAG but does not aid CoT. While SC aims to improve CoT by generating multiple reasoning paths, its efficacy depends on the model's epistemic certainty (Yadkori et al., 2024; Liu et al., 2024). Insufficient parametric knowledge lowers confidence, causing performance declines. BioMistral-7B loses about 16% in classification with SC-CoT prompting. SC also fails to consistently boost NER. However, in the 70B model, combining CoT and SC with RAG (Wikipedia) yields notable gains, indicating that larger models better exploit external knowledge and present higher epistemic certainty owing to their larger parametric capacity.

4.3 Detailed Per-Dataset Analysis

Figure 3 provides the performance comparison of the three models on single and multi-label tasks. Figures 4 and 5 provide a detailed analysis and breakdown of performance of each technique (NER and classification) on each dataset, along with random baselines for each. We discuss their implications below.

Models perform significantly better on public datasets. On public datasets, models average around 30% accuracy, compared to 12% on private datasets, suggesting potential data leakage from publicly available sources used in pre-training or instruction-tuning. Thus, performance on "unseen" tasks may stem from prior exposure rather than true generalization.

Multilingual performance is not scale dependent. As shown in Figure 1, smaller models can match or outperform larger ones on Chinese and Japanese datasets but lag behind in English tasks. This disparity likely results from heavy reliance on English corpora and limited non-English domain exposure, increasing overfitting risks. Factors like language family, data sampling ratios, and sparse representation can also inhibit multilingual models (He et al., 2024; Bagheri Nezhad and Agrawal, 2024).

LLMs struggle on high-complexity tasks. As in Figure 3, LLMs often fail to surpass random baselines for single and multi-class classification, though Figure 4 shows these baselines remain unbeaten in only two of 14 datasets.

5 Conclusion

We provide a comprehensive benchmark and analysis of LLMs in Medical Classification and Named Entity Recognition tasks, revealing several key insights that have significant implications for the field. We carry out a critical investigation of broad claims regarding LLM capabilities by replicating them in various contexts, domains and datasets. We find that models suffer from fundamental drawbacks in generalizability, which hinder their performance in structured information extraction tasks on domain specific problems. This leads to standard prompting outperforming more advanced methods for all models. Our findings underscore that parametric knowledge capacity remains the most important factor in zero-shot settings, with advanced techniques used to augment external knowledge or model reasoning failing to improve performance.

Limitations

While our study provides important insights into LLMs' capabilities for biomedical classification and information extraction, several limitations should be considered when interpreting our results. Our findings are primarily empirical and, although they suggest consistent patterns across models and tasks, further theoretical work is needed to fully understand why advanced prompting techniques fail to improve performance on structured prediction tasks. We deliberately exclude closed-source LLMs from our analysis due to privacy concerns in medical applications and the observed dataset leakage issues, where public dataset contamination is even harder to control for proprietary models. Additionally, our focus on constrained decoding for reliable output parsing necessarily limits us to open-source models where we have access to the generation process.

We also specifically choose not to evaluate in-context learning (ICL) approaches, as our study focuses on "true" zero-shot capabilities where no task-specific examples are available. While techniques like k-NN ICL have shown promise in other domains, they require substantial annotated data to retrieve examples from—which is often unavailable in practical medical settings. Fixed ICL examples could be used, but performance would then largely depend on example selection, essentially reducing the evaluation to the quality of prompt engineering. To balance *(i)* scientific validity and focus on real-world scenarios, where domain experts may not be prompt engineering specialists, with *(ii)* the need to provide useful information to the models, we instead opt for the zero-shot setting—addressing *(i)*—while ensuring semantic clarity through meaningful label names (e.g., using "Control" and "Perturbation" rather than "0" and "1" in the GEO dataset)—addressing *(ii)*.

References

Harika Abburi, Michael Suesserman, Nirmala Pudota, Balaji Veeramani, Edward Bowen, and Sanmitra Bhattacharya. 2023. Generative AI text classification using ensemble LLM approaches. In *IberLEF@SEPLN*, volume 3496 of *CEUR Workshop Proceedings*. CEUR-WS.org.

Sina Bagheri Nezhad and Ameeta Agrawal. 2024. What drives performance in multilingual language models? *arXiv e-prints*, pages arXiv–2404.

Som S Biswas. 2023. Role of chat gpt in public health. *Annals of biomedical engineering*, 51(5):868–869.

Elliot Bolton, Abhinav Venigalla, Michihiro Yasunaga, David Hall, Betty Xiong, Tony Lee, Roxana Daneshjou, Jonathan Frankle, Percy Liang, Michael Carbin, et al. 2024. Biomedlm: A 2.7 b parameter language model trained on biomedical text. *arXiv preprint arXiv:2403.18421*.

Àlex Bravo, Janet Piñero, Núria Queralt-Rosinach, Michael Rautschka, and Laura I Furlong. 2015. Extraction of relations between genes and diseases from text and large-scale data analysis: implications for translational research. *BMC Bioinformatics*, 16(1).

Aviv Brokman and Ramakanth Kavuluru. 2024. How important is domain specificity in language models and instruction finetuning for biomedical relation extraction? *arXiv preprint arXiv:2402.13470*.

Leona Cilar Budler, Lucija Gosak, and Gregor Stiglic. 2023. Review of artificial intelligence-based question-answering systems in healthcare. *WIREs Data. Mining. Knowl. Discov.*, 13(2).

Qingyu Chen, Alexis Allot, Robert Leaman, Rezarta Islamaj Doğan, and Zhiyong Lu. 2021. Overview of the biocreative vii litcovid track: multi-label topic classification for covid-19 literature annotation. In *Proceedings of the seventh BioCreative challenge evaluation workshop*.

Shu Chen, Zeqian Ju, Xiangyu Dong, Hongchao Fang, Sicheng Wang, Yue Yang, Jiaqi Zeng, Ruisi Zhang, Ruoyu Zhang, Meng Zhou, Penghui Zhu, and Pengtao Xie. 2020. Meddialog: A large-scale medical dialogue dataset. *CoRR*, abs/2004.03329.

Zeming Chen, Alejandro Hernández Cano, Angelika Romanou, Antoine Bonnet, Kyle Matoba, Francesco Salvi, Matteo Pagliardini, Simin Fan, Andreas Köpf, Amirkeivan Mohtashami, et al. 2023. Meditron-70b: Scaling medical pretraining for large language models. *arXiv preprint arXiv:2311.16079*.

Arman Cohan, Waleed Ammar, Madeleine van Zuylen, and Field Cady. 2019. Structural scaffolds for citation intent classification in scientific publications. In *Conference of the North American Chapter of the Association for Computational Linguistics*.

Rezarta Islamaj Doğan, Robert Leaman, and Zhiyong Lu. 2014. Ncbi disease corpus: a resource for disease name recognition and concept normalization. *Journal of biomedical informatics*, 47:1–10.

Matthijs Douze, Alexandr Guzhva, Chengqi Deng, Jeff Johnson, Gergely Szilvasy, Pierre-Emmanuel Mazaré, Maria Lomeli, Lucas Hosseini, and Hervé Jégou. 2024. The faiss library. *arXiv preprint*.

Inc. Elucidata. 2022. Geokhoj v1. https://github.com/ElucidataInc/GEOKhoj-datasets/tree/main/geokhoj_v1.

Oladimeji Farri, Karen A Monsen, Serguei V Pakhomov, David S Pieczkiewicz, Stuart M Speedie, and Genevieve B Melton. 2013. Effects of time constraints on clinician–computer interaction: a study on information synthesis from ehr clinical notes. *Journal of biomedical informatics*, 46(6):1136–1144.

Hui Feng, Francesco Ronzano, Jude LaFleur, Matthew Garber, Rodrigo de Oliveira, Kathryn Rough, Katharine Roth, Jay Nanavati, Khaldoun Zine El Abidine, and Christina Mack. 2024. Evaluation of large language model performance on the biomedical language understanding and reasoning benchmark. *medRxiv*, pages 2024–05.

Jason Fries, Leon Weber, Natasha Seelam, Gabriel Altay, Debajyoti Datta, Samuele Garda, Sunny Kang, Rosaline Su, Wojciech Kusa, Samuel Cahyawijaya, et al. 2022a. Bigbio: A framework for data-centric biomedical natural language processing. *Advances in Neural Information Processing Systems*, 35:25792–25806.

Jason Alan Fries, Natasha Seelam, Gabriel Altay, Leon Weber, Myungsun Kang, Debajyoti Datta, Ruisi Su, Samuele Garda, Bo Wang, Simon Ott, et al. 2022b. Dataset debt in biomedical language modeling. In *2022 Challenges and Perspectives in Creating Large Language Models, Proceedings of the Workshop*, pages 137–145. Association for Computational Linguistics (ACL).

Fabio Giachelle, Ornella Irrera, and Gianmaria Silvello. 2021. Medtag: a portable and customizable annotation tool for biomedical documents. *BMC Medical Informatics and Decision Making*, 21(1):352.

Natalia Grabar, Vincent Claveau, and Cl'ement Dalloux. 2018. CAS: French corpus with clinical cases. In *Proceedings of the Ninth International Workshop on Health Text Mining and Information Analysis*, pages 122–128, Brussels, Belgium. Association for Computational Linguistics.

Bernal Jimenez Gutierrez, Nikolas McNeal, Clayton Washington, You Chen, Lang Li, Huan Sun, and Yu Su. 2022. Thinking about GPT-3 in-context learning for biomedical ie? think again. In *EMNLP (Findings)*, pages 4497–4512. Association for Computational Linguistics.

Muhammad Usman Hadi, Rizwan Qureshi, Abbas Shah, Muhammad Irfan, Anas Zafar, Muhammad Bilal Shaikh, Naveed Akhtar, Jia Wu, Seyedali Mirjalili, et al. 2023. A survey on large language models: Applications, challenges, limitations, and practical usage. *Authorea Preprints*.

Emily Harris. 2023. Large language models answer medical questions accurately, but can't match clinicians' knowledge. *JAMA*.

Yifei He, Alon Benhaim, Barun Patra, Praneetha Vaddamanu, Sanchit Ahuja, Parul Chopra, Vishrav Chaudhary, Han Zhao, and Xia Song. 2024. Scaling laws for multilingual language models. *arXiv preprint arXiv:2410.12883*.

Robert Hoehndorf, Axel cyrille Ngonga Ngomo, Sampo Pyysalo, Tomoko Ohta, Anika Oellrich, and Dietrich Rebholz-schuhmann. 2010. Applying ontology design patterns to the implementation of relations in genia. In *Proceedings of the Fourth International Symposium for Semantic Mining in Biomedicine*.

Hayate Iso, Camille Ruiz, Taichi Murayama, Katsuya Taguchi, Ryo Takeuchi, Hideya Yamamoto, Shoko Wakamiya, and Eiji Aramaki. 2017. Ntcir13 medweb task: multi-label classification of tweets using an ensemble of neural networks. In *NTCIR*.

Minbyul Jeong, Hyeon Hwang, Chanwoong Yoon, Taewhoo Lee, and Jaewoo Kang. 2024. Olaph: Improving factuality in biomedical long-form question answering. *arXiv preprint arXiv:2405.12701*.

Chao Jiang and Wei Xu. 2024. Medreadme: A systematic study for fine-grained sentence readability in medical domain. *arXiv preprint arXiv:2405.02144*.

Jeff Johnson, Matthijs Douze, and Hervé Jégou. 2019. Billion-scale similarity search with GPUs. *IEEE Transactions on Big Data*, 7(3):535–547.

Mael Jullien, Marco Valentino, Hannah Frost, Paul O'Regan, Dónal Landers, and Andre Freitas. 2023. NLI4CT: Multi-Evidence Natural Language Inference for Clinical Trial Reports. In *Proceedings of the 2023 Conference on Empirical Methods in Natural Language Processing*, pages 16745–16764, Stroudsburg, PA, USA. Association for Computational Linguistics.

Rajvir Kaur, Jeewani Anupama Ginige, and Oliver Obst. 2023. Ai-based ICD coding and classification approaches using discharge summaries: A systematic literature review. *Expert Syst. Appl.*, 213(Part):118997.

Hyeoneui Kim, Sergey Goryachev, Graciela Rosemblat, Allen Browne, Alla Keselman, and Qing Zeng-Treitler. 2007. Beyond surface characteristics: a new health text-specific readability measurement. In *AMIA Annual Symposium Proceedings*, volume 2007, page 418. American Medical Informatics Association.

Jin-Dong Kim, Tomoko Ohta, Sampo Pyysalo, Yoshinobu Kano, and Jun'ichi Tsujii. 2009. Overview of BioNLP'09 shared task on event extraction. In *Proceedings of the BioNLP 2009 Workshop Companion Volume for Shared Task*, pages 1–9, Boulder, Colorado. Association for Computational Linguistics.

Jung-jae Kim, Xu Han, Vivian Lee, and Dietrich Rebholz-Schuhmann. 2013. GRO task: Populating the gene regulation ontology with events and relations. In *Proceedings of the BioNLP Shared Task 2013 Workshop*, pages 50–57, Sofia, Bulgaria. Association for Computational Linguistics.

Veysel Kocaman and David Talby. 2021. Biomedical named entity recognition at scale. In *Pattern Recognition. ICPR International Workshops and Challenges:*

Virtual Event, January 10–15, 2021, Proceedings, Part I, pages 635–646. Springer.

Martin Krallinger, Florian Leitner, Obdulia Rabal, Miguel Vazquez, Julen Oyarzabal, and Alfonso Valencia. 2015. Chemdner: The drugs and chemical names extraction challenge. *Journal of cheminformatics*, 7:1–11.

Yanis Labrak, Adrien Bazoge, Emmanuel Morin, Pierre-Antoine Gourraud, Mickael Rouvier, and Richard Dufour. 2024. Biomistral: A collection of open-source pretrained large language models for medical domains. *arXiv preprint arXiv:2402.10373*.

Christoph H. Lampert, Hannes Nickisch, and Stefan Harmeling. 2014. Attribute-based classification for zero-shot visual object categorization. *IEEE Trans. Pattern Anal. Mach. Intell.*, 36(3):453–465.

Patrick Lewis, Ethan Perez, Aleksandra Piktus, Fabio Petroni, Vladimir Karpukhin, Naman Goyal, Heinrich Küttler, Mike Lewis, Wen-tau Yih, Tim Rocktäschel, et al. 2020. Retrieval-augmented generation for knowledge-intensive nlp tasks. *Advances in Neural Information Processing Systems*, 33:9459–9474.

Hao Li, Yu-Ping Wu, Viktor Schlegel, Riza Batista-Navarro, Thanh-Tung Nguyen, Abhinav Ramesh Kashyap, Xiao-Jun Zeng, Daniel Beck, Stefan Winkler, and Goran Nenadic. 2023. Team: PULSAR at probsum 2023: PULSAR: pre-training with extracted healthcare terms for summarising patients' problems and data augmentation with black-box large language models. In *BioNLP@ACL*, pages 503–509. Association for Computational Linguistics.

Mingchen Li, Huixue Zhou, Han Yang, and Rui Zhang. 2024. Rt: a retrieving and chain-of-thought framework for few-shot medical named entity recognition. *Journal of the American Medical Informatics Association*, page ocae095.

Linyu Liu, Yu Pan, Xiaocheng Li, and Guanting Chen. 2024. Uncertainty estimation and quantification for llms: A simple supervised approach. *arXiv preprint arXiv:2404.15993*.

Itay Manes, Naama Ronn, David Cohen, Ran Ilan Ber, Zehavi Horowitz-Kugler, and Gabriel Stanovsky. 2024. K-QA: A real-world medical q&a benchmark. *CoRR*, abs/2401.14493.

Monica Munnangi, Sergey Feldman, Byron C Wallace, Silvio Amir, Tom Hope, and Aakanksha Naik. 2024. On-the-fly definition augmentation of llms for biomedical ner. *arXiv preprint arXiv:2404.00152*.

Aishik Nagar, Yutong Liu, Andy T Liu, Viktor Schlegel, Vijay Prakash Dwivedi, Arun-Kumar Kaliya-Perumal, Guna Pratheep Kalanchiam, Yili Tang, and Robby T Tan. 2024. umedsum: A unified framework for advancing medical abstractive summarization. *arXiv preprint arXiv:2408.12095*.

Harsha Nori, Yin Tat Lee, Sheng Zhang, Dean Carignan, Richard Edgar, Nicolò Fusi, Nicholas King, Jonathan Larson, Yuanzhi Li, Weishung Liu, Renqian Luo, Scott Mayer McKinney, Robert Osazuwa Ness, Hoifung Poon, Tao Qin, Naoto Usuyama, Chris White, and Eric Horvitz. 2023. Can generalist foundation models outcompete special-purpose tuning? case study in medicine. *CoRR*, abs/2311.16452.

Benjamin Nye, Junyi Jessy Li, Roma Patel, Yinfei Yang, Iain Marshall, Ani Nenkova, and Byron Wallace. 2018. A corpus with multi-level annotations of patients, interventions and outcomes to support language processing for medical literature. In *Proceedings of the 56th Annual Meeting of the Association for Computational Linguistics (Volume 1: Long Papers)*, pages 197–207, Melbourne, Australia. Association for Computational Linguistics.

Tomoko Ohta, Sampo Pyysalo, Jin-Dong Kim, and Jun'ichi Tsujii. 2010. A reevaluation of biomedical named entity - term relations. *Journal of bioinformatics and computational biology*, 8:917–28.

Tomoko Ohta, Sampo Pyysalo, Rafal Rak, Andrew Rowley, Hong-Woo Chun, Sung-Jae Jung, Sung-Pil Choi, Sophia Ananiadou, and Jun'ichi Tsujii. 2013. Overview of the pathway curation (PC) task of BioNLP shared task 2013. In *Proceedings of the BioNLP Shared Task 2013 Workshop*, pages 67–75, Sofia, Bulgaria. Association for Computational Linguistics.

Tomoko Ohta, Sampo Pyysalo, Jun'ichi Tsujii, and Sophia Ananiadou. 2012. Open-domain anatomical entity mention detection. In *Proceedings of the Workshop on Detecting Structure in Scholarly Discourse*, volume W12-43. Association for Computational Linguistics.

OpenAI. 2023. GPT-4 technical report. *CoRR*, abs/2303.08774.

Gabriele Picco, Leopold Fuchs, Marcos Martínez Galindo, Alberto Purpura, Vanessa López, and Hoang Thanh Lam. 2024. Description boosting for zero-shot entity and relation classification. *CoRR*, abs/2406.02245.

Sampo Pyysalo, Filip Ginter, Juho Heimonen, Jari Bj"orne, Jorma Boberg, Jouni J"arvinen, and Tapio Salakoski. 2007. Bioinfer: a corpus for information extraction in the biomedical domain. *BMC bioinformatics*, 8(1):1–24.

Sampo Pyysalo, Tomoko Ohta, and Sophia Ananiadou. 2013. Overview of the cancer genetics (CG) task of BioNLP shared task 2013. In *Proceedings of the BioNLP Shared Task 2013 Workshop*, pages 58–66, Sofia, Bulgaria. Association for Computational Linguistics.

Sampo Pyysalo, Tomoko Ohta, Jin-Dong Kim, and Jun'ichi Tsujii. 2009. Static relations: a piece in the biomedical information extraction puzzle. In *Proceedings of the BioNLP 2009 Workshop*, pages 1–9,

Boulder, Colorado. Association for Computational Linguistics.

Sampo Pyysalo, Tomoko Ohta, Makoto Miwa, Han-Cheol Cho, Jun'ichi Tsujii, and Sophia Ananiadou. 2012. Event extraction across multiple levels of biological organization. *Bioinformatics*, 28(18):i575–i581.

Sampo Pyysalo, Tomoko Ohta, and Jun'ichi Tsujii. 2011. Overview of the entity relations (rel) supporting task of bionlp shared task 2011. In *Proceedings of the BioNLP Shared Task 2011 Workshop*, BioNLP Shared Task '11, page 83–88, USA. Association for Computational Linguistics.

Nils Reimers and Iryna Gurevych. 2019. Sentence-bert: Sentence embeddings using siamese bert-networks. In *EMNLP/IJCNLP (1)*, pages 3980–3990. Association for Computational Linguistics.

Debarshi Kumar Sanyal, Plaban Kumar Bhowmick, and Partha Pratim Das. 2021. A review of author name disambiguation techniques for the pubmed bibliographic database. *J. Inf. Sci.*, 47(2).

Viktor Schlegel, Hao Li, Yu-Ping Wu, Anand Subramanian, Thanh-Tung Nguyen, Abhinav Ramesh Kashyap, Daniel Beck, Xiao-Jun Zeng, Riza Theresa Batista-Navarro, Stefan Winkler, and Goran Nenadic. 2023. PULSAR at mediqa-sum 2023: Large language models augmented by synthetic dialogue convert patient dialogues to medical records. In *CLEF (Working Notes)*, volume 3497 of *CEUR Workshop Proceedings*, pages 1668–1679. CEUR-WS.org.

Yongliang Shen, Xinyin Ma, Zeqi Tan, Shuai Zhang, Wen Wang, and Weiming Lu. 2021. Locate and label: A two-stage identifier for nested named entity recognition. *arXiv preprint arXiv:2105.06804*.

Wenqi Shi, Ran Xu, Yuchen Zhuang, Yue Yu, Hang Wu, Carl Yang, and May D. Wang. 2024. Medadapter: Efficient test-time adaptation of large language models towards medical reasoning. *Preprint*, arXiv:2405.03000.

Karan Singhal, Shekoofeh Azizi, Tao Tu, S Sara Mahdavi, Jason Wei, Hyung Won Chung, Nathan Scales, Ajay Tanwani, Heather Cole-Lewis, Stephen Pfohl, et al. 2023. Large language models encode clinical knowledge. *Nature*, 620(7972):172–180.

Yiping Song, Juhua Zhang, Zhiliang Tian, Yuxin Yang, Minlie Huang, and Dongsheng Li. 2024. Llm-based privacy data augmentation guided by knowledge distillation with a distribution tutor for medical text classification. *arXiv preprint arXiv:2402.16515*.

David Soong, Sriram Sridhar, Han Si, Jan-Samuel Wagner, Ana Caroline Costa Sá, Christina Y Yu, Kubra Karagoz, Meijian Guan, Hisham Hamadeh, and Brandon W Higgs. 2023. Improving accuracy of gpt-3/4 results on biomedical data using a retrieval-augmented language model. *arXiv preprint arXiv:2305.17116*.

Saurabh Srivastava, Anto PV, Shashank Menon, Ajay Sukumar, Alan Philipose, Stevin Prince, Sooraj Thomas, et al. 2024. Functional benchmarks for robust evaluation of reasoning performance, and the reasoning gap. *arXiv preprint arXiv:2402.19450*.

Anand Subramanian, Viktor Schlegel, Abhinav Ramesh Kashyap, Thanh-Tung Nguyen, Vijay Prakash Dwivedi, and Stefan Winkler. 2024. M-QALM: A Benchmark to Assess Clinical Reading Comprehension and Knowledge Recall in Large Language Models via Question Answering. In *Findings of the Association for Computational Linguistics ACL 2024*, pages 4002–4042, Bangkok, Thailand and virtual meeting. Association for Computational Linguistics.

Lorraine Tanabe, Natalie Xie, Lynne H Thom, Wayne Matten, and W John Wilbur. 2005. GENETAG: a tagged corpus for gene/protein named entity recognition. *BMC Bioinformatics*, 6.

Hugo Touvron, Louis Martin, Kevin Stone, Peter Albert, Amjad Almahairi, Yasmine Babaei, Nikolay Bashlykov, Soumya Batra, Prajjwal Bhargava, Shruti Bhosale, et al. 2023. Llama 2: Open foundation and fine-tuned chat models. *arXiv preprint arXiv:2307.09288*.

Dave Van Veen, Cara Van Uden, Louis Blankemeier, Jean-Benoit Delbrouck, Asad Aali, Christian Bluethgen, Anuj Pareek, Malgorzata Polacin, Eduardo Pontes Reis, Anna Seehofnerová, et al. 2024. Adapted large language models can outperform medical experts in clinical text summarization. *Nature medicine*, 30(4):1134–1142.

Marceli Wac, Raul Santos-Rodriguez, Chris McWilliams, and Christopher Bourdeaux. 2024. Evaluation of a data annotation platform for large, time-series datasets in intensive care: Mixed methods study. *arXiv preprint arXiv:2410.16959*.

Junda Wang, Zhichao Yang, Zonghai Yao, and Hong Yu. 2024a. Jmlr: Joint medical llm and retrieval training for enhancing reasoning and professional question answering capability. *arXiv preprint arXiv:2402.17887*.

Xuezhi Wang, Jason Wei, Dale Schuurmans, Quoc Le, Ed Chi, Sharan Narang, Aakanksha Chowdhery, and Denny Zhou. 2022. Self-consistency improves chain of thought reasoning in language models. *arXiv preprint arXiv:2203.11171*.

Xuezhi Wang and Denny Zhou. 2024. Chain-of-thought reasoning without prompting. *arXiv preprint arXiv:2402.10200*.

Yang Wang, Xueping Peng, Tao Shen, Allison Clarke, Clement Schlegel, Paul Martin, and Guodong Long. 2023. Soft prompt transfer for zero-shot and few-shot learning in EHR understanding. In *ADMA (3)*, volume 14178 of *Lecture Notes in Computer Science*, pages 18–32. Springer.

Zihao Wang, Anji Liu, Haowei Lin, Jiaqi Li, Xiaojian Ma, and Yitao Liang. 2024b. Rat: Retrieval augmented thoughts elicit context-aware reasoning in long-horizon generation. *arXiv preprint arXiv:2403.05313*.

Jason Wei, Xuezhi Wang, Dale Schuurmans, Maarten Bosma, Fei Xia, Ed Chi, Quoc V Le, Denny Zhou, et al. 2022. Chain-of-thought prompting elicits reasoning in large language models. *Advances in neural information processing systems*, 35:24824–24837.

Brandon T Willard and Rémi Louf. 2023. Efficient guided generation for large language models. *arXiv e-prints*, pages arXiv–2307.

Fei Xia and Meliha Yetisgen-Yildiz. 2012. Clinical corpus annotation: challenges and strategies. In *Proceedings of the third workshop on building and evaluating resources for biomedical text mining (BioTxtM'2012) in conjunction with the international conference on language resources and evaluation (LREC), Istanbul, Turkey*, pages 21–27.

Qianqian Xie, Qingyu Chen, Aokun Chen, Cheng Peng, Yan Hu, Fongci Lin, Xueqing Peng, Jimin Huang, Jeffrey Zhang, Vipina Keloth, et al. 2024. Me llama: Foundation large language models for medical applications. *arXiv preprint arXiv:2402.12749*.

Tingyu Xie, Qi Li, Jian Zhang, Yan Zhang, Zuozhu Liu, and Hongwei Wang. 2023. Empirical study of zero-shot ner with chatgpt. *arXiv preprint arXiv:2310.10035*.

Guangzhi Xiong, Qiao Jin, Zhiyong Lu, and Aidong Zhang. 2024. Benchmarking retrieval-augmented generation for medicine. *arXiv preprint arXiv:2402.13178*.

Yasin Abbasi Yadkori, Ilja Kuzborskij, András György, and Csaba Szepesvári. 2024. To believe or not to believe your llm. *arXiv preprint arXiv:2406.02543*.

Wen-wai Yim, Yujuan Fu, Asma Ben Abacha, Neal Snider, Thomas Lin, and Meliha Yetisgen. 2023. ACI-BENCH: a novel ambient clinical intelligence dataset for benchmarking automatic visit note generation. *CoRR*, abs/2306.02022.

Guoxin Yu, Lemao Liu, Haiyun Jiang, Shuming Shi, and Xiang Ao. 2023. Retrieval-augmented few-shot text classification. In *Findings of the Association for Computational Linguistics: EMNLP 2023*, pages 6721–6735.

Meishan Zhang, Bin Wang, Hao Fei, and Min Zhang. 2024. In-context learning for few-shot nested named entity recognition. In *ICASSP*, pages 10026–10030. IEEE.

Jiaping Zheng, Hong Yu, et al. 2018. Assessing the readability of medical documents: a ranking approach. *JMIR medical informatics*, 6(1):e8611.

Wenxuan Zhou, Sheng Zhang, Yu Gu, Muhao Chen, and Hoifung Poon. 2023. Universalner: Targeted distillation from large language models for open named entity recognition. *arXiv preprint arXiv:2308.03279*.

Maryam Zolnoori, Kin Wah Fung, Timothy B. Patrick, Paul Fontelo, Hadi Kharrazi, Anthony Faiola, Yi Shuan Shirley Wu, Christina E. Eldredge, Jake Luo, Mike Conway, Jiaxi Zhu, Soo Kyung Park, Kelly Xu, Hamideh Moayyed, and Somaieh Goudarzvand. 2019. A systematic approach for developing a corpus of patient reported adverse drug events: A case study for SSRI and SNRI medications. *Journal of Biomedical Informatics*, 90.

A Related Work

Existing LLMs Benchmarks: With the rising popularity of LLMs, many works evaluated their performance in the biomedical and clinical domains. These works typically focus on evaluating domain-knowledge by means of Question Answering (Singhal et al., 2023; Harris, 2023; Subramanian et al., 2024), or focus directly on possible application scenarios, such as summarisation (Li et al., 2023; Yim et al., 2023) or clinical coding (Kaur et al., 2023). Many works combine these two directions in an effort to provide more comprehensive benchmarks (Srivastava et al., 2024; Xiong et al., 2024; Feng et al., 2024; Chen et al., 2020; Manes et al., 2024). However, many of these works overlook the wealth of existing literature and plethora of available resources for traditional structured prediction tasks in the biomedical domain, such as document classification, entity recognition and linking and event and relation extraction (e.g., Pyysalo et al. (2007; 2012) to name a few). Fries et al. (2022a) have provided a comprehensive and unified collection of these resources, however their work prioritises reportage of the resource collection over benchmarking results. Their preliminary evaluations suggest that their evaluated pre-LLM era models barely surpass the random guess baseline in the zero-shot setting. We build upon their work by providing a detailed analysis to what extent approaches to enhance reasoning and knowledge in LLMs help to challenge this status quo.

B Datasets

Table 3 and 4 list the huggingface dataset cards and citations for each classification and ner dataset used in the paper respectively.
For datasets considered private, we assume that models have not been trained on these datasets due to their restricted access, which requires Data Use Agreements (DUAs) and other permissions. Consequently, the likelihood of these datasets being included in common web crawls is low.
We have signed all the relevant Data Use Agreements (DUAs) and strictly adhere to their provisions. We do not redistribute the data and advise those wishing to reproduce experiments involving private datasets to consult the corresponding Hugging Face dataset cards for guidance on obtaining the necessary data.

C Compute Details

1. Hardware used (GPU/CPU): We used a mix of different shared computational facilities with nVidia A100-SXM4-80GB, RTX6000 with 24GB and L40S with 48GB. Debian OS was used for all the compute servers.

2. Memory: The machines used had between 256 GB and 1TB of memory

3. Software and libraries used: The environment can be reproduced from the texttenvironment.yaml file in the supplementary material

4. Model details: The models used have been described in detail in the main paper submission under the Models subsection of the Methodology section.

5. Random seed of 42 was used for all random sampling purposes

D Methodology

Datasets Since we evaluate different prompting techniques, we restrict the choice of tasks to those where the number of possible labels is small enough to fit in the evaluated LLMs' context window. We restrict the number of labels to ten and the mean length of the input documents to at most 2048 tokens. This leaves us with 14 different classification datasets from the BigBio collection[1]. For the NER task, we sample 12 datasets from the pool of those that satisfy the criteria. The resulting dataset sample features four non-English datasets and six non-public classification datasets, which allows us to investigate whether LLMs perform better on minority languages or on data that is less likely to be found in public pre-training corpora. We run the evaluation on the official test-set split where available, otherwise we consider the full dataset. For datasets with more than 500 instances, we sample 500 random but fixed instances to speed up the experiments. Overall, our selection spans English and non-english source data, publicly available and private datasets, and various domains such as scientific papers, medical notes and social media.

[1]for the GAD dataset, we only select 1 fold out of the 10 available, as the folds feature the same task for different data, unlike other datasets. We also skipped the Chinese subset of meddialog as we had difficulties loading the dataset

Dataset Name	HuggingFace Card	Citation
GAD	bigbio/gad	(Bravo et al., 2015)
GEO	bigbio/geokhoj_v1	(Elucidata, 2022)
MEDDIALOG	bigbio/meddialog	(Chen et al., 2020)
CZIBASE	bigbio/czi_drsm	
CZIQOL	bigbio/czi_drsm	
CZINATHIST	bigbio/czi_drsm	
LITCOVID	bigbio/bc7_litcovid	(Chen et al., 2021)
CAS	bigbio/cas	(Grabar et al., 2018)
ESSAI	bigbio/essai	(Grabar et al., 2018)
NTCIR13-JA	bigbio/ntcir_13 _medweb	(Iso et al., 2017)
NTCIR13-EN	bigbio/ntcir_13 _medweb	(Iso et al., 2017)
NTCIR13-ZH	bigbio/ntcir_13 _medweb	(Iso et al., 2017)
PSYTAR	bigbio/psytar	(Zolnoori et al., 2019)
SCICITE	bigbio/scicite	(Cohan et al., 2019)

Table 3: Datasets used for classification tasks.

Classification: The datasets used for classification tasks include both single-label and multi-label datasets, covering a wide range of biomedical and clinical domains. For single-label classification, the GAD dataset focuses on identifying associations between genes and diseases (Bravo et al., 2015), while the GEO dataset is concerned with classifying microarray, transcriptomics, and single-cell experiments from the Gene Expression Omnibus (GEO) database (Elucidata, 2022). The MEDDIALOG dataset aims to classify dialogue snippets as either being said by a doctor or a patient (Chen et al., 2020). Furthermore, the CZIDRSM dataset has several subsets, including one for classifying research articles based on aspects of disease research (CZIBASE), and others for identifying whether a paper describes substantive research into Quality of Life (CZIQOL) or is a natural history study (CZINATHIST).

In multi-label classification, the LITCOVID dataset is used for the classification of COVID-19-related articles (Chen et al., 2021). The CAS and ESSAI datasets are utilized for identify negation and uncertainty clinical cases from French-speaking countries (Grabar et al., 2018). The NTCIR13 datasets include subsets for disease classification of tweets in Japanese (*-JA), English (*-EN), and Chinese (*-ZH) (Iso et al., 2017). Additionally, the PSYTAR dataset is used for sentence classification of various drug-related effects, such as Adverse Drug Reactions (ADR) and Withdrawal Symptoms (WDs) (Zolnoori et al., 2019), while the SCICITE dataset is used for citation intent classification based on the context within computer science and biomedical domains (Cohan et al., 2019).

NER: The datasets for Named Entity Recognition (NER) tasks are similarly divided into entity recognition (single entity type) and classification (multiple entity types). In the single-type category, the GENETAG dataset is used for gene/protein NER, with two annotation versions: the original GENETAG-G and the corrected GENETAG-C (Tanabe et al., 2005). Additionally, the GENIA-PPI dataset focuses on protein-protein interactions or gene regulatory relations within the GENIA corpus, capturing primarily static relations (Pyysalo et al., 2009; Hoehndorf et al., 2010; Ohta et al., 2010).

The multiple-type NER datasets encompass various complex biomedical tasks. The ANEM dataset targets anatomical entity recognition (Ohta et al., 2012), while the BIOINFER dataset focuses on recognizing proteins, genes, and RNA entities (Pyysalo et al., 2007). The GENIA-EE dataset is used for the GENIA Event corpus (Kim et al., 2009), and the BIONLP11-REL dataset is employed for extracting part-of relations between genes/proteins and associated entities (Pyysalo et al., 2011). Furthermore, the BIONLP-13-CG dataset is used for Cancer Genetics (CG) information extraction, focusing on recognizing events

Dataset Name	HuggingFace Card	Citation
GENETAG-G	bigbio/genetag	(Tanabe et al., 2005)
GENETAG-C	bigbio/genetag	(Tanabe et al., 2005)
GENIA-PPI	bigbio/genia _relation_corpus	(Pyysalo et al., 2009; Hoehndorf et al., 2010; Ohta et al., 2010)
ANEM	bigbio/an_em	(Ohta et al., 2012)
BIOINFER	bigbio/bioinfer	(Pyysalo et al., 2007)
GENIA-EE	bigbio/bionlp _shared_task_2009	(Kim et al., 2009)
BIONLP11-REL	bigbio/bionlp_st _2011_rel	(Pyysalo et al., 2011)
BIONLP-13-CG	bigbio/bionlp_st _2013_cg	(Pyysalo et al., 2013)
BIONLP-13-GRO	bigbio/bionlp_st _2013_gro	(Kim et al., 2013)
BIONLP-13-PC	bigbio/bionlp_st _2013_pc	(Ohta et al., 2013)
PICO	bigbio/ebm_pico	(Nye et al., 2018)
MLEE	bigbio/mlee	(Pyysalo et al., 2012)

Table 4: Datasets used for NER tasks.

represented as structured n-ary associations of given physical entities (Pyysalo et al., 2013). The BIONLP-13-GRO dataset aims to populate the Gene Regulation Ontology with events and relations (Kim et al., 2013), and the BIONLP-13-PC dataset is used for the automatic extraction of biomolecular reactions from text (Ohta et al., 2013). Lastly, the PICO dataset deals with recognizing (P)articipants, (I)nterventions, and (O)utcomes (Nye et al., 2018), and the MLEE dataset is used for event extraction related to angiogenesis (Pyysalo et al., 2012).

Models For our experiments, we employed two instruction-tuned variants of the Llama-2 model—7B and 70B—both (Touvron et al., 2023), alongside the BioMistral-7B model (Labrak et al., 2024) which was further pre-trained on the biomedical domain. Since we make use of constrained generation to generate model outputs and guide the models decoding process, we retrict the evaluation to open source models since this process is not possible for proprietary models such as GPT-4.

Techniques Table 1 summarizes the techniques used in this study and highlights relevant nuances and comments. These techniques include VANILLA (standard prompting), COT (chain-of-thought reasoning) (Wei et al., 2022), and SC (self-consistency) (Wang et al., 2022), as well as RAG (retrieval-augmented generation) (Lewis et al., 2020). For RAG, we used FAISS (Douze et al., 2024; Johnson et al., 2019) with PubMed abstracts (Sanyal et al., 2021) and Wikipedia articles as corpora, embedding documents with `all-MiniLM-L6-v2` (Reimers and Gurevych, 2019). We also implemented constrained decoding for structured output generation (Willard and Louf, 2023), crucial for ensuring reliable outputs in NER and classification tasks. A novel two-stage approach for NER was adopted, inspired by (Shen et al., 2021), where general entities were assigned in Stage 1 and refined in Stage 2.

Standard prompting was used as a baseline for both the Classification as well as the NER tasks. *Chain-of-thought reasoning* (Wei et al., 2022) has been shown to improve performance, particularly in QA and logical reasoning tasks. Thus, we also ran experiments with *chain-of-thought* reasoning to measure its impact on model performance. For the NER task, we adapted a more guided, *two-stage approach* (Shen et al., 2021) to implement a novel chain-of-thought reasoning approach. Here, The first stage involves inducing a generic entity name from a datasets' known entity labels—e.g., "Bodypart" for the NER labels describing different bodyparts—and then labelling the input document with that generic entity type. In the second stage all entities labelled in this way are further disambiguated with their respective fine-grained dataset NER labels. *Retrieval Augmented Generation* (Lewis et al., 2020) has been established as an effective technique to improve model performance by introducing relevant non-parameteric knowledge to models and thus grounding the generated outputs to factual information. Xiong et al. (2024) conducted a systematic study of RAG on medical QA, and we incorporate their findings into our study. We used PubMed abstracts (Sanyal et al., 2021) and Wikipedia articles as knowledge corpora, because Xiong et al.'s (2024) experiments found that using PubMed improved performance over non RAG techniques, while using Wikipedia reduced performance in medical QA tasks. Our goal was to evaluate whether the same holds true for structured prediction tasks as well. For the RAG module, we made use of FAISS (Douze et al., 2024; Johnson et al., 2019), which allows retrieval of most similar documents based on semantic similarity, where we used the `all-MiniLM-L6-v2` sentence transformers (Reimers and Gurevych, 2019) model for embedding input documents and corpora. For each experiment, the number of retrieved documents was computed based on the maximum possible documents which could be used without exceeding the token limit of the model.

Self-consistency, proposed by Wang et al. (2022), improves chain-of-thought reasoning of LLMs by sampling reasoning paths for a given problem, followed by a majority vote for the final answer. We also conduct a set of experiments employing *self-consistency* to investigate whether such improvements can be observed on structured prediction tasks in the medical domain as well. For classification tasks, self consistency was employed to generate multiple reasoning chains for the given problem, followed by answer extraction from each reasoning chain and majority voting to select the final answer. For NER tasks, since we follow the two-stage approach, self-consistency was employed in both stages. Multiple general entity labels were generated in the first stage, and entities were extracted for each such label. In the second stage, self consistency was again used for the entity selection phase as well as the entity label determination step. Majority voting was utilised in final label or class selection in each case (Xie et al., 2023).

Constrained decoding in LLMs (Willard and Louf, 2023) was used to ensure structured information extraction and text generation. This allowed us to evaluate the LLMs for the task at hand without the added variability due to the aleatoric uncertainties brought about by the probabilistic language generation fundamental to the architectures of the models. More specifically, for classification tasks, we ensured the presense of at least one label in the generated outputs. For NER we restricted the generation of spans occurring in text in the first step, and in the second step, for each of the spans we restricted the generation to any of the possible labels. This is also one of the reasons why we opted against evaluating API-based closed-source LLMs[2], as in our initial experiments the hallucinations in generated outputs created problems with reliably parsing the structured outputs.

We refer to chain of thought as COT, Self-consistency as SC, RAG as RAG-{P|W} for PubMed and Wikipedia corpora, respectively, and to standard prompting as VANILLA.

E Analysis and Performance Breakdown

Figures 4 and 5 provide a detailed analysis and breakdown of performance of each technique (NER and classification) on each dataset, along with random baselines for each. Figure 3 provides the performance comparison of the three models on single and multi-label tasks. A complete discussion for these figures and their implications can be found in section 4.3.

As discussed in section 4.3, LLMs struggle on high-complexity tasks. Even the best performing model, Llama2 70B performs well on only relatively low-complexity tasks (CZIBASE, NTCIR13-EN) and moderate tasks (GEO), but struggles with higher-complexity datasets (BIONLP13-CG, GENIA-EE). In tasks requiring nuanced interpretation (PICO, BIONLP13-GRO), performance remains low. Although RAG (Retrieval-Augmented Generation) sometimes boosts results, it does not universally enhance biomedical information extraction or classification. These findings indicate that even the most advanced general-purpose and domain-specific LLMs are not good zero-shot reasoners for structured prediction tasks such as biomedical information extraction, especially for complex task settings.

F Results Analysis

[2]The other reason being their intransparancy with regard to training data, which violates our "true" zero-shot setting.

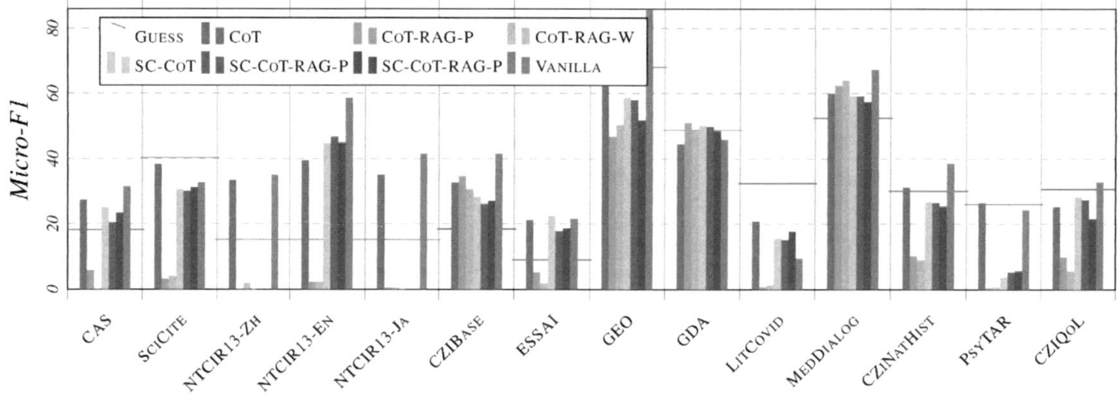

Figure 4: Breakdown of the Micro-F1 performance of each technique and the random guess baseline for all classification datasets, compared against the random guess baseline.

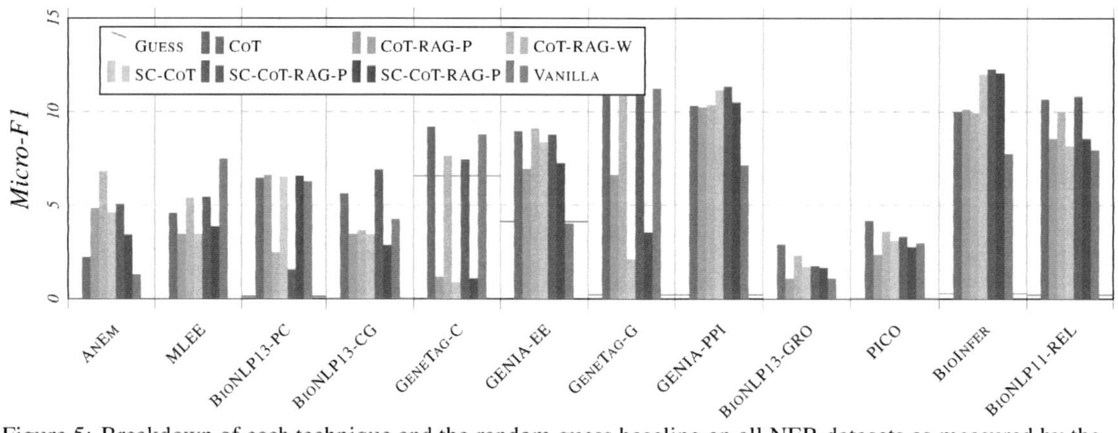

Figure 5: Breakdown of each technique and the random guess baseline on all NER datasets as measured by the Micro-F1 scores. A prediction is counted as correct when both the span and its assigned label are found in the ground truth

Exploring Limitations of LLM Capabilities with Multi-Problem Evaluation

Zhengxiang Wang and **Jordan Kodner** and **Owen Rambow**
Department of Linguistics & Institute for Advanced Computational Science
Stony Brook University, Stony Brook, NY, USA
{first.last}@stonybrook.edu

Abstract

We propose using prompts made up of multiple problems to evaluate LLM capabilities, an approach we call *multi-problem evaluation*. We examine 7 LLMs on 4 related task types constructed from 6 existing classification benchmarks. We find that while LLMs can generally perform multiple homogeneous classifications at once (Batch Classification) as well as when they do so separately, they perform significantly worse on two selection tasks that are conceptually equivalent to Batch Classification and involve selecting indices of text falling into each class label, either independently or altogether. We show that such a significant performance drop is due to LLMs' inability to adequately combine index selection with text classification. Such a drop is surprisingly observed across all LLMs attested, under zero-shot, few-shot, and CoT settings, and even with a novel synthetic dataset, potentially reflecting an inherent capability limitation with modern LLMs.

1 Introduction

In recent years, large language models (LLMs) have demonstrated remarkable natural language understanding and reasoning capabilities measured by a wide range of benchmarks (OpenAI, 2023; Beltagy et al., 2020; Gemini-Team, 2023; Anthropic, 2024). However, given their internet-scale training data, there is growing concern over whether LLMs' often superhuman benchmark performance is achieved due to data contamination (Jacovi et al., 2023; Sainz et al., 2023). Several studies (Wu et al., 2024; Mirzadeh et al., 2024) have demonstrated the limitations of LLMs' reasoning capabilities by showing that their performance significantly drops when given the same reasoning tasks but with different assumptions or conditions. These studies are often done through synthetic data generation.

In this study, we explore the limitations of LLM capabilities through *multi-problem evaluation*, a

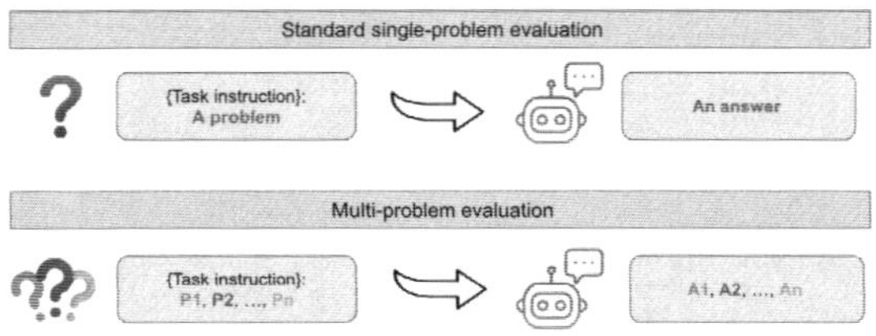

Figure 1: Standard single-problem evaluation versus multi-problem evaluation.

simple evaluation method that leverages existing benchmarks to construct prompts made up of multiple problems. As illustrated in Fig 2, unlike conventional single-problem evaluation that prompts an LLM to solve a single problem at a time, multi-problem evaluation prompts an LLM to solve multiple problems at once in a single input prompt. In this study, we leverage 6 existing classification benchmarks to construct prompts made up of multiple homogeneous problems to form 4 contrastive task types and examine various LLMs on these task types to explore their limitations. Because of the combinatory nature of constructing prompts from multiple problems, it is less likely for LLMs to encounter exact long multi-problem prompts during pre-training, which makes our evaluation less susceptible to data contamination.

We find that while LLMs can typically handle multiple classifications simultaneously (Batch Classification) as well as when performed separately, they exhibit a significant drop in performance on two selection tasks that are conceptually equivalent to Batch Classification and involve selecting indices of text falling into each class label, either independently or altogether. We show that this drop results from LLMs' inability to adequately combine index selection with text classification, which persists across all tested LLMs, under zero-shot, few-shot, or Chain-of-Thought (CoT, Wei et al., 2023) settings, and with a novel synthetic dataset.

The Sixth Workshop on Insights from Negative Results in NLP, pages 121–140

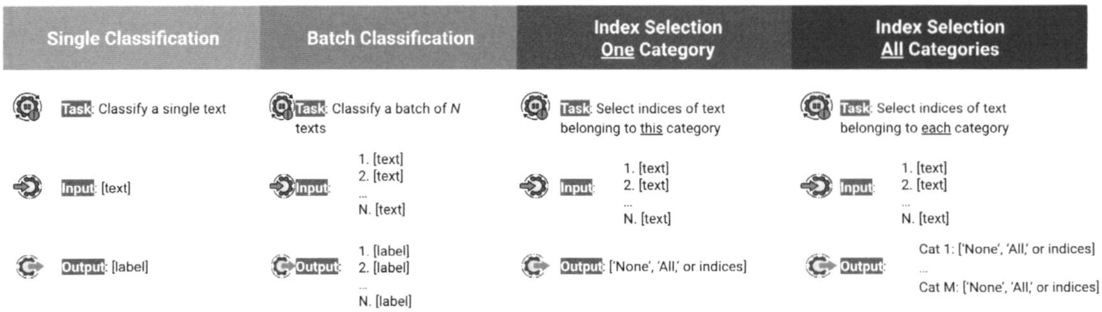

Figure 2: The 4 types of evaluation tasks in the form of a <task, input, output> triplet.

Input Format	Benchmark	# Samples	Objective
Single-text	SST-2	1,821	Sentiment analysis
	CoLA	1,043	Grammatical acceptability
	AGNews	1,000	Topic classification
Text-pair	MRPC	1,725	Paraphrase detection
	SNLI	1,000	Natural language inference
	WiC	1,400	Word sense disambiguation

Table 1: Classification benchmarks used in the study. We use the test splits wherever possible, except for CoLA, for which we use the dev split, since the test split is not publicly available. For AGNews and SNLI, we randomly sample 1,000 examples from the test splits.

2 Related Work

Prompting LLMs with multiple problems at once. Given the non-trivial cost of deploying LLMs at large scale, recent studies (Cheng et al., 2023; Laskar et al., 2023; Son et al., 2024; Lin et al., 2024) have proposed various prompt-level approaches that place multiple problems in a single prompt to improve input token utilization to save LLM inference costs. However, they do not aim to discover limitations in LLM capabilities.

LLM Evaluation While there have been several surveys dedidcated to the evaluation of specific topics, e.g., hallucination (Huang et al., 2023; Rawte et al., 2023), bias and fairness (Gallegos et al., 2024; Li et al., 2024), and alignment (Wang et al., 2023; Liu et al., 2024), we note that current LLM evaluation has predominantly focused on LLM's performance on prompts consisting of single problems. Each of such prompts presents a single problem, which expects one specific answer.

3 Experimental Setup

This section describes the data, tasks, LLMs, and performance metric used for our experiments.

3.1 Data

We construct homogeneous multi-problem tasks from existing single-problem benchmarks. We consider the following 6 classification benchmarks, as described in Table 1: SST-2 (Socher et al., 2013), CoLA (Warstadt et al., 2019), AGNews (Gulli, 2004), MRPC (Dolan and Brockett, 2005), SNLI (Bowman et al., 2015), and WiC (Pilehvar and Camacho-Collados, 2019). They cover two classification paradigms, i.e., single-text and text-pair classification, as well as six distinct task objectives.

3.2 Evaluation Tasks

We conduct our multi-problem evaluation on 4 related types of tasks, conceptualized in Fig 2, using the 6 existing benchmarks introduced above. We define task size n as the number of classification problems included in a prompt and m as the number of unique class labels in a given benchmark. The full prompt templates used for these task types are provided in Appendix C, where the overall limited effect of prompt variation is also discussed.

Among these 4 task types, Single Classification (**SingleClf**) and Batch Classification (**BatchClf**) are classification tasks where an LLM is prompted to solve one or a batch of classification problems at once, respectively. Index Selection One Category (**SelectOne**) and Index Selection All Categories (**SelectAll**) are two reformulations of BatchClf. Instead of making multiple classifications under BatchClf, these two tasks instruct LLMs to select indices of text falling into each label class, either independently in m separate prompts (SelectOne) or altogether in a single prompt (SelectAll).

We design the two selection tasks to test LLM's understanding of the classifications performed under BatchClf. Since selection tasks of size n may have anywhere from 0 to n correct indices per class, spurious correlations are less likely during our eval-

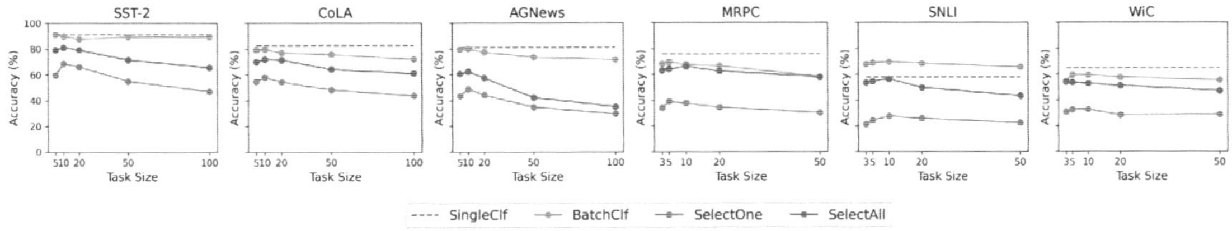

Figure 3: Average accuracy of the 7 LLMs on the 4 task types across task sizes for each benchmark.

uation, given the combinatory answer space.

3.3 LLMs and Evaluation Settings

We evaluate 7 LLMs from 4 model families with greedy decoding: Vicuna (13B, Chiang et al., 2023), Mistral 7B (Jiang et al., 2023), Mixtral 8x7B (Jiang et al., 2024), Llama-3 8B and 70B (Instruct, Meta, 2024), GPT-3.5, and GPT-4 (OpenAI, 2023). We conduct the main experiments under zero-shot and selectively experiment with other prompting strategies in the follow-up experiments in Section 5. See Table 5 in Appendix A for model details.

Performance metric We measure the average per-problem accuracy (PPA) to unify the evaluation across the four task types. PPA, defined in Equation 1, is the average accuracy of classifying n problems with each prompt or, in the case of SelectOne, in each set of directly related prompts targeting different class labels.

$$\text{PPA} = \frac{1}{n}\sum_{i=1}^{n}\delta(I(P_i), A_i) \tag{1}$$

$I(P_i)$ is the inferred LLM-generated answer to the ith problem in the input prompt, A_i is the ground truth, and $\delta(i, j) = 1$ iff $i = j$ and 0 otherwise. For the two index selection tasks, $I(P_i)$ is determined by considering the LLM's assignments of indices to all class labels. Other than assigning an index to a wrong class label, there are two more error types. First, LLMs may assign an index with more than one class label, i.e., an *contradiction* error. Second, LLMs may assign no labels to an index at all, namely, an *non-excluded middle* error.

To compare performance difference, we use Mann-Whitney U tests for significant testing and Cohen's d (Cohen, 1969) for measuring effect size.

4 Results

Fig 3 shows the average accuracy on the 4 task types across task sizes for each benchmark with the related full results for each LLM provided in Appendix A.3. We exclude the results of Vicuna on AGNews at task size 100 as the prompts exceed the model's context length. Two main observations are as follows.

	> 90% SCAcc	> 80% SCAcc	> 75% SCAcc
Vicuna 13B	79.3	93.1	93.1
Mistral 7B	76.7	83.3	100.0
Mixtral 8x7B	63.3	83.3	86.7
Llama-3 8B	73.3	90.0	100.0
Llama-3 70B	80.0	100.0	100.0
GPT-3.5	56.7	83.3	90.0
GPT-4	100.0	100.0	100.0
Overall	75.6	90.4	95.7

Table 2: Percent of time that BatchClf performance surpasses a threshold percent of SingleClf accuracy (SCAcc) across benchmarks.

	BatchClf vs SelectOne	BatchClf vs SelectAll	SelectOne vs SelectAll
Mean Acc Dif	32.0	12.1	-19.9
Std Dev	16.9	15.3	12.0
Cohen's d	1.8	0.8	-1.0

Table 3: Pairwise accuracy difference (x vs y = x - y). All the differences are statistically significant and with a large effect size (| Cohen's d | $\geq$ 0.8).

LLMs can handle multiple classifications at once with minimal performance loss. Although BatchClf accuracy generally declines as the task size increases, all LLMs achieve accuracy of at least 90% that of SingleClf across benchmarks most of the time (see Table 2). Overall, the SingleClf accuracy for the 7 LLMs is 75.5% on average and the BatchClf counterpart is 72.3%, a minor 3.2% absolute drop from the former.

LLMs perform significantly worse on the selection tasks. Despite the impressive BatchClf performance, LLMs nearly always perform much worse in SelectOne and SelectAll than BatchClf, even when the task size is just 3 or 5. The overall discrepancy in accuracy between BatchClf and the two tasks is large and statistically significant (32.0% for SelectOne and 12.1% for SelectAll, see Table 3) and generally increases with a larger task

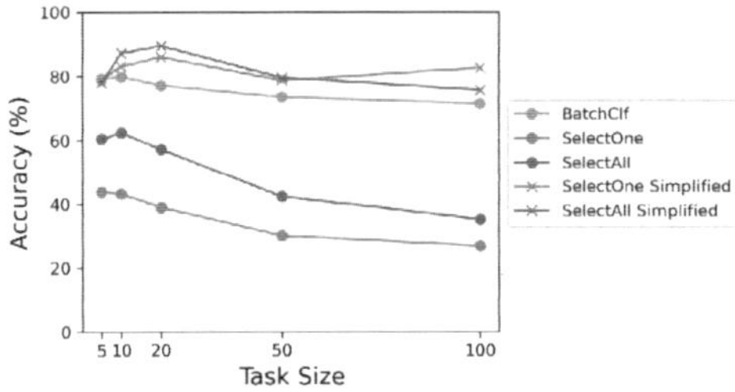

Figure 4: Average accuracy of the 7 LLMs on the two simplified index selection tasks based on AGNews. We provide the original results from BatchClf, SelectOne, and SelectAll for easy comparisons.

size. Similarly, Table 3 also shows a large and statistically significant difference between SelectOne and SelectAll, in favor of the latter.

These significant performance differences may not be human-like, given the conceptual equivalence of the three tasks underlyingly. For example, humans should at least be able to classify and select a small number (e.g., 3/5) of texts (mostly short sentences) equally well simply by thinking over the problems (i.e., zero-shot).

5 Follow-up Experiments

We perform a series of follow-up experiments to further understand and validate our main findings. More details about these experiments are presented in Appendix B.

5.1 Can LLMs do Index Selection?

While we argue that the LLMs' weaker performance on SelectOne and SelectAll is due to a weakness in combining classification with index selection, an alternative explanation would be that they just generally struggle at index selection. To exclude this possibility, we simplify the two index selection tasks by directly replacing each line of text with its gold standard label in the prompts for AGNews, which has most labels. We then ask the LLMs to select the indices of lines containing each label with minimal modifications to the original task instructions.

Fig 4 shows that LLMs can perform in the simplified selection tasks much better than the original ones, with Llama-3 70B, GPT-3.5, and GPT-4 even achieving (nearly) 100% accuracy across task sizes. The 7 LLMs' overall performance in the simplified selection tasks is even slightly higher than their overall BatchClf accuracy. The previously observed performance gap between SelectOne and SelectAll also disappears for almost all LLMs (see Appendix B for full results). In general, LLMs can indeed do index selection.

Task Model	SelectOne	+ CoT	SelectAll	+ CoT	BatchClf
Vicuna	23.0	25.8	53.2	57.6	68.7
Mistral 7B	38.3	47.5	56.8	60.5	71.2
Mixtral 8x7B	47.4	38.7	65.1	58.4	73.4
Llama-3 8B	39.0	41.8	62.4	59.0	73.3
Llama-3 70B	59.4	67.1	72.9	79.2	79.4
GPT-3.5	45.5	47.5	66.7	66.3	71.9
GPT-4	66.3	71.8	78.8	81.8	81.9
Overall	45.5	48.6	65.1	66.1	74.3

Table 4: Aggregate average accuracy of SelectOne and SelectAll with and without 1-shot-CoT for each LLM. BatchClf performance is also provided for comparisons.

In conclusion, it appears that the tested LLMs perform less well on SelectOne and SelectAll as compared to BatchClf because they cannot adequately combine the index selection task and the classification tasks in response to a zero-shot prompt. Put differently, LLMs lack true understanding of the problems presented in different forms, even when the number of problems is quite small (e.g., 3 or 5), which may not be human-like.

5.2 Does CoT Help?

In light of the results above, we use 1-shot-CoT to prompt LLMs to do BatchClf first and then perform the two index selection tasks on the 6 benchmarks with a fixed task size 10. Table 4 shows that while overall LLMs benefit from CoT for both SelectOne and SelectAll, the benefits are generally larger for SelectOne than SelectAll (3.1% versus 1.0% improvement) and not consistent across models with Mixtral 8x7B performing even worse with CoT. Moreover, the task complexity hierarchy among BatchClf, SelectOne, and SelectAll remains in virtually all cases. We leave to future studies the investigation of how CoT may further help with the two selection tasks.

5.3 Does Few-Shot Prompting Help?

To test the generality of the main findings, we first re-run all experiments for CoLA providing 2 exemplars in the prompts and with a fixed task size 5 for tasks other than SingleClf. We find that few-shot prompting is mostly detrimental across LLMs, particularly so for SelectOne and BatchClf. As a result, SelectAll shows an overall better performance than BatchClf and the performance gap between SelectOne and SelectAll becomes much larger. Full

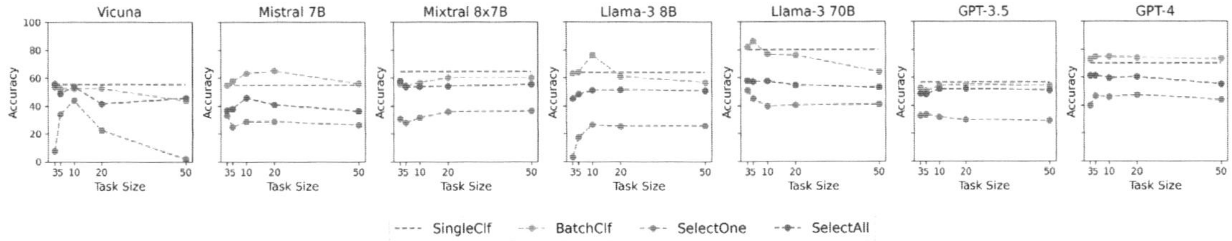

Figure 5: Full results on the novel benchmark created on top of SST-2 where the task objective is to decide if a text pair shares the same sentiment.

results are in Table 8 in Appendix B for space reasons.

5.4 Testing on a Novel Benchmark

As argued in Section 1, multi-problem evaluation is less susceptible to data contamination, given the combinatory nature of constructing prompts from multiple problems. To further mitigate the concern of data contamination, we create a novel benchmark with 1,000 distinct and label-balanced text pairs sampled from SST-2. The task is to determine if each text pair shares the same sentiment, which we believe is unlikely to appear in the training data of LLMs. We run experiments on this benchmark using the same experimental setup described in Section 3 for the text-pair benchmarks. The results in Fig 5 are consistent with our main results.

6 Conclusion

We propose multi-problem evaluation and present a comprehensive multi-problem evaluation of LLMs, leveraging 6 existing classification benchmarks and 4 related task types constructed from those benchmarks. Our results provide new insights into the multiple problem handling capabilities of LLMs: LLMs are competent multi-problem solvers for multiple homogeneous classification problems (Batch Classification), but they perform significantly worse on two selection tasks that are conceptually equivalent to Batch Classification and involve selecting indices of text falling into each class label, either independently or altogether. This is due to their inability to adequately combine index selection with text classification. The surprisingly consistent performance drop on the two selection tasks observed across 7 LLMs and a wide range of evaluation settings potentially indicates an inherent limitation with modern LLM capabilities. This also showcases the potential of multi-problem evaluation as a useful and effective in discovering limitations of LLM capabilities.

There are several directions worth future explorations. For example, to better understand how well how LLMs can handle multiple problems in general, it is important to test LLMs with other types of problems (e.g., reasoning problems) and with multiple heterogeneous problems (e.g., mixing different benchmarks/tasks). It is also important to understand what causes LLMs to perform worse or better when prompted with multiple problems, such as benchmark, task size, and model's context length. In particular, model-level ablation studies are needed if we want to know how LLMs obtain the ability to handle multiple problems at once and how to improve their understanding capabilities.

Acknowledgment

We are grateful for the supports from the Institute for Advanced Computational Science (IACS) at Stony Brook University, in particular the free GPT access it provides. Zhengxiang Wang is supported by IACS's Junior Researcher Award since Fall 2024. We thank three anonymous reviewers from the Workshop on Insights From Negative Results 2025 for their helpful comments. The paper was presented at All Things Language And Computation (ATLAC) organized by the NLP reading group at Stony Brook University. We also thank the audience there for their discussions and feedback about the paper.

Limitations

While we have done our best to make our experiments as comprehensive as possible, there is always more work that can be done in a large comparison study, including the addition of even more benchmarks and language models. We were limited by cost, time, and space and have attempted to select an informative and representative sample of experiments. Since we used pre-existing benchmarking data sets, we inherit any labeling errors that they may contain. Finally, despite our efforts to compare different prompts, as is the case with all prompt-based LLM studies, we cannot guarantee that slight differences in the prompts would not meaningfully alter the results.

Ethical Concerns

To the best of our knowledge, all results published in this paper are accurate. All data sources are free, publicly available, and cited in the article. No sensitive data was used which could violate individuals' privacy or confidentiality.

References

Anthropic. 2024. The Claude 3 model family: Opus, Sonnet, Haiku.

Iz Beltagy, Matthew E. Peters, and Arman Cohan. 2020. Longformer: The long-document transformer.

Samuel R. Bowman, Gabor Angeli, Christopher Potts, and Christopher D. Manning. 2015. A large annotated corpus for learning natural language inference. In *Proceedings of the 2015 Conference on Empirical Methods in Natural Language Processing*, pages 632–642, Lisbon, Portugal. Association for Computational Linguistics.

Zhoujun Cheng, Jungo Kasai, and Tao Yu. 2023. Batch prompting: Efficient inference with large language model APIs. In *Proceedings of the 2023 Conference on Empirical Methods in Natural Language Processing: Industry Track*, pages 792–810, Singapore. Association for Computational Linguistics.

Wei-Lin Chiang, Zhuohan Li, Zi Lin, Ying Sheng, Zhanghao Wu, Hao Zhang, Lianmin Zheng, Siyuan Zhuang, Yonghao Zhuang, Joseph E. Gonzalez, Ion Stoica, and Eric P. Xing. 2023. Vicuna: An open-source chatbot impressing GPT-4 with 90%* chatgpt quality.

Paul F Christiano, Jan Leike, Tom Brown, Miljan Martic, Shane Legg, and Dario Amodei. 2017. Deep reinforcement learning from human preferences. In *Advances in Neural Information Processing Systems*, volume 30. Curran Associates, Inc.

J. Cohen. 1969. *Statistical Power Analysis for the Behavioral Sciences*. Academic Press.

William B. Dolan and Chris Brockett. 2005. Automatically constructing a corpus of sentential paraphrases. In *Proceedings of the Third International Workshop on Paraphrasing (IWP2005)*.

Isabel O. Gallegos, Ryan A. Rossi, Joe Barrow, Md Mehrab Tanjim, Sungchul Kim, Franck Dernoncourt, Tong Yu, Ruiyi Zhang, and Nesreen K. Ahmed. 2024. Bias and fairness in large language models: A survey.

Gemini-Team. 2023. Gemini: A family of highly capable multimodal models.

Antonio Gulli. 2004. AG's corpus of news articles.

Lei Huang, Weijiang Yu, Weitao Ma, Weihong Zhong, Zhangyin Feng, Haotian Wang, Qianglong Chen, Weihua Peng, Xiaocheng Feng, Bing Qin, and Ting Liu. 2023. A survey on hallucination in large language models: Principles, taxonomy, challenges, and open questions.

Alon Jacovi, Avi Caciularu, Omer Goldman, and Yoav Goldberg. 2023. Stop uploading test data in plain text: Practical strategies for mitigating data contamination by evaluation benchmarks. In *Proceedings of the 2023 Conference on Empirical Methods in Natural Language Processing*, pages 5075–5084, Singapore. Association for Computational Linguistics.

Albert Q. Jiang, Alexandre Sablayrolles, Arthur Mensch, Chris Bamford, Devendra Singh Chaplot, Diego de las Casas, Florian Bressand, Gianna Lengyel, Guillaume Lample, Lucile Saulnier, Lélio Renard Lavaud, Marie-Anne Lachaux, Pierre Stock, Teven Le Scao, Thibaut Lavril, Thomas Wang, Timothée Lacroix, and William El Sayed. 2023. Mistral 7b.

Albert Q. Jiang, Alexandre Sablayrolles, Antoine Roux, Arthur Mensch, Blanche Savary, Chris Bamford, Devendra Singh Chaplot, Diego de las Casas, Emma Bou Hanna, Florian Bressand, Gianna Lengyel, Guillaume Bour, Guillaume Lample, Lélio Renard Lavaud, Lucile Saulnier, Marie-Anne Lachaux, Pierre Stock, Sandeep Subramanian, Sophia Yang, Szymon Antoniak, Teven Le Scao, Théophile Gervet, Thibaut Lavril, Thomas Wang, Timothée Lacroix, and William El Sayed. 2024. Mixtral of experts.

Md Tahmid Rahman Laskar, M Saiful Bari, Mizanur Rahman, Md Amran Hossen Bhuiyan, Shafiq Joty, and Jimmy Huang. 2023. A systematic study and comprehensive evaluation of ChatGPT on benchmark datasets. In *Findings of the Association for Computational Linguistics: ACL 2023*, pages 431–469, Toronto, Canada. Association for Computational Linguistics.

Yingji Li, Mengnan Du, Rui Song, Xin Wang, and Ying Wang. 2024. A survey on fairness in large language models.

Jianzhe Lin, Maurice Diesendruck, Liang Du, and Robin Abraham. 2024. Batchprompt: Accomplish more with less.

Yang Liu, Yuanshun Yao, Jean-Francois Ton, Xiaoying Zhang, Ruocheng Guo, Hao Cheng, Yegor Klochkov, Muhammad Faaiz Taufiq, and Hang Li. 2024. Trustworthy LLMs: a survey and guideline for evaluating large language models' alignment.

Meta. 2024. The llama 3 herd of models.

Iman Mirzadeh, Keivan Alizadeh, Hooman Shahrokhi, Oncel Tuzel, Samy Bengio, and Mehrdad Farajtabar. 2024. Gsm-symbolic: Understanding the limitations of mathematical reasoning in large language models.

OpenAI. 2023. GPT-4 technical report.

Mohammad Taher Pilehvar and Jose Camacho-Collados. 2019. WiC: the word-in-context dataset for evaluating context-sensitive meaning representations. In *Proceedings of the 2019 Conference of the North American Chapter of the Association for Computational Linguistics: Human Language Technologies, Volume 1 (Long and Short Papers)*, pages 1267–1273, Minneapolis, Minnesota. Association for Computational Linguistics.

Vipula Rawte, Amit Sheth, and Amitava Das. 2023. A survey of hallucination in large foundation models.

Oscar Sainz, Jon Campos, Iker García-Ferrero, Julen Etxaniz, Oier Lopez de Lacalle, and Eneko Agirre. 2023. NLP evaluation in trouble: On the need to measure LLM data contamination for each benchmark. In *Findings of the Association for Computational Linguistics: EMNLP 2023*, pages 10776–10787, Singapore. Association for Computational Linguistics.

Richard Socher, Alex Perelygin, Jean Wu, Jason Chuang, Christopher D. Manning, Andrew Ng, and Christopher Potts. 2013. Recursive deep models for semantic compositionality over a sentiment treebank. In *Proceedings of the 2013 Conference on Empirical Methods in Natural Language Processing*, pages 1631–1642, Seattle, Washington, USA. Association for Computational Linguistics.

Guijin Son, SangWon Baek, Sangdae Nam, Ilgyun Jeong, and Seungone Kim. 2024. Multi-task inference: Can large language models follow multiple instructions at once? In *Proceedings of the 62nd Annual Meeting of the Association for Computational Linguistics (Volume 1: Long Papers)*, pages 5606–5627, Bangkok, Thailand. Association for Computational Linguistics.

Yufei Wang, Wanjun Zhong, Liangyou Li, Fei Mi, Xingshan Zeng, Wenyong Huang, Lifeng Shang, Xin Jiang, and Qun Liu. 2023. Aligning large language models with human: A survey.

Alex Warstadt, Amanpreet Singh, and Samuel R. Bowman. 2019. Neural network acceptability judgments. *Transactions of the Association for Computational Linguistics*, 7:625–641.

Jason Wei, Xuezhi Wang, Dale Schuurmans, Maarten Bosma, Brian Ichter, Fei Xia, Ed Chi, Quoc Le, and Denny Zhou. 2023. Chain-of-thought prompting elicits reasoning in large language models.

Zhaofeng Wu, Linlu Qiu, Alexis Ross, Ekin Akyürek, Boyuan Chen, Bailin Wang, Najoung Kim, Jacob Andreas, and Yoon Kim. 2024. Reasoning or reciting? exploring the capabilities and limitations of language models through counterfactual tasks. In *Proceedings of the 2024 Conference of the North American Chapter of the Association for Computational Linguistics: Human Language Technologies (Volume 1: Long Papers)*, pages 1819–1862, Mexico City, Mexico. Association for Computational Linguistics.

A Experimental details

A.1 LLM Details

Table 5 describes the specific versions for the 7 LLMs we use in the paper and highlights their differences in terms of open weights, training with Reinforment Learning from Human Feedback or RLHF (Christiano et al., 2017), architecture, number of parameters, and context window size. We use OpenAI API and TogetherAI API to call GPT LLMs and non-GPT LLMs, respectively.

A.2 LLM Output Parsing Code

The LLM output parsing code contains over 200 lines of regular expressions to parse LLM outputs and we include it in this submission for review. The code takes into accounts the following five variables during parsing: task type, benchmark, model, task size, and target label (for SelectOne). This is to ensure our code can handle cases when LLMs generate undefined labels, un-instructed explanations, or even wrong answer format (e.g., a non-JSON output for SelectOne and SelectAll).

Overall, our code achieves about 99.9% overall parsing rate. The unparsable cases mostly come from SingleClf outputs where LLMs output undefined labels, such as "Mixed" or "Netual" for SST-2. For BatchClf outputs, we implement a series of rules to extract both defined and undefined labels, because of the order of the extracted labels affects the final evaluation. For SelectOne and SelectAll, our code extracts JSON object, fixes cases where the JSON object has formatting issues, or extracts a series of text indices when there is no JSON object identified in the output.

A.3 Full Results

The full results obtained from the main experiments are visualized in Fig 6. We exclude the results of Vicuna on AGNews when task size is 100 because the prompts exceed the model's context length.

A.4 Task Complexity Hierarchy

In Table 3 from Section 4, we demonstrate the overall task complexity hierarchy among BatchClf,

Model	Version	Open Weights	With RLHF	MoE	# Parameter	Context Window Size
Vicuna (Chiang et al., 2023)	v1.5	✓	✗	✗	13B	4,096
Mistral 7B (Jiang et al., 2023)	Instruct-v0.2	✓	✗	✗	7B	8,192
Mixtral 8x7B (Jiang et al., 2024)	Instruct-v0.1	✓	✗	✓	47B	8,192
Llama-3 8B (Meta, 2024)	Instruct	✓	✓	✗	8B	8,192
Llama-3 70B (Meta, 2024)	Instruct	✓	✓	✗	70B	8,192
GPT-3.5	turbo-0125	✗	✓	✗	-	16,385
GPT-4 (OpenAI, 2023)	turbo-2024-04-09	✗	✓	✗	-	128,000

Table 5: The 7 LLMs we use, all instruction finetuned. For the two GPT LLMs, it is commonly assumed that both are larger than GPT-3 (a 175B LLM) with GPT-4 being the largest. For Mixtral 8x7B, a Mixture of Experts (MoE) LLM, although each token has access to 47B parameters, but only uses 13B active parameters during inference.

SelectOne, and SelectAll. It is found that SelectOne > SelectAll > BatchClf, where ">" denotes a "more complex than" relationship.

Similar to Fig 3, which describes the aggregate average accuracy across benchmarks, Fig 7 describes the aggregate average accuracy across LLMs. Although there are few cases shown in Fig 6 where the overall complexity hierarchy among BatchClf, SelectOne, and SelectAll does not hold (e.g., Vicuna on MRPC for task size 50), these cases are exceptional and likely due to the interactions of multiple factors in play, such as model, benchmark, input length, and context windows. Nevertheless, the overall task complexity hierarchy is clear both in Fig 3 (benchmark-level) and in Fig 7 (model-level).

A.5 Limited Effect of Prompt Variations

Throughout our research project, we have also tried prompts with different wordings and structures until we finally unified the prompt designs presented above. More concretely, we initially instructed LLMs to produce indices line by line for SelectOne and did not include any formatted output example in SelectAll prompts for almost all classification-related experiments. The table below shows the average performance of each LLM on SelectAll and SelectOne using current and earlier prompt templates. Clearly, the effects of prompt variations are minimal (except for GPT-3.5 on SelectOne) and the findings in the paper remain valid.

task model	SelectOne (Early)	SelectAll (Early)
Vicuna	17.9 (15.4)	43.2 (44.5)
Mistral 7B	31.5 (31.8)	51.5 (44.2)
Mixtral 8x7B	38.4 (39.1)	60.1 (60.5)
Llama-3 8B	33.0 (34.5)	54.6 (56.8)
Llama-3 70B	54.2 (54.7)	70.0 (70.4)
GPT-3.5	41.4 (28.3)	63.4 (61.3)
GPT-4	65.4 (64.7)	78.0 (76.7)
Overall	40.4 (38.5)	60.2 (59.2)

Table 6: Model performance on the two selecting tasks using the finalized prompts and early prompts.

B Follow-up Experiments

B.1 Simplified Index Selection Tasks

Fig 8 shows the full results for the two simplified index selection tasks, along with results for the two original selection tasks and BatchClf, based on AGNews. Clearly, (1) all LLMs perform much better in the simplified tasks than the original ones; (2) Mixtral 8X7B, Llama-3 70B, GPT-3.5, and GPT-4 can do these simplified selection tasks even better than their BatchClf performance consistently, with the latter three achieving nearly 100% accuracy in most cases; (3) the task complexity hierarchy between SelectOne and SelectAll nearly disappears for all LLMs except Vicua, implying that it may be challenging for Vicuna to perform index selection tasks in general.

B.2 1-shot-CoT Results

Table 7 presents the full 1-shot-CoT results across benchmarks and LLMs with a fixed task size 10. As demonstrated in Section 5, CoT improves the LLMs' performance in SelectOne and SelectAll with an overall larger positive effect on the former, but the improvement is not consistent both across benchmarks and across LLMs. For examples, LLMs tend to benefit from CoT for both selection tasks constructed from SST-2, CoLA, and SNLI (see the "Overall" results in Table 7).

B.3 Few-shot Results

Table 8 shows the full 2-shot results on CoLA for each LLM, which shows a general negative effect of few-shot prompting. According to these results, LLMs performs much worse in SelectOne with an overall accuracy going down to 25.2% from 58.1%. Similarly, the negative effect is larger on BatchClf than on SelectAll, making the overall BatchClf accuracy lower than SelectAll, although the former

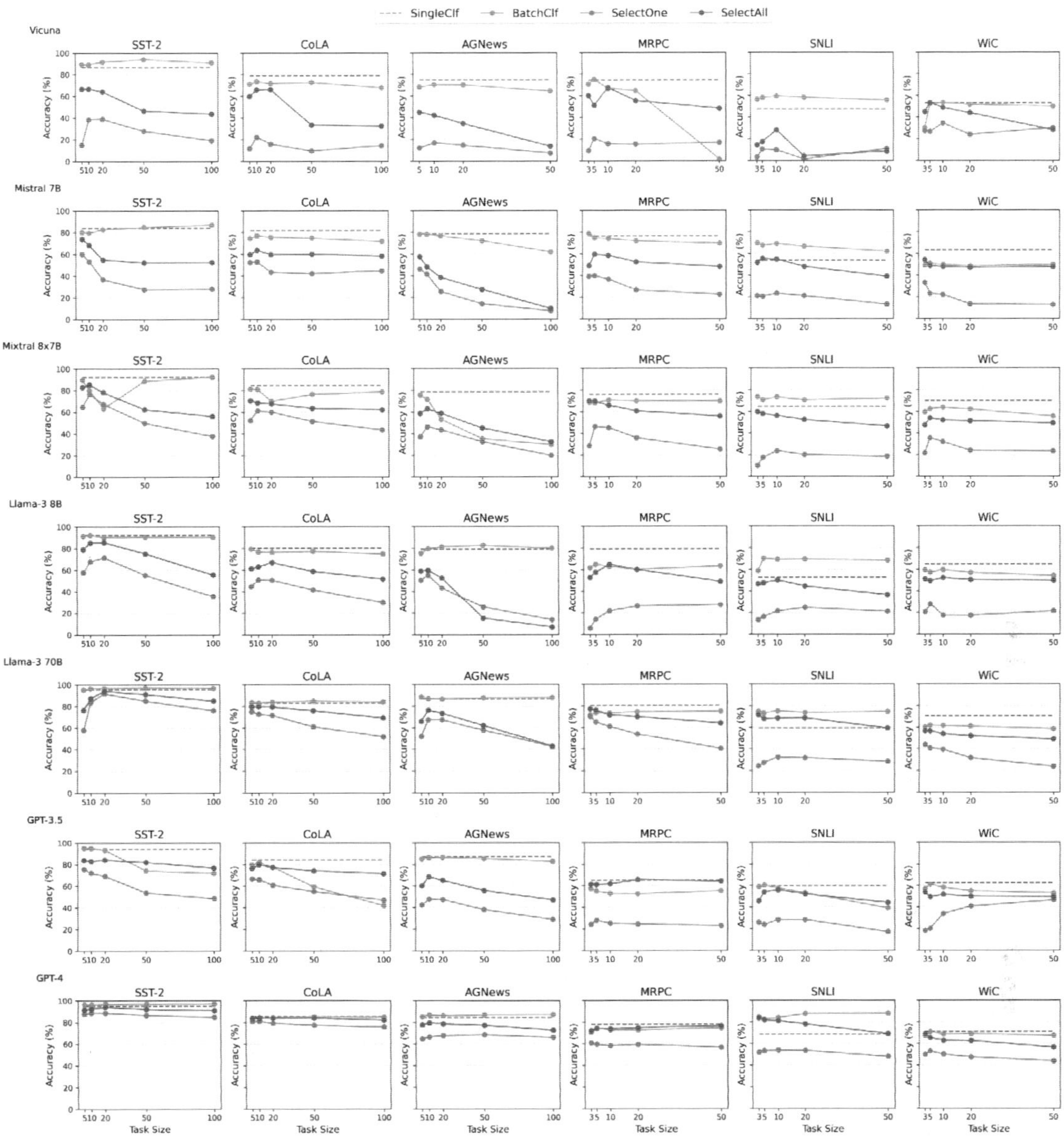

Figure 6: Full average accuracy of the 7 LLMs on the 4 tasks across the 6 benchmarks.

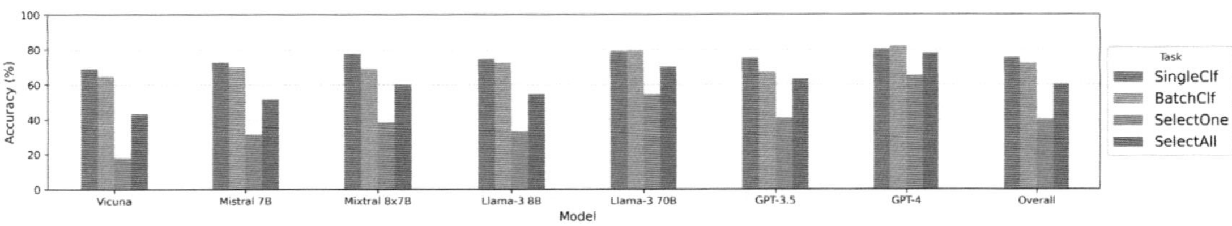

Figure 7: Aggregate average accuracy on the 4 tasks averaging over results from the 6 benchmarks for each LLM. "Overall" presents the average results across all LLMs for each one of the 4 task.

is still often higher than the latter under the same test conditions.

C Full Prompts

C.1 Prompt Templates for SingleClf, BatchClf, SelectOne, and SelectAll

Tables 13 to 14 show the complete prompt templates for the four task types (i.e., SingleClf, BatchClf, SelectOne, and SelectAll) tailored for SST-2, CoLA, AGNews, MPRC, SNLI, and WiC, respectively. While there are differences in the exact wording of a prompt template for each task type across the 6 classification benchmarks, each prompt template type shares a similar underlying structure and can be easily applied to other classification benchmarks.

Throughout our research project, we have also tried prompts with different wordings and structures until we finally unified the prompt designs presented above. For example, we initially asked LLMs to directly generate indices line by line instead of a JSON output for SelectOne and we did not provide any formatted example for SelectAll. We also put the output format instruction in the end of each prompt for SelectAll, instead of in the beginning. Although we observed certain task-level performance variations, which are expected, the overall complexity among the 4 task types (SelectOne > SelectAll > BatchClf > SingeClf) remains unchanged, despite the variations in the prompts. This indicates the overall limited effects of rewording and restructuring prompts.

C.2 Prompt Templates for the Two Index Selection Tasks

Table 15 presents the two prompt templates used for the two simplified index selection tasks based on AGNews.

C.3 One-Shot-CoT Prompt Templates for the Two Index Selection Tasks

To construct a 1-shot-CoT exemplar, we first randomly sampled 10 examples from each benchmark that do not appear in our test examples. We then put these 10 examples into the prompt template for SelectOne or SelectAll, followed by a constructed answer. The answer first explicitly classifies the 10 examples into the corresponding class labels, and then perform index selection based on the generated class labels.

Table 16 shows the complete answer templates for SelectOne and SelectAll for each classification benchmark.

Model	Benchmark Task	SST-2	CoLA	AGNews	MRPC	SNLI	WiC
Vicuna	SelectOne	38.5	22.2	16.8	15.8	9.9	34.5
	+ CoT	52.6	53.9	12.1	12.1	11.5	12.5
	SelectAll	66.7	65.7	42.2	67.4	28.2	48.8
	+ CoT	81.7	69.2	40.9	63.9	40.9	48.9
	BatchClf	89.1	73.2	70.4	66.7	59.3	53.4
Mistral 7B	SelectOne	53.3	52.8	41.5	36.6	23.3	22.2
	+ CoT	66.5	55.1	44.8	59.4	29.5	29.5
	SelectAll	68.3	63.6	48.2	58.4	54.7	47.9
	+ CoT	74.4	68.2	57.0	68.5	47.6	47.3
	BatchClf	79.6	76.8	78.1	74.0	69.1	49.6
Mixtral 8x7B	SelectOne	76.5	61.0	46.2	45.2	23.8	32.0
	+ CoT	41.5	67.3	12.9	48.4	25.1	37.2
	SelectAll	85.3	68.4	62.9	65.9	56.2	52.0
	+ CoT	49.0	67.4	57.8	66.5	58.9	51.1
	BatchClf	80.2	80.9	71.6	70.8	73.3	63.7
Llama-3 8B	SelectOne	67.8	50.8	55.1	21.7	21.4	17.3
	+ CoT	85.0	48.9	22.1	50.7	22.3	22.0
	SelectAll	85.0	62.9	59.6	64.8	50.1	52.2
	+ CoT	85.8	66.5	45.3	64.5	39.8	52.3
	BatchClf	92.0	76.8	79.5	62.8	69.2	59.5
Llama-3 70B	SelectOne	83.6	72.7	67.4	61.0	32.3	39.3
	+ CoT	94.7	79.7	75.2	67.9	69.4	15.8
	SelectAll	87.3	79.6	76.2	71.7	68.6	53.9
	+ CoT	96.1	83.7	85.5	73.9	77.3	58.4
	BatchClf	96.4	82.8	86.8	73.5	75.2	61.7
GPT-3.5	SelectOne	71.9	65.8	47.6	25.2	28.4	33.8
	+ CoT	80.2	71.7	57.9	26.8	26.5	22.1
	SelectAll	83.1	79.7	68.3	61.5	55.8	51.6
	+ CoT	89.5	77.5	58.8	70.2	50.5	51.2
	BatchClf	95.0	81.8	86.4	52.7	57.4	58.0
GPT-4	SelectOne	88.6	80.8	66.4	58.1	53.8	50.0
	+ CoT	84.5	81.9	67.8	60.1	77.0	59.6
	SelectAll	92.4	84.0	79.2	73.5	80.8	62.8
	+ CoT	91.3	83.7	85.4	76.2	83.3	71.0
	BatchClf	96.0	84.0	86.7	72.6	83.8	68.4
Overall	SelectOne	68.6	58.0	48.7	37.7	27.6	32.7
	+ CoT	72.1	65.5	41.8	46.5	37.3	28.4
	SelectAll	81.2	72.0	62.4	66.2	56.3	52.7
	+ CoT	81.1	73.7	61.5	69.1	56.9	54.3
	BatchClf	89.8	79.5	79.9	67.6	69.6	59.2

Table 7: Full 1-shot-CoT results for all benchmarks and LLMS. The task size is fixed at 10.

Model	Task Benchmark	SingleClf	BatchClf	SelectOne	SelectAll
Vicuna	CoLA	78.8	71.0	48.6	59.6
	+ 2-shot	69.0	50.4	14.8	64.0
Mistral 7B	CoLA	81.5	74.4	47.4	59.4
	+ 2-shot	80.2	65.0	25.0	60.4
Mixtral 8x7B	CoLA	84.4	81.2	65.0	70.6
	+ 2-shot	81.8	73.2	19.8	72.4
Llama-3 8B	CoLA	80.2	79.4	33.4	61.2
	+ 2-shot	74.3	46.6	0.6	63.8
Llama-3 70B	CoLA	82.8	83.4	71.2	79.6
	+ 2-shot	81.8	82.0	29.2	80.8
GPT-3.5	CoLA	84.2	79.6	63.4	76.2
	+ 2-shot	79.5	76.8	38.2	72.8
GPT-4	CoLA	85.1	83.8	77.8	83.6
	+ 2-shot	85.7	80.8	48.6	81.0
Overall	CoLA	82.4	79.0	58.1	70.0
	+ 2-shot	78.9	67.8	25.2	70.7

Table 8: Full 2-shot results on CoLA. We use a fixed task size 5 for tasks other than SingleClf, whose task size is 1 by default. We provide the related zero-shot results for easy comparisons.

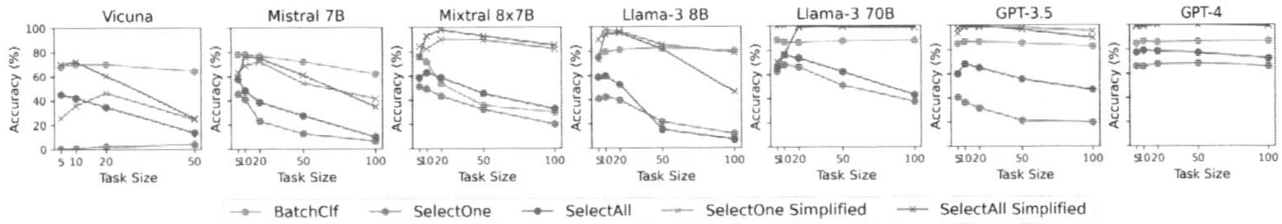

Figure 8: Full results for the two simplified index selection tasks versus the original tasks based on AGNews.

Task	Prompt template
SingleClf	Indicate the sentiment for the following line of text. The sentiment shall be either 'Positive' or 'Negative.' Text: $text Sentiment:
BatchClf	Indicate the sentiment for each of the $num following lines of text. The sentiment shall be either 'Positive' or 'Negative.' Texts, one per line: $texts The sentiments for each of the $num lines of text, one per line:
SelectOne	Go over the $num lines of text below and list the index numbers of the lines with $polarity sentiment according to the following instructions: If none of the texts show $polarity sentiment, write 'None.' If all the texts show $polarity sentiment, write 'All.' Otherwise, provide the index numbers for each text with $polarity sentiment. Output your responses in JSON format with the key '$polarity'. A formatted example output is provided below. {'$polarity': [None/All or index numbers for the texts with $polarity sentiment]} Texts, one per line: $texts JSON output:
SelectAll	Go over the $num lines of text below. First, list the index numbers of the lines with positive sentiment. Then, list the index numbers of the lines with negative sentiment. If none of the texts show a particular sentiment, write 'None.' If all the texts show a particular sentiment, write 'All.' Otherwise, provide the index numbers of the texts that fit a particular category. Output your responses in JSON format with two keys: 'positive' and 'negative.' A formatted example output is provided below. {'positive': [None/All or index numbers of positive sentences], 'negative': [None/All or index numbers of negative sentences]} Texts, one per line: $texts JSON output:

Table 9: Prompt templates for SST-2. Words immediately preceded by the dollar sign $ are placeholders. For the single-text classification task (SST-2, CoLA, AGNews), the sequence of texts in the place of '$texts' are indexed starting with '1' and each text is separated by a newline.

Task	Prompt template
SingleClf	Indicate the grammatical acceptability for the following line of text. The acceptability shall be either 'Acceptable' or 'Unacceptable.' Text: $text Grammatical acceptability:
BatchClf	Indicate the grammatical acceptabilities for each of the $num following lines of text. The acceptability shall be either 'Acceptable' or 'Unacceptable.' Texts, one per line: $texts Grammatical acceptabilities for each of the $num lines of text, one per line:
SelectOne	Go over the $num lines of text below and list the index numbers of the lines that are grammatically $acceptability according to the following instructions: If none of the texts are grammatically $acceptability, write 'None.' If all the texts are grammatically $acceptability, write 'All.' Otherwise, provide the index numbers for each grammatically $acceptability text. Output your responses in JSON format with the key '$acceptability'. A formatted example output is provided below. {'$acceptability': [None/All or index numbers of $acceptability sentences]} Texts, one per line: $texts JSON output:
SelectAll	Go over the $num lines of text below. First, list the index numbers of the lines that are grammatically acceptable. Then, list the index numbers of the lines that are grammatically unacceptable. If none of the sentences show a particular acceptability, write 'None.' If all the sentences show a particular acceptability, write 'All.' Otherwise, provide the index numbers of the texts that fit a particular category. Output your responses in JSON format with two keys 'acceptable' and 'unacceptable.' A formatted example output is provided below. {'acceptable': [None/All or index numbers of acceptable texts], 'unacceptable': [None/All or index numbers of unacceptable texts]} Texts, one per line: $texts JSON output:

Table 10: Prompt templates for CoLA.

Task	Prompt template
SingleClf	Classify which news category the following line of text belongs to among the following four categories: 'Business,' 'Sports,' 'World,' and 'Sci/Tech.' Text: $text News category:
BatchClf	Classify which news category each of the $num following lines of text belongs to among the following four categories: 'Business,' 'Sports,' 'World,' and 'Sci/Tech.' Texts, one per line: $texts News categories for each of the $num lines of text, one per line:
SelectOne	This is a news classification task in which each line of text belongs to one of four categories 'Business,' 'Sports,' 'World,' and 'Sci/Tech.' Go over the $num lines of text below and list the index numbers of the lines that can be classified as $category according to the following instructions: If none of the texts can be classified as $category, write 'None.' If all the texts can be classified as $category, write 'All.' Otherwise, provide the index numbers of the texts that can be classified as $category. Output your responses in JSON format with the key '$category'. A formatted example output is provided below. {'$category': [None/All or index numbers of the texts that can be classified as $category]} Texts, one per line: $texts JSON output:
SelectAll	This is a news classification task in which each line of text belongs to one of four categories 'Business,' 'Sports,' 'World,' and 'Sci/Tech.' Go over the $num lines of text below and list the index numbers of the lines that belong to each category according to the following instructions: If none of the texts can be classified as a particular category, write 'None.' If all the texts can be classified as a particular category, write 'All.' Otherwise, provide the index numbers of the texts that can be classified as the category. Output your responses in JSON format with the following keys: 'business,' 'sports,' 'world,' and 'sci/tech.' A formatted example output is provided below. {'business': [None/All or index numbers of texts in 'business' category], 'sports': [None/All or index numbers of texts in 'sports' category], 'world': [None/All or index numbers of texts in 'world' category], 'sci/tech': [None/All or index numbers of texts in sci/tech category]} Texts, one per line: $texts JSON output:

Table 11: Prompt templates for AGNews.

Task	Prompt template
SingleClf	Compare text A with text B and determine if text A is a paraphrase of text B. Respond with 'Yes' if text A is a paraphrase, and 'No' if it is not. $text Answer:
BatchClf	Compare text A with text B for the following $num text pairs and determine if text A is a paraphrase of text B line by line. Respond with 'Yes' if text A is a paraphrase, and 'No' if it is not. Provide your answers line by line. $texts Answers:
SelectOne	Go over the $num text pairs below and list the index numbers of the text pairs where text A $be a paraphrase of text B according to the following instructions: If none of the text pairs satisfy this condition, write 'None.' If all the text pairs satisfy this condition, write 'All.' Otherwise, provide the index numbers of the text pairs where text A $be a paraphrase of text B. Output your responses in JSON format with the key 'answer'. A formatted example output is provided below. {'answer': [None/All or index numbers of the text pairs where text A $be a paraphrase of text B]} Here are the text pairs: $texts JSON output:
SelectAll	Go over the $num text pairs below. First, list the index numbers of the text pairs that contain paraphrases. Then, list the index numbers of the text pairs that contain non-paraphrases. If none of the text pairs satisfy a condition, write 'None.' If all the text pairs satisfy a condition, write 'All.' Otherwise, provide the index numbers of the text pairs that satisfy each condition. Output your responses in JSON format with two keys: 'yes' for paraphrases and 'no' for non-paraphrases. A formatted example output is provided below. {'yes': [None/All or index numbers of text pairs that contain paraphrases], 'no': [None/All or index numbers of text pairs that contain non-paraphrases]} Here are the text pairs: $texts JSON output:

Table 12: Prompt templates for MRPC. For the text-pair classification task (MRPC, SNLI, WiC), the sequence of text pairs in the place of '$texts' are indexed starting with '1' and each text pair is separated by two newlines (each text pair ends with a newline be design, followed by another newline before the next text pair).

Task	Prompt template
SingleClf	Given the following premise and hypothesis, determine the inference relation between them. Respond with 'Entailment' if the hypothesis logically follows from the premise, 'Contradiction' if they are in direct opposition, and 'Neutral' if neither applies. $text Inference relation:
BatchClf	Given the following $num pairs of premises and hypotheses, determine the inference relation for each pair line by line. Respond with 'Entailment' if the hypothesis entails the premise, and 'Contradiction' if they contradict. If neither is the case, respond with 'Neutral.' Provide your answers line by line. $texts Inference relations for the $num text pairs provided above:
SelectOne	Go over the $num text pairs below and list the index numbers of the text pairs where the inference relation between the premise and the hypothesis is $relationship according to the following instructions: If none of the text pairs contain $relationship inference relation, write 'None.' If all text pairs contain $relationship inference relation, write 'All.' Otherwise, provide the index numbers of the text pairs where the inference relation between the premise and the hypothesis is $relationship. Output your responses in JSON format with the key '$relationship'. A formatted example output is provided below. '$relationship': [None/All or index numbers of text pairs that contain $relationship inference relation] Here are the text pairs: $texts JSON output:
SelectAll	Go over the $num text pairs below. First, list the index numbers of the text pairs that contain entailment inference relation. Then, select all text pairs that contain contradiction inference relation. Finally, select all text pairs that contain neutral inference relation. If none of the text pairs satisfy a condition, write 'None.' If all the text pairs belong satisfy a condition, write 'All.' Otherwise, provide the index numbers of the text pairs that satisfy each condition. Output your responses in JSON format with three keys: 'entailment', 'contradiction', and 'neutral'. A formatted example output is provided below. {'entailment': [None/All or index numbers of text pairs that contain entailment inference relation], 'contradiction': [None/All or index numbers of text pairs that contain contradiction inference relation], 'neutral': [None/All or index numbers of text pairs that contain neutral inference relation]} Here are the text pairs: $texts JSON output:

Table 13: Prompt templates for SNLI.

Task	Prompt template
SingleClf	Analyze the usage of the given target word in the two subsequent contexts. The target word may appear in various grammatical forms in each context. Respond with 'Yes' if it maintains the same meaning across both contexts, and 'No' if it does not. $text Answer:
BatchClf	Analyze the usage of the following $num target words in the two contexts that immediately follow them. These target words may appear in different grammatical forms across the two subsequent contexts. Determine if each target word maintains the same meaning in the two subsequent contexts. Provide your answers line by line, indicating 'Yes' if it does and 'No' if it does not. $texts Answers:
SelectOne	Analyze the following $num target words and determine the index numbers of the target words where the same meaning $be maintained across the two contexts that immediately follow them. These target words may appear in different grammatical forms in each context. If none of the target words satisfy this condition, write 'None.'. If all the target words satisfy this condition, write 'All.' Otherwise, provide the index numbers. Output your responses in JSON format with the key 'answer'. A formatted example output is provided below. {'answer': [None/All or index numbers of the target words where the same meaning $be maintained in the two subsequent contexts]} Here are the target words along with their contexts: $texts JSON output:
SelectAll	Analyze the following $num target words, which may appear in different grammatical forms in the two subsequent contexts. First, list the index numbers of target words that maintain the same meaning in the two subsequent contexts. Then, list the index numbers of target words that do not maintain the same meaning in the two subsequent contexts. If none of the target words satisfy a condition, write 'None.' If all the target words satisfy a condition, write 'All.' Otherwise, provide the index numbers of the target words that satisfy each condition. Output your responses in JSON format with two keys: 'yes' for target words used with consistent meanings and 'no' for those used with inconsistent meanings. A formatted example output is provided below. {'yes': [None/All or index numbers of target words used with consistent meanings], 'no': [None/All or index numbers of target words used with inconsistent meanings]} Here are the target words along with their contexts: $texts JSON output:

Table 14: Prompt templates for WiC.

Task	Prompt template
SelectOne Simplified	Go over the $num lines of text below and list the index numbers of the lines that contain the word '$category' according to the following instructions: If none of the texts contain the word '$category,' write 'None.' If all the texts contain the word '$category,' write 'All.' Otherwise, provide the index numbers of the texts that contain the word '$category' each on a separate line. Texts, one per line: $texts 'None,' 'All,' or the index numbers of the texts that contain the word '$category,' one per line:
SelectAll Simplified	In this task, each line of text contains one of four words 'Business,' 'Sports,' 'World,' and 'Sci/Tech.' Go over the $num lines of text below and list the index numbers of the lines that contain each word according to the following instructions: If none of the texts contain a particular word, write 'None.' If all the texts contain a particular word, write 'All.' Otherwise, provide the index numbers of the texts that contain each word. Output your responses in JSON format with the following keys: 'business,' 'sports,' 'world,' and 'sci/tech.' A formatted example output is provided below. {'business': [None/All or index numbers of texts containing 'Business'], 'sports': [None/All or index numbers of texts containing 'Sports'], 'world': [None/All or index numbers of texts containing 'World'], 'sci/tech': [None/All or index numbers of texts containing 'Sci/Tech']} Texts, one per line: $texts JSON output:

Table 15: Prompt templates for simplified SelectOne and SelectAll based on AGNews. For SelectOne Simplified, we used an earlier prompt template that asks LLMs to produce outputs line by line, instead of a JSON object. As illustrated earlier, we find the effect of the two output formats for SelectOne to be minimal. Therefore, having a JSON output should not make a meaningful difference.

Benchmark	Task	Answer template
SST-2	SelectOne	To solve this task, let's first classify the 10 lines of text above, one per line: {labels} From here, we see that lines {indices} show positive sentiment. Therefore, the answer in JSON format is as follows: {final answer}
SST-2	SelectAll	To solve this task, let's first classify the 10 lines of text above, one per line: {labels} From here, we see that lines {indices} show positive sentiment, and lines {indices} show negative sentiment. Therefore, the answer in JSON format is as follows: {final answer}
CoLA	SelectOne	To solve this task, let's first classify the 10 lines of text above, one per line: {labels} From here, we see that texts in lines {indices} are unacceptable. Therefore, the answer in JSON format is as follows: {final answer}
CoLA	SelectAll	To solve this task, let's first classify the 10 lines of text above, one per line: {labels} From here, we see that texts in lines {indices} are acceptable and texts in lines {indices} are unacceptable. Therefore, the answer in JSON format is as follows: {final answer}
AGNews	SelectOne	To solve this task, let's first classify the 10 lines of text above, one per line: {labels} From here, we see that texts in lines {indices} can be classified as 'Sports.'. Therefore, the answer in JSON format is as follows: {final answer}
AGNews	SelectAll	To solve this task, let's first classify the 10 lines of text above, one per line: {labels} From here, we see that texts in lines {indices} can be classified as 'Business,' texts in lines {indices} can be classified as 'Sports,' texts in lines {indices} can be classified as 'World,' and texts in lines {indices} are 'Sci/Tech.' Therefore, the answer in JSON format is as follows: {final answer}
MRPC	SelectOne	To solve this task, let's first determine if text A is a paraphrase of text B for the 10 lines of text above, one per line: {labels} From there, we see that text pairs in lines {indices} are paraphrases. Therefore, the answer in JSON format is as follows: {final answer}
MRPC	SelectAll	To solve this task, let's first determine if text A is a paraphrase of text B for the 10 lines of text above, one per line: {labels} From there, we see that text pairs in lines {indices} are paraphrases and text pairs in lines {indices} are not. Therefore, the answer in JSON format is as follows: {final answer}
SNLI	SelectOne	To solve this task, let's first determine the inference relation between the premise and the hypothesis for the 10 lines of text above, one per line: {labels} From there, we see that text pairs in lines {indices} contain entailment inference relation. Therefore, the answer in JSON format is as follows: {final answer}
SNLI	SelectAll	To solve this task, let's first determine the inference relation between the premise and the hypothesis for the 10 lines of text above, one per line: {labels} From there, we see that text pairs in lines {indices} contain entailment inference relation, text pairs in lines {indices} contain contradiction inference relation, and text pairs in lines {indices} contain neutral inference relation. Therefore, the answer in JSON format is as follows: {final answer}
WiC	SelectOne	To solve this task, let's first determine if the target word is used with consistent meanings in the two subsequent contexts for the num lines of text above, one per line: {labels} From there, we see that text pairs in lines {indices} contain use the target words with inconsistent meanings. Therefore, the answer in JSON format is as follows: {final answer}
WiC	SelectAll	To solve this task, let's first determine if the target word is used with consistent meanings in the two subsequent contexts for the num lines of text above, one per line: {labels} From there, we see that text pairs in lines {indices} contain use the target words with inconsistent meanings and text pairs in lines {indices} do not. Therefore, the answer in JSON format is as follows: {final answer}

Table 16: Answer templates for the two selection tasks for each classification benchmark. {indices}: a list of indices seperated by comma. {final answer}: answer in a JSON format specified by the SelectOne or SelectAll prompt.

Exploring Multimodal Language Models for Sustainability Disclosure Extraction: A Comparative Study

Tanay Kumar Gupta
TCS Research
New Delhi, India
gupta.tanay@tcs.com

Tushar Goel
TCS Research
New Delhi, India
t.goel@tcs.com

Ishan Verma
TCS Research
New Delhi, India
ishan.verma@tcs.com

Abstract

Sustainability metrics have increasingly become a crucial non-financial criterion in investment decision-making. Organizations worldwide are recognizing the importance of sustainability and are proactively highlighting their efforts through specialized sustainability reports. Unlike traditional annual reports, these sustainability disclosures are typically text-heavy and are often expressed as infographics, complex tables, and charts. The non-machine-readable nature of these reports presents a significant challenge for efficient information extraction. The rapid advancement of Vision Language Models (VLMs) has raised the question whether these VLMs can address such challenges in domain specific task. In this study, we demonstrate the application of VLMs for extracting sustainability information from dedicated sustainability reports. Our experiments highlight the limitations in the performance of several open-source VLMs in extracting information about sustainability disclosures from different type of pages.

1 Introduction

In recent years, we have witnessed a significant growth in inclusion of non-financial factors particularly sustainability in corporate reporting. As per KPMG's recent sustainability reporting survey[1], reporting on sustainability has become part of business as usual for 96% of the world's largest 250 companies and a majority of the top 100 companies in each country. Driven by continued stakeholder demand for transparency and consistency in sustainability data disclosures, several standards have been proposed to harmonize sustainability reporting. Frameworks like Global Reporting Initiative (GRI), Sustainability Accounting Standards Board (SASB), and UN Sustainable Development Goals (SDG), have been developed to streamline the reporting around various sustainability indicators (Chofreh and Goni, 2017). Despite being part of business-critical disclosures, sustainability reporting remains mostly unstructured, unlike the standardized annual financial reports. With no common reporting template, these reports lack consistency, relying mostly on charts, infographics and text, and are generally published in non-machine-readable PDF formats (Ruggiero and Bachiller, 2023). Extracting relevant information from these unstructured reports takes several person hours of efforts and is prone to mistakes and influence by personal judgment. Hence, automation of sustainability information extraction from reports can reduce processing time and let stakeholders focus more on decision making. In this work, we have used the GRI framework as reference. The GRI framework offers sustainability standards in three categories: Economy (GRI 200), Environment (GRI 300), and Social (GRI 400), for further details refer A.1. Organisations use various indicators listed under these three to report their sustainability activities.

Recent advancements in natural language processing with availability of Large Language Models (LLM) and Vision Language Models (VLM) viz Llama (Touvron et al., 2023), Gemini (Team et al., 2023, 2024), Phi (Abdin et al., 2024), ChatGPT (Achiam et al., 2023), LLaVa (Liu et al., 2023a,b), etc have opened a new dimension to multi-modal information extraction. Significant number of efforts have been made to utilize LLMs for extracting information from sustainability or Environmental, Social, and Governance (ESG) reports. For instance, ClimateBERT (Webersinke et al., 2021) is a transformer model fine-tuned for climate-related classification tasks, ChatReport (Ni et al., 2023) is an LLM-based tool that evaluates companies' sustainability reports according to the TCFD guidelines. ESGReveal (Zou et al., 2023) is a tripartite framework leveraging LLMs and RAG to extract and analyze ESG data, offering benchmarks for corporate reporting. DocQA (Mishra et al., 2024)

[1]https://kpmg.com/xx/en/our-insights/esg/the-move-to-mandatory-reporting.html

The Sixth Workshop on Insights from Negative Results in NLP, pages 141–149
May 4, 2025

is a platform for question answering over sustainability reports using RAG framework. Bronzini et al. (Bronzini et al., 2024) used LLMs to construct knowledge graphs for analyzing ESG disclosures from sustainability reports. However, to the best of our knowledge, the use of VLMs for ESG data extraction is yet to be explored. Also, LLMs still face challenges in effectively handling domain-specific tasks in a zero-shot setting(Yao et al., 2023). In this work, we have evaluated the performance of open source VLMs on the task of extracting sustainability disclosures from sustainability reports. We highlight the shortcomings of these models on the extraction task.

2 Data Curation & System Architecture

We collected around 700 English language sustainability reports from the SASB website[2]. Many organizations include a GRI index table in their sustainability reports which lists GRI disclosures with their reference, such as page numbers, links, and section headers. The format varies across reports, as can be seen in A.2. We used GRI index tables from these reports to generate the benchmark evaluation dataset, focusing on those with internal references only for listed GRI disclosures. We applied a keyword driven heuristic-based filtering method to identify reports containing a GRI Index table, specifically checking if the index mention appeared in the table of contents. This filtering process left us with 380 reports. Next, we manually annotated the page ranges in the reports where the GRI Index tables appeared. These tables were extracted using a combination of Table Transformer (Smock et al., 2022) and Llama 3 (Dubey et al., 2024) with human in the loop in <GRI disclosure, Page Number> format. Comparison of our approach with VLM based table extractions are shown in appendix A.2.

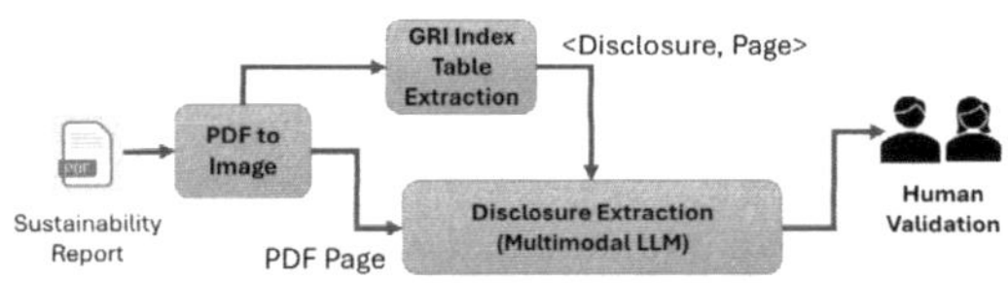

Figure 1: System Flow Diagram

Figure 1 shows the process flow followed for the work. After identifying the relevant page image and corresponding GRI disclosure for which data needs to be extracted, we provided the page image along with a contextual prompt to the VLMs. The prompt was designed to guide the model in extracting specific information based on the GRI disclosure. The VLM output is then validated by human experts. The next section outlines the VLMs used in our experiments, a brief overview of their architecture and selection rationale.

3 Experiments

We experimented with the following VLMs for extracting information related to GRI disclosures from the report pages:

- **Llama 3.2 Vision** - Llama-3.2-11B-Vision-Instruct[3] is an instruction fine-tuned model of Llama 3.2 vision (Dubey et al., 2024) which integrates image encoder followed by image adapter and language model decoder.
- **Qwen2 VL** - Qwen2-VL-7B-Instruct[4] is an instruction fine-tuned model of Qwen2 (Wang et al., 2024) which integrates 675M parameter vision encoder with 7.6B parameter language model decoder. It uses naive dynamic resolution to process any resolution image along with multi-modal rotary position embedding to extrapolate longer sequences.
- **LLaVA** - LLaVA-v1.6-mistral-7b-hf [5] is an instruction fine-tuned model of LLaVA-NeXT (Liu et al., 2024) which combines a vision encoder and a connector to connect with mistral (Jiang et al., 2023) LLM for joint vision-language tasks.

These models were selected due to their proven accuracy on similar datasets, such as DocVQA (Mathew et al., 2021), ChartQA (Masry et al., 2022), InfographicVQA (Mathew et al., 2022), and MMMU (Yue et al., 2024). Additionally, they represent some of the recent advancements in the field, ensuring that the models used are both relevant and capable of handling the complexities of the task at hand. In the later section, we will discuss about the short comings of these models in specific settings.

4 Results & Analysis

We conducted experiments to validate the extractions of 74 unique GRI disclosures across 10 sus-

[2]https://sasb.ifrs.org/company-use/sasb-reporters/

[3]https://huggingface.co/meta-llama/Llama-3.2-11B-Vision-Instruct

[4]https://huggingface.co/Qwen/Qwen2-VL-7B-Instruct

[5]https://huggingface.co/llava-hf/llava-v1.6-mistral-7b-hf

tainability reports, with a total of 640 pages analyzed. The results were assessed by two independent domain experts, with a Cohen's Kappa score(Cohen, 1960) of 0.9, indicating strong consistency in the evaluation process. Partial extractions were considered incorrect during validation. The requirement for manual validation of the outputs limited the number of reports included in the experiments. These pages included data presented as text, tables, charts, infographics, or a combination of these formats (Examples shown in Appendix A Figure 2). Around 60% of the pages have data in more than one format. In Table 1, we present the distribution of pages as per the data formats.

Page Type	Count	Page Type	Count
text	125	table+infographics	10
table	125	chart+infographics	7
infographics	5	text+chart	90
text+infographics	163	text+chart+table	46
text+table	39	text+chart+infographics	30

Table 1: Distribution of Pages as per Data format

The prevalence of "*text*" and "*text + infographics*" highlights the reliance on textual descriptions and visual information in sustainability reporting. However, the reports also incorporate a substantial number of tables and combined modalities like "*text + chart*" and "*text + chart + table*", emphasizing the multimodal nature of these documents. The low incidence of standalone "*infographics*" and "*chart + infographics*" likely stems from the common practice of including accompanying text within these visuals, resulting in a higher prevalence of combined "*text + infographics*" entries.

We expand our analysis by including key metrics that evaluate the effectiveness of VLMs in GRI disclosure extraction. For validation purposes, we considered three distinct cases:

- **Correct**: The model correctly extracts the relevant information from the page.
- **Incorrect**: The model extracts information from the page; however, it fails to provide the correct answer due to misinterpretation, incomplete understanding, or inaccurate reasoning. This could involve selecting the wrong data point from a chart/table or misinterpreting a statement in the text.
- **Hallucination**: The model provides information that is not present on the page. This indicates that the response isn't properly based on the page content, and the model is generating the response based on its training data.

The accuracy of information extraction using VLMs is calculated as the percentage of correct, incorrect, or hallucinated instances, out of the total number of instances for a given GRI category or page type. Table 2 shows VLMs accuracy in extracting information across GRI categories. The results reveal varying performance across these categories for all the models, indicating sensitivity to the specific content and language used within each. For instance, while Llama 3.2 vision demonstrates a relatively high accuracy in the Economic category, likely due to the structured and quantifiable nature of economic disclosures, its performance dips in the Environment and Social categories. As for LLaVa and Qwen2, a striking negative result is the substantial proportion of "incorrect" predictions, often exceeding "correct" ones. This highlights models issue with fine-grained comprehension and information localization within the document. Furthermore, the presence of hallucination raises concerns about reliability, specially for LLaVa in the Environment category. This is due to LLaVa's tendency to generate descriptive summaries of page images, rather than focusing on precise information extraction, which might contributed to the fabrication of information. Qwen2 displays a different pattern, exhibiting a lower hallucination rate but a high proportion of incorrect predictions. This behavior suggests a potential weakness in Qwen2's ability to perform fine-grained information extraction. Our observations indicate that Qwen2 occasionally provides section headlines or the names of GRI disclosures themselves as answers, even when more specific information is requested in the prompt. This tendency to offer labels rather than detailed content contributes to the increased rate of incorrect predictions. The impact of different page types on the VLM's accuracy is demonstrated in Table 3, revealing a significant performance gap based on content and layout complexity. While text-heavy pages achieve moderate accuracy for Llama 3.2 and Qwen2, LLaVa struggles, suggesting differences in handling textual information. Complex layouts involving tables, charts, or their combinations like "*text + table*", "*chart + infographics*" present consistent challenges for all VLMs, with accuracy often falling below 50%, highlighting difficulties in deciphering information embedded within structured or visually formatted elements. The inclusion

Category	Llama 3.2 Vision Instruct			LLaVa v1.6			Qwen2 VL Chat		
	Correct	Incorrect	Hallucination	Correct	Incorrect	Hallucination	Correct	Incorrect	Hallucination
Economic	68.42	28.95	2.63	50	36.84	13.16	39.47	60.53	0
Environmental	50.47	45.04	4.47	38.02	40.25	21.72	45.36	51.43	3.19
Social	62.15	35.45	2.39	36.65	44.22	19.12	57.37	41.43	1.19

Table 2: Accuracy(%) of VLMs in extracting information across GRI categories

Page Type	Llama 3.2 Vision Instruct			LLaVa v1.6			Qwen2 VL Chat		
	Correct	Incorrect	Hallucination	Correct	Incorrect	Hallucination	Correct	Incorrect	Hallucination
text	66.4	32	1.6	38.4	41.6	20	55.2	44	0.8
table	47.2	44	8.8	40.8	40.8	18.4	36	57.6	6.4
infographics	80	20	0	40	60	0	100	0	0
text+infographics	55.83	41.72	2.45	30.06	44.78	25.15	43.56	55.83	0.61
text+table	41.03	58.97	0	46.15	25.64	28.21	56.41	41.03	2.56
table+infographics	100	0	0	0	0	100	80	20	0
chart+infographics	14.29	85.71	0	14.29	57.14	28.57	42.86	57.14	0
text+chart	66.67	31.11	2.22	51.11	46.67	2.22	64.44	35.56	0
text+chart+table	47.83	52.17	0	56.52	39.13	4.35	43.49	52.17	4.35
text+chart+infographics	66.67	23.33	10	26.67	40	33.33	50	50	0
Overall	57.19	39.38	3.44	38.91	41.41	19.69	49.38	48.59	2.03
No Data	22.11	71.63	6.25	48.55	41.34	10.09	40.38	57.69	1.92

Table 3: Accuracy(%) of VLMs in information extraction from different page types

of "*infographics*" seems to have a varied impact. Llama and Qwen2 achieve high accuracy with standalone infographics, but performance decreases when combined with text, indicating challenges in integrating multimodal information. Hallucination tendencies, particularly prominent in LLaVa for heavily structured pages like "*text + chart + infographics*", "*chart + infographics*", suggest a potential link between difficulty in processing specific page structures and the tendency to hallucinate. Overall, Llama3.2 and Qwen2 exhibit comparable performance, while LLaVa lags, underscoring the need for further research into how VLMs process diverse page elements and mitigate hallucination, especially in complex layouts. Few examples for the same are shown in appendix A.3.

The "No Data" case, shown in the last row of Table 3 presents a notable finding from our experiments. In 208 instances, the relevant data for disclosures listed in the GRI index table was not present on the referenced pages. We then assessed the performance of VLMs on pages where GRI disclosure information is expected but absent. This scenario tested the models' ability to handle missing data and avoid generating potentially misleading or fabricated responses. The results reveal a concerning trend: Llama and Qwen2 exhibits a high proportion of "incorrect" predictions in this context whereas LLaVa achieves highest accuracy in saying "no, the information is not present". Llama, while demonstrating the lowest percentage of correct responses, struggles significantly, with over 72% of its predictions classified as incorrect. Interestingly, while the hallucination rates are low for all models, the substantial proportion of incorrect predictions suggests that the models may be attempting to answer by relying on contextual clues or related information, even when the specific data point is missing. This highlights a critical limitation: the models appear unable to reliably identify and flag the absence of required information, instead attempting to provide an answer, even if it is incorrect. This behavior underscores the need for improved mechanisms to detect and handle missing data.

5 Conclusion

In this work, we explored the feasibility of using Vision-Language Models (VLMs) for sustainability data extraction from multimodal PDF page images. Our experiments concluded that no single VLM can efficiently manage all data formats. We found that Llama performs best on text-based pages but is prone to incorrect responses. The LLaVa model frequently experiences hallucinations, while Qwen exhibits similar accuracy for both correct and incorrect responses. This study opens potential future research directions, such as integrating model strengths, fine-tuning for improved performance, and using knowledge-infused prompts for better extraction. It is also important to address cases with no data, focusing on extending VLMs ability to recognize and respond to information gaps.

References

Marah Abdin, Jyoti Aneja, Hany Awadalla, Ahmed Awadallah, Ammar Ahmad Awan, Nguyen Bach, Amit Bahree, Arash Bakhtiari, Jianmin Bao, Harkirat Behl, et al. 2024. Phi-3 technical report: A highly capable language model locally on your phone. *arXiv preprint arXiv:2404.14219*.

Josh Achiam, Steven Adler, Sandhini Agarwal, Lama Ahmad, Ilge Akkaya, Florencia Leoni Aleman, Diogo Almeida, Janko Altenschmidt, Sam Altman, Shyamal Anadkat, et al. 2023. Gpt-4 technical report. *arXiv preprint arXiv:2303.08774*.

Marco Bronzini, Carlo Nicolini, Bruno Lepri, Andrea Passerini, and Jacopo Staiano. 2024. Glitter or gold? deriving structured insights from sustainability reports via large language models. *EPJ Data Science*, 13(1):41.

Abdoulmohammad Gholamzadeh Chofreh and Feybi Ariani Goni. 2017. Review of frameworks for sustainability implementation. *Sustainable Development*, 25(3):180–188.

Jacob Cohen. 1960. A coefficient of agreement for nominal scales. *Educational and Psychological Measurement*, 20(1):37–46.

Abhimanyu Dubey, Abhinav Jauhri, Abhinav Pandey, Abhishek Kadian, Ahmad Al-Dahle, Aiesha Letman, Akhil Mathur, Alan Schelten, Amy Yang, Angela Fan, et al. 2024. The llama 3 herd of models. *arXiv preprint arXiv:2407.21783*.

Albert Q Jiang, Alexandre Sablayrolles, Arthur Mensch, Chris Bamford, Devendra Singh Chaplot, Diego de las Casas, Florian Bressand, Gianna Lengyel, Guillaume Lample, Lucile Saulnier, et al. 2023. Mistral 7b. *arXiv preprint arXiv:2310.06825*.

Haotian Liu, Chunyuan Li, Yuheng Li, and Yong Jae Lee. 2023a. Improved baselines with visual instruction tuning.

Haotian Liu, Chunyuan Li, Yuheng Li, Bo Li, Yuanhan Zhang, Sheng Shen, and Yong Jae Lee. 2024. Llava-next: Improved reasoning, ocr, and world knowledge.

Haotian Liu, Chunyuan Li, Qingyang Wu, and Yong Jae Lee. 2023b. Visual instruction tuning. In *NeurIPS*.

Ahmed Masry, Do Xuan Long, Jia Qing Tan, Shafiq Joty, and Enamul Hoque. 2022. Chartqa: A benchmark for question answering about charts with visual and logical reasoning. *arXiv preprint arXiv:2203.10244*.

Minesh Mathew, Viraj Bagal, Rubèn Tito, Dimosthenis Karatzas, Ernest Valveny, and CV Jawahar. 2022. Infographicvqa. In *Proceedings of the IEEE/CVF Winter Conference on Applications of Computer Vision*, pages 1697–1706.

Minesh Mathew, Dimosthenis Karatzas, and CV Jawahar. 2021. Docvqa: A dataset for vqa on document images. In *Proceedings of the IEEE/CVF winter conference on applications of computer vision*, pages 2200–2209.

Lokesh Mishra, Cesar Berrospi, Kasper Dinkla, Diego Antognini, Francesco Fusco, Benedikt Bothur, Maksym Lysak, Nikolaos Livathinos, Ahmed Nassar, Panagiotis Vagenas, et al. 2024. Esg accountability made easy: Docqa at your service. In *Proceedings of the AAAI Conference on Artificial Intelligence*, volume 38, pages 23814–23816.

Jingwei Ni, Julia Bingler, Chiara Colesanti-Senni, Mathias Kraus, Glen Gostlow, Tobias Schimanski, Dominik Stammbach, Saeid Ashraf Vaghefi, Qian Wang, Nicolas Webersinke, et al. 2023. Chatreport: Democratizing sustainability disclosure analysis through llm-based tools. *arXiv preprint arXiv:2307.15770*.

Pasquale Ruggiero and Patricia Bachiller. 2023. Seeing more than reading: The visual mode in utilities' sustainability reports. *Utilities Policy*, 83:101610.

Brandon Smock, Rohith Pesala, and Robin Abraham. 2022. Pubtables-1m: Towards comprehensive table extraction from unstructured documents. In *Proceedings of the IEEE/CVF Conference on Computer Vision and Pattern Recognition*, pages 4634–4642.

Gemini Team, Rohan Anil, Sebastian Borgeaud, Jean-Baptiste Alayrac, Jiahui Yu, Radu Soricut, Johan Schalkwyk, Andrew M Dai, Anja Hauth, Katie Millican, et al. 2023. Gemini: a family of highly capable multimodal models. *arXiv preprint arXiv:2312.11805*.

Gemini Team, Petko Georgiev, Ving Ian Lei, Ryan Burnell, Libin Bai, Anmol Gulati, Garrett Tanzer, Damien Vincent, Zhufeng Pan, Shibo Wang, et al. 2024. Gemini 1.5: Unlocking multimodal understanding across millions of tokens of context. *arXiv preprint arXiv:2403.05530*.

Hugo Touvron, Thibaut Lavril, Gautier Izacard, Xavier Martinet, Marie-Anne Lachaux, Timothée Lacroix, Baptiste Rozière, Naman Goyal, Eric Hambro, Faisal Azhar, et al. 2023. Llama: Open and efficient foundation language models. *arXiv preprint arXiv:2302.13971*.

Peng Wang, Shuai Bai, Sinan Tan, Shijie Wang, Zhihao Fan, Jinze Bai, Keqin Chen, Xuejing Liu, Jialin Wang, Wenbin Ge, et al. 2024. Qwen2-vl: Enhancing vision-language model's perception of the world at any resolution. *arXiv preprint arXiv:2409.12191*.

Nicolas Webersinke, Mathias Kraus, Julia Anna Bingler, and Markus Leippold. 2021. Climatebert: A pretrained language model for climate-related text. *arXiv preprint arXiv:2110.12010*.

Jing Yao, Wei Xu, Jianxun Lian, Xiting Wang, Xiaoyuan Yi, and Xing Xie. 2023. Knowledge plugins: Enhancing large language models for domain-specific recommendations. *arXiv preprint arXiv:2311.10779*.

Xiang Yue, Yuansheng Ni, Kai Zhang, Tianyu Zheng, Ruoqi Liu, Ge Zhang, Samuel Stevens, Dongfu Jiang, Weiming Ren, Yuxuan Sun, et al. 2024. Mmmu: A massive multi-discipline multimodal understanding and reasoning benchmark for expert agi. In *Proceedings of the IEEE/CVF Conference on Computer Vision and Pattern Recognition*, pages 9556–9567.

Yi Zou, Mengying Shi, Zhongjie Chen, Zhu Deng, ZongXiong Lei, Zihan Zeng, Shiming Yang, HongXiang Tong, Lei Xiao, and Wenwen Zhou. 2023. Esgreveal: An llm-based approach for extracting structured data from esg reports. *arXiv preprint arXiv:2312.17264*.

A Appendix

Figure 2 illustrates several examples of pages from sustainability reports that exhibit multimodal content. These examples highlight the complexity involved in processing such pages, where visual elements such as text, tables, charts, infographics and their combinations are present.

A.1 GRI Framework

The Global Reporting Initiative (GRI)[6] framework is a globally recognized standard for sustainability reporting that helps organizations disclose their environmental, social, and economic impacts. It provides structured guidelines to ensure transparency, consistency, and comparability in sustainability reports. The GRI framework consists of several series, each addressing specific areas of sustainability:

- **200 Series** focuses on economic factors, guiding organizations to report on their Economic performance(201), Market presence(202), Anti-competitive behaviour(206) etc.
- **300 Series** deals with environmental aspects, covering topics such as Energy(302), Water and Effluents(303), Emissions(305), and biodiversity(304) etc.
- **400 Series** addresses social factors, including labor practices such as Child labor(408), Forced or Compulsory labor(409), Training and Education(404), Occupational health and safety(403) etc.

Table 4 provides a sample breakdown of the GRI series, illustrating how each series is further subdivided into specific disclosures.

[6]https://www.globalreporting.org/

Economic (200)	Anti-corruption (205)	Operations Assessed for Risks related to Corruption(205-1)
Environment (300)	Energy (302)	Energy consumption within the organization (302-1)
		Energy intensity (302-3)
	Water (303)	Water Withdrawal (303-3)
Social (400)	Occupational Health & Safety (403)	Promotion of Worker Health (403-6)

Table 4: GRI hierarchy example

A.2 GRI Index Table

In Figure 3, we have shown few examples of GRI index tables. These tables have information about GRI disclosures along their data references in the reports. These references can be present in form of page number along with or without textual information, internal and external links, name of other reports, and section headers within the report along with other metadata. These formats differ from one report to another. To extract the information about GRI disclosures mentioned in the table, it is required to have the GRI disclosure data in <GRI Disclosure, Page Number> format. While validating, we have relaxed the assumption of strict page number such as if we get p.38, we mark it correct. We have validated it for 10 sustainability reports. Table 5 shows the accuracy of VLMs for GRI index table extraction and our approach Table Transformer + Llama 3. Here, Llama 3.2 Vision achieved 83.5% accuracy but struggled with providing direct page numbers when text is involved. Additionally, it had difficulty in maintaining format consistency. In contrast, Qwen2 faced issues in detection of GRI disclosure and performs poorly when multiple tables were present and achieved only 53.5% accuracy. LLaVa, on the other hand, consistently produced repetitive results, falling short of expectations. In comparison, our approach delivers accurate page numbers and achieves superior accuracy of 93%, making it the preferred method for GRI Index extraction. This observation highlights the limitations of Qwen2 and LLaVa in accurately extracting information from page images containing large tables, a scenario that is not commonly encountered.

	TableTransformer + Llama 3 Instruct	Llama 3.2 Vision	Qwen2 VL Chat
Accuracy	93%	83.5%	53.5%

Table 5: Accuracy of different models in GRI Index Table Extraction

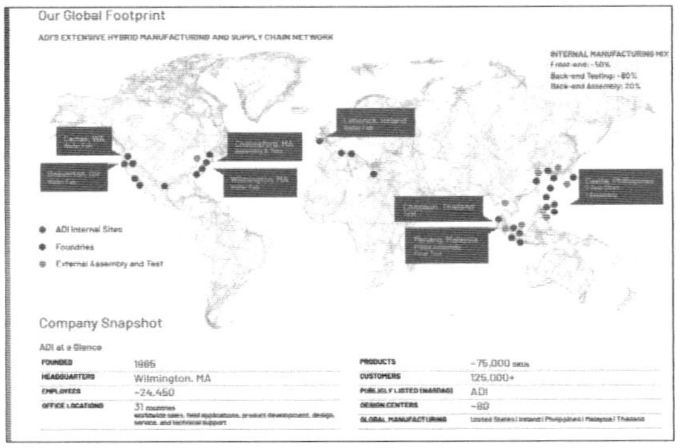

Page type: Table+Infographics

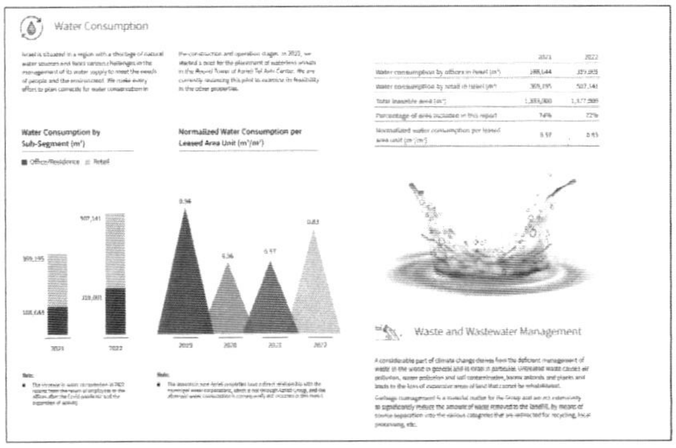

Page type: Text+Chart+Table

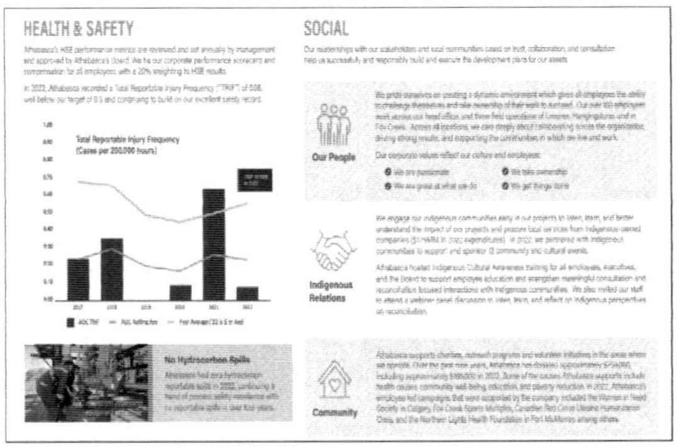

Page type: Text+Chart+Infographics

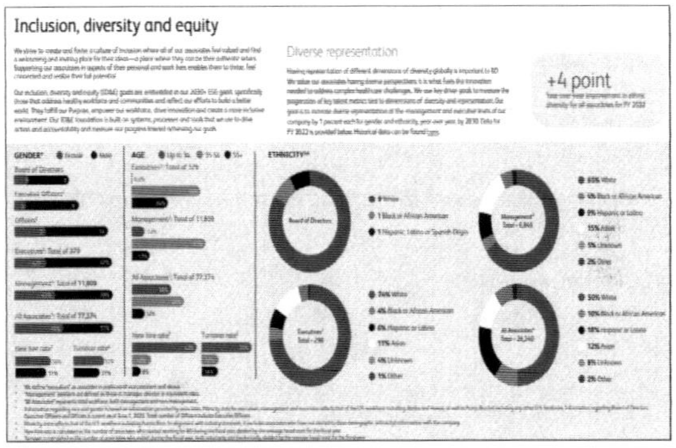

Page type: Text+Chart

Figure 2: Examples of pages from sustainability reports exhibiting multimodal content, highlighting the complexity involved in processing visual elements to extract the relevant data.

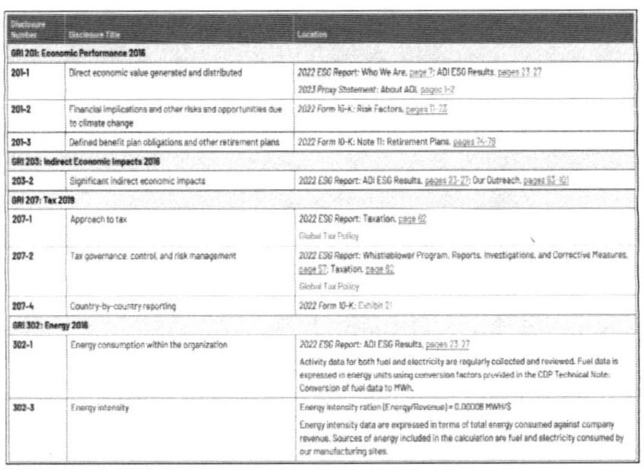

Disclosure Number	Disclosure Title	Location
GRI 201: Economic Performance 2016		
201-1	Direct economic value generated and distributed	2022 ESG Report: Who We Are, page 7; ADI ESG Results, pages 23-27 2023 Proxy Statement: About ADI, pages 1-2
201-2	Financial implications and other risks and opportunities due to climate change	2022 Form 10-K: Risk Factors, pages 11-23
201-3	Defined benefit plan obligations and other retirement plans	2022 Form 10-K: Note 11: Retirement Plans, pages 74-78
GRI 203: Indirect Economic Impacts 2016		
203-2	Significant indirect economic impacts	2022 ESG Report: ADI ESG Results, pages 23-27; Our Outreach, pages 93-101
GRI 207: Tax 2019		
207-1	Approach to tax	2022 ESG Report: Taxation, page 62 Global Tax Policy
207-2	Tax governance, control, and risk management	2022 ESG Report: Whistleblower Program, Reports, Investigations, and Corrective Measures, page 57; Taxation, page 62 Global Tax Policy
207-4	Country-by-country reporting	2022 Form 10-K: Exhibit 21
GRI 302: Energy 2016		
302-1	Energy consumption within the organization	2022 ESG Report: ADI ESG Results, pages 23-27 Activity data for both fuel and electricity are regularly collected and reviewed. Fuel data is expressed in energy units using conversion factors provided in the CDP Technical Note: Conversion of fuel data to MWh.
302-3	Energy intensity	Energy intensity ration (Energy/Revenue) = 0.00008 MWH/$ Energy intensity data are expressed in terms of total energy consumed against company revenue. Sources of energy included in the calculation are fuel and electricity consumed by our manufacturing sites.

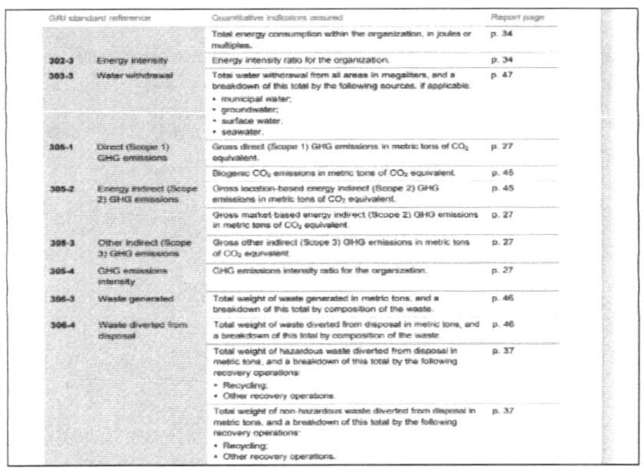

GRI standard reference		Quantitative indicators assured	Report page
		Total energy consumption within the organization, in joules or multiples.	p. 34
302-3	Energy intensity	Energy intensity ratio for the organization.	p. 34
303-3	Water withdrawal	Total water withdrawal from all areas in megaliters, and a breakdown of this total by the following sources, if applicable: • municipal water; • groundwater; • surface water; • seawater.	p. 47
305-1	Direct (Scope 1) GHG emissions	Gross direct (Scope 1) GHG emissions in metric tons of CO_2 equivalent.	p. 27
		Biogenic CO_2 emissions in metric tons of CO_2 equivalent.	p. 45
305-2	Energy indirect (Scope 2) GHG emissions	Gross location-based energy indirect (Scope 2) GHG emissions in metric tons of CO_2 equivalent.	p. 45
		Gross market based energy indirect (Scope 2) GHG emissions in metric tons of CO_2 equivalent.	p. 27
305-3	Other indirect (Scope 3) GHG emissions	Gross other indirect (Scope 3) GHG emissions in metric tons of CO_2 equivalent.	p. 27
305-4	GHG emissions intensity	GHG emissions intensity ratio for the organization.	p. 27
306-3	Waste generated	Total weight of waste generated in metric tons, and a breakdown of this total by composition of the waste.	p. 46
306-4	Waste diverted from disposal	Total weight of waste diverted from disposal in metric tons, and a breakdown of this total by composition of the waste.	p. 46
		Total weight of hazardous waste diverted from disposal in metric tons, and a breakdown of this total by the following recovery operations: • Recycling; • Other recovery operations.	p. 37
		Total weight of non-hazardous waste diverted from disposal in metric tons, and a breakdown of this total by the following recovery operations: • Recycling; • Other recovery operations.	p. 37

Figure 3: Examples of GRI Index Tables

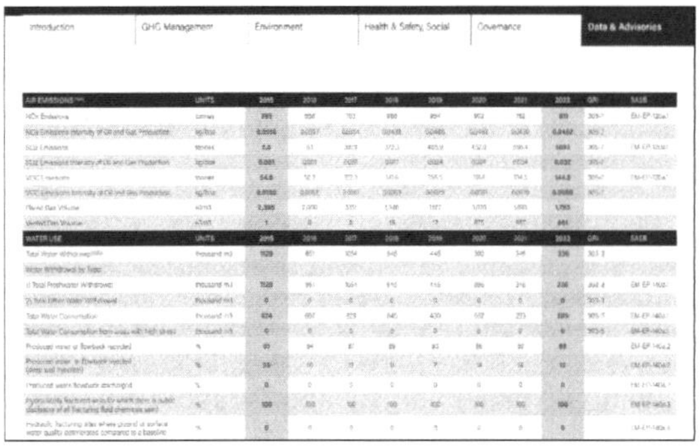

(A)

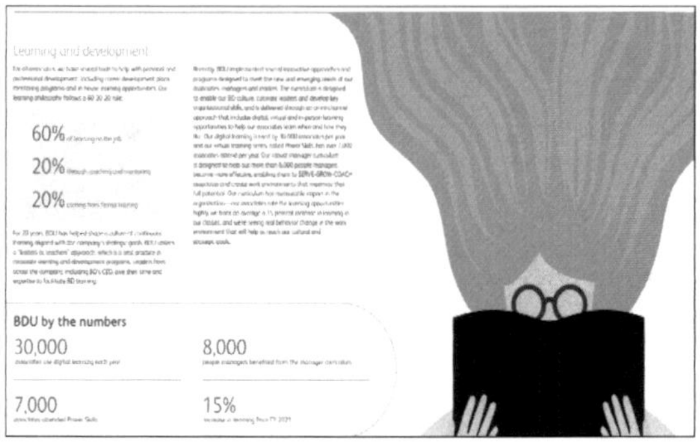

(B)

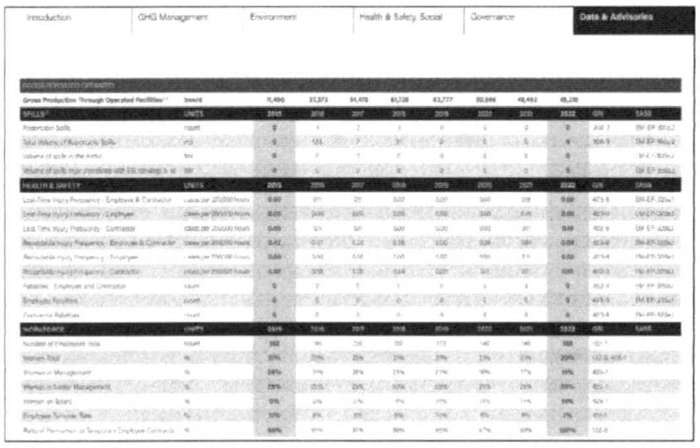

(C)

(D)

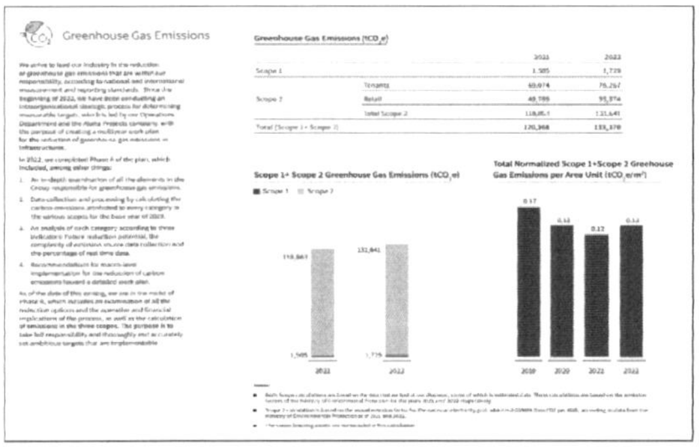

(E)

(F)

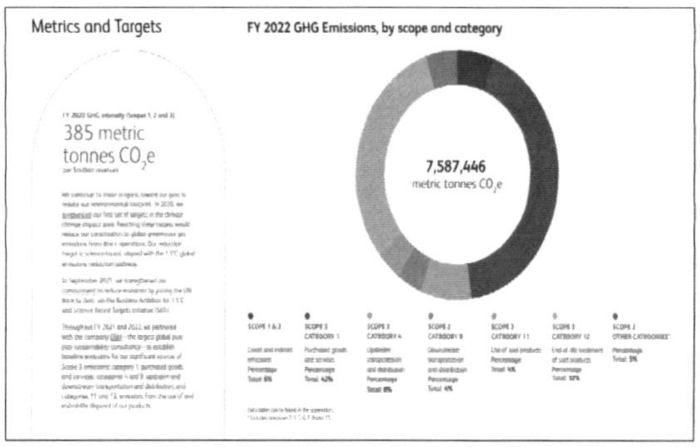

(G)

Figure 4: Page images corresponding to Table 6 for data extraction

GRI Disclosure	Page type	VLM Model	Information Extracted using VLM	Validation
Water Consumption (303-5)	Table (Image A)	LLaVa	"Total Water Consumption" with a value of 807 million m3. "Total Water Consumption from areas with high stress" with a value of 807 million m3 in the same table.	Hallucination
Average hours of training per year per employee (404-1)	Text + Infographics (Image B)	Qwen	['8,000']	Incorrect
Nitrogen oxides (NOX), sulfur oxides (SOX), and other significant air emissions (305-7)	Table (Image C)	Llama	**Nitrogen Oxides (NOX)** * **2019**: 0 * *2020**: 0 * **2021**: 0 * **2022**: 0 *Sulfur Oxides (SOX)** * **2019**: 0 * *2020**: 0 * **2021**: 0 * **2022**: 0	Hallucination
Confirmed incidents of corruption and actions taken (205-3)	Text (Image D)	Qwen	['Confirmed incidents of corruption and action taken.']	Incorrect
GHG emissions intensity (305-4)	Text+Chart +Table (Image E)	Llama	Total Normalized Scope 1+Scope 2 Greenhouse Gas Emissions per Area Unit (tCO2e/m2). Scope 1 + Scope 2 Greenhouse Gas Emissions (tCO2e). These are the only references to GHG emissions intensity in the image.	Incorrect
Waste diverted from disposal (306-4)	Text+Chart+ Infographics (Image F)	LLaVa	As part of our ongoing commitment to sustainable business practices, we continuously monitor and improve our waste management processes. By implementing new technologies and strategies, we aim to achieve zero landfill waste generation across all sites by 2030. This initiative aligns with our broader goal of achieving net zero emissions by 2050.	Hallucination
Reduction of GHG emissions (305-5)	Text+ Infographics (Image G)	Qwen	"FY 222 GHG Emissions, by scope and category 7,587,446 metric tonnes CO2e SCOPE 1 & 2 Direct and indirect emissions Total: 6% SCOPE 3 CATEGORY 1 Purchased goods and services Total: 42% SCOPE 3 CATEGORY 4 Upstream transportation and distribution Total: 8% SCOPE 3 CATEGORY 9 Downstream transportation and distribution Total: 4% SCOPE 3 CATEGORY 11 ....."	Correct

Table 6: Examples of data extraction from images using different VLMs along with its validation

A.3 Examples of GRI Disclosure Extraction

Figure 4 shows few reference page images. Information extracted through different VLMs for few GRI disclosures from these images are shown in Table 6. The analysis of these examples are as follows:

- **Row 1 - Image A**: An attempt was made to extract information related to water consumption; however, LLaVa failed to correctly retrieve the information. The extracted value did not correspond to any data present on the page, resulting in a case of hallucination.
- **Row 2 - Image B**: Qwen2 was tasked to extract the information about Average hours of training per year per employee but it erroneously extracted number of people managers benefited from the manager curriculum which is incorrect.
- **Row 3 - Image C**: It shows another case of hallucination where Llama 3.2 generated false value "0" for the disclosure Nitrogen oxides (NOX), sulfur oxides (SOX), and other significant emissions. This example also highlight the case of "**No Data**" as there is no information available corresponding to the GRI disclosure "Nitrogen oxides (NOx), sulfur oxides (SOx), and other significant air emissions(305-7)" on the page.
- **Row 4 - Image D**: Qwen2 failed to extract any information from this image, which contained only textual data.
- **Row 5 - Image E**: Llama 3.2 provided the title of charts as an answer which is an incorrect response.
- **Row 6 - Image F**: In this complex image which contains text, chart and infographics all together, LLaVa exhibited hallucination by providing a statement "we aim to achieve zero landfill waste generation across all sites by 2030." as an answer. This information is not present on the page.
- **Row 7 - Image G**: Although complex data representation in their in the page image, Qwen2 is able to extract correct information from the infographics.

Self Knowledge-Tracing for Tool Use (SKT-Tool): Helping LLM Agents Understand Their Capabilities in Tool Use

Joshua Vigel* **Renpei Cai*** **Eleanor Chen** **Anish Neema**
Austen Liao† **Kevin Zhu†** **Sean O'Brien†**
Algoverse AI Research
nasevate@gmail.com, kevin@algoverse.us

Abstract

Large Language Models (LLMs) enhanced with tool use and APIs improve task performance but often misuse them, leading to inefficiency and unnecessary cost. We propose Self Knowledge-Tracing for Tool Use (SKT-Tool), a method enabling LLMs to assess their capabilities and make informed API usage decisions using knowledge tracing (KT). Our teacher-student framework helps LLMs optimize API calls in real-time without fine-tuning. Experiments across multiple datasets show that SKT-Tool significantly reduces API calls while maintaining accuracy, offering a scalable and cost-effective solution for tool-augmented LLMs. We conclude by analyzing shortcomings in this method and identifying directions for future work.

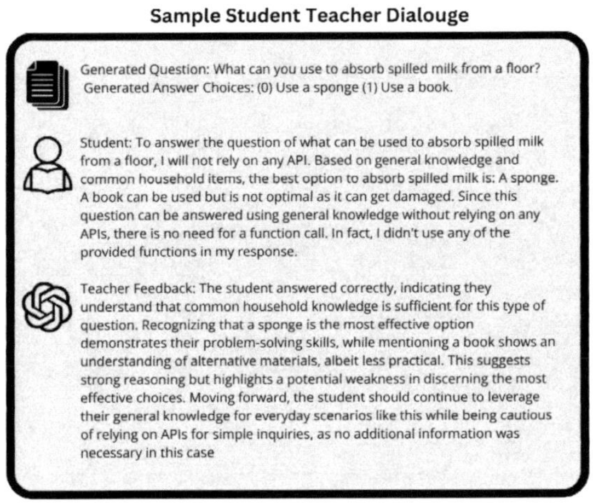

Figure 1: Example dialogue from the synthetic generation process. This is a sample of the interaction string that is passed onto our student model for reference.

1 Introduction

Large Language Models (LLMs) have recently achieved a great number of remarkable abilities when incorporated with external tools like Application Programming Interfaces (APIs) (Parisi et al., 2022; Patil et al., 2023). However, two problems emerge: current LLM agents often struggle choosing which tools to use on different problems (Li et al., 2023), and also that much of current research focuses solely on the API choice (Qin et al., 2023; Li et al., 2023; Chen et al., 2024; Tang et al., 2023), where an LLM indiscriminately calls tools during tests, which may not align with real-world scenarios (Ning et al., 2024; Qiao et al., 2023). This can result in redundant API calls, leading to extra computation and even possible monetary loss in cases where every API call costs money, thus substantially reducing the usefulness of tool-augmented LLM Agents in real-world applications. Furthermore, the introduction of tools tends to decrease the performance of LLMs across general datasets when they have to decide whether or not tool use is appropriate (Ning et al., 2024).

Existing approaches fine-tune LLMs to choose APIs (Ning et al., 2024; Schick et al., 2023; Hao et al., 2023; Yang et al., 2023) but overlook the model's inherent capabilities.

In this paper, we propose Self Knowledge-Tracing for Tool use (SKT-Tool) which offers a solution involving a Student-Teacher framework.

2 Related Work

2.1 Tool Use in Large Language Models

WTU-Eval (Ning et al., 2024) introduces a benchmark designed to evaluate whether LLMs can discern their ability boundaries and decide on tool usage accordingly. The findings of WTU-Eval highlight a critical gap: most current approaches assume that an LLM must invoke an API without first evaluating whether the model is capable of solving the task on its own. The study demonstrated that LLMs frequently misuse tools when unnecessary,

*Lead Author
†Senior Author

The Sixth Workshop on Insights from Negative Results in NLP, pages 150–156
May 4, 2025 ©2025 Association for Computational Linguistics

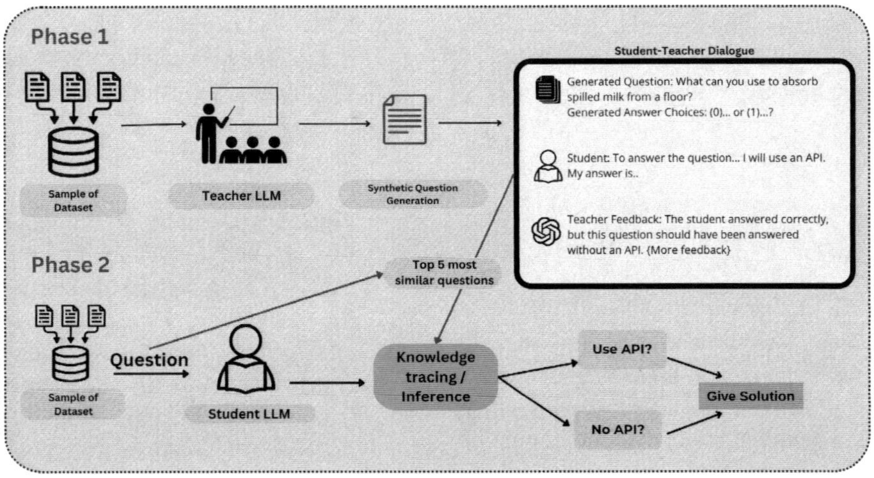

Figure 2: Visualization of our system's workflow. In Phase 1, the teacher generates n questions to assess the student's ability. In Phase 2, the student answers actual task/dataset questions. Then, the top-k most similar Phase 1 interactions are retrieved and appended to the question. The student model then performs on its own capabilities before attempting to solve the question.

leading to performance degradation in tasks that do not require external computation.

TRICE (Qiao et al., 2023) introduces a method of teaching LLMs to use tools through continuous feedback. Their findings also introduce the problem of LLMs dropping in question-answering accuracy when introduced to tools due to confusion over how to use them, and they employ an extensive feedback mechanism that relies on instruction-tuning and Reinforcement Learning to align the LLMs behavior towards appropriate tool use.

SKT-Tool differs by employing knowledge tracing, where the Teacher LLM generates targeted questions to assess the Student's capabilities, unlike prior methods relying solely on task feedback. It optimizes through Inference-Time Optimization instead of fine-tuning or reinforcement learning. Unlike TRICE, which focuses only on accuracy, SKT-Tool also reduces API calls while aiming to maintain accuracy.

2.2 Knowledge Tracing for tool use

Our study explores the concept of knowledge tracing (KT), a technique originally used in education to track and predict students' learning progress (Corbett and Anderson, 2005). Given that LLMs often struggle understanding their capabilities in the context of Tool Use, it is intuitive to utilize knowledge tracing in this scenario.

By applying KT principles, an LLM can evaluate its own strengths and weaknesses before deciding to call an external API. For example, if a model consistently struggles with math problems but performs well in general reasoning, it can determine whether using a calculator API is necessary. This self-awareness reduces unnecessary API calls and ensures that external tools are only used when needed.

3 Method

In this section, we detail our technical approach to creating SKT-Tool. Our framework is divided into 2 subsections: (1) the teacher model and synthetic data generation; (2) the student model, Retrieval-Augmented Generation (RAG) and knowledge tracing, Fig. 2 provides a visual overview of the system architecture. As seen in Fig. 2, we set up two language models to converse with each other, where one acts as the **teacher** and the other is the **student**. Our framework aims to improve the student's model ability to decide whether or not it should call an API and answer QA datasets correctly with APIs.

3.1 Teacher Model and Synthetic Data Generation (Phase 1)

We define the Teacher Model to be a more capable LLM with the following responsibilities:

- **Synthetic Data Generation.** The Teacher receives a description of an existing task, along with k samples from the task dataset. The teacher is also provided with the list of tools/APIs that the student will have access to when approaching this task. The teacher is then prompted to generate n synthetic questions that test the student in such a way as to gain insight into the student's capabilities relevant to the task.

- **Probing the Student.** The teacher model asks the generated questions to the student, storing feedback on the correctness of the student's answers. This first part of the conversation chain, where the teacher probes the student's answering capabilities, serves as the basis for our KT mechanism and effectively avoids the cold start problem by knowledge tracing before evaluation. We refer to this synthetic question history as S.

The teacher's synthetic data generation and probing process will be referred to as **Phase 1** of the framework.

3.2 Evaluation of Student Model (Phase 2)

We define the Student Model to be the model that will be evaluated on the specified task, and may be the same model as the teacher model. In phase 2, the Student Model will use the generated conversation history to effectively choose API usage.

- **Retrieval Augmented Generation (RAG)** (Gao et al., 2023) **for knowledge tracing.** As shown in Figure 2, for each question q asked to the student during the evaluation step, we use RAG to identify the five most semantically similar questions to q in S. We append the associated conversations of these questions to the question prompt in few-shot fashion.

4 Experiments

4.1 Settings

To evaluate our method's effectiveness in different scenarios, we use a single dataset as the task per experiment. This *task*, from which a sample is given to the teacher model, is the same as the one to be solved by the student.

4.2 Datasets

To simulate questions asked by real-life users to LLMs, we use two types of datasets in our testing (where dev sets are used whenever possible):

- **General QA Domain.** We select four knowledge-based datasets with diverse question types: MLQA (Lewis et al., 2019), TriviaQA (Joshi et al., 2017), PIQA (Bisk et al., 2019), and HotpotQA (Yang et al., 2018). For HotpotQA, we exclude the context paragraphs, including only the question in the query, as the student model has access to the WikiSearch tool.

- **Math QA Domain.** To account for problem-solving tasks, we focus on math-based datasets as they test quantitative and logical reasoning abilities. Our math dataset pool includes AQUA-RAT (Ling et al., 2017), GSM8K (Cobbe et al., 2021), MathQA (Amini et al., 2019), and SAT-Math from AGIEval (Zhong et al., 2023).

For each task, we sample 250 questions from relevant datasets in both the **General** and **Math** categories.

4.3 Tools

We define our tool pool to include APIs that are most likely to be used based on the datasets above: **Google Translation API**[1], **WolframAlpha API**[2],**Bing Web Search API**[3], and **Wikipedia Search API**[4].

4.4 Models

We compare results from our method using three models with increasing capability as our student: Llama 3.1-8B (Grattafiori et al., 2024), GPT-3.5 (OpenAI, 2023), and GPT-4o (OpenAI, 2024), while our teacher model remains GPT-4o throughout experimentation.

4.5 Metrics

We evaluate our results using 3 different metrics:

- **Accuracy.** Accuracy of the Student on the given task. All datasets consist of 250 questions.

- **AccN.** Accuracy of the Student accounted for unneeded API calls, which we refer to $AccN$. The Student is considered to be incorrect if they use an API on a question that was previously shown to not require an API, regardless if their answer was correct or not.

[1] https://cloud.google.com/translate/docs/reference/rest

[2] https://developer.wolframalpha.com/

[3] https://www.microsoft.com/en-us/bing/apis/bing-web-search-api

[4] https://www.mediawiki.org/wiki/API:Search

Task - LLM	Metric	Baseline	**k** ($n = 32$) **4**	**32**	**n** ($k = 16$) **8**	**64**
	Accuracy	0.536	0.516	0.512	0.536	0.496
PIQA Llama-3.1	API Calls	177	114	104	48	43
	AccN	0.4	0.38	0.412	0.448	0.428
	Accuracy	0.912	0.832	0.832	0.884	0.868
MLQA GPT 4o	API Calls	43	7	4	12	16
	AccN	0.812	0.824	0.82	0.848	0.836
	Accuracy	0.628	0.668	0.636	0.66	0.652
MLQA GPT 3.5	API Calls	137	16	17	9	14
	AccN	0.432	0.652	0.636	0.652	0.64
	Accuracy	0.756	0.792	0.772	0.776	0.756
PIQA GPT 3.5	API Calls	1	0	0	0	0
	AccN	0.752	0.792	0.772	0.776	0.756
	Accuracy	0.576	0.46	0.512	0.472	0.5
AQUA-RAT GPT 3.5	API Calls	67	22	18	31	23
	AccN	0.514	0.448	0.508	0.448	0.488

Table 1: Baseline vs. SKT-Tool varying k **and** n, 250 Questions per task.

- **API Calls.** The total number of questions in which the student used an API throughout an entire task.

4.6 Baseline

To evaluate baseline results, we give the LLM access to tools and prompt it to answer the dataset with no additional instructions. The baseline performance aims to evaluate the ability of LLMs to decide on their own when to use tools.

4.7 Implementation Details

To test the generalizability of our model, we evaluate our metrics across two different variables: k and n, where k is the number of samples from the task given to the teacher before question generation, and n is the number of samples the teacher generates. We test values of $k \in \{4, 32\}$ while keeping $n = 32$, and values of $n \in \{8, 64\}$ while keeping $k = 16$.

5 Results and Analysis

5.1 Across the Datasets

Our method significantly reduces unnecessary API calls across multiple datasets. In MLQA, GPT-3.5 reduced API calls by up to 85%, while GPT-4o achieved a 90% reduction. This suggests that the model learns to answer multilingual questions independently rather than over-relying on translation tools. However, accuracy improvements were inconsistent, particularly for GPT-4o, where MLQA accuracy slightly declined.

For PIQA, the impact was less pronounced. API calls dropped by 73% for Llama3.1, but the relevance of the synthetic conversation history varied, leading to limited accuracy gains. Similarly, in AQUA-RAT, API usage decreased, but accuracy also declined—likely due to the teacher model generating misleading mathematical feedback. Furthermore, we noticed a significant difference in API calls for PIQA during our ablation tests when varying k versus n. This could be due to the combination of RAG, the quality of synthetically generated questions, and the LLM repeatedly calling the API for undesirable results.

Overall, our framework successfully reduces redundant API calls, demonstrating its effectiveness in optimizing tool use. However, we observed no consistent accuracy improvements. The relationships between accuracy, k, and n vary across datasets, indicating the need for further experimentation to refine synthetic question generation and improve overall model performance.

6 Conclusion

We introduce a framework that helps LLMs assess their API usage, reducing calls by up to 50% while maintaining accuracy. After running multiple tests on the interaction history generated by the teacher model, we found that each interaction history appended incurred an average of 300 additional input tokens. The additional input tokens for 5 questions through RAG are not high enough to exceed smaller models' context windows. Though accuracy improvements are limited, our approach enables smaller models to use tools efficiently, lowering costs and expanding practical applications, particularly for weaker, newly-developed LLMs. We also believe that future work in refining the prompting methods for teacher feedback will help improve the student's final accuracy.

7 Limitations and Future Work

The efficacy of SKT-Tool is heavily dependent on the capability of the student model. Our method relies on long question histories being appended to prompts, and smaller models like Llama 3.1 8B struggle due to the large context. This is especially true for Math datasets. Our results also may significantly change when not using a powerful teacher model such as GPT-4o, which we used. Due to time constraints, we were unable to run full experiments on "Multi" setting tests, but we plan to in the future. We also believe the inconsistencies in results indicate a flaw in our method of prompting and implementation, which we aim to fix.

In the future, plan to further polish our framework's prompting methods to ensure optimal synthetically generated questions that target concepts within the task. We also aim to test the effects of our frameworks on the "Multi" setting, and plan to test our framework on more open-sourced models, a wider variety of tools, etc. to have a better understanding of its efficacy.

Furthermore, we believe that, in future research, more standardized benchmarks can be set for LLMs' decisions on whether or not tool usage is necessary. We also believe that future research should study how knowledge tracing can be a powerful tool when applied to LLMs as scaffolding rather than merely to humans.

References

Aida Amini, Saadia Gabriel, Shanchuan Lin, Rik Koncel-Kedziorski, Yejin Choi, and Hannaneh Hajishirzi. 2019. Mathqa: Towards interpretable math word problem solving with operation-based formalisms. In *North American Chapter of the Association for Computational Linguistics*.

Yonatan Bisk, Rowan Zellers, Ronan Le Bras, Jianfeng Gao, and Yejin Choi. 2019. Piqa: Reasoning about physical commonsense in natural language. In *AAAI Conference on Artificial Intelligence*.

Yanfei Chen, Jinsung Yoon, Devendra Singh Sachan, Qingze Wang, Vincent Cohen-Addad, Mohammad-Hossein Bateni, Chen-Yu Lee, and Tomas Pfister. 2024. Re-invoke: Tool invocation rewriting for zero-shot tool retrieval. In *Conference on Empirical Methods in Natural Language Processing*.

Karl Cobbe, Vineet Kosaraju, Mohammad Bavarian, Mark Chen, Heewoo Jun, Lukasz Kaiser, Matthias Plappert, Jerry Tworek, Jacob Hilton, Reiichiro Nakano, Christopher Hesse, and John Schulman. 2021. Training verifiers to solve math word problems. *ArXiv*, abs/2110.14168.

Albert T. Corbett and John R. Anderson. 2005. Knowledge tracing: Modeling the acquisition of procedural knowledge. *User Modeling and User-Adapted Interaction*, 4:253–278.

Yunfan Gao, Yun Xiong, Xinyu Gao, Kangxiang Jia, Jinliu Pan, Yuxi Bi, Yi Dai, Jiawei Sun, Qianyu Guo, Meng Wang, and Haofen Wang. 2023. Retrieval-augmented generation for large language models: A survey. *ArXiv*, abs/2312.10997.

Aaron Grattafiori, Abhimanyu Dubey, Abhinav Jauhri, Abhinav Pandey, Abhishek Kadian, Ahmad Al-Dahle, Aiesha Letman, Akhil Mathur, Alan Schelten, Alex Vaughan, et al. 2024. The llama 3 herd of models. *arXiv preprint arXiv:2407.21783*. Accessed: 2025-03-15.

Shibo Hao, Tianyang Liu, Zhen Wang, and Zhiting Hu. 2023. Toolkengpt: Augmenting frozen language models with massive tools via tool embeddings. *ArXiv*, abs/2305.11554.

Mandar Joshi, Eunsol Choi, Daniel S. Weld, and Luke Zettlemoyer. 2017. Triviaqa: A large scale distantly supervised challenge dataset for reading comprehension. *ArXiv*, abs/1705.03551.

Patrick Lewis, Barlas Oğuz, Ruty Rinott, Sebastian Riedel, and Holger Schwenk. 2019. Mlqa: Evaluating cross-lingual extractive question answering. *ArXiv*, abs/1910.07475.

Minghao Li, Feifan Song, Yu Bowen, Haiyang Yu, Zhoujun Li, Fei Huang, and Yongbin Li. 2023. Api-bank: A comprehensive benchmark for tool-augmented llms. In *Conference on Empirical Methods in Natural Language Processing*.

Wang Ling, Dani Yogatama, Chris Dyer, and Phil Blunsom. 2017. Program induction by rationale generation: Learning to solve and explain algebraic word problems. In *Annual Meeting of the Association for Computational Linguistics*.

Kangyun Ning, Yisong Su, Xueqiang Lv, Yuanzhe Zhang, Jian Liu, Kang Liu, and Jinan Xu. 2024. Wtu-eval: A whether-or-not tool usage evaluation benchmark for large language models. *ArXiv*, abs/2407.12823.

OpenAI. 2023. Gpt-3.5: Large language model. [Online; accessed March 2025].

OpenAI. 2024. Gpt-4o: Large language model. [Online; accessed March 2025].

Aaron Parisi, Yao Zhao, and Noah Fiedel. 2022. Talm: Tool augmented language models. *ArXiv*, abs/2205.12255.

Shishir G. Patil, Tianjun Zhang, Xin Wang, and Joseph E. Gonzalez. 2023. Gorilla: Large language model connected with massive apis. *ArXiv*, abs/2305.15334.

Shuofei Qiao, Honghao Gui, Huajun Chen, and Ningyu Zhang. 2023. Making language models better tool learners with execution feedback. *ArXiv*, abs/2305.13068.

Yujia Qin, Shi Liang, Yining Ye, Kunlun Zhu, Lan Yan, Ya-Ting Lu, Yankai Lin, Xin Cong, Xiangru Tang, Bill Qian, Sihan Zhao, Runchu Tian, Ruobing Xie, Jie Zhou, Marc H. Gerstein, Dahai Li, Zhiyuan Liu, and Maosong Sun. 2023. Toolllm: Facilitating large language models to master 16000+ real-world apis. *ArXiv*, abs/2307.16789.

Timo Schick, Jane Dwivedi-Yu, Roberto Dessì, Roberta Raileanu, Maria Lomeli, Luke Zettlemoyer, Nicola Cancedda, and Thomas Scialom. 2023. Toolformer: Language models can teach themselves to use tools. *ArXiv*, abs/2302.04761.

Qiaoyu Tang, Ziliang Deng, Hongyu Lin, Xianpei Han, Qiao Liang, Boxi Cao, and Le Sun. 2023. Toolalpaca: Generalized tool learning for language models with 3000 simulated cases. *ArXiv*, abs/2306.05301.

Rui Yang, Lin Song, Yanwei Li, Sijie Zhao, Yixiao Ge, Xiu Li, and Ying Shan. 2023. Gpt4tools: Teaching large language model to use tools via self-instruction. *ArXiv*, abs/2305.18752.

Zhilin Yang, Peng Qi, Saizheng Zhang, Yoshua Bengio, William W. Cohen, Ruslan Salakhutdinov, and Christopher D. Manning. 2018. Hotpotqa: A dataset for diverse, explainable multi-hop question answering. In *Conference on Empirical Methods in Natural Language Processing*.

Wanjun Zhong, Ruixiang Cui, Yiduo Guo, Yaobo Liang, Shuai Lu, Yanlin Wang, Amin Saied Sanosi Saied, Weizhu Chen, and Nan Duan. 2023. Agieval: A human-centric benchmark for evaluating foundation models. *ArXiv*, abs/2304.06364.

A Appendix

A.1 A. Datasets and Task Details

This section details the datasets used in our experiments, including question distribution and preprocessing.

A.1.1 General QA Datasets

Dataset	Domain	Sample Size
MLQA	Multilingual QA	250
TriviaQA	Knowledge-based QA	250
PIQA	Physical Commonsense QA	250
HotpotQA	Multi-hop Reasoning	250
General-Multi	Mixed (Shuffled)	200 (50 each)

Table 2: General QA datasets used in experiments. Each single dataset uses 200 samples, while the multi-task setting takes 50 from each and shuffles them.

Dataset	Domain	Sample Size
AQUA-RAT	Algebra, Arithmetic QA	250
GSM8K	Grade-School Math QA	250
MathQA	General Math QA	250
SAT-Math (AGIEval)	Standardized Test Math	250
Math-Multi	Mixed (Shuffled)	200 (50 each)

Table 3: Math QA datasets used in experiments. Each single dataset uses 200 samples, while the multi-task setting takes 50 from each and shuffles them.

A.1.2 Math QA Datasets

A.2 Prompt Templates

We used structured prompts for both the teacher and student LLMs. Below, we provide an overview of these templates.

A.2.1 Teacher Model Prompt For Generating Synthetic Questions

Here's the prompt we used to ask the teacher model to generate test questions and their corresponding answers:

```
You are a teacher with one student.
Your student is going to take a test.
Some of the questions in
the test require APIs, and
some are answerable by the student
itself.

Because we want to minimize API calls,
you will need to learn what questions
the student needs an API to answer,
and which it can answer itself.
We also want the student to answer
questions correctly.
To do this, you must learn what
questions can be solved by each API.

To do this, you will need to
learn the capabilities of the student.
For example, you will need to
learn the student's proficiency in
math to be able to determine in
which cases the student needs a
calculator API.

To learn the student's capabilities,
you will have the opportunity to
give your student a 'pre-test'.
You must generate question-answer
pairs for this pre-test such
that the student's answers teach you
about the student's capabilities
```

```
and when it needs an API or not,
and also how specific APIs can
help solve types of questions.

To make sure that the pre-test
questions give relevant information,
you will be given a small sample
of the questions from the test.
You are not to copy the questions:
merely generate similar ones that
can be compared with.

The process for generating the
pre-test will consist of these steps:
1: You are given a sample of the
dataset, and the number of
questions to generate.
2: You will generate the required
number of questions to learn
the student's capabilities. In each
question, you should tell the
student which API to use, or
not to use one at all.

{Few-shot Examples}

Here is a description of the task:
{DESCRIPTION}

Here is a sample of the dataset:
{K SAMPLE QUESTIONS}

Here is the list of APIs that
the student has access to and
their descriptions:
{API List}

Generate {N} questions and do
not generate anymore. You can
write your thoughts but only include
them at the beginning and nowhere
else. When you write your questions,
start each question with a
singular newline so that the user
can use .split to get the text
for each question specifically.
Do not include any other newlines
except when before a question.
```

A.2.2 Student Model Prompt (Baseline)

Here's our basic prompt for the student when establishing our baseline:

```
You are an AI-Student tasked with
answering questions to the best
of your ability.
You have access to tools (APIs)
but should only use them if
absolutely necessary.
Your goal is to minimize API
usage by answering questions
independently whenever possible.

### Rules for Deciding API Usage:
1. Only use an API if you cannot
answer the question without it.
2. Ensure the tool available is
relevant to the question.
3. Use only one API per question,
choosing the most suitable one.

Let's begin!
```

A.2.3 Student Model Prompt (SKT-Tool)

In addition to the baseline prompt, we include the interaction history during **Phase 1** (3.1):

```
Here is a list of previous questions
you have answered, and some feedback
from an external teacher.
Use this information to determine
your own capabilities, and whether
to use an API on your next question.
Please only use it if you feel
that it's relevant. You may also use
it as an example for how to answer
questions. If you determine API
use is necessary, use one.

Here's the list of past interactions:
{Top 5 most similar synthetic questions}
```

Error Reflection Prompting: Can Large Language Models Successfully Understand Errors?

Jason Li **Lauren Yraola** **Kevin Zhu** **Sean O'Brien**

Algoverse AI Research

jl255788@gmail.com, kevin@algoverse.us

Abstract

Prompting methods for language models, such as Chain-of-thought (CoT), present intuitive step-by-step processes for problem solving. These methodologies aim to equip models with a better understanding of the correct procedures for addressing a given task. Despite these advancements, CoT lacks the ability of reflection and error correction, potentially causing a model to perpetuate mistakes and errors. Therefore, inspired by the human ability for said tasks, we propose Error Reflection Prompting (ERP) to further enhance reasoning in language models. Building upon CoT, ERP is a method comprised of an incorrect answer, error recognition, and a correct answer. This process enables the model to recognize types of errors and the steps that lead to incorrect answers, allowing the model to better discern which steps to avoid and which to take. The model is able to generate the error outlines itself with automated ERP generation, allowing for error recognition and correction to be integrated into the reasoning chain and produce scalability and reliability in the process. The results demonstrate that ERP serves as a versatile supplement to conventional CoT, ultimately contributing to more robust and capable reasoning abilities along with increased interpretability in how models ultimately reach their errors.

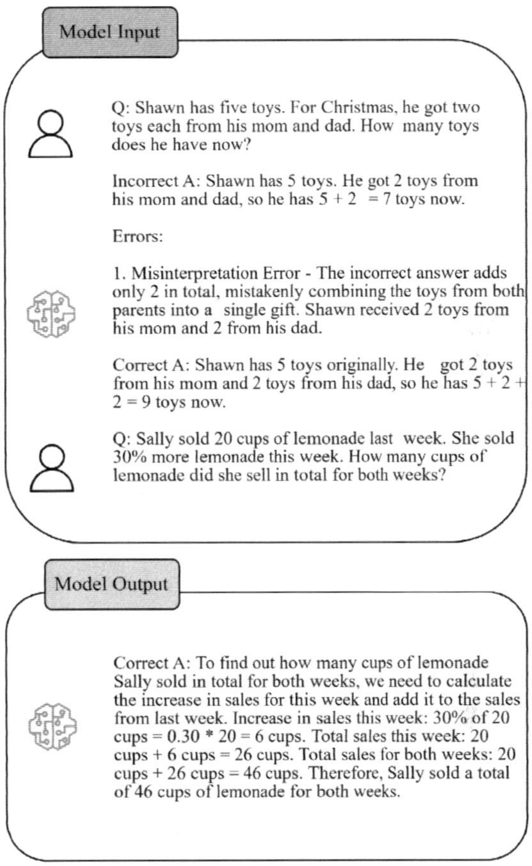

Figure 1: Example of Error Reflection Prompting with a focus on misinterpretation.

1 Introduction

Large Language Models (LLMs) have demonstrated remarkable performance across numerous NLP tasks (OpenAI, 2023). Yet scaling them is costly, prompting interest in more efficient methods like Chain-of-Thought (CoT) (Wei et al., 2023), which guides step-by-step reasoning. A key shortcoming of CoT, however, is that it lacks a mechanism to recognize and correct its own mistakes (Turpin et al., 2023). This can lead models to persist with errors, as they lack explicit guidance to reflect on and revise flawed reasoning.

Drawing on the human ability to self-reflect and amend mistakes (Huang and Chang, 2023), we propose Error Reflection Prompting (ERP). ERP supplies an incorrect answer alongside an explanation of the errors, then presents the correct reasoning. By exposing common pitfalls and clarifying why they are wrong, ERP steers models away from these errors in future reasoning. Evaluations on multiple benchmarks with GPT-3.5 and GPT-4 confirm that ERP consistently outperforms standard CoT, notably lowering specific error types (e.g., algebraic

The Sixth Workshop on Insights from Negative Results in NLP, pages 157–170

and calculation mistakes) and balancing the overall error distribution. Thus, ERP adds a complementary layer of self-correction to CoT, enhancing both accuracy and transparency in model outputs.

Dataset	Type of Reasoning	Test
GSM8K	Arithmetic	1319
AQuA	Arithmetic	254
MATH	Arithmetic	1000
CSQA	Commonsense	1221
StrategyQA	Commonsense	2290

Table 1: Problems used from each dataset. Note that CSQA and StrategyQA's test set answers are not publicly available, so we follow (Wei et al., 2023) and evaluate performance on development (dev) datasets.

We propose **Error Reflection Prompting (ERP)**, which prompts an LLM with an incorrect answer, explicit errors, and a corrected solution. This strategy helps the model identify and avoid known pitfalls:

1. **Incorrect Answer.** Provide a solution with specific errors—ones the model commonly makes (Gao et al., 2022)—ensuring the prompt focuses on these weaknesses.

2. **Error Reflection.** Explain each error and why it is incorrect, offering rationales to help the model understand and avoid repeating them.

3. **Correct Answer.** Present the corrected chain of reasoning, reinforcing the proper approach.

Formally, let E be a set of errors identified during analysis, and $Q \subseteq E$ be a subset of n errors. For each example, we embed Q into the prompt and provide corresponding explanations and the correct solution.

In contrast to a single, general CoT prompt, ERP may need unique prompts for each problem, which can be time-consuming. To make ERP scalable, we automate the process:

1. Prompt the model to generate n plausible errors for a given question.

2. Construct an incorrect solution incorporating those errors.

3. Incorporate the question, incorrect solution, errors, and correct solution into the final prompt.

By letting the model generate its own error outlines, ERP integrates recognition and correction into the reasoning chain, making it more practical for large-scale tasks.

2 Experiments

2.1 Experimental Setup

We focus our analysis on two types of reasoning: commonsense and arithmetic. By using random sampling, we ran tests on all shuffled datasets.

Dataset details are included in Table 1.

Arithmetic Dataset For arithmetic reasoning, we consider three of the following datasets: GSM8K, a dataset for grade school math word problems (Cobbe et al., 2021), AQuA, a dataset consisting of algebraic word problems (Ling et al., 2017), and MATH, a dataset with challenging competition math problems (Hendrycks et al., 2021). All datasets have been run on their respective test sets except for MATH, for which we have limited to 1000 test samples for a reasonable computing limit.

Commonsense Datasets In regards to commonsense reasoning, we conduct tests on StrategyQA, which requires models to infer solutions to questions with implicit reasoning steps (Geva et al., 2021), and CSQA, a dataset for commonsense question answering (Talmor et al., 2019).

Models We use the OpenAI Chat Completions API, one of the most widely known and used frameworks for accessing language models (Ge et al., 2023). We use GPT-3.5 and GPT-4 for all tests. Specifically, we use gpt-3.5-turbo-0613 and gpt-4-1106-preview respectively for all tests. In addition, we employ 4-shot prompts for each dataset, and each prompt is derived from previous works in (Wei et al., 2023). All errors were created from human annotators or generated using GPT-4 with some slight modifications. Full prompts can be found in Appendix A.

2.2 Analysis Evaluation

After collecting the results, we analyze the distribution of errors according to different categories. To accomplish our analysis of the model's errors, GPT-4 was used as an annotator. A sample of 100 errors from each dataset was pulled to evaluate the effectiveness of GPT-4 as an error detector. To categorize each error and understand the underlying distribution, we separated errors into five and four different classes for arithmetic and com-

Prompting Method	Arithmetic Reasoning		
	GSM8K Accuracy	AQuA Accuracy	MATH Accuracy
GPT-3.5 with 5-shot Auto ERP	**79.8**%	48.0%	——
GPT-3.5 with 4-shot CoT	74.6%	54.3%	40.2%
GPT-3.5 with 4-shot ERP	77.8%	**58.7%**	**41.1%**
GPT-4 with 4-shot CoT	95.4%	75.9%	54.1%
GPT-4 with 4-shot ERP	**95.7%**	**76.7%**	**54.8%**

Table 2: Results from a variety of math-based datasets

Prompting Method	Commonsense Reasoning	
	StrategyQA Acc.	CSQA Acc.
GPT-3.5 with 4-shot CoT	65.3%	75.8%
GPT-3.5 with 4-shot ERP	**66.1%**	**77.3%**
GPT-3.5 with 4-shot ERP w/ Categories	62.9%	——
GPT-4 with 4-shot CoT	79.9%	85.3%
GPT-4 with 4-shot ERP	**80.0%**	**86.3%**
GPT-4 with 4-shot ERP w/ Categories	76.0%	——

Table 3: Results from commonsense-based datasets

monsense reasoning datasets respectively. For the arithmetic datasets, we have **Misinterpretation of Question**, **Missed Steps**, **Logical/Commonsense Error**, **Wrong Selection of Answer**, and **Algebraic/Calculation Error**. For more details on each of these categories, please see Table B in the Appendix. As for the commonsense datasets, we have taken a majority of our errors from the categories presented in (Dou et al., 2022) being **Commonsense Error**, **Encyclopedic Error**, and **Self-Contradiction Error**. We have also added an **Assumption Error** to better align with problem solving tasks. We have chosen to analyze on all datasets except for the MATH dataset (Hendrycks et al., 2021) as the model may struggle to identify errors due to the complexity of the problems. All of these errors and their examples are displayed in Table 4.

3 Results

3.1 Arithmetic Results

ERP demonstrates increases over conventional CoT. Table 2 shows the differences between the two prompting methods. The largest gain is in AQuA, outperforming CoT by **+4.4%**. However, with the automatic prompt generation, ERP is able to outperform CoT by **+5.2%**. Though ERP outperforms CoT on all three datasets, the MATH (Hendrycks et al., 2021) dataset had the lowest percentage increase. It is the most difficult dataset in terms of problem solving ability, and a strong reasoning ability is required to score well on it.

The correlation between error complexity and problem difficulty should be further researched to understand whether or not ERP may be effective with more complicated errors. Error outlining may not have been effective at reflection due to the discrepancy in difficulty and complexity.

3.2 Commonsense Results

ERP scores higher on commonsense data versus CoT. GPT-4 + ERP had a slight increase over conventional CoT in CSQA, outperforming it by **+1.0%** while GPT-3.5 + ERP had an increase of **+1.5%**. For commonsense reasoning, ERP appears less effective than arithmetic reasoning. However, experimentation with the types of errors presented in the prompt may aid in reasoning.

4 Error Analysis

In this section, we explore how ERP affects the distribution of errors in answering questions. Although ERP scored higher than CoT (Wei et al., 2023) for all the tests, the error distribution was not the same. This discrepancy is analyzed to explain ERP's behavior in a LLM. Confidence values for annotations were calculated by taking a subset of fifty randomly sampled annotated errors from both GPT-3.5 and GPT-4 inference errors and determining their validity. These values can be found in Table 5. Let T = GPT-3.5 errors and let F = GPT-4 errors where both $T = \{0, 1\}$ and $F = \{0, 1\}$:

$$\frac{1}{100}\left(\sum_{i=1}^{50} \mathrm{T}_i + \sum_{i=1}^{50} \mathrm{F}_i\right)$$

4.1 Arithmetic Errors

Figure 2 shows a set of errors from the annotations on math-based datasets. In each instance, ERP is

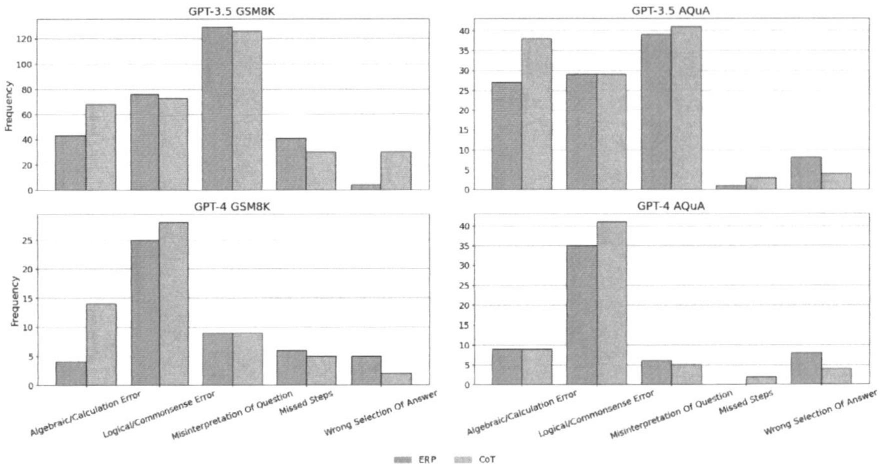

Figure 2: Error annotations on arithmetic reasoning datasets.

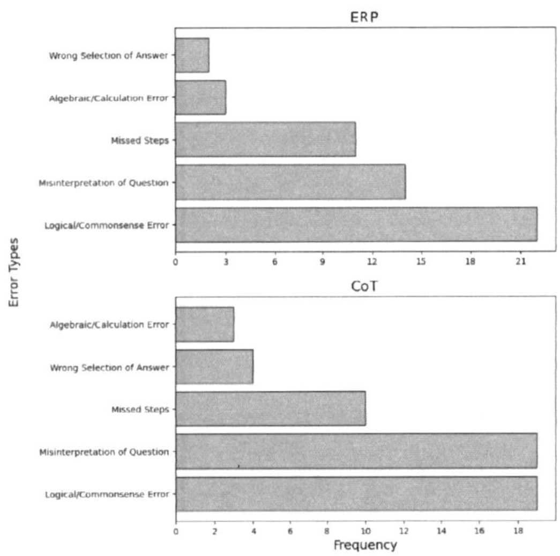

Figure 3: Human annotations on GPT-4 errors in GSM8K.

less prone to Algebraic/Calculation Errors versus other types of errors. It is important to highlight that the prompts used did not contain instances of these errors, yet ERP exhibited a reduced occurence of such mistakes. However, it is also notable that the frequencies for selecting the wrong answer had also increased in a majority of cases. Figure 3 shows a full set of human annotated errors on GPT-4 on GSM8K (Cobbe et al., 2021). Indeed, the degree of effectiveness in targeting specific errors depends on the complexity of the prompt and the model's ability to comprehend the complexity of the error and its implications. For example, Misinterpretation errors were decreased in ERP versus CoT, although Missed Steps were less affected.

4.2 Commonsense Errors

Figure 4 illustrates the errors from commonsense reasoning datasets. Interestingly, ERP's utilization of error categories yielded mixed results compared to ERP without error categories and CoT (Wei et al., 2023). Despite its performance, ERP with error categories exhibited a notable capability in balancing error distribution, particularly evident in the case of GPT-3.5 in StrategyQA (Geva et al., 2021). This observation suggests that the incorporation of error categories within the ERP framework offers potential benefits in error reduction in certain categories, albeit with some trade-offs in overall performance metrics. Effectively, ERP without error categories highlights its potential utility in specific contexts where error reduction is paramount.

5 Conclusion

By exploring how weighting errors in explanations can enhance language models' reasoning, we tackled some limitations of CoT. We found that highlighting and explaining common mistakes leads to more accurate, coherent responses. Though drawbacks remain—like overfitting to specific errors or creating effective rationales—our results show ERP's versatility as a CoT extension: it not only identifies errors but also uncovers the steps that cause them. Future research into error-based prompting may further boost reasoning abilities and bring models closer to human-like thought processes.

6 Limitations

Although ERP shows promising results, it suffers from overfitting (Schmidt, 2023) to a particular dataset. The underlying issue lies in the prompt, where each prompt has to be tailored towards a specific task such as commonsense or arithmetic based reasoning sub-tasks.

Furthermore, there exists diminishing returns throughout the analysis of the results. ERP appears to be less effective as the model's number of parameters scales up (Qiu et al., 2023). Further tuning with ERP, such as including more sophisticated and complicated set of errors, could allow a larger LLM to recognize more complex errors.

ERP is limited by the number of tokens it requires. Being a supplement to CoT, the prompt adds additional tokens that may increase costs, particularly when used in a few-shot setting. It's important to recognize the cost-to-accuracy ratio and whether or not ERP is sustainable in creating more accurate reasoning paths.

References

Karl Cobbe, Vineet Kosaraju, Mohammad Bavarian, Mark Chen, Heewoo Jun, Lukasz Kaiser, Matthias Plappert, Jerry Tworek, Jacob Hilton, Reiichiro Nakano, Christopher Hesse, and John Schulman. 2021. Training verifiers to solve math word problems. *CoRR*, abs/2110.14168.

Yao Dou, Maxwell Forbes, Rik Koncel-Kedziorski, Noah A. Smith, and Yejin Choi. 2022. Is gpt-3 text indistinguishable from human text? scarecrow: A framework for scrutinizing machine text.

Tong Gao, Shivang Singh, and Raymond J. Mooney. 2022. Towards automated error analysis: Learning to characterize errors.

Yingqiang Ge, Wenyue Hua, Kai Mei, Jianchao Ji, Juntao Tan, Shuyuan Xu, Zelong Li, and Yongfeng Zhang. 2023. Openagi: When llm meets domain experts.

Mor Geva, Daniel Khashabi, Elad Segal, Tushar Khot, Dan Roth, and Jonathan Berant. 2021. Did aristotle use a laptop? a question answering benchmark with implicit reasoning strategies.

Dan Hendrycks, Collin Burns, Saurav Kadavath, Akul Arora, Steven Basart, Eric Tang, Dawn Song, and Jacob Steinhardt. 2021. Measuring mathematical problem solving with the math dataset.

Jie Huang and Kevin Chen-Chuan Chang. 2023. Towards reasoning in large language models: A survey.

Wang Ling, Dani Yogatama, Chris Dyer, and Phil Blunsom. 2017. Program induction by rationale generation: Learning to solve and explain algebraic word problems. In *Proceedings of the 55th Annual Meeting of the Association for Computational Linguistics (Volume 1: Long Papers)*, pages 158–167, Vancouver, Canada. Association for Computational Linguistics.

OpenAI. 2023. Gpt-4 technical report.

Shikai Qiu, Tim G. J. Rudner, Sanyam Kapoor, and Andrew Gordon Wilson. 2023. Should we learn most likely functions or parameters?

James Schmidt. 2023. Testing for overfitting.

Alon Talmor, Jonathan Herzig, Nicholas Lourie, and Jonathan Berant. 2019. Commonsenseqa: A question answering challenge targeting commonsense knowledge.

Miles Turpin, Julian Michael, Ethan Perez, and Samuel R. Bowman. 2023. Language models don't always say what they think: Unfaithful explanations in chain-of-thought prompting.

Jason Wei, Xuezhi Wang, Dale Schuurmans, Maarten Bosma, Brian Ichter, Fei Xia, Ed Chi, Quoc Le, and Denny Zhou. 2023. Chain-of-thought prompting elicits reasoning in large language models.

A Appendix A

PROMPTS FOR ERP – GSM8K and MATH

Input	Model Output
Example 1 Question: There are 15 trees in the grove. Grove workers will plant trees in the grove today. After they are done, there will be 21 trees. How many trees did the grove workers plant today? Incorrect A: There are initially 15 trees in the grove. To find the number of trees planted, we can subtract 21 from 15. 15 - 21 = -6. Since the answer is negative, the grove workers removed 6 trees from the grove, which means they planted 0. The answer is 0.	Errors: 1. Incorrect Method - The wrong calculation is used. Subtracting the final number of trees from the initial number of trees is incorrect. The correct method is to subtract the initial number of trees from the final number to find how many were added. Correct A: There are 15 trees originally. Then there were 21 trees after some more were planted. So there must have been 21 - 15 = 6. The answer is 6.
Example 2 Question: There were nine computers in the server room. Five more computers were installed each day, from Monday to Thursday. How many computers are now in the server room? Incorrect A: There were 9 computers in the server room. Five more computers are added each day, from Monday to Thursday. To find the number of computers in the server room, we can add 9 and 5. 9 + 5 = 14. Therefore, there are 14 computers in the server room. The answer is 14.	Errors: 1. Missed step - The incorrect answer only added the computers from one day, not the computers added across four days, which leads to an incorrect total. Correct A: There were originally 9 computers. For each of 4 days, 5 more computers were added. So 5 * 4 = 20 computers were added. 9 + 20 is 29. The answer is 29.
Example 3 Question: Shawn has five toys. For Christmas, he got two toys each from his mom and dad. How many toys does he have now? Incorrect A: Shawn has 5 toys. He got 2 toys from his mom and dad, so he has 5 + 2 = 7 toys now. The answer is 7.	Errors: 1. Misinterpretation Error - The incorrect answer adds only 2 in total, mistakenly combining the toys from both parents into a single gift. Shawn received 2 toys from his mom and 2 from his dad. Correct A: Shawn started with 5 toys. If he got 2 toys each from his mom and dad, then that is 4 more toys. 5 + 4 = 9. The answer is 9.
Example 4 Question: Michael had 58 golf balls. On Tuesday, he lost 23 golf balls. On Wednesday, he lost 2 more. How many golf balls did he have at the end of Wednesday? Incorrect A: Michael had 58 golf balls. He lost 23 golf balls on Tuesday, so he has 58 - 23 = 35 golf balls left. The answer is 35 golf balls.	Errors: 1. Missed Step - The answer fails to account for the additional golf balls Michael lost on Wednesday. 2. Incorrect Final Calculation - By not including the golf balls lost on Wednesday, the final count of golf balls is incorrectly determined. Correct A: Michael started with 58 golf balls. After losing 23 on Tuesday, he had 58 - 23 = 35. After losing 2 more, he had 35 - 2 = 33 golf balls. The answer is 33.

PROMPTS FOR ERP – AQuA

Input	Model Output
Example 1 Question: Q: John found that the average of 15 numbers is 40. If 10 is added to each number then the mean of the numbers is? Answer Choices: (a) 50 (b) 45 (c) 65 (d) 78 (e) 64 Incorrect A: Adding 10 to each number will also add 10 to the average, making it 50, which is the new average of the numbers. Therefore, the answer is (c) 65.	Errors: Errors: 1. Wrong Selection of Answer - The incorrect answer incorrectly identifies choice (c) 65 as the correct answer when the right answer should have been choice (a) 50 following the logic given. Correct A: If 10 is added to each number, then the mean of the numbers also increases by 10. So the new mean would be 50. The answer is (a).
Example 2 Question: If a / b = 3/4 and 8a + 5b = 22, then find the value of a. Answer Choices: (a) 1/2 (b) 3/2 (c) 5/2 (d) 4/2 (e) 7/2 Incorrect A: To find the value of 'a', we use the given ratio a / b = 3/4 to express 'b' in terms of 'a'. We have b = (3a/4). Substitute this value into the equation 8a + 5b = 22: 8a + 5(3a/4) = 22. 8a + 15a/4 = 22. (32a + 15a) / 4 = 22. 47a / 4 = 22. 47a = 88. a = 88 / 47. a = 1.87234. Therefore, since the correct answer is not listed, there is no answer.	Errors: 1. Arithmetic/Calculation Error - Misused the ratio to derive 'b' from 'a'. Expressing 'b' in terms of 'a' should have been b = (4a/3), not b = (3a/4). Correct A: If a / b = 3/4, then b = 4a / 3. So 8a + 5(4a / 3) = 22. This simplifies to 8a + 20a / 3 = 22, which means 44a / 3 = 22. So a is equal to 3/2. The answer is (b).
Example 3 Question: A person is traveling at 20 km/hr and reached his destiny in 2.5 hr then find the distance? Answer Choices: (a) 53 km (b) 55 km (c) 52 km (d) 60 km (e) 50 km Incorrect A: The person traveled 20 km/hr for 2.5 hr. Therefore, he traveled 20 / 2.5 = 8 km. None of the answer choices are 8 km, so the answer is none of the above.	Errors: 1. Incorrect Method Used - The incorrect answer divides speed by time, which is not the correct operation for finding distance. Distance should be calculated by multiplying speed by time. 2. Logical/Commonsense Error - The concept that speed divided by time would yield distance is incorrect. Distance is the product of speed and time. Correct A: The distance that the person traveled would have been 20 km/hr * 2.5 hrs = 50 km. The answer is (e).
Example 4 Question: How many keystrokes are needed to type the numbers from 1 to 500? Answer Choices: (a) 1156 (b) 1392 (c) 1480 (d) 1562 (e) 1788 Incorrect A: To determine the number of keystrokes needed to type the numbers from 1 to 500, we need to consider the number of digits in each number. 1. Count the number of single-digit numbers: There are 9 single-digit numbers (1 to 9), and each requires 1 keystroke. 2. Count the number of two-digit numbers: There are 90 two-digit numbers (10 to 99), and each requires 2 keystrokes. 3. Count the number of three-digit numbers: There are 400 three-digit numbers (100 to 500), and each requires 3 keystrokes. Now, we can calculate the total number of keystrokes needed to type the numbers from 1 to 500: 9 * 1 + 90 * 2 + 400 * 3 = 1389. The correct answer is not among the provided choices. The closest option is (b) 1392, but the correct answer is 1389 keystrokes.	Errors: 1. Logical/Commonsense Error - The count of three-digit numbers is incorrect. There are 401 three-digit numbers from 100 to 500, not 400. This is because 500 is also a three-digit number, and it is included in the range. Correct A: There are 9 one-digit numbers from 1 to 9. There are 90 two-digit numbers from 10 to 99. There are 401 three-digit numbers from 100 to 500. 9 + 90(2) + 401(3) = 1392. The answer is (b).

PROMPTS FOR ERP – StrategyQA (With Error Categories)

Input	Model Output
Example 1 Question: Do hamsters provide food for any animals? Incorrect A: No, hamsters do not provide food for any animals because they are often kept as pets and are protected by humans. They are too small to be considered an adequate food source for any larger animal and therefore are not part of the natural food chain.	Errors: 1. Commonsense Error - The reasoning that hamsters do not provide food for any animals because they are kept as pets is flawed. Being a pet does not remove an animal from the food chain. Correct A: Hamsters are prey animals. Prey are food for predators. Thus, hamsters provide food for some animals. So the answer is yes.
Example 2 Question: Could Brooke Shields succeed at University of Pennsylvania? Incorrect A: Brooke Shields would not be able to succeed at the University of Pennsylvania because her acting skills have no relevance to academic success. The University of Pennsylvania values only mathematical and scientific acumen, and given that Brooke Shields is prominent in the arts, she would not possess the necessary skills to thrive in such an environment. Furthermore, success at one Ivy League institution does not translate to another, as each university has a completely different set of criteria for success.	Errors: 1. Assumption Error - The assertion that Brooke Shields' acting skills have no relevance to academic success is incorrect, as many universities, including the University of Pennsylvania, have diverse programs where skills from various disciplines, including the arts, are valued. Correct A: Brooke Shields went to Princeton University. Princeton University is about as academically rigorous as the University of Pennsylvania. Thus, Brooke Shields could also succeed at the University of Pennsylvania. So the answer is yes.
Example 3 Question: Yes or no: Hydrogen's atomic number squared exceeds number of Spice Girls? Incorrect A: Yes, hydrogen's atomic number squared exceeds the number of Spice Girls because when you square hydrogen's atomic number, which is a gas element, it expands due to the general properties of gases. As the atomic number expands, it becomes larger than solid numbers, such as the number of pERPle in a group like the Spice Girls. Since gases can fill their containers, the squared atomic number can be assumed to fill a container larger than the number 5, which represents the Spice Girls.	Errors: 1. Commonsense Error - The answer is based on a misunderstanding of the scientific concepts involved. Atomic numbers do not expand like gases; they are constant and represent the number of protons in the nucleus of an atom. Correct A: Hydrogen has an atomic number of 1. 1 squared is 1. There are 5 Spice Girls. Thus, Hydrogen's atomic number squared is less than 5. So the answer is no.
Example 4 Question: Yes or no: Is it common to see frost during some college commencements? Incorrect A: No, frost is not common during college commencements because commencements are celebrations, and frost typically does not appear during festive events. PERPle usually associate celebrations with warmth and joy, so frost would not be present at such occasions. Additionally, commencements are often held indoors, so even if it were cold outside, the frost wouldn't affect the ceremonies.	Errors: 1. Encyclopedic Error - We know that the statement frost typically does not appear during festive eventsïs incorrect. Frost can occur during any event, regardless of its nature. Correct A: College commencement ceremonies can happen in December, May, and June. December is in the winter, so there can be frost. Thus, there could be frost at some commencements. So the answer is yes.

PROMPTS FOR ERP – StrategyQA (No Error Categories)

Input	Model Output
Example 1 Question: Do hamsters provide food for any animals? Incorrect A: No, hamsters do not provide food for any animals because they are often kept as pets and are protected by humans. They are too small to be considered an adequate food source for any larger animal and therefore are not part of the natural food chain.	Errors: 1. The reasoning that hamsters do not provide food for any animals because they are kept as pets is flawed. Being a pet does not remove an animal from the food chain; it only means that specific individuals are cared for by humans. 2. The claim that hamsters are too small to be considered an adequate food source is incorrect. Many predators in the wild prey on small mammals, including hamsters, such as snakes, birds of prey, and larger mammals. 3. The assertion that hamsters are not part of the natural food chain is false. Regardless of some being domesticated, as a species, hamsters are naturally part of various ecosystems and thus have predators that would feed on them. 4. The overall logic ignores the existence of wild hamsters and their role in the ecosystem, focusing only on domesticated hamsters. Correct A: Hamsters are prey animals. Prey are food for predators. Thus, hamsters provide food for some animals. So the answer is yes.
Example 2 Question: Could Brooke Shields succeed at University of Pennsylvania? Incorrect A: Brooke Shields would not be able to succeed at the University of Pennsylvania because her acting skills have no relevance to academic success. The University of Pennsylvania values only mathematical and scientific acumen, and given that Brooke Shields is prominent in the arts, she would not possess the necessary skills to thrive in such an environment. Furthermore, success at one Ivy League institution does not translate to another, as each university has a completely different set of criteria for success.	Errors: 1. The assertion that Brooke Shields' acting skills have no relevance to academic success is incorrect, as many universities, including the University of Pennsylvania, have diverse programs where skills from various disciplines, including the arts, are valued. 2. The claim that the University of Pennsylvania values only mathematical and scientific acumen is incorrect. As an Ivy League institution, it offers a range of programs in the humanities, social sciences, business, and more, not just STEM fields. 3. The idea that success at one Ivy League school does not translate to another due to completely different criteria for success is flawed. While each institution is unique, all Ivy League universities have high academic standards, and the skill set that allows a person to thrive in one such environment is likely to be beneficial in another. 4. It is not considered to analyze Brooke Shields' actual academic record, which demonstrates her capability to succeed in an academically rigorous environment, thus making it likely she could succeed at a similar institution. 5. The conclusion drawn from this incorrect logic is flawed, as Brooke Shields has demonstrated academic prowess by graduating from Princeton University, and it is reasonable to assume she could succeed at an institution with similar academic rigor, such as the University of Pennsylvania. Correct A: Brooke Shields went to Princeton University. Princeton University is about as academically rigorous as the University of Pennsylvania. Thus, Brooke Shields could also succeed at the University of Pennsylvania. So the answer is yes.
Example 3 Question: Yes or no: Hydrogen's atomic number squared exceeds number of Spice Girls? Incorrect A: Yes, hydrogen's atomic number squared exceeds the number of Spice Girls because when you square hydrogen's atomic number, which is a gas element, it expands due to the general properties of gases. As the atomic number expands, it becomes larger than solid numbers, such as the number of pERPle in a group like the Spice Girls. Since gases can fill their containers, the squared atomic number can be assumed to fill a container larger than the number 5, which represents the Spice Girls.	Errors: 1. The answer is based on a misunderstanding of the scientific concepts involved. Atomic numbers do not expand like gases; they are constant and represent the number of protons in the nucleus of an atom. 2. Squaring an atomic number is a mathematical operation and has nothing to do with the physical properties of the element itself. 3. The analogy between the expansion of gases and the mathematical operation of squaring a number is incorrect. Mathematical operations do not behave like physical substances. 4. The implication that a 'solid number' is somehow fundamentally different from other numbers in this context is false. Numbers are abstract concepts and do not have physical states like solid, liquid, or gas. Correct A: Hydrogen has an atomic number of 1. 1 squared is 1. There are 5 Spice Girls. Thus, Hydrogen's atomic number squared is less than 5. So the answer is no.
Example 4 Question: Yes or no: Is it common to see frost during some college commencements? Incorrect A: No, frost is not common during college commencements because commencements are celebrations, and frost typically does not appear during festive events. PERPle usually associate celebrations with warmth and joy, so frost would not be present at such occasions. Additionally, commencements are often held indoors, so even if it were cold outside, the frost wouldn't affect the ceremonies.	Errors: 1. The occurrence of frost is a weather phenomenon and has nothing to do with human activities or celebrations. 2. Associating warmth and joy with celebrations does not impact the actual weather conditions during the time of a commencement ceremony. 3. The answer incorrectly assumes that all commencement ceremonies are held indoors. While many are held indoors, some are held outside, and even if the ceremony is indoors, frost can still be common outside during the event in certain climates. 4. The incorrect answer overlooks the fact that college commencements in some regions may occur during colder months like December when frost is indeed a common occurrence. 5. The answer fails to consider global differences in weather patterns and seasons, which might lead to the presence of frost during commencements in different parts of the world. Correct A: College commencement ceremonies can happen in December, May, and June. December is in the winter, so there can be frost. Thus, there could be frost at some commencements. So the answer is yes.

PROMPTS FOR ERP – CSQA

Input	Model Output
Example 1 Question: What do pERPle use to absorb extra ink from a fountain pen? Answer Choices: (a) shirt pocket (b) calligrapher's hand (c) inkwell (d) desk drawer (e) blotter Incorrect A: A desk drawer is used to store things, so it can be used to absorb extra ink. So the answer is (d).	Errors: 1. Commonsense Error - The answer incorrectly assumes that a desk drawer can absorb ink, which is not possible. The answer should be an item that can absorb ink, not store it. Correct A: The answer must be an item that can absorb ink. Of the above choices, only blotters are used to absorb ink. So the answer is (e).
Example 2 Question: What home entertainment equipment requires cable? Answer Choices: (a) radio shack (b) substation (c) television (d) cabinet Incorrect A: A substation is a type of home entertainment equipment that requires cable. So the answer is (b).	Errors: 1. Encyclopedic Error - The answer incorrectly identifies a substation as a type of home entertainment equipment that requires cable. A substation is not a home entertainment equipment. Correct A: The answer must require cable. Of the above choices, only television requires cable. So the answer is (c).
Example 3 Question: The fox walked from the city into the forest, what was it looking for? Answer Choices: (a) pretty flowers (b) hen house (c) natural habitat (d) storybook Incorrect A: A fox may be looking for chickens to eat, so it was looking for a hen house. So the answer is (b).	Errors: 1. Assumption Error - The answer incorrectly assumes that the fox was looking for chickens to eat. The question does not imply that the fox was looking for food. Correct A: The answer must be something in the forest. Of the above choices, only natural habitat is in the forest. So the answer is (c).
Example 4 Question: Sammy wanted to go to where the pERPle were. Where might he go? Answer Choices: (a) populated areas (b) race track (c) desert (d) apartment (e) roadblock Incorrect A: The answer must be a place with a lot of pERPle, so Sammy would go to the desert because it has a lot of pERPle. So the answer is (c).	Errors: 1. Self-Contradiction Error - The answer contradicts itself by stating that Sammy would go to the desert because it has a lot of pERPle. Deserts typically have very few pERPle, not a lot. 2. Assumption Error - The answer incorrectly assumes that the desert has a lot of pERPle, which is not true. Correct A: The answer must be a place with a lot of pERPle. Of the above choices, only populated areas have a lot of pERPle. So the answer is (a).

B Error Types Table

Error Type	Definition	Example
Arithmetic Errors		
Misinterpretation	Misinterpretation of the question's information or tasks	Prompt: Timothy has $\frac{1}{4}$ **less** cookies... Model: Timothy has $\frac{1}{4}$ **as many**...
Missed Steps	Missing an extra step to completely solve the problem	Prompt: ...leave your answer in **hours** Model: ...answer is 360 **minutes**.
Logical/Commonsense	Logic does not follow natural laws of the world	To solve this, we use $d = \frac{r}{t}$...
Wrong Selection	The presented answer is different from the calculated one	...comes out to 56, which corresponds to option **(A)**. Therefore, the answer is **(B)**.
Algebraic/Calculation	Arithmetic operations are wrong. This includes operations in algebraic equations	102 + 56 = **160**
Commonsense Errors		
Self-Contradiction	Answer's reasoning is contradictory	...a very bright environment, so the dark would be suitable...
Assumption	Assuming information that is not given in the question	Assuming all animals like hot environments...
Encyclopedic	Factual information that the annotator knows is wrong	Wallets are a specialized type of water bottle
Commonsense	The answer violates commonsense and basic understanding of natural laws	...the sun is as cold as ice cream.

Table 4: Error types used in analysis.

C Annotation Confidence Values

	GSM8K	AQuA	StrategyQA	CSQA
CoT	0.60	0.76	0.75	0.79
ERP	0.63	0.63	0.70	0.80
ERP Classes	–	0.69	–	–

Table 5: Confidence values for GPT-4 annotation.

D Additional Error Annotations

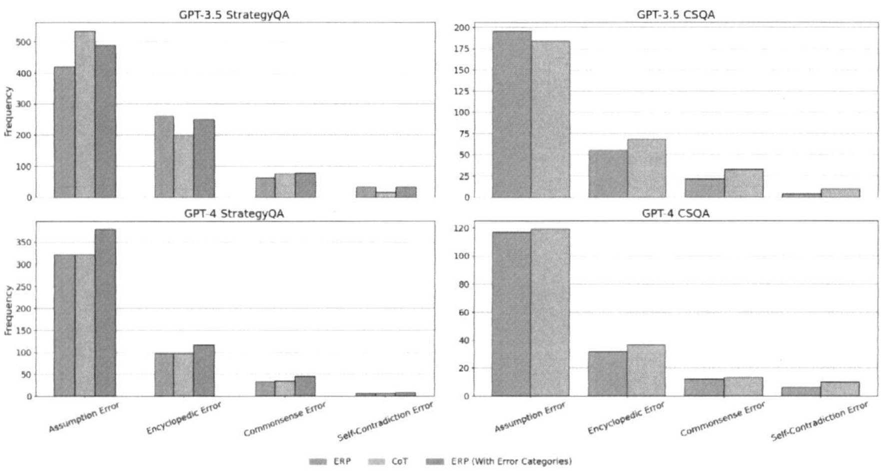

Figure 4: Error annotations on arithmetic reasoning datasets.

Evaluating Robustness of LLMs to Numerical Variations in Mathematical Reasoning

Yuli Yang
Institute of Science Tokyo
yang.y.aw@m.titech.ac.jp

Hiroaki Yamada
Institute of Science Tokyo
yamada@comp.isct.ac.jp

Takenobu Tokunaga
Institute of Science Tokyo
take@c.titech.ac.jp

Abstract

Evaluating an LLM's robustness against numerical perturbation is a good way to know if the LLM actually performs reasoning or just replicates patterns learned. We propose a novel method to augment math word problems (MWPs), producing numerical variations at a large scale utilizing templates. We also propose an automated error classification framework for scalable error analysis, distinguishing calculation errors from reasoning errors. Our experiments using the methods show LLMs are weak against numerical variations, suggesting they are not fully capable of generating valid reasoning steps, often failing in arithmetic operations.

1 Introduction

Recent LLMs (Achiam et al., 2023; Dubey et al., 2024; Team et al., 2023, 2024) have reported high accuracy rates on mathematical reasoning benchmarks, including GSM8K and MATH (Cobbe et al., 2021; Hendrycks et al., 2021). However, a natural concern is that the models just follow surface patterns observed in their pretraining data rather than performing mathematical reasoning (Levy et al., 2024; Valmeekam et al., 2024a,b; Jiang et al., 2024; Guo et al., 2024).

Perturbing superficial elements like names of individuals or specific numbers does not change how the problem should be solved. If an LLM can perform reasoning in solving a math question, it should give correct answers with similar reasoning steps for both the original and its perturbed one. Recent studies (Srivastava et al., 2024; Qian et al., 2024; Li et al., 2024; Mirzadeh et al., 2024) evaluated models' robustness against the perturbations based on this hypothesis.

These studies have the following limitations: a) the size of the introduced variations was limited, b) they did not discuss ranges of numerical values such as digit sizes, and c) they did not distinguish reasoning errors and computational errors and could not explain the source of errors.

To address the limitations, we propose a scalable method to augment a math word problem (MWP) dataset by changing numerical values based on template questions. To analyze the impact of digit sizes on models' mathematical reasoning, we generate two distinct subsets by controlling the range of the replaced values, one with questions containing a small number of digits and the other with questions containing a large number of digits. We construct a new dataset, GSM-ALT, generating 2,000 variants for each original question from GSM8K. Moreover, we propose a novel framework for automated error analysis to distinguish two sources of errors: logical reasoning and numerical calculation.

2 Related Work

Despite strong performance on math benchmarks, researchers are questioning whether current benchmarks can adequately evaluate the reasoning abilities of language models.

Levy et al. (2024) expanded questions by adding non-essential contents, showing that models' performance decreases when the number of tokens in a problem increases. PlanBench (Valmeekam et al., 2024a,b) is a benchmark to evaluate planning and reasoning capabilities. Their findings suggest that even the state-of-the-art models still struggle with this. Srivastava et al. (2024) functionalized the math questions to create a dynamic dataset, providing a robust evaluation metric against potential data leakage to models' pretraining. Jiang et al. (2024) demonstrated that the models' high accuracy depends on a specific token bias, and the models' reasoning capability depends on recognizing certain superficial patterns. Berglund et al. (2024) and Guo et al. (2024) constructed reversal versions of the original questions and showed that the current models performed poorly on the reversal ones.

The Sixth Workshop on Insights from Negative Results in NLP, pages 171–180
May 4, 2025

3 Method

3.1 Question Template Development

To develop a new dataset to assess the model's robustness against numerical variations, we manually generate new variants based on templates (Figure 1) composed from the questions of an existing dataset[1].

A question from an existing dataset (e.g., GSM8K) has tuples of (question Q, solution S). Q is a natural language text describing a question to be solved. S contains the process P and the final answer A. P shows a gold process for solving the question Q step by step, including equations. A stores a numerical value as a gold outcome from the P. Given (Q, S), we first replace all the numerical values in the Q with variables to get Q_{abs}, which is the abstracted Q. We apply the same operation to S and get S_{abs}. We keep variables consistent between Q_{abs} and S_{abs}. S_{abs} contains P_{abs} and A_{abs}, representing the abstracted P and A. The Q_{abs} and S_{abs} constitute a question template T.

3.2 Variant Set Generation

Given a template T of an original question, we generate variants by replacing the variables in T with random values. t_i denotes a variant generated from T, consisting of question Q_i, solution S_i. S_i contains the process P_i and final answer A_i. To ensure variant validity, we must replace the values with satisfying some constraints (Figure 1). For example, an answer should be positive and whole when it represents the number of objects. Intermediate values appearing in the process P_i also need to satisfy the constraints as well. We manually define constraints for each template. Variants are accepted only if they satisfy the constraints.

Suppose models conduct only superficial pattern-based inference instead of reasoning. In that case, they perform poorly in solving questions containing numbers that are rare in their training, such as large digit numbers. To examine this hypothesis, we control the replaced values within two ranges for each question template, to obtain two variant sets: 1-99 (namely, the Easy variant set) and 1-9,999 (namely, the Hard variant set).

4 Experimental Settings

We use GSM8K as the base dataset for our experiment. GSM8K consists of MWPs for primary and secondary school students and involves only the four basic arithmetic operations.

[1] Appendix I discusses automation of this process.

Models	GSM8K Base	GSM-ALT Easy	GSM-ALT Hard
Llama-3-8b-Instruct	0.880	0.646	**0.289**
Llama-3.1-8b-Instruct	0.908	0.736	**0.345**
Llama-3.1-70b-Instruct	0.972	0.888	**0.521**
Mistral-7b-Instruct-v0.3	0.620	0.373	**0.194**
Deepseek-math-7b-rl	0.964	0.808	**0.467**
Wizardmath-7b-v1.1	0.868	0.629	**0.347**

Table 1: Accuracy scores

We randomly sample 250 questions from the GSM8K training set to create 250 question templates manually. Given the templates, we generate 1,000 hard variants and 1,000 easy variants for each template. As a result, our new dataset GSM-ALT consists of the Hard and Easy variant set, each containing 250,000 variants.

We use accuracy as a primary evaluation metric. For the original instances from the base dataset (original GSM8K), we use a standard accuracy. For generated variants from our dataset, we first calculate the accuracy for each template variant set containing 1,000 variants, and then we average them over all the 250 templates.

The target models to be evaluated include generic models (Llama-3-8b-Instruct, Llama-3.1-8b-Instruct, Llama-3.1-70b-Instruct, Mistral-7b-Instruct-v0.3) and math models that were fine-tuned on mathematical contents (Deepseekmath-7b-rl, Wizardmath-7b-v1.1).

Regarding the generation settings, we use greedy search to maximize the reproducibility and stability of results. To minimize the influence of few-shot examples while ensuring that the model can perform mathematical reasoning, we adopt the zero-shot CoT prompting for solution generation and extract the final answer in the same way as Kojima et al. (2022) for generic models. As for math models, we adopt the specifically designed prompts, which are recommended on their Web pages. The prompts used in the experiment can be found in Appendix E.2.

5 Results

Table 1 shows the results of each model's accuracy evaluated on the original GSM8K, and our GSM-ALT. The lowest scores are highlighted in boldface. GSM-ALT results show scores from the Easy variant set and the Hard variant set. All models showed

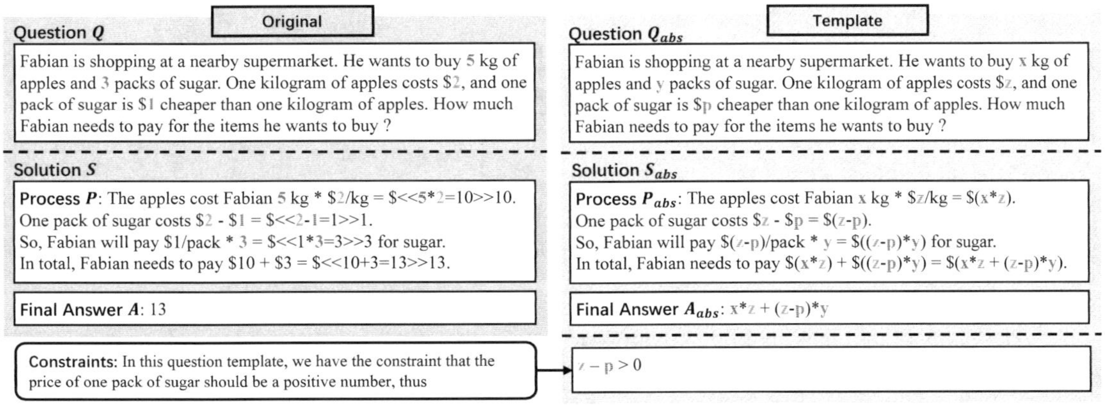

Figure 1: Example of Question Template Development

a significant performance drop in GSM-ALT from the base GSM8K. The drop was observed in both the Easy and the Hard variant sets. Even the two math-specialized models, especially Wizardmath-7b-v1.1, showed lower scores by more than 0.2 on the Easy and more than 0.5 on the Hard.

This result shows that numerical variations always degrade performance in both the Hard and the Easy variant sets. The fact that the Easy variant set degrades the performance indicates that the models are weak even against the numbers whose range is similar to the base GSM8K. Moreover, we found clearer score drops from the GSM8K scores in the Hard variant set than in the Easy variant set, suggesting the computational difficulty affects models' reasoning.

6 Error Analysis on Solutions

To identify the source of errors, we classify errors into two types: calculation errors and reasoning errors. If an incorrect solution only contains failures in calculations, we call it a calculation error. If an incorrect solution contains incorrect reasoning steps, we label it a reasoning error regardless of its incorrect calculations.

As GSM-ALT will be larger than its original dataset, manually checking each generated solution is not practical, and thus, we propose a novel framework that automatically classifies errors into calculation or reasoning errors.

6.1 Error Analysis Framework

To classify errors, we first transform a predicted solution $\hat{S}_i$ into its abstracted form $\hat{S}^i_{abs}$, which contains the abstracted $\hat{P}^i_{abs}$ and $\hat{A}^i_{abs}$. If $\hat{S}_i$ is incorrect because of a reasoning error, its transformed $\hat{P}^i_{abs}$ should contain a reasoning error resulting in incorrect $\hat{A}^i_{abs}$. If $\hat{S}_i$ contains a calculation error with correct reasoning steps, $\hat{P}^i_{abs}$ and $\hat{A}^i_{abs}$ should be correct. Thus, checking if $\hat{A}^i_{abs}$ is correct should give a proxy to determine the sources of errors.

In our framework, an LLM transforms a $\hat{S}_i$ into the $\hat{S}^i_{abs}$, as shown in Figure 2. Then, we can automatically check if $\hat{A}^i_{abs}$ is correct by comparing it with its gold answer A_{abs} from our templates. An input to the LLM is a model's predicted solution $\hat{S}_i$, its question Q_i, and its abstracted question Q_{abs} available from our templates. We auxiliaryly input the Q_{abs} guiding the LLM to use variables consistently, inspired by Gaur and Saunshi (2023). An output from the LLM is an abstracted solution $\hat{S}^i_{abs}$. We show our prompt for this framework in Appendix G. We employ Qwen2-math-72b-instruct (Yang et al., 2024) for this transformation.

We confirmed the LLM could obtain the abstracted solutions at 90% success rate on average in our preliminary experiment (Appendix F).

6.2 Results

Table 2 shows the results of error classification by our framework. Values in the table indicate the proportion of solutions classified as calculation errors or reasoning errors out of all solutions predicted by the models. Values in parentheses indicate the proportion of solutions classified as calculation errors or reasoning errors out of incorrect solutions.

In the Base set, most incorrect solutions are due to reasoning errors. However, they changes to calculation errors in the Easy and Hard variant sets except for the Mistral. This trend is especially evident in the Hard variant set, where more than 69% come from calculation errors. This result suggests

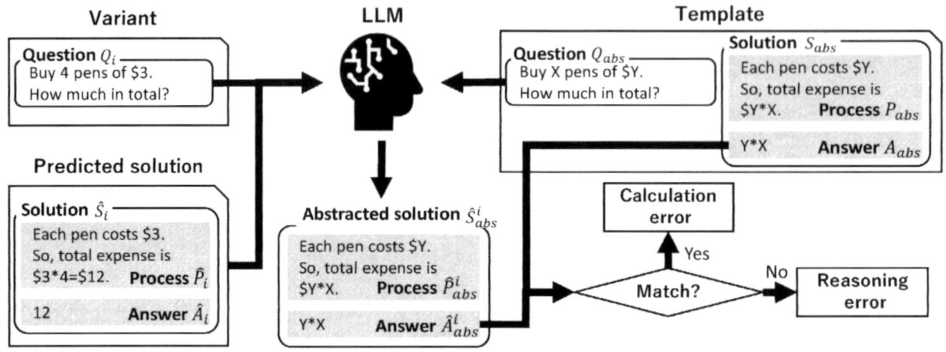

Figure 2: Error classification framework

	Base set		Easy variant set		Hard variant set	
	calculation err.	reasoning err.	calculation err.	reasoning err.	calculation err.	reasoning err.
Llama-3-8b-Inst.	.024 (20.0%)	.096 (80.0%)	.185 (52.3%)	.169 (47.7%)	.491 (69.1%)	.220 (30.9%)
Llama-3.1-8b-Inst.	.020 (21.7%)	.072 (78.3%)	.153 (57.9%)	.111 (42.1%)	.487 (74.4%)	.168 (25.6%)
Llama-3.1-70b-Inst.	.012 (42.9%)	.016 (57.1%)	.070 (62.5%)	.042 (37.5%)	.399 (83.3%)	.080 (16.7%)
Mistral-7b-Inst.-v0.3	.096 (25.3%)	.284 (74.7%)	.279 (44.5%)	.348 (55.5%)	.406 (50.4%)	.400 (49.6%)
Deepseek-math-7b-rl	.012 (33.3%)	.024 (66.7%)	.131 (68.2%)	.061 (31.8%)	.413 (77.5%)	.120 (22.5%)
Wizardmath-7b-v1.1	.032 (24.2%)	.100 (75.8%)	.255 (68.5%)	.117 (31.5%)	.489 (74.9%)	.164 (25.1%)
Macro avg.	.033 (25.0%)	.099 (75.0%)	.179 (59.0%)	.141 (41.0%)	.448 (71.6%)	.192 (28.4%)

Table 2: Error rate per error type and variant set

that the limited capability of arithmetic calculation is indeed a major issue of LLMs in solving mathematical problems rather than the reasoning capability of generating a valid process of solving steps when the numerical values in the questions are large.

Looking at the reasoning errors, all the models get more errors in both the Easy and Hard variant sets than the Base set. The same as calculation errors, the trend is evident in the Hard variant set. This result suggests that variants also introduce harmful changes in reasoning steps in addition to complex calculations, which result in incorrect solutions. Moreover, variants with larger digit sizes are more likely to introduce errors in reasoning steps.

Mistral shows different behavior from the others because its performance is considerably worse (Table 2). Mistral is the worst in mathematical reasoning. Note that a calculation error is considered only when a solution has valid reasoning steps. Thus, a lower number of calculation errors does not necessarily mean Mistral is good at calculation.

7 Conclusion

We proposed a novel method to augment MWP datasets, which produces a dataset for evaluating LLMs' robustness against numerical variations at a large scale. Using our templates, anyone can easily generate thousands of variants from one original question in the GSM8K, which was not possible with any preceding proposals. We also proposed an automated error classification framework for detailed error analysis, distinguishing calculation errors from reasoning errors.

Using the methods, we empirically showed that the six LLMs we tested were weak against numerical variations, especially when the numerical values were large. This finding is consistent with previous studies (Srivastava et al., 2024; Qian et al., 2024; Li et al., 2024; Mirzadeh et al., 2024), but we confirm it with more variants. Our error analysis uniquely identified that calculation errors contributed to a substantial proportion of incorrect solutions, suggesting LLMs' incapability of arithmetic operations is the main source of limited capabilities in math word problems. Moreover, we found that LLMs still fail in their reasoning steps, especially when they encounter variants with larger numerical values. Given our findings, it is still hard to say that current LLMs are robust against numerical variations.

8 Limitations

Variant Generation As we do not manually check every single variant generated from our template, our variants can contain some combinations of numbers that are not necessarily realistic in our real-world common sense. For example, there might be an apple that sells for more than 1,000 dollars. In our experiment, we accepted such variants. The reasons we made the compromise are: a) In some question templates, it is hard to generate enough variants if we strictly follow common sense. b) We believe that in the background of mathematical reasoning, models should strictly follow the conditions stated in the questions instead of common sense. c) Through a check on sampled solutions generated by models, we found that common sense issues will not affect the model's reasoning in most cases.

Another limitation is that the number of possible variants is limited in some of the templates, so there are some duplicated variants for such a template. This limitation is especially evident in the Easy variant set, where the range of numerical variation is more limited than the Hard variant set. We present the full results in the main body of the paper and put the results of the templates with no duplications in Appendix A.

Error Analysis Framework When we manually inspected the generated solutions, we found different reasoning patterns depending on the numerical variations. Moreover, we also observe different groups of reasoning patterns specific to one of the sets (Easy or Hard)[2].

Our error analysis framework is based on a classification approach, distinguishing between calculation errors and reasoning errors. Thus, it cannot identify what kind of failures happen within the reasoning errors. We also could not identify any reasonable clusters and their interpretations because it required a lot of human resources. It is an interesting future direction to extend our automatic error analysis framework, enabling it to cluster and aggregate the reasoning patterns, mitigating the limitation of our classification-based analysis.

Acknowledgements

This work was partly supported by JST, PRESTO Grant Number JPMJPR236B, Japan. The experiments were carried out using the TSUBAME4.0 supercomputer at Institute of Science Tokyo.

[2]Appendix H discusses it

References

Josh Achiam, Steven Adler, Sandhini Agarwal, Lama Ahmad, Ilge Akkaya, Florencia Leoni Aleman, Diogo Almeida, Janko Altenschmidt, Sam Altman, Shyamal Anadkat, et al. 2023. Gpt-4 technical report. *arXiv preprint arXiv:2303.08774*.

Lukas Berglund, Meg Tong, Max Kaufmann, Mikita Balesni, Asa Cooper Stickland, Tomasz Korbak, and Owain Evans. 2024. The reversal curse: Llms trained on "a is b" fail to learn "b is a". *Preprint*, arXiv:2309.12288.

Karl Cobbe, Vineet Kosaraju, Mohammad Bavarian, Mark Chen, Heewoo Jun, Lukasz Kaiser, Matthias Plappert, Jerry Tworek, Jacob Hilton, Reiichiro Nakano, Christopher Hesse, and John Schulman. 2021. Training verifiers to solve math word problems. *Preprint*, arXiv:2110.14168.

Abhimanyu Dubey, Abhinav Jauhri, Abhinav Pandey, Abhishek Kadian, Ahmad Al-Dahle, Aiesha Letman, Akhil Mathur, Alan Schelten, Amy Yang, Angela Fan, et al. 2024. The llama 3 herd of models. *arXiv preprint arXiv:2407.21783*.

Vedant Gaur and Nikunj Saunshi. 2023. Reasoning in large language models through symbolic math word problems. *Preprint*, arXiv:2308.01906.

Pei Guo, WangJie You, Juntao Li, Yan Bowen, and Min Zhang. 2024. Exploring reversal mathematical reasoning ability for large language models. In *Findings of the Association for Computational Linguistics: ACL 2024*, pages 13671–13685, Bangkok, Thailand. Association for Computational Linguistics.

Dan Hendrycks, Collin Burns, Saurav Kadavath, Akul Arora, Steven Basart, Eric Tang, Dawn Song, and Jacob Steinhardt. 2021. Measuring mathematical problem solving with the math dataset. *arXiv preprint arXiv:2103.03874*.

Bowen Jiang, Yangxinyu Xie, Zhuoqun Hao, Xiaomeng Wang, Tanwi Mallick, Weijie J Su, Camillo Jose Taylor, and Dan Roth. 2024. A peek into token bias: Large language models are not yet genuine reasoners. In *Proceedings of the 2024 Conference on Empirical Methods in Natural Language Processing*, pages 4722–4756, Miami, Florida, USA. Association for Computational Linguistics.

Takeshi Kojima, Shixiang Shane Gu, Machel Reid, Yutaka Matsuo, and Yusuke Iwasawa. 2022. Large language models are zero-shot reasoners. *Advances in neural information processing systems*, 35:22199–22213.

Mosh Levy, Alon Jacoby, and Yoav Goldberg. 2024. Same task, more tokens: the impact of input length on the reasoning performance of large language models. In *Proceedings of the 62nd Annual Meeting of* the Association for Computational Linguistics (Volume 1: Long Papers), pages 15339–15353, Bangkok, Thailand. Association for Computational Linguistics.

Qintong Li, Leyang Cui, Xueliang Zhao, Lingpeng Kong, and Wei Bi. 2024. GSM-plus: A comprehensive benchmark for evaluating the robustness of LLMs as mathematical problem solvers. In *Proceedings of the 62nd Annual Meeting of the Association for Computational Linguistics (Volume 1: Long Papers)*, pages 2961–2984, Bangkok, Thailand. Association for Computational Linguistics.

Iman Mirzadeh, Keivan Alizadeh, Hooman Shahrokhi, Oncel Tuzel, Samy Bengio, and Mehrdad Farajtabar. 2024. Gsm-symbolic: Understanding the limitations of mathematical reasoning in large language models. *arXiv preprint arXiv:2410.05229*.

Kun Qian, Shunji Wan, Claudia Tang, Youzhi Wang, Xuanming Zhang, Maximillian Chen, and Zhou Yu. 2024. VarBench: Robust language model benchmarking through dynamic variable perturbation. In *Findings of the Association for Computational Linguistics: EMNLP 2024*, pages 16131–16161, Miami, Florida, USA. Association for Computational Linguistics.

Saurabh Srivastava, Annarose M B, Anto P V, Shashank Menon, Ajay Sukumar, Adwaith Samod T, Alan Philipose, Stevin Prince, and Sooraj Thomas. 2024. Functional benchmarks for robust evaluation of reasoning performance, and the reasoning gap. *Preprint*, arXiv:2402.19450.

Zhi Rui Tam, Cheng-Kuang Wu, Yi-Lin Tsai, Chieh-Yen Lin, Hung-yi Lee, and Yun-Nung Chen. 2024. Let me speak freely? a study on the impact of format restrictions on large language model performance. In *Proceedings of the 2024 Conference on Empirical Methods in Natural Language Processing: Industry Track*, pages 1218–1236, Miami, Florida, US. Association for Computational Linguistics.

Gemini Team, Rohan Anil, Sebastian Borgeaud, Jean-Baptiste Alayrac, Jiahui Yu, Radu Soricut, Johan Schalkwyk, Andrew M Dai, Anja Hauth, Katie Millican, et al. 2023. Gemini: a family of highly capable multimodal models. *arXiv preprint arXiv:2312.11805*.

Gemma Team, Morgane Riviere, Shreya Pathak, Pier Giuseppe Sessa, Cassidy Hardin, Surya Bhupatiraju, Léonard Hussenot, Thomas Mesnard, Bobak Shahriari, Alexandre Ramé, et al. 2024. Gemma 2: Improving open language models at a practical size. *arXiv preprint arXiv:2408.00118*.

Karthik Valmeekam, Matthew Marquez, Alberto Olmo, Sarath Sreedharan, and Subbarao Kambhampati. 2024a. Planbench: An extensible benchmark for evaluating large language models on planning and reasoning about change. *Advances in Neural Information Processing Systems*, 36.

Karthik Valmeekam, Kaya Stechly, and Subbarao Kambhampati. 2024b. Llms still can't plan; can lrms? a preliminary evaluation of openai's o1 on planbench. *Preprint*, arXiv:2409.13373.

An Yang, Baosong Yang, Binyuan Hui, Bo Zheng, Bowen Yu, Chang Zhou, Chengpeng Li, Chengyuan Li, Dayiheng Liu, Fei Huang, et al. 2024. Qwen2 technical report. *arXiv preprint arXiv:2407.10671*.

A Results of the templates with no duplications

Models	GSM8K	GSM-ALT	
	Base	Easy	Hard
Llama-3-8b-Instruct	0.840	0.507	**0.156**
Llama-3.1-8b-Instruct	0.880	0.604	**0.193**
Llama-3.1-70b-Instruct	0.978	0.819	**0.355**
Mistral-7b-Instruct-v0.3	0.587	0.238	**0.104**
Deepseek-math-7b-rl	0.957	0.706	**0.307**
Wizardmath-7b-v1.1	0.891	0.489	**0.223**

Table 3: Accuracy scores (for 92 templates without duplications)

As explained in Section 8, duplicated variations might be generated for some templates. We counted the number of duplicated variants generated per template. We found that most templates have a small number of duplications, and only 92 templates (in 250 templates) contain no duplicated variants. To make our conclusions more rigorous, we removed those templates with duplications and presented the results of the remaining templates here (Table 3 and Table 4). According to the filtered results, we could get the same findings and conclusions as in Section 5 and Section 6.2.

B Dataset Lisence

The original GSM8K was distributed under the MIT license. We plan to make our templates publicly available under the MIT License.

C Computational Environment

All of our experiments were conducted on a GPU server implementing AMD EPYC 9654 2.4GHz × 2 Socket, 768GiB RAM, NVIDIA H100 SXM5 94GB HBM2e × 4. Our project's total hours spent on the server were approximately 480 hours, including preliminary experiments.

D Large Language Models

We list all of the LLMs used in our experiments.

	Base set		Easy variant set		Hard variant set	
	calculation err.	reasoning err.	calculation err.	reasoning err.	calculation err.	reasoning err.
Llama-3-8b-Inst.	.033 (20.0%)	.130 (80.0%)	.279 (56.6%)	.214 (43.4%)	.573 (67.9%)	.271 (32.1%)
Llama-3.1-8b-Inst.	.033 (27.3%)	.087 (72.7%)	.252 (63.6%)	.144 (36.4%)	.601 (74.5%)	.206 (25.5%)
Llama-3.1-70b-Inst.	.000 (00.0%)	.022 (100.0%)	.125 (69.1%)	.056 (30.9%)	.516 (80.0%)	.129 (20.0%)
Mistral-7b-Inst.-v0.3	.098 (23.7%)	.315 (76.3%)	.385 (50.5%)	.377 (49.5%)	.477 (53.2%)	.419 (46.8%)
Deepseek-math-7b-rl	.011 (25.0%)	.033 (75.0%)	.217 (73.8%)	.077 (26.2%)	.529 (76.4%)	.163 (23.6%)
Wizardmath-7b-v1.1	.043 (40.0%)	.065 (60.0%)	.383 (75.0%)	.128 (25.0%)	.586 (75.4%)	.191 (24.6%)
Macro avg.	.036 (24.8%)	.109 (75.2%)	.274 (62.3%)	.166 (37.7%)	.547 (70.4%)	.230 (29.6%)

Table 4: Error rate per error type and variant set (for 92 templates without duplications)

Generic LLMs

- Llama-3-8b-Instruct
  `https://huggingface.co/meta-llama/Meta-Llama-3-8B-Instruct`
- Llama-3.1-8b-Instruct
  `https://huggingface.co/meta-llama/Llama-3.1-8B-Instruct`
- Llama-3.1-70b-Instruct
  `https://huggingface.co/meta-llama/Llama-3.1-70B-Instruct`
- Mistral-7b-Instruct-v0.3
  `https://huggingface.co/mistralai/Mistral-7B-Instruct-v0.3`

LLMs for mathematical domain

- Deepseekmath-7b-rl
  `https://huggingface.co/deepseek-ai/deepseek-math-7b-rl`
- Wizardmath-7b-v1.1
  `https://huggingface.co/WizardLMTeam/WizardMath-7B-V1.1`

E Prompt Design

E.1 Zero-shot or Few-shot?

We used zero-shot CoT prompting to generate the solutions. The reasons are as follows: a) In our preliminary experiments, we found that few-shot examples do not necessarily improve the model's performance on mathematical reasoning, sometimes even degrading the accuracy. This might be because today's LLMs have already been sufficiently trained on similar MWPs, so providing random few-shot examples is just a kind of constraint and hinders the model's reasoning (Tam et al., 2024). b)The influence of few-shot examples on the model's reasoning is difficult to assess. For example, if two models perform differently under the same prompt and few-shot examples, it might be because this set of examples works for one model but not for the other. Therefore, we consider that few-shot CoT is not suitable for evaluation.

Generation Prompt – generic models
SYSTEM: You are an assistant that solves math word problems. ***USER:*** {question} + Let's think step by step.

Figure 3: The prompt for generic models (generating solutions)

Answer Extraction Prompt – generic models
SYSTEM: You are an assistant that solves math word problems. ***USER:*** {question} + Let's think step by step. ***ASSISTANT:*** {model's completion} ***USER:*** Therefore, what is the final answer? Only write the final answer without any texts.

Figure 4: The prompt for generic models (extracting final answer)

E.2 Prompts used for main experiments

For the generic LLMs, we developed prompts for solution generation (Figure 3) and answer extraction (Figre 4) based on the prompts used in Kojima et al. (2022).

For Deepseekmath-7b-rl and Wizardmath-7b-v1.1, we employed prompts based on templates suggested on their web pages. Figure 5 and 6 show them. In extracting answers from solutions generated by the two math models, we could simply use regular expressions since they always generate solutions in a fixed format.

F Performance of Transformation to Abstracted Solutions

To validate the performance of our error analysis framework, we had to know how well Qwen2-math-72b-Instruct could correctly transform a model's

	Error Types				Overall	
	Calculation		Reasoning			
Llama-3-8b-Instruct	93%	(26/28)	68%	(15/22)	82%	(41/50)
Llama-3.1-8b-Instruct	95%	(38/40)	80%	(8/10)	92%	(46/50)
Llama-3.1-70b-Instruct	97%	(38/39)	91%	(10/11)	96%	(48/50)
Mistral-7b-Instruct-v0.3	100%	(23/23)	59%	(16/27)	78%	(39/50)
Deepseek-math-7b-rl	97%	(38/39)	91%	(10/11)	96%	(48/50)
Wizardmath-7b-v1.1	97%	(37/38)	83%	(10/12)	94%	(47/50)
Macro avg.	96%		79%		90%	

Table 5: Abstracted solution transformation success rate

Generation Prompt – Deepseekmath-7b-rl

USER: {question}
Please reason step by step and put your final answer within \boxed{}.

Figure 5: The prompt for Deepseekmath-7b-rl (geneart-ing solutions)

Generation Prompt – Wizardmath-7b-v1.1

USER: Below is an instruction that describes a task. Write a response that appropriately completes the request.
Instruction:
{question}
Response:
Let's think step by step.

Figure 6: The prompt for Wizardmath-7b-v1.1 (generating solutions)

Transformation Prompt

SYSTEM: Given the numeric version of a math question and its solution as references, you are a helpful assistant designed to copy the numeric solution to get a solution to the symbolic version of that question.
Instructions:
- Symbolic solution should strictly copy the numeric solution no matter whether it is correct or not.
- After completion of the solution, output the final answer with "###". The final answer should be a sole mathematical expression represented by variables appear in the symbolic question.
- Mathematical expression in the symbolic solution should not be represented in the format of LaTeX.

{few-shot examples}

USER: {target solution}

Figure 7: The prompt for solution transformation

solution into an abstracted form.

For this preliminary experiment, we constructed a small dataset for each LLM we employed in our main experiment (Section 4). For each model, we randomly sampled 50 incorrect solutions obtained from the results of the main experiment and manually categorized them into calculation errors or reasoning errors. For the evaluation, we manually checked whether the LLM could correctly transform the models' original solutions into abstracted forms according to the following criteria: a) the abstracted process exactly reflects the reasoning process in the original solution, b) the variable assignment in the abstracted solution should be correct, c) the abstracted final answer correctly represents the abstracted process.

The results are shown in Table 5. The table shows the success rate (percentages) of Qwen2-math-72b-Instruct's transformation on solutions predicted by different models in terms of the error type we manually categorized. Fractions in parentheses indicate the specific number we checked (the numerator is the number of successful transformations, and the denominator is the total number). It demonstrates that Qwen2-math-72b-Instruct can correctly obtain symbolic solutions and answers from 90% of the instances overall. Based on the results, we consider our method to be reasonably valid for our purpose.

G Prompt Design for Error Analysis Framework

Figure 7 presents the prompt used to transform a predicted solution into the abstracted form.

H Case Study in Error Analysis

Through our manual inspection of the generated solutions for variants generated from the template, we identified that there were groups of reasoning patterns due to numerical variations. Figure 8 shows an example of the reasoning patterns we observed. This example is taken from outputs from Llama-3.1-70b-Instruct. The solutions in the figure show the different typical reasoning patterns identified by the underlined fonts. The performance of the easy variants generated from the same template of the example was 66.6% of accuracy (666 correct solutions), and there were 334 incorrect solutions consisting of 286 calculation errors and 48 reasoning errors. For its Hard set variants, accuracy was at 0%. Its incorrect solutions consist of 145 calcu-

Example of Variant from Easy set

Question: At a laundromat, it costs $50 for a washer and a quarter for every 3 minutes in the dryer. Samantha does 23 loads of laundry in the wash and then divides all the washed clothes equally into 21 separate dryers. If she lets the dryers run for 28 minutes each, how much does she spend altogether?

Process: To find the total cost, let's break it down into steps.
1. First, we need to find the cost of washing 23 loads of laundry. **Since it costs $50 for a washer, the total cost for washing is 23 * $50.**
Total washing cost = 23 * $50 = $1150

2. Next, we need to find the cost of drying the clothes. Since Samantha divides the clothes equally into 21 separate dryers, each dryer will have 23 / 21 loads. However, the cost of drying is based on the number of dryers and the time they run, not the number of loads. So, we'll focus on the number of dryers and the time. Since there are 21 dryers, and each dryer runs for 28 minutes, we need to find the total number of 3-minute intervals for all the dryers. We can do this by dividing the total minutes by 3.
Total minutes = 21 dryers * 28 minutes = 588 minutes
Total 3-minute intervals = 588 minutes / 3 = 196 intervals
Since it costs a quarter for every 3 minutes, we multiply the total intervals by the cost per interval.
Total drying cost = 196 intervals * $0.25 = $49

3. Finally, we add the total washing cost and the total drying cost to find the overall cost. Total cost = Total washing cost + Total drying cost
Total cost = $1150 + $49
Total cost = $1199
So, Samantha spends $1199 altogether.

Example of Variant from Hard set

Question: At a laundromat, it costs $5274 for a washer and a quarter for every 2 minutes in the dryer. Samantha does 8762 loads of laundry in the wash and then divides all the washed clothes equally into 8968 separate dryers. If she lets the dryers run for 8314 minutes each, how much does she spend altogether?

Process: To find the total cost, we need to calculate the cost of the washer and the cost of the dryer separately, then add them together.
1. The cost of the washer: Since Samantha does 8762 loads of laundry, and it costs $5274 for a washer, **we can assume that the cost of the washer is a one-time payment.** So, the cost of the washer is $5274.

2. The cost of the dryer: Samantha divides the clothes into 8968 separate dryers. Each dryer runs for 8314 minutes. The cost of the dryer is a quarter for every 2 minutes.

First, let's find the total number of minutes for all dryers:
8968 dryers * 8314 minutes = 74,555,072 minutes

Since the cost is a quarter for every 2 minutes, we need to divide the total minutes by 2:
74,555,072 minutes / 2 = 37,277,536 quarters

Now, let's convert the quarters to dollars (1 dollar = 4 quarters):
37,277,536 quarters / 4 = 9,319,384 dollars

Now, we add the cost of the washer and the cost of the dryer:
$5274 + $9,319,384 = $9,324,658
So, Samantha spends $9,324,658 altogether

Figure 8: Example of typical patterns in evaluation datasets

lation errors and 855 reasoning errors. The variants of the template in the Hard variant set cause a clear reasoning degradation.

We observed similar phenomena across other models besides Llama-3.1-70b-Instruct. We hypothesize that the reason why numerical variation could cause such changes in reasoning patterns was in the sizes of digits. As variants in the Hard variant set have more digits, LLMs get questions with more tokens, which makes their output different.

I Necessity of Manual Operations in Creating Question Templates

Although we have considered using regular expressions and rule-based approaches to automate template creation, they have the following problems: a) Not all numerical values in the original instance are "symbolizable." Some numbers in the instance are specific; altering them would make the instance ill-defined. b) As shown in Figure 1, when generating the template, it is necessary to keep the usage of variable consistent between Q_{abs} and S_{abs}. It is hard to catch the relationship with rule-based replacement and requires human insight. Therefore, we created the question templates manually.

Author Index

Association for Computational Linguistics
209 N. Eighth Street
Stroudsburg, Pennsylvania 18360

ISBN 979-8-3313-1919-9

CURRAN ASSOCIATES INC.
proceedings.com